Lecture Notes in Computer Science   8855

Commenced Publication in 1973
Founding and Former Series Editors:
Gerhard Goos, Juris Hartmanis, and Jan van Leeuwen

T0212920

Eran Yahav (Ed.)

Hardware and Software: Verification and Testing

10th International
Haifa Verification Conference, HVC 2014
Haifa, Israel, November 18-20, 2014
Proceedings

 Springer

Volume Editor

Eran Yahav
Technion
Faculty of Computer Science
Haifa 32000, Israel,
E-mail: yahave@cs.technion.ac.il

ISSN 0302-9743   e-ISSN 1611-3349
ISBN 978-3-319-13337-9   e-ISBN 978-3-319-13338-6
DOI 10.1007/978-3-319-13338-6
Springer Cham Heidelberg New York Dordrecht London

Library of Congress Control Number: 2014953963

LNCS Sublibrary: SL 2 – Programming and Software Engineering

Typesetting: Camera-ready by author, data conversion by Scientific Publishing Services, Chennai, India

Printed on acid-free paper

Springer is part of Springer Science+Business Media (www.springer.com)

Preface

This volume contains the proceedings of the 10th Haifa Verification Conference (HVC 2014). The conference was hosted by IBM Research - Haifa and took place during November 18–20, 2014. It was the tenth event in this series of annual conferences dedicated to advancing the state of the art and state of the practice in verification and testing. The conference provided a forum for researchers and practitioners from academia and industry to share their work, exchange ideas, and discuss the future directions of testing and verification for hardware, software, and complex hybrid systems.

Overall, HVC 2014 attracted 43 submissions in response to the call for papers. Each submission was assigned to at least three members of the Program Committee and in many cases additional reviews were solicited from external experts. The Program Committee selected 21 papers for presentation.

In addition to the 21 contributed papers, the program included five invited talks by Moshe Vardi (Rice University), Bradley McCredie (IBM), Martin Vechev (ETH Zurich), Harry Foster (Mentor Graphics), and Ziv Binyamini (Cadence).

I would like to extend our appreciation and sincere thanks to Ronny Morad for serving as general chair and handling the conference details. Our thanks also go to Raviv Gal for arranging the tutorials day, and Rachel Tzoref-Brill for serving as the publicity chair. I would like to thank the Organizing Committee: Moshe Levinger, Laurent Fournier, Amir Nahir, Karen Yorav, Avi Ziv, and Sharon Keidar Barner.

Finally, I would like to thank our support team: Eti Jahr for managing the technical aspects of the conference, and Gili Aizen and Chani Sacharen handling communication.

HVC 2014 received sponsorships from IBM, Cadence, Mellanox, Mentor Graphics, Quallcom, SanDisk, and Technion TCE.

Submissions and evaluations of papers, as well as the preparation of this proceedings volume, were handled by the EasyChair conference management system.

October 2014   Eran Yahav

Organization

Program Committee

Earl Barr	University College London, UK
Valeria Bertacco	University of Michigan, USA
Tevfik Bultan	University of California at Santa Barbara, USA
Swarat Chaudhuri	Rice University, USA
Hana Chockler	King's College, UK
Isil Dillig	UT Austin, USA
Kerstin Eder	University of Bristol, UK
Franco Fummi	University of Verona, Italy
Patrice Godefroid	Microsoft Research
Aarti Gupta	NEC Laboratories America
Barbara Jobstmann	EPFL, Jasper DA, and CNRS-Verimag, France
Laura Kovacs	Chalmers University of Technology, Sweden
Daniel Kroening	University of Oxford, UK
Florian Letombe	Synopsys
João Lourenço	CITI - Universidade Nova de Lisboa, Portugal
Shan Lu	University of Wisconsin, Madison, USA
Rupak Majumdar	MPI-SWS
Darko Marinov	University of Illinois at Urbana-Champaign, USA
Mayur Naik	Intel Labs
Aditya Nori	MSR India
Corina Pasareanu	CMU/NASA Ames Research Center, USA
Ruzica Piskac	Yale University, USA
Itai Segall	IBM Haifa Research Labs, Israel
Martina Seidl	Johannes Kepler University Linz, Austria
Ohad Shacham	Yahoo! Labs
Sharon Shoham	Academic College of Tel Aviv Yaffo, Isreal
Zhendong Su	UC Davis, USA
Rachel Tzoref	IBM Haifa Research Labs, Israel
Jan Vitek	Purdue University, USA
Heike Wehrheim	University of Paderborn, Germany

Additional Reviewers

Bocic, Ivan	Dimitrova, Rayna
Busany, Nimrod	Dragan, Ioan
Chakarov, Aleksandar	Ferreira, Bernardo
Cobb, Jake	Forejt, Vojtech

Fu, Zhoulai
Gabmeyer, Sebastian
Grumberg, Orna
Gyori, Alex
Heule, Marijn
Horn, Alexander
Isenberg, Tobias
Itzhaky, Shachar
Joshi, Saurabh
Karbyshev, Aleksandr
Kloos, Johannes
Konnov, Igor
Kuncak, Viktor
Landsberg, David
Le, Vu
Legunsen, Owolabi
Mangal, Ravi
Maoz, Shahar
Milicevic, Aleksandar

Parikh, Ritesh
Qiu, Rui
Rinetzky, Noam
Ringert, Jan Oliver
Schäf, Martin
Sen, Shayak
Shi, August
Sun, Chengnian
Tentrup, Leander
Torfah, Hazem
Van Delft, Bart
van Den Elsen, Susanne
Vizel, Yakir
Wachter, Björn
Yahav, Eran
Yorav, Karen
Zhang, Xin
Ziegert, Steffen
Ziv, Avi

Abstracts

SAT Counting and Sampling - From Theory to Practice

Moshe Vardi

Rice University

Abstract. Counting the the number of satisfying truth assignments of a given Boolean formula or sampling such assignments uniformly at random are fundamental computational problems in computer science with numerous applications. In computer-aided design, these problems come up in constrained-random verification, where test input vectors are described by means of constraints. While the theory of these problems has been thoroughly investigated in the 1980s, approximation algorithms developed by theoreticians do not scale up to industrial-sized instances. Algorithms used by the industry offer better scalability, but give up certain correctness guarantees to achieve scalability. We describe a novel approach, based on universal hashing and SMT, that scales to formulas with hundreds of thousands of variable without giving up correctness guarantees.

Joint work with Supratik Chaudhuri, Daniel Fremont, Kuldeep Meel, and Sanjit Sheshia.

Statistical Program Analysis and Synthesis

Martin Vechev

Department of Computer Science
ETH Zurich

Abstract. The increased availability of massive codebases, sometimes referred to as "Big Code", creates a unique opportunity for new kinds of program analysis and synthesis techniques based on statistical reasoning. These approaches will extract useful information from existing codebases and will use that information to provide statistically likely solutions to problems that are difficult or impossible to solve with traditional techniques.

As an example, I will present several statistical engines developed in our lab which instantiate this vision. I will highlight the key challenges when designing such systems including the importance of carefully combining and interfacing programming language techniques (*e.g.* static analysis) with powerful machine learning approaches (*e.g.* graphical models).

Navigating the Perfect Storm: New Trends in Functional Verification

Harry Foster

Mentor Graphics

Abstract. Between 2006 and 2014, the average number of IPs integrated into an advanced SoC increased from about 30 to over 120. In the same period, the average number of embedded processors found in an advanced SoC increased from one to as many as 20. However, increased design size is only one dimension of the growing verification complexity challenge. Beyond this growing functionally phenomenon are new layers of requirements that must be verified. Many of these verification requirements did not exist ten years ago, such as multiple asynchronous clock domains, interacting power domains, security domains, and complex HW/SW dependencies. Add all these challenges together, and you have the perfect storm brewing. This talk introduces todays trends and challenges in SoC design and then discusses emerging verification strategy to navigate the perfect storm.

Table of Contents

Using Coarse-Grained Abstractions to Verify Linearizability on TSO Architectures

John Derrick[1], Graeme Smith[2], Lindsay Groves[3], and Brijesh Dongol[1]

[1]Department of Computing, University of Sheffield, UK
[2]School of Information Technology and Electrical Engineering,
The University of Queensland, Australia
[3] School of Engineering and Computer Science,
Victoria University of Wellington, New Zealand

Abstract. Most approaches to verifying linearizability assume a sequentially consistent memory model, which is not always realised in practice. In this paper we study correctness on a *weak* memory model: the TSO (Total Store Order) memory model, which is implemented in x86 multicore architectures.

Our central result is a proof method that simplifies proofs of linearizability on TSO. This is necessary since the use of local buffers in TSO adds considerably to the verification overhead on top of the already subtle linearizability proofs. The proof method involves constructing a coarse-grained abstraction as an intermediate layer between an abstract description and the concurrent algorithm. This allows the linearizability proof to be split into two smaller components, where the effect of the local buffers in TSO is dealt with at a higher level of abstraction than it would have been otherwise.

1 Introduction

There has been extensive work on correctness of fine-grained concurrent algorithms over the last few years, where linearizability is the key criteria that is applied. This requires that fine-grained implementations of access operations (e.g., insertion or removal of an element of a data structure) appear as though they take effect "instantaneously at some point in time" [12], thereby achieving the same effect as an atomic operation. There has been considerable work on verifying linearizability, and a variety of proof techniques have been developed, some of them with automated support.

However, most of this work assumes a particular memory model; specifically a *sequentially consistent* (SC) memory model, whereby program instructions are executed by the hardware in the order specified by the program. Typical multicore systems communicate via shared memory and, to increase efficiency, use (local) store buffers. Whilst these *relaxed memory models* give greater scope for optimisation, sequential consistency is lost, and because memory accesses may be reordered in various ways it is even harder to reason about correctness. Typical multiprocessors that provide such weaker memory models include the x86 [16], Power [17] and ARM [1] multicore processor architectures.

In this paper we focus on one such memory model, the TSO (Total Store Order) model [17] which is implemented in the x86 architecture. The notion of correctness

E. Yahav (Ed.): HVC 2014, LNCS 8855, pp. 1–16, 2014.

we adopt for this architecture is TSO-linearizability as defined in [9]. If verifying linearizability was not hard enough, the reordering of the memory accesses in TSO brings an additional layer of complexity. The purpose of this paper is to simplify this complexity as much as we can. To do so we use the key observation that in many cases for an algorithm on TSO the conditions that linearizability require can be split into two. One aspect deals with the fine-grained nature of the concurrent algorithm, and the other with the effect the local buffers have on when effects become visible in the shared memory.

We exploit this in our proof method, which uses an intermediate description, specifically a coarse-grained abstraction that lies between the abstract specification and the concurrent algorithm. The coarse-grained abstraction captures the semantics of the concurrent algorithm when there is no fine-grained interleaving of operations by different processes. Our simplified proof method then requires one set of proof obligations between the concurrent algorithm and the coarse-grained abstraction, and a different set of proof obligations between the coarse-grained abstraction and the abstract description.

The structure of the paper is as follows. In Section 2 we introduce the TSO model as well as our running example, the *spinlock* algorithm along with an abstract and concrete specification of it in Z. (We assume the reader is familiar with Z — for details see [18]). In Section 3 we provide a coarse-grained abstraction of spinlock. In Section 4 we adapt the standard definition of linearizability to allow the concrete specification to be proved linearizable to the coarse-grained specification. In Section 5 we define a transformation from the coarse-grained abstraction to the abstract one which together with the results of Section 4 allows us to prove overall correctness of the concrete specification with the abstract one. This is shown to be sound in Section 6 with respect to a notion of linearizability on TSO previously published in [9]. We conclude in Section 7.

2 The TSO Memory Model

In the TSO architecture [17] each processor core uses a write buffer, which is a FIFO queue that stores pending writes to memory. A processor core performing a *write* to a memory location enqueues the write to the buffer and continues computation without waiting for the write to be committed to memory. Pending writes do not become visible to other cores until the buffer is *flushed*, which commits (some or all) pending writes to memory. The value of a memory location *read* by a process is the most recent in the processor's local buffer. If there is no such value (e.g., initially or when all writes corresponding to the location have been flushed), the value of the location is fetched from memory. The use of local buffers allows a read by one process, occurring after a write by another, to return an older value as if it occurred before the write.

In general, flushes are controlled by the CPU, and from the programmer's perspective occur non-deterministically. However, a programmer may explicitly include a *fence*, or *memory barrier*, instruction in a program's code to force a flush to occur. Therefore, although TSO allows some non-sequentially consistent executions, it is used in many modern architectures on the basis that these can be prevented, where necessary, by programmers using fence instructions. A pair of *lock* and *unlock* commands allows a process to acquire sole access to the memory. Both commands include a fence which forces the store buffer of that process to be flushed completely.

2.1 Example – Spinlock

Spinlock is a locking mechanism designed to avoid operating system overhead associated with process scheduling and context switching. The **abstract** specification simply describes a lock, with operations $Acquire_p$, $Release_p$ and $TryAcquire_p$ parameterised by the identifier of the process $p \in P$ performing the operation (P is the set of all process identifiers). A global variable x represents the lock and is set to 0 when the lock is held by a thread, and 1 otherwise. As in [16], we assume that only a process that has acquired the lock will release it, and a process will only attempt to acquire the lock if it doesn't already hold it.

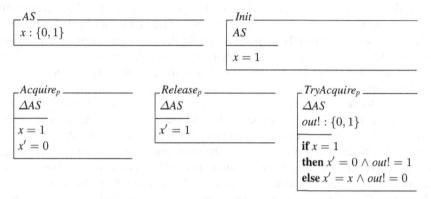

A typical implementation of spinlock [11] is shown in Figure 1, given as pseudo-code (where a1, etc. are line numbers). A thread trying to acquire the lock *spins*, i.e., waits in a loop, while repeatedly checking x for availability.

```
    word x=1;

    void acquire()            void release()           int tryacquire()
       {                         {                        {
a1     while(1) {        r1       x=1;             t1       lock;
a2       lock;                  }                  t2       if (x==1) {
a3       if (x==1) {                               t3         x=0;
a4         x=0;                                    t4         unlock;
a5         unlock;                                 t5         return 1;
a6         return;                                          }
         }                                         t6       unlock;
a7       unlock;                                   t7       return 0;
a8       while(x==0){};                                   }
       }}
```

Fig. 1. Spinlock implementation

A terminating acquire operation will always succeed to acquire the lock. It will lock[1] the global memory so that no other process can write to x. If, however, another

---

[1] Locking the global memory using the TSO lock command should not be confused with acquiring the lock of this case study by setting x to 0.

thread has already acquired the lock (i.e., x==0) then it will unlock the global memory and spin, i.e., loop in the while-loop until it becomes free, before starting over. Otherwise, it acquires the lock by setting x to 0.

The operation release releases the lock by setting x to 1. The tryacquire operation differs from acquire in that it only makes one attempt to acquire the lock. If this attempt is successful it returns 1, otherwise it returns 0.

The lock and unlock commands act as memory barriers on TSO. Hence, writes to x by the acquire and tryacquire operations are not delayed. For efficiency, however, release does not have a memory barrier and so its write to x can be delayed until a flush occurs. The spinlock implementation will still work correctly, the only effect that the absence of a barrier has is that a subsequent acquire may be delayed until a flush occurs, or a tryacquire operation by a thread q may return 0 after the lock has been released by another thread p. For example, the following execution is possible, where we write $(q, \text{tryacquire}(0))$ to denote process q performing a tryacquire operation and returning 0, and $\text{flush}(p)$ to denote the CPU flushing a value from process p's buffer: $\langle (p, \text{acquire}), (p, \text{release}), (q, \text{tryacquire}(0)), \text{flush}(p) \rangle$.

Thus p performs an acquire, then a release, and then q a tryacquire that returns 0 even though it occurs immediately after the release. This is because the $\text{flush}(p)$, which sets the value of x in memory to 0 has not yet occurred.

The Z specification that corresponds to the **concrete** system has one operation per line of pseudo-code, and each operation can be invoked by a given process. The concrete state consists of the shared memory, given as a global state GS and local state LS for each process. GS includes the value of the shared variable x (initially 1), a variable $lock$ which has value $\{p\}$ when a process p currently has the global memory locked (and is $\varnothing$ otherwise), and a buffer for each process modelled as a sequence of 0 and 1's.[2]

$\begin{array}{l}
\underline{\;GS\;} \\
x : \{0, 1\} \\
lock : \mathbb{P}\,P \\
buffer : P \to \text{seq}\{0, 1\} \\
\hline
\#lock \le 1
\end{array}$
$\qquad$
$\begin{array}{l}
\underline{\;GSInit\;} \\
GS \\
\hline
x = 1 \\
lock = \varnothing \\
\forall p : P \bullet buffer(p) = \langle\rangle
\end{array}$

For a given process, LS is specified in terms a program counter, PC, indicating which operations (i.e., lines of code) can next be performed. Let

$$PC ::= 1 \mid a1 \mid \ldots \mid a8 \mid t1 \mid \ldots \mid t7 \mid r1$$

The value 1 denotes that the process is not executing any of the three operations. The values ai, for $i \in 1 .. 8$, denote the process is ready to perform the ith line of code of acquire, and similarly for ti and tryacquire. The value $r1$ denotes the process is ready to perform the first line of release.

$\begin{array}{l}
\underline{\;LS\;} \\
pc : PC
\end{array}$
$\qquad$
$\begin{array}{l}
\underline{\;LSInit\;} \\
LS \\
\hline
pc = 1
\end{array}$

---

[2] In a more complex example, the buffer would also store the name of the variable assigned.

Given this specification, the lines of code are formalised as Z operations.[3] For a given process p, we have an operation $A0_p$ corresponding to the invocation of the `acquire` operation, and an operation $A1_p$ corresponding to the line of code `while(1)`.

```
┌─A0ₚ ─────────────────────
│ ΞGS; ΔLS
├──────────────────────────
│ pc = 1 ∧ pc' = a1
```

```
┌─A1ₚ ─────────────────
│ ΞGS; ΔLS
├──────────────────────
│ pc = a1 ∧ pc' = a2
```

The operation $A2_p$ corresponds to the line of code `lock`. To model the next line of code, `if (x==1)`, we use two operations: $A31_p$ for the case when $x = 1$, and $A30_p$ for the case when $x = 0$. These operations are only enabled when the buffer is empty, modelling the fact that the lock of $A2_p$ is a fence, i.e., a sequence of flush operations on p's buffer (specified below) must occur immediately after $A2_p$ if the buffer is non-empty.

```
┌─A2ₚ ─────────────────────
│ ΔGS; ΔLS
├──────────────────────────
│ pc = a2 ∧ lock = ∅
│ pc' = a3 ∧ lock' = {p}
```

```
┌─A31ₚ ──────────────
│ ΞGS; ΔLS
├────────────────────
│ buffer(p) = ⟨⟩
│ pc = a3 ∧ x = 1
│ pc' = a4
```

```
┌─A30ₚ ──────────
│ ΞGS; ΔLS
├────────────────
│ buffer(p) = ⟨⟩
│ pc = a3 ∧ x = 0
│ pc' = a7
```

The operation $A4_p$, corresponding to the line `x=0`, adds the value 0 to the buffer. The operations corresponding to the other lines of `acquire` are modelled similarly. The two operations corresponding to `while(x==0)`, $A80_p$ and $A81_p$, are only enabled when either x can be read from the buffer, i.e., $buffer \neq \langle\rangle$, or the buffer is empty and the memory is not locked (and so x can be read from the global memory).

```
┌─A4ₚ ──────────────────────
│ ΔGS; ΔLS
├───────────────────────────
│ pc = a4
│ buffer'(p) = buffer(p) ⌢ ⟨0⟩
│ pc' = a5
```

```
┌─A5ₚ ──────────────────────────────
│ ΔGS; ΔLS
├───────────────────────────────────
│ buffer(p) = ⟨⟩
│ pc = a5 ∧ pc' = a6 ∧ lock' = ∅
```

```
┌─A6ₚ ─────────────────────
│ ΞGS; ΔLS
├──────────────────────────
│ pc = a6 ∧ pc' = 1
```

```
┌─A7ₚ ──────────────────────────────
│ ΔGS; ΔLS
├───────────────────────────────────
│ buffer(p) = ⟨⟩
│ pc = a7 ∧ pc' = a8 ∧ lock' = ∅
```

```
┌─A80ₚ ─────────────────────────────────
│ ΞGS; ΞLS
├───────────────────────────────────────
│ pc = a8
│ buffer(p) = ⟨⟩ ⇒ lock = ∅ ∧ x = 0
│ buffer(p) ≠ ⟨⟩ ⇒ last buffer(p) = 0
```

```
┌─A81ₚ ─────────────────────────────────
│ ΞGS; ΔLS
├───────────────────────────────────────
│ pc = a8
│ buffer(p) = ⟨⟩ ⇒ lock = ∅ ∧ x = 1
│ buffer(p) ≠ ⟨⟩ ⇒ last buffer(p) = 1
│ pc' = a1
```

---

[3] To simplify the presentation we adopt the convention that the values (of variables or in the range of a function) that are not explicitly changed by an operation remain unchanged.

The operations for `tryacquire` are similar to those of `acquire`. Those for `release` are given below. We also have an operation, $Flush_{cpu}$, corresponding to a CPU-controlled flush which outputs the process whose buffer it flushes.

```
┌─ R0_p ─────────────────────────┐   ┌─ R1_p ─────────────────────────┐
│ ΞGS                             │   │ ΞGS                             │
│ ΔLS                             │   │ ΔLS                             │
├─────────────────────────────────┤   ├─────────────────────────────────┤
│ pc = 1 ∧ pc' = r1               │   │ pc = r1 ∧ pc' = 1               │
│                                 │   │ buffer'(p) = buffer(p) ⌢ ⟨1⟩    │
└─────────────────────────────────┘   └─────────────────────────────────┘
```

We also have an operation, $Flush_{cpu}$, corresponding to a CPU-controlled flush which outputs the process whose buffer it flushes.

```
┌─ Flush_cpu ──────────────────────────────────────────────────────────┐
│ ΔGS                                                                    │
│ p! : P                                                                 │
├────────────────────────────────────────────────────────────────────────┤
│ lock = ∅ ∨ lock = {p!}                                                 │
│ buffer(p!) ≠ ⟨⟩ ⇒ x' = head buffer(p!) ∧ buffer'(p!) = tail buffer(p!) │
│ buffer(p!) = ⟨⟩ ⇒ x' = x ∧ buffer'(p!) = buffer(p!)                    │
└────────────────────────────────────────────────────────────────────────┘
```

The task in its most general setting is to prove that this concrete specification is linearizable with respect to the abstract one given earlier. The rest of this paper is concerned with a method by which one can show this and similar algorithms correct. First we recap on the notion of linearizability and then discuss how it can be used to provide a coarse-grained abstraction of our concrete specification.

3   Coarse-Grained Abstraction

Linearizability [12] is the standard notion of correctness for concurrent algorithms, and allows one to compare a fine-grained implementation against its abstract specification. For example, in spinlock the concurrent system might perform an execution such as: $\langle (p, \text{A0}), (q, \text{R0}), (p, \text{A1}), (q, \text{R1}) \rangle$. The idea of linearizability is that any such concrete sequence must be consistent with *some* abstract execution (i.e., a sequence of *Acquire*'s, *Release*'s etc. also performed by p and q):

> (1) Linearizability provides the illusion that each operation applied by concurrent processes takes effect instantaneously at some point between its invocation and its return. This point is known as the *linearization point* [12].

In other words, if two operations overlap, then they may take effect in any order from an abstract perspective, but otherwise they must take effect in program order.

There has been an enormous amount of interest in deriving techniques for verifying linearizability. These range from using shape analysis [2, 4] and separation logic [4] to rely-guarantee reasoning [20] and refinement-based simulation methods [7, 10]. Most of this work has been for sequentially consistent architectures, but some work has been done for TSO [3, 9, 11, 19]. In particular, in [9] we have defined a simulation-based proof method for linearizability on TSO. The key point in defining linearizability on TSO is to take into account the role of the local buffers. Since the flush of a process's buffer is sometimes the point that the effect of an operation's changes to memory become globally visible, the flush can be viewed as being the final part of the operation. For example, the flush of a variable, such as x, after an operation, such as `release`, can be taken as the return of that operation. Under this interpretation, the `release` operation extends from its invocation to the flush which writes its change to x to the global memory. Thus [19] and [9] use the following principle:

> (2) The return point of an operation on a TSO architecture is not necessarily the point where the operation ceases execution, but can be any point up to the last flush of the variables written by that operation.

However, any proof method will be complicated by having to deal with both the inherent interleaving handled by linearizability and the additional potential overlapping of concrete operations resulting from the above principle. For example, in spinlock, a process may perform a `release` but not have its buffer flushed before invoking its next operation.

The idea in this paper is simple. We use an intermediate specification (between the abstract and concrete) to split the original proof obligations into two simpler components. The first (between the concrete and intermediate specifications) deals with the underlying linearizability, and the second (between intermediate and abstract) deals with the effects of local buffers. The intermediate specification is a *coarse-grained abstraction* that captures the semantics of the concrete specification with no fine-grained interleaving of operations by different processes. We describe how to define such a coarse-grained abstraction in the next section.

Figure 2 illustrates this idea for a specific execution: at the bottom is a concrete execution, and in the middle is an execution of the intermediate specification which linearizes it (as per Section 4). Finally at the top is an execution of the abstract specification that is related to the intermediate one by the transformation *TRANS* defined in Section 5. Overall this will guarantee that the concrete execution is TSO-linearizable to the abstract one, as we show in Section 6.

3.1 Defining the Coarse-Grained Abstraction

The coarse-grained abstraction is constructed by adding local buffers to the abstract specification. Thus, it is still a description on the TSO architecture – since it has buffers and flushes – but does not decompose the operations. The state space is the abstract state space with the addition of a buffer for each process (as in the concrete state space *GS*). Like in the concrete state space, all buffers are initially empty. Hence for spinlock we have:

_BS_____	_BSInit_____
$x : \{0, 1\}$	BS
buffer $: P \to \mathrm{seq}\{0, 1\}$	$x = 1 \wedge \forall p : P \bullet \textit{buffer}(p) = \langle \rangle$

Each operation is like that of the abstract specification except that

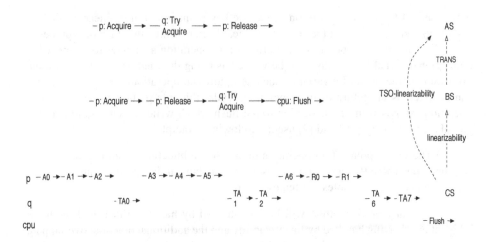

Fig. 2. Three executions in abstract, intermediate and concrete models

- reads are replaced by reads from the process's buffer or from memory, i.e., the operation refers to the latest values of variables in the buffer, and to their actual values otherwise,
- writes are replaced by writes to the buffer (unless the corresponding concrete operation has a fence),
- because we have buffers in the intermediate state space we need to include fences and flushes: the buffer is set to empty when the corresponding concrete operation has a fence, and a flush is modelled as a separate operation.

For example, for the abstract operation $Acquire_p$, $x = 1$ represents a read, and $x' = 0$ represents a write. Using the above heuristic, we replace $x = 1$ by $buffer(p) \neq \langle \rangle \Rightarrow last\,buffer(p) = 1 \wedge buffer(p) = \langle \rangle \Rightarrow x = 1$ since the latest value of x is that in the buffer when the buffer is not empty, and the actual value of x otherwise. We also replace $x' = 0$ by $buffer'(p) = \langle \rangle \wedge x' = 0$ since the corresponding concrete operation has a fence. Similarly, while the operation $TryAcquire_p$ writes directly to x and sets the buffer to empty (since it has a fence), the operation $Release_p$ writes only to the buffer.

┌─ $Acquire_p$ ───────────────
ΔBS
$buffer(p) \neq \langle \rangle \Rightarrow last\,buffer(p) = 1$ $buffer(p) = \langle \rangle \Rightarrow x = 1$ $buffer'(p) = \langle \rangle \wedge x' = 0$

┌─ $Release_p$ ───────────────
ΔBS
$buffer'(p) = buffer(p) \frown \langle 1 \rangle$

┌─ $TryAcquire_p$ ──────────────────────────────
ΔBS $out! : \{0, 1\}$
if $buffer(p) \neq \langle \rangle \wedge last\,buffer(p) = 1 \vee buffer(p) = \langle \rangle \wedge x = 1$ **then** $buffer'(p) = \langle \rangle \wedge x' = 0 \wedge out! = 1$ **else** $buffer'(p) = \langle \rangle \wedge x' = 0 \wedge out! = 0$

Note that $x' = 0$ in the else-predicate of *TryAcquire$_P$* since if the buffer is empty, x is 0 and does not change, and if the buffer is not empty, the last element in buffer is 0 and the buffer is completely flushed by the `lock` command in `tryacquire`.

Finally, the course-grained abstraction is completed with the *Flush$_{cpu}$* operation. As in the concrete specification, this operation is performed by the CPU process.

Flush$_{cpu}$
ΔBS
$p! : P$

$buffer(p!) \neq \langle \rangle \Rightarrow x' = head\,buffer(p!) \wedge buffer'(p!) = tail\,buffer(p!)$
$buffer(p!) = \langle \rangle \Rightarrow x' = x \wedge buffer'(p!) = buffer(p!)$

The coarse-grained abstraction is chosen purposefully to reflect the abstract specification; this facilitates the final part of the proof. The inclusion of buffers and flush operations, however, means it can be shown to linearize the concrete specification using standard proof methods.

4 Linearizability: From Concrete to Intermediate Specification

To prove the concrete specification is correct with respect to the intermediate one, we can use a slight adaption of the standard notion of linearizability. Below we describe how we adapt the formal definition and proof method for linearizability given in [7].

In the standard definition of linearizability, *histories* are sequences of *events* which can be invocations or returns of operations from a set I and performed by a particular process from a set P. On the TSO architecture, operations can be flushes and we assume that a flush is only executed by a CPU process $cpu \in P$, different from all other processes. We also assume that invocations of flushes are immediately followed by their returns. Invocations have an associated input from domain In, and returns an output from domain Out.

$Event ::= inv\langle\!\langle P \times I \times In \rangle\!\rangle \mid ret\langle\!\langle P \times I \times Out \rangle\!\rangle$
$History == seq\,Event$

For a history h, $\#h$ is the *length* of the sequence, and $h(n)$ its nth element (for n : $1..\#h$). Predicates $inv?(e)$ and $ret?(e)$ determine whether an event $e \in Event$ is an invoke or return, respectively. We let $e.\pi \in P$ and $e.i \in I$ be the process executing the event e and the operation to which the event belongs, respectively.

Let $mp(p, m, n, h)$ denote matching pairs of invocations and returns by process p in history h as in [7]. Its definition requires that $h(m)$ and $h(n)$ are executed by the same process p and are an invocation and return event, respectively, of the same operation. Additionally, it requires that for all k between m and n, $h(k)$ is not an invocation or return event of p. That is, $mp(p, m, n, h)$ holds iff

$0 < m < n \leq \#h \wedge$
$inv?(h(m)) \wedge ret?(h(n)) \wedge h(m).\pi = h(n).\pi = p \wedge h(m).i = h(n).i \wedge$
$\forall k \bullet m < k < n \Rightarrow h(k).\pi \neq p$

We say a history h is *legal* iff for each $n : 1..\#h$ such that $ret?(h(n))$, there exists an earlier $m : 1..n - 1$ such that $mp(p, m, n, h)$.

A formal definition of linearizability is given below. A history is *incomplete* if it has either (i) an operation which has been invoked and has linearized but not yet returned, or (ii) results in a non-empty buffer. An incomplete history h is extended with a sequence h_0 of flushes and returns of non-flush operations, then matched to a sequential history hs by removing the remaining pending invocations using a function *complete*. Let $Hist_{FR}$ be the set of histories that are sequences of flushes and returns of non-flush operations.

Definition 1 (Linearizability). *A history* $h : History$ *is* linearizable *with respect to some sequential history* hs *iff* $lin(h, hs)$ *holds, where*

$$lin(h, hs) \; \widehat{=} \; \exists h_0 : Hist_{FR} \bullet legal(h \frown h_0) \wedge linrel(complete(h \frown h_0), hs)$$

where

$$\begin{aligned}
linrel(h, hs) \; \widehat{=} \; &\exists f : 1..\#h \rightarrowtail 1..\#hs \bullet (\forall n : 1..\#h \bullet h(n) = hs(f(n))) \wedge \\
&(\forall p : P; \; m, n : 1..\#h \bullet m < n \wedge mp(p, m, n, h) \Rightarrow f(n) = f(m) + 1) \; \wedge \\
&(\forall p, q : P; \; m, n, m', n' : 1..\#h \bullet \\
&\quad n < m' \wedge mp(p, m, n, h) \wedge mp(q, m', n', h) \Rightarrow f(n) < f(m')) \qquad \square
\end{aligned}$$

That is, operations in hs do not overlap (each invocation is followed immediately by its matching return) and the order of non-overlapping operations in h is preserved in hs.

For example, the history h corresponding to the concrete execution in Figure 2 is

$\langle inv(p, \texttt{acquire},), inv(q, \texttt{tryacquire},), ret(p, \texttt{acquire},), inv(p, \texttt{release},),$
$ret(p, \texttt{release},), ret(q, \texttt{tryacquire}, 0), inv(cpu, \texttt{flush},), ret(cpu, \texttt{flush}, p) \rangle$

This history is complete and legal, and is linearized by the history hs

$\langle inv(p, Acquire,), ret(p, Acquire,), inv(p, Release,), ret(p, Release,),$
$inv(q, TryAcquire,), ret(q, TryAcquire, 0), inv(cpu, Flush,), ret(cpu, Flush, p) \rangle$

which corresponds to the intermediate-level execution in Figure 2.

Correctness requires showing all concrete histories are linearizable. Existing proof methods for showing this include the simulation-based approach in [7]. This is based on showing that the concrete specification is a non-atomic refinement of the abstract one. Examples of its use are given in [5–8, 14, 15]. This approach is fully encoded in a theorem proving tool, KIV [13], and has been proved sound and complete — the proofs themselves being done within KIV. The key point for us is that, for this portion of the correctness proof, we do not have to adapt the proof method.

5   Transforming the Intermediate Specification to an Abstract One

The previous section has shown how to prove that a concrete specification is linearizable with respect to an intermediate, coarse-grained abstraction. The inclusion of local buffers in this intermediate specification avoided us needing to deal with the effects of the TSO architecture. In this section, we introduce a deterministic history transformation which when coupled with the linearization method of the previous section guarantees the overall correctness of concrete specification with respect to the abstract one. Correctness involves showing every history of the intermediate specification is transformed to a history of the abstract one. Soundness of this approach is proved in Section 6.

The histories of the intermediate specification are sequential, i.e., returns of operations occur immediately after their invocations, but the specification includes buffers and flush operations. The transformation turns the histories of the intermediate specification into histories of an abstract one, i.e., without buffers, with the same behaviour. It does this according to principle (2) in Section 3, i.e., it moves the return of an operation to the flush that make its global behaviour visible. To keep histories sequential, we also move the invocation of the operation to immediately before the return.

To define the transformation, denoted *TRANS*, we need to calculate which flush an operation's return (and invocation) should be moved to. This is done by a function *mpf* (standing for *matching pair flush*) which in turn uses *mp* defined in Section 4. A flush returns an operation, i.e., makes its effects visible globally, when it writes the last variable which was updated by that operation to memory. Let $bs(p, m, h)$ denote the size of process p's buffer at point m in the history h. Given an operation whose invocation is at point m and return at point n, if the buffer is empty when the operation is invoked, then the number of flushes to be performed before the operation returns is equal to the size of the buffer at the end of the operation, i.e., $bs(p, n, h)$; if this number is 0 then the return does not move. Similarly, if an operation contains a fence then the number of flushes before the operation returns is also equal to $bs(p, n, h)$. In all other cases, we need to determine whether the operation has written to any global variables. If it has written to one or more global variables then again the number of flushes to be performed before the operation returns is $bs(p, n, h)$.

To determine whether an operation has written to global variables, we compare the size of the buffer at the start and end of the operation taking into account any flushes that have occurred in between. Let $nf(p, m, n, h)$ denote the number of flushes of process p's buffer from point m up to and including point n in h. The number of writes between the two points is given by

$$nw(p, m, n, h) \mathrel{\widehat{=}} bs(p, n, h) - bs(p, m, h) + nf(p, m, n, h) .$$

The function *mpf* is then defined below where m, n and l are indices in h such that (m, n) is a matching pair and l corresponds to the point to which the return of the matching pair must be moved.

$$mpf(p, m, n, l, h) \mathrel{\widehat{=}} mp(p, m, n, h) \wedge n \leq l \wedge$$
$$\textbf{if } nw(p, m, n, h) = 0 \vee bs(p, n, h) = 0 \textbf{ then } l = n$$
$$\textbf{else } h(l) = ret(cpu, Flush, p) \wedge nf(p, n, l, h) = bs(p, n, h)$$

The first part of the if states that $l = n$ if no items are put on the buffer by the operation invoked at point m, or all items put on the buffer have already been flushed when the operation returns. The second states that l corresponds to a flush of p's buffer and the number of flushes between n and l is precisely the number required to flush the contents of the buffer at n.

The history transformation *TRANS* is then defined as follows. It relies on the fact that the intermediate histories are sequential, i.e., comprise a sequence of matching pairs. Each matching pair of a history is either moved to the position of the flush which acts as its return (given by *mpf*), or left in the same position relative to the other matching pairs. The transformation also removes all flushes from the history. Informally we can think of *TRANS(hs)* creating a new history determined by applying two steps to the history *hs*. The first step introduces a new history hs_1 which includes dummy events δ and invocations and returns of flushes. The second step removes these resulting in an abstract history:

Step 1. For all indices *m*, *n* and *l* such that $mpf(p, m, n, l, h)$ holds for some *p*:

   if $n = l$ then $hs_1(m) := hs(m)$ and $hs_1(n) := hs(n)$
   else $hs_1(l) := hs(n)$ and $hs_1(l-1) := hs(m)$ and $hs_1(n) := \delta$ and $hs_1(m) := \delta$

Step 2. All δ and flush invocations and returns are removed.

Although this is the best intuition of *TRANS*, the formal definition is based on identifying the matching pairs, and ordering them by the positions that invocations and returns are moved to. The key point is that the positions that returns get moved to are different for each event, so we can order them, and this order defines our new history.

Definition 2 (TRANS). *Let hs be a history of the intermediate specification, $S = \{(m, n, l) \mid \exists p : P \bullet mpf(p, m, n, l, hs) \wedge hs(m).i \neq Flush\}$, and $k = \#S$. We can order elements of S by the 3rd element in the tuple: $l_1 < l_2 < \ldots < l_k$. Then TRANS(hs) is an abstract history with length 2k defined (for $i : 1 .. 2k$) as:*

$$TRANS(hs)(i) = \begin{cases} hs(n) & \text{if } i \text{ is even and } (m, n, l_{i/2}) \in S \\ hs(m) & \text{if } i \text{ is odd and } (m, n, l_{(i+1)/2}) \in S \end{cases}$$

Furthermore, this mapping induces a function G which identifies the index that any particular invocation or return has been moved to. G is defined (for $j : 1 .. \#hs$) by:

$$G(j) = \begin{cases} 2i & \text{if } (m, j, l_i) \in S \text{ and so } hs(j) \text{ is a return} \\ 2i - 1 & \text{if } (j, n, l_i) \in S \text{ and so } hs(j) \text{ is an invocation} \end{cases} \qquad \square$$

Definition 3 (TSO-equivalence). *An intermediate specification BS is TSO-equivalent to an abstract specification AS whenever for every history hs of BS, TRANS(hs) is a history of AS.* $\qquad \square$

For example, given the intermediate-level history *hs* in Section 4, the indices which are related by *mpf* are as follows: for *Acquire* we get $mpf(p, 1, 2, 2, hs)$, for *Release* we get $mpf(p, 3, 4, 8, hs)$, for *TryAcquire* we get $mpf(q, 5, 6, 6, hs)$ and for *Flush* we get $mpf(cpu, 7, 8, 8, hs)$. *S* will include the first three tuples which are then ordered: $(1, 2, l_1), (5, 6, l_2), (3, 4, l_3)$ (where $l_1 = 2, l_2 = 6$ and $l_3 = 8$). Thus, $TRANS(hs)(1) = hs(1)$ since 1 is odd and $(1, 2, l_1) \in S$. Similarly, $TRANS(hs)(6) = hs(4)$ as 6 is even and $(3, 4, l_3) \in S$. Overall, *TRANS(hs)* is the following which corresponds to the abstract execution in Figure 2: $\langle inv(p, Acquire,), ret(p, Acquire,), inv(q, TryAcquire,), ret(q, TryAcquire, 0), inv(p, Release,), ret(p, Release,)\rangle$.

6   Gluing it Together: From Concrete to Abstract Specification

Overall, we want to show the correctness of the concrete specification with respect to the abstract one. The notion of correctness we adopt is TSO-linearizability as defined in

[9]. We summarise this definition below before proving that the effect of linearizability followed by TSO-equivalence implies TSO-linearizability.

6.1 TSO-Linearizability

To prove linearizability on TSO, we introduce a history transformation *Trans* which (according to principle (2) in Section 3) moves the return of each operation to the flush which makes its global behaviour visible, if any. *Trans* is similar to *TRANS* of Section 5 except it does not also move the invocation of the operation. The informal intuition for *Trans* alters the first step of the transformation to the following:

Step 1. For all indices m, n and l such that $mpf(p, m, n, l, h)$ holds for some p:

if $n = l$ then $h_1(m) := h(m)$ and $h_1(n) := h(n)$

else $h_1(m) := h(m)$ and $h_1(l) := h(n)$ and $h_1(n) := \delta$

In a manner similar to *TRANS*, this is formalised in the following definition:

Definition 4 (Trans). *Let h be a history of the concrete specification, $S_1 = \{(m, n, l, x) \mid \exists p : P \bullet mpf(p, m, n, l, h) \wedge h(m).i \neq Flush \wedge x \in \{m, l\}\}$, and $k_1 = \#S_1$. We can order the elements of S_1 by their 4th elements: $x_1 < x_2 < \ldots < x_{k_1}$. Then $Trans(h)$ is an abstract history with length k_1 defined (for $i : 1 \ldots k_1$) as:*

$$Trans(h)(i) = \begin{cases} h(x_i), & \text{if } (x_i, n, l, x_i) \in S, \text{for some } n \text{ and } l \\ h(n), & \text{if } (m, n, x_i, x_i) \in S, \text{for some } m \end{cases}$$

Furthermore, this mapping induces a function g which identifies the index that any particular invocation or return has been moved from. g is defined (for $i : 1 \ldots k_1$) by:

$$g(i) = \begin{cases} x_i, & \text{if } (x_i, n, l, x_i) \in S, \text{for some } n \text{ and } l \\ n, & \text{if } (m, n, x_i, x_i) \in S, \text{for some } m \end{cases} \qquad \Box$$

For example, given the concrete history h in Section 4, the indices which are related by *mpf* are as follows: for `acquire` we get $mpf(p, 1, 3, 3, h)$, for `tryacquire` we get $mpf(q, 2, 6, 6, h)$, for `release` we get $mpf(p, 4, 5, 8, h)$ and for `flush` we get $mpf(cpu, 7, 8, 8, h)$. The elements of set S_1 are ordered as follows: $(x_1, 3, 3, x_1)$, $(x_2, 6, 6, x_2)$, $(1, 3, x_3, x_3)$, $(x_4, 5, 8, x_4)$, $(2, 6, x_5, x_5)$, $(4, 5, x_6, x_6)$ (where $x_1 = 1$, $x_2 = 2$, $x_3 = 3$, $x_4 = 4$, $x_5 = 6$ and $x_6 = 8$). Thus, $Trans(h)(1) = h(1)$ since $x_1 = 1$, and $Trans(h)(6) = h(8)$ since $x_6 = 8$. Overall $Trans(h)$ is

$\langle inv(p, Acquire,), inv(q, TryAcquire,), ret(p, Acquire,), inv(p, Release,),$
$ret(q, TryAcquire, 0), ret(p, Release,)\rangle$.

A key part of adapting the definition of linearizability from Section 4 to TSO is what we mean by a matching pair of invocations and returns. The formal definition of the function mp requires that for all k between m and n, $h(k)$ is not an invocation or return event of p. This is not true for our transformed histories on TSO since operations by the same process may overlap. Therefore, we will use a new version of matching pairs mp_{TSO} defined as follows.

$mp_{TSO}(p, m, n, h)$ iff $mpf(p, x, n, z, y, h)$
where $m = x - \sum_{p:P} nf(p, 1, x, h)$ and $n = y - \sum_{p:P} nf(p, 1, y, h)$ and $x < z \le y$

We then adopt the definition of TSO-linearizability from [9]. After extending an incomplete concrete history with flushes and returns of non-flush operations, we apply *Trans* to it before matching it to an abstract history.

Definition 5 (TSO-linearizability). *A history* h : *History is* TSO-linearizable *with respect to some sequential history hs iff* $lin_{TSO}(h, hs)$ *holds, where*

$$lin_{TSO}(h, hs) \cong \exists h_0 : Hist_{FR} \bullet legal(h \frown h_0) \wedge linrel_{TSO}(Trans(complete(h \frown h_0)), hs)$$

where

$$linrel_{TSO}(h, hs) \cong \exists f : 1..\#h \rightarrowtail 1..\#hs \bullet (\forall n : 1..\#h \bullet h(n) = hs(f(n))) \wedge$$
$$(\forall p : P; \ m, n : 1..\#h \bullet m < n \wedge mp_{TSO}(p, m, n, h) \Rightarrow f(n) = f(m) + 1) \wedge$$
$$(\forall p, q : P; \ m, n, m', n' : 1..\#h \bullet$$
$$n < m' \wedge mp_{TSO}(p, m, n, h) \wedge mp_{TSO}(q, m', n', h) \Rightarrow f(n) < f(m'))$$

We say that a concrete specification is TSO-linearizable with respect to an abstract specification if and only if for all concrete histories h, *there exists an abstract history* hs *such that* $lin_{TSO}(h, hs)$.   □

The new matching pairs in the example history $Trans(h)$ above are $mp_{TSO}(p, 1, 3, h_1)$, $mp_{TSO}(q, 2, 5, h_1)$ and $mp_{TSO}(p, 4, 6, h_1)$. It is easy to see that this is linearized by the abstract history corresponding to the execution in Figure 2.

6.2 Soundness

Assume a concrete specification *CS* is linearizable with respect to an intermediate specification *BS*, and *BS* is TSO-equivalent to an abstract specification *AS*. Given a concrete history h, to prove our approach sound we have to find an abstract history hs such that $lin_{TSO}(h, hs)$. It is clear that any incomplete concrete history can be extended to a complete and legal history, therefore we assume h is complete and legal.

Since *CS* is linearizable with respect to *BS*, there exists an hs_1 such that $lin(h, hs_1)$ and an associated bijection f_1. Let $hs \cong TRANS(hs_1)$. To show *CS* is TSO-linearizable with respect to *AS*, we define a bijection f between the indices of $Trans(h)$ and hs as follows. Let $f(n) = G(f_1(g(n)))$ where $n \in 1 .. \#Trans(h)$, and G and g are given in Definitions 2 and 4 respectively. f is a bijection since:

(i) Since $\#h = \#hs_1$ (property of *lin*), we get $\#Trans(h) = \#TRANS(hs_1)$ (since both remove flush invocation and returns) and hence $\#hs = \#Trans(h)$.

(ii) f is surjective since each event in $TRANS(hs_1)$ is either an invocation or return of a non-flush operation. Therefore, there exists an invocation or return of a non-flush operation in hs_1 that is mapped to this event by G. Then surjectivity of f_1 implies there exists an invocation or return of a non-flush operation in h which maps to the event in hs_1. Since this event is of a non-flush operation, there exists an invocation or return in $Trans(h)$ which is mapped to it by g.

(iii) f is injective since g, f_1 and G are all injective.

We now show that f satisfies the three conjuncts of $linrel_{TSO}$ and hence that TSO-linearizability holds.

(i) $Trans(h)(n) = hs(f(n))$ follows by construction of f.

(ii) Given $m, n : 1 .. \#Trans(h)$ and $p : P$, suppose that $m < n \wedge mp_{TSO}(p, m, n, h)$. In the case where $h(g(n))$ is the return of a non-flush operation, $mp(p, g(m), g(n), h)$ holds so we know $f_1(g(n)) = f_1(g(m)) + 1$ (property of lin). G does not change this relationship between $f_1(g(n))$ and $f_1(g(m))$. Hence, $f(n) = f(m) + 1$.

On the other hand if $h(g(n))$ is the return of a flush operation, G moves $f_1(g(m))$ and $f_1(g(m+1))$ to $f_1(g(n-1))$ and $f_1(g(n))$ respectively. Again, we get $f(n) = f(m) + 1$.

(iii) Given $m, n, m', n' : 1 .. \#Trans(h)$ and $p, q : P$ such that $n < m' \wedge mp_{TSO}(p, m, n, h) \wedge mp_{TSO}(q, m', n', h)$, it follows that $mp(p, g(m), g(n), h) \wedge mp(q, g(m'), g(n'), h)$. This means $f_1(g(n)) < f_1(g(m'))$ (property of lin). G does not change this relationship between $f_1(g(n))$ and $f_1(g(m'))$. Hence, $f(n) < f(m')$.

7 Conclusions

In this paper we have developed a method by which to simplify proofs of linearizability for algorithms running on the TSO memory model. Instead of having to deal with the effects of both fine-grained atomicity and local buffers in one set of proof obligations, we have used an intermediate specification to partition the proof obligations in two. One set of proof obligations is simply the standard existing notion of linearizability (where flushes are treated as normal operations), and any existing proof method can be employed to verify this step (we in fact use our mechanised simulation-based method). The second set of proof obligations involves verifying that an appropriate transformation (given by *TRANS* defined in Section 5) holds.

Although there is existing work on defining linearizability on TSO, to the best of our knowledge this is the first work that provides simplified reasoning for showing *how* linearizability can be verified for algorithms running on TSO, although mention should be made of the approach in [19] that uses SPIN to check specific runs for TSO-linearizability. Clearly this work could be extended in a number of directions. Specifically, we would like to mechanise the proof obligations inherent in *TRANS* using KIV in the same way that the existing proof methods for standard linearizability, such as those in [5–8, 14, 15], have already been encoded in the theorem prover. Additionally, we aim to look at the issue of completeness and related to this will be how one can *calculate* the required intermediate description from the concrete algorithm and abstract and concrete state spaces.

References

1. Alglave, J., Fox, A., Ishtiaq, S., Myreen, M.O., Sarkar, S., Sewell, P., Nardelli, F.Z.: The Semantics of Power and ARM Multiprocessor Machine Code. In: Petersen, L., Chakravarty, M.M.T. (eds.) DAMP 2009, pp. 13–24. ACM (2008)

2. Amit, D., Rinetzky, N., Reps, T.W., Sagiv, M., Yahav, E.: Comparison under abstraction for verifying linearizability. In: Damm, W., Hermanns, H. (eds.) CAV 2007. LNCS, vol. 4590, pp. 477–490. Springer, Heidelberg (2007)
3. Burckhardt, S., Gotsman, A., Musuvathi, M., Yang, H.: Concurrent library correctness on the TSO memory model. In: Seidl, H. (ed.) ESOP 2012. LNCS, vol. 7211, pp. 87–107. Springer, Heidelberg (2012)
4. Calcagno, C., Parkinson, M., Vafeiadis, V.: Modular safety checking for fine-grained concurrency. In: Riis Nielson, H., Filé, G. (eds.) SAS 2007. LNCS, vol. 4634, pp. 233–248. Springer, Heidelberg (2007)
5. Derrick, J., Schellhorn, G., Wehrheim, H.: Proving linearizability via non-atomic refinement. In: Davies, J., Gibbons, J. (eds.) IFM 2007. LNCS, vol. 4591, pp. 195–214. Springer, Heidelberg (2007)
6. Derrick, J., Schellhorn, G., Wehrheim, H.: Mechanizing a correctness proof for a lock-free concurrent stack. In: Barthe, G., de Boer, F.S. (eds.) FMOODS 2008. LNCS, vol. 5051, pp. 78–95. Springer, Heidelberg (2008)
7. Derrick, J., Schellhorn, G., Wehrheim, H.: Mechanically verified proof obligations for linearizability. ACM Trans. Program. Lang. Syst. 33(1), 4 (2011)
8. Derrick, J., Schellhorn, G., Wehrheim, H.: Verifying linearisability with potential linearisation points. In: Butler, M., Schulte, W. (eds.) FM 2011. LNCS, vol. 6664, pp. 323–337. Springer, Heidelberg (2011)
9. Derrick, J., Smith, G., Dongol, B.: Verifying linearizability on TSO architectures. In: Albert, E., Sekerinski, E. (eds.) IFM 2014. LNCS, vol. 8739, pp. 341–356. Springer, Heidelberg (2014)
10. Doherty, S., Groves, L., Luchangco, V., Moir, M.: Formal verification of a practical lock-free queue algorithm. In: de Frutos-Escrig, D., Núñez, M. (eds.) FORTE 2004. LNCS, vol. 3235, pp. 97–114. Springer, Heidelberg (2004)
11. Gotsman, A., Musuvathi, M., Yang, H.: Show no weakness: Sequentially consistent specifications of TSO libraries. In: Aguilera, M.K. (ed.) DISC 2012. LNCS, vol. 7611, pp. 31–45. Springer, Heidelberg (2012)
12. Herlihy, M., Wing, J.M.: Linearizability: A correctness condition for concurrent objects. ACM Trans. Program. Lang. Syst. 12(3), 463–492 (1990)
13. Reif, W., Schellhorn, G., Stenzel, K., Balser, M.: Structured specifications and interactive proofs with KIV. In: Automated Deduction, pp. 13–39. Kluwer (1998)
14. Schellhorn, G., Wehrheim, H., Derrick, J.: How to prove algorithms linearisable. In: Madhusudan, P., Seshia, S.A. (eds.) CAV 2012. LNCS, vol. 7358, pp. 243–259. Springer, Heidelberg (2012)
15. Schellhorn, G., Wehrheim, H., Derrick, J.: A sound and complete proof technique for linearizability of concurrent data structures. ACM Trans. on Computational Logic (2014)
16. Sewell, P., Sarkar, S., Owens, S., Nardelli, F.Z., Myreen, M.O.: x86-TSO: a rigorous and usable programmer's model for x86 multiprocessors. Commun. ACM 53(7), 89–97 (2010)
17. Sorin, D.J., Hill, M.D., Wood, D.A.: A Primer on Memory Consistency and Cache Coherence. Synthesis Lectures on Computer Architecture. Morgan & Claypool Publishers (2011)
18. Spivey, J.M.: The Z Notation: A Reference Manual. Prentice Hall (1992)
19. Travkin, O., Mütze, A., Wehrheim, H.: SPIN as a linearizability checker under weak memory models. In: Bertacco, V., Legay, A. (eds.) HVC 2013. LNCS, vol. 8244, pp. 311–326. Springer, Heidelberg (2013)
20. Vafeiadis, V.: Modular fine-grained concurrency verification. PhD thesis, University of Cambridge (2007)

Enhancing Scenario Quality Using Quasi-Events

Yoav Katz, Eitan Marcus, and Avi Ziv

IBM Research Laboratory in Haifa, Israel
{katz,marcus,aziv}@il.ibm.com

Abstract. A major challenge for processor-level stimuli generators is the need to generate stimuli that exercise deep micro-architectural mechanisms. Advanced generators address this challenge by applying expert testing knowledge that bias the stimuli toward interesting verification events. In this paper, we present a new approach whereby scenarios are not just enhanced, but are actually modified by testing knowledge. By allowing such mutations, scenarios are diverted toward quasi-events that are semantically related, though not identical, to the original intent of the scenario. We describe the importance of quasi-events and the usefulness of automated scenario mutations for improving the verification of speculative execution.

1 Introduction

Modern processors use a combination of architectural and micro-architectural innovations to improve performance and power consumption [7]. This significantly increases the complexity of a processor's design and its verification. Generating processor-level stimuli is one of the main challenges in the verification of processors. The need to thoroughly exercise the micro-architecture and reach all its corners led to the development of sophisticated stimuli generators that are based on techniques such as machine learning [6], constraints satisfaction [2,4], and formal methods [11].

The input to a processor-level stimuli generator is a test template, which describes the desired characteristics of the test cases to be generated on a high level. Given a test template as input, the stimuli generator produces a large set of architecturally valid tests that satisfy the template request by filling all unspecified details in a pseudo-random way.

Existing processor-level test generators (such as [1,5]) provide a rich language for specifying requests at the instruction-level. As processor micro-architecture complexity increases, the ability of these generators to reach all desired corner cases has been strained. Advances in verification methodologies and test-generation tools led to new features that target the micro-architecture. For example, tools embed testing knowledge [1] to increase the probability of generating interesting micro-architectural events (e.g., creating register dependency between instructions to trigger pipeline forwarding). The tools also include elaborate user control in the test template to help the stimuli reach specific micro-architectural events.

E. Yahav (Ed.): HVC 2014, LNCS 8855, pp. 17–29, 2014.
© Springer International Publishing Switzerland 2014

Nevertheless, we observe a growing gap between the goals of the verification plan, which targets events deep inside the processor, and the capabilities of available test generation tools. This impacts both the quality of the verification and the effort needed to complete the verification process. A major cause of this gap is that the goals of the verification plan are typically formulated in terms of high-level scenarios, whereas existing template languages focus on individual instructions and the interactions between them.

Test Plan Automation (TPA) [8,9] bridges this semantic gap by introducing a test template language that more closely resembles the level of abstraction found in the verification plan. The basic construct of TPA's language is the *scenario*, which targets events that are associated with some micro-architectural mechanism modeled in the tool. A simple scenario is expressed as a set of instructions and the required constraints between them. An example of such a scenario is two instructions that access the same cache line to create a cache hit. Additionally, the language provides constructs to combine existing scenarios into hierarchically more complex ones. For example, the simple cache hit and cache miss scenarios can be combined to create a scenario that hits the L1 cache but misses the L2.

To improve the quality of the test cases it generates, TPA extends the notion of testing knowledge from the instruction to the scenario level. Testing knowledge is the embodiment of expert verification knowledge in a stimuli generator so that it biases the stimuli toward interesting verification events without the need for explicit direction from the user. Scenario level testing knowledge automatically elaborates the original scenario to reach interesting variants of the targeted events. This is accomplished in TPA in two ways: by selectively ordering and placing the instructions in the scenario, and by adding background instructions. For example, TPA may choose to place two instructions involved in a collision scenario close to each other to increase the probability that the instructions collide. In addition, it may insert a background instruction that causes the first instruction in the collision to stall, so that the instructions have a greater chance of executing out of order.

In this paper, we propose a new approach to testing knowledge in which scenarios are not just enhanced by the testing knowledge, but are actually modified by it. This allows scenarios to be diverted toward novel areas of the verification space that would not likely be explored by the original scenario. The purpose of these mutations is to generate stimuli that cover simulation events that were not the original intent of the scenario but are semantically related to it.

There are a number of different mutation strategies that TPA can use: changing program order and control flow, modifying the contents of individual instructions, and exchanging the micro-architectural mechanisms used by the scenario. One mutation strategy, which we describe in depth, is to take existing instructions of a scenario and move them onto the speculative path of some branch instruction. The handling of speculative executed instructions significantly complicates a processor's design, and exercising a processor's speculation mechanism is an important component of its verification plan. By modifying a scenario so that some of its instructions are speculatively executed, TPA provides greater testing and coverage of a design's speculation mechanism.

The rest of the paper is organized as follows. Section 2 describes a simple scenario that we use as an example throughout this paper. In Section 3, we describe scenario mutations in general, while Section 4 looks at speculation mutations in particular. Section 5 provides experimental results. Finally, we present our conclusions in Section 6.

2   Simple Scenario Example

To illustrate the power and usefulness of scenarios, we define a scenario that combines two sub-scenarios – a load-hit-store (LHS) and a store-hit-load (SHL). As shown in Figure 1, both of these sub-scenarios involve collisions in buffers commonly found in the load store units of a processor. In the case of LHS, the collision occurs in the store reorder queue (SRQ) buffer, whereas for the SHL scenario, it occurs in the load reorder queue (LRQ) buffer.

Both the SRQ and LRQ buffers store memory access requests until they have completed. When a memory access is stored in one of these buffers, additional accesses to the same memory location cause collisions that may lead to special treatment of the colliding instructions. More specifically, in the implementation of the SRQ of the verified processor, data write accesses to memory are stored in the SRQ until the instruction completes. However, if a read access hits an address that is in the SRQ, it may be forwarded its value even if the corresponding write access has not yet completed. Furthermore, for designs which support out-of-order execution, a write access stored in the SRQ will be flushed whenever it is executed before an earlier read access to the same address.

As shown in Figure 1, the LHS and SHL scenarios both call for a read-after-write (RAW) collision in their respective buffers. The RAW collision scenario is defined generically for all memory buffers with the following specification: The scenario includes two instructions, one (wr) which writes to the buffer, while the other (rd) reads, but does not write to it. Furthermore, the two instructions must collide with each other, with the writer ordered before, but close to the reader. Finally, it is necessary to disable exceptions since exceptions clear the buffers of the processor and must be avoided if a read-after-write is to occur.

The readers and writers of a buffer, as well as the criteria for when instructions collide in a buffer, depend upon the particular buffer. For the SRQ, instructions that write data to memory also write to the SRQ, and instructions that read data from memory read from the SRQ. For the LRQ, it is the opposite. In both cases, collisions occur when the reader from the buffer shares the same address as the writer, and its data is fully contained in the writer's data. The details for the readers, writers, and collision criteria of a buffer is defined in the TPA micro-architecture model of a design [9].

In TPA, the order in which instructions are defined in a scenario does not necessarily determine the order in which instructions will be generated or where they will be placed in the resulting test program. This is also true with regard to the order in which sub-scenarios are invoked by a scenario. TPA therefore has great flexibility in deciding where to place generated instructions. In the RAW

```
scenario LSUCollisions {
  SRQ.RAW()   // LHS
  LRQ.RAW()   // SHL
}
```

```
scenario MemoryBuffer:RAW {
  Instruction wr : writers()
  Instruction rd : readers()

  collision(wr, rd)
  Order(wr,rd)
  Distance(wr,rd) < 5

  Directive: NoException
}
```

Fig. 1. Scenario construction

scenario, the writer to the buffer has been explicitly ordered before the reader using the Order directive. This ensures that the scenario does indeed generate a read after write. In the case of the LSUCollisions scenario on the other hand, no order is specified between the LHS and the SHL sub-scenarios. Therefore, TPA is free to generate these sub-scenarios in any order it chooses, whether randomly or by applying some relevant testing knowledge. It can decide to generate the two sub-scenarios in different threads, or in the same thread with any combination of interleaving between their instructions.

3   Scenario Mutations

As we explained, advanced stimuli generators use testing knowledge to bias stimuli toward interesting verification events. A generator's testing knowledge base contains information verification engineers have accumulated over years of experience that describe the error-prone areas of a design and the test conditions needed to verify them. For example, testing knowledge may bias a generated arithmetic instruction to produce more interesting results such as underflow or overflow, or it may create address collisions between memory access instructions to exercise some cache or memory buffer mechanism.

A fundamental principle of traditional testing knowledge is the need to be faithful to what was specified by the user in the input test template. This means that any testing knowledge rule that contravenes what appears or is implied by the scenario must be disregarded. As a consequence, the application of testing knowledge yields stimuli that are directed toward a subset of the events that make up the solution space of a scenario. Events that were previously unreachable however remain unreachable even when testing knowledge is considered.

While fulfilling scenario requirements is important to achieve quality verification, it is also useful to produce stimuli that almost meet these requirements. *Quasi-events* are events that are different, yet semantically related, to those targeted by a scenario. For example, if the test template contains a scenario to fill some buffer in the design, thereby ensuring that the design stalls until there is a vacancy in the buffer, then generating a stimuli that almost fills the buffer is also important, since it ensures that the design does not stall unnecessarily. As shown in Figure 2(a), scenarios are specifically written to reach their intended targeted events, which often leaves quasi-events outside their solution space. Frequently quasi-events are overlooked when drawing up a test plan since these events may be of secondary importance, or they may be less precisely defined and therefore harder to target.

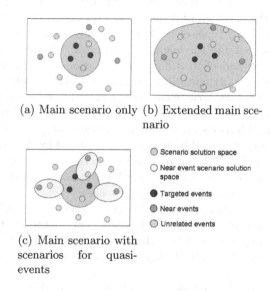

(a) Main scenario only   (b) Extended main scenario

(c) Main scenario with scenarios for quasi-events

○ Scenario solution space

○ Near event scenario solution space

● Targeted events

◍ Near events

○ Unrelated events

Fig. 2. Quasi-events

Currently, there are two main approaches for dealing with quasi-events. The first is to relax the scenario defined in the test template and use the modified scenario to try and reach the quasi-events. As shown in Figure 2(b), a relaxed scenario has an enlarged solution space which, in addition to containing targeted and quasi-events, potentially contains many unrelated events as well. As a result, such a scenario may sacrifice reaching targeted events without significantly increasing the probability of reaching quasi ones. A second approach is to specifically define the desired quasi-events and create scenarios that target them explicitly, as shown in Figure 2(c). The drawback to this approach is that it may require significant effort by the user to define these events and to create the necessary test templates to cover them.

We introduce a new technique in TPA, called *scenario mutation*, which automatically mutates a given input scenario so that the generated stimuli intentionally misses the original requirements of the scenario but targets quasi-events instead. This technique saves the need to manually specify the quasi-events and create specific test templates to hit them. Furthermore, it does not rely on the stimuli generator to "accidentally" hit these quasi-events.

Mutations have many uses in hardware verification. Mutations of the target design are used to detect simple bugs, such as wrong operator in an expression [10], and to quantify the quality of a verification environment [13]. Mutations are also used in coverage directed generation (CDG) systems to improve the ability of test cases to hit specific coverage events [3]. While our scenario mutation approach relies on mutations, it is not related to these other uses of mutations. Specifically, [3] uses mutation to modify test cases and test templates to hit a given event. Scenario mutation, on the other hand, uses mutations to intentionally miss the event and hit unspecified quasi-events instead.

TPA can perform many types of scenario mutations on a given scenario. These can be broadly classified into the following categories: (1) mutations on the generated program order and control flow, (2) mutations on specific instructions that are generated, and (3) mutations on some underlying micro-architectural mechanisms used by the scenario. Examples of program order mutations include swapping the order of two instructions or generating part of the scenario in a speculative path. Mutations on specific instructions may involve replacing an instruction with another or modifying constraints placed by the user on a particular instruction. Finally, TPA can replace or generalize a scenario's mechanism with another mechanism (e.g., LRQ with SRQ) or change the behavior of some aspect of the mechanism itself (e.g., a buffer's size).

Mutations can be further augmented with additional testing knowledge to increase the likelihood of reaching quasi-events. The mutation that swaps two instructions for example, may decide that it is preferable to swap instructions that are close to each other in the test program, or are related by some property or constraint.

Scenario mutations are a special form of testing knowledge, albeit one that relaxes the scenario fidelity principle mentioned earlier. Like traditional testing knowledge, mutations are applied heuristically during some invocations of the tool. TPA may therefore decide to mutate a given input scenario to increase the likelihood of reaching some quasi-events.

4 Speculation Mutations

Hardware-based branch speculation is performed by most modern processor designs to increase parallel execution and throughput of instructions [12]. The mechanism works by predicting the outcome of conditional branch instructions in a program and executing instructions immediately following these branches, as if the prediction was known to be correct. With speculation, the processor fetches, issues, and executes instructions as normal, but results of the execution are not written back into architected resources until the speculation is resolved. If the speculation was incorrect, that is, if the branch was mis-predicted, all instructions executed speculatively after the branch must be flushed from the pipeline.

Speculative execution considerably complicates a processor's design since it triggers a complex undo chain that must be performed before the processor can continue fetching and executing instructions from the correct path. Furthermore, it necessitates additional hardware buffers to hold the results of all executed but not yet committed instructions, as well as hardware support to pass results among speculatively executing instructions. Hence, hardware-based speculation is a challenging and bug-prone feature of a design, and a critical feature to verify.

Scenarios are presumably written to cover events that are triggered by complex architectural or micro-architectural mechanisms. For each such mechanism, there exists a corresponding recovery mechanism that is activated whenever speculation occurs. Typically, the more complex a mechanism, the more complex its recovery. Therefore an event targeted by a scenario often has a corresponding quasi-event for when the scenario, or part of the scenario, is speculatively executed. While it is true that speculatively executing a scenario makes it unlikely that the events originally intended by the scenario will be reached, it does however significantly increase the chance of hitting corresponding speculative quasi-events.

Consider the load-hit-store scenario previously described. This scenario targets, among other events, the event that is triggered when a store forwards its value to a subsequent load. By speculatively executing the store (and leaving the load in the actual program), the load no longer obtains its value from the store. This means that the original store forwarding event will not be covered. The chances however of hitting its corresponding speculative quasi-event (i.e., flushing the speculatively executed store from the SRQ buffer) will have greatly increased. Thus speculatively executing the store in the load-hit-store scenario no longer tests that store forwarding happens when it should, but rather, that store forwarding does not happen when it shouldn't.

Existing processor stimuli generators typically enable users to define instructions that should be generated both for the leg taken and the leg not taken of a conditional branch. This allows users to hit events caused by speculation. The drawback to this approach, as we have already seen with quasi-events in general, is that it requires the user to define these events and to construct specific test templates to target them.

An alternative approach, and the one adopted by TPA, is to use scenario mutations to handle speculation. With *speculation mutations*, TPA randomly injects conditional branches into the stimuli, and moves or copies existing scenario instructions onto the speculative path of these branches. This enables some of the instructions of the scenario to be executed speculatively (assuming the branch was mis-predicted) leaving the other instructions to execute on the true program path. As a result, quasi-events caused by the recovery from speculatively executing instructions will be tested. The advantage of speculation mutation is that no special scenarios need to be written to explicitly test for speculation. Furthermore, all existing scenarios in a design's verification plan can be mutated to execute speculatively. Therefore, all scenarios in the plan can be used not only to test for the events specifically targeted by the scenario, but to test for corresponding speculative quasi-events as well.

In TPA, speculation mutation is implemented as a multiple step process. First, TPA chooses the number of conditional branches to inject into the test. This is a weighted random selection based on the total number of instructions found in the scenario. Next, for each injected branch, TPA chooses the number of instructions to move or copy to the branch's speculative path. This too is a weighted random selection based on the total number of instructions in the scenario as well as the number of injected branches. Finally, TPA iteratively selects instructions until the desired number of instructions per speculation is reached.

4.1   Handling Ordered Instructions

When an order directive is specified between instructions in a scenario (e.g., between the wr and rd instructions in the RAW scenario), TPA ensures that the instructions appear in the generated test program according to the order given. Program order, however, only makes sense for non-speculatively executed instructions. Still, TPA tries to retain some notion of order even for instructions that are speculatively executed.

Consider a scenario with instructions i_1 and i_2 with i_1 ordered before i_2 in the scenario. Figure 3 shows the different ways these instructions can be placed in the generated program. In the case in which both i_1 and i_2 are placed on the same leg of the branch, i_1 will appear before i_2 in the test, regardless if they are on the non-speculative (Figure 3(a)) or speculative (Figure 3(b)) leg of the branch. More interesting is when one of the instructions is speculatively transferred and the other is not. If i_1 is the speculatively transferred instruction, then i_2 is placed after the injected branch in the program (Figure 3(c)). This ensures that if i_1 is executed, it will be executed before i_2. Conversely, i_1 will be placed before the branch when i_2 is the instruction that is speculatively transferred (Figure 3(d)).

4.2   Eliminating Speculation Candidates

Before choosing the next instruction to transfer to the speculative path, TPA may need to eliminate certain instructions from consideration. This can happen for a number of reasons, such as the user explicitly stating in the test template that an instruction should not be mutated. Another possibility is when the user specifies that two instructions should be generated in different threads. In this case, it is not legal to move both instructions onto the same speculative path. Finally, TPA must be careful when moving an instruction to a speculative path if an instruction already exists on the path which is ordered, either before it or after it, in the scenario. This may lead to an impossible situation if there is an intervening instruction between them not on the speculative path.

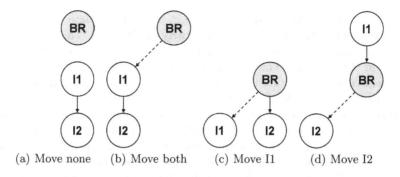

(a) Move none   (b) Move both   (c) Move I1   (d) Move I2

Fig. 3. Moving two ordered instructions to speculative path

4.3   Selecting Speculative Instructions

Once instructions that are illegal to transfer have been eliminated from consideration, TPA must choose the next instruction to move or copy from the list of remaining candidates. Instead of selecting instructions totally at random, TPA uses heuristics to determine which instruction would most likely increase the probability of hitting quasi-events if placed on a speculative path. The heuristic ranking of an instruction is based on three properties, the size of its footprint, the strength of its connectivity with other instructions, and its order relative to other instructions.

An instruction's footprint is related to the amount of residue it leaves after it has been executed. It is a measure of the complexity of the micro-architectural mechanism that is involved in its execution. The larger an instruction's footprint, the more complicated the recovery needed if it was speculatively executed. Indications of the size of an instruction's footprint comes from the type of the instruction, the unit in which it is to be executed, and the number of resources it needs to access, all which can be extracted automatically with static analysis from the design. An example of an instruction with a large footprint is one that accesses memory. Because of their footprint size, TPA assigns a higher ranking to such instructions.

The connectivity of an instruction is based on a number of static properties of the instruction in the test template. These properties include whether the instruction is part of a scenario (as opposed to being a background instruction), and the number of constraints and order directives in which the instruction participates. Inter-connected instructions are more likely to play a crucial role in exercising some underlying micro-architectural mechanism. In contrast, isolated instructions with low connectivity are less likely to have an impact. TPA attempts to break interconnected components by placing some, but not all, of their instructions onto the speculative path. By favoring mutating instructions that participate in different connected components, TPA increases the probability that some mechanism will be speculatively activated and the mechanism's corresponding quasi-events will be reached.

Finally, for instructions that are ordered in the test template, a preference is given to transfer instructions that appear early in the order. This is because an instruction is more likely to impact instructions that appear after it rather than before it in the program. This can be seen in the load-hit-store example where the consequence of executing the store affects the subsequent load since it can forward its value to the load. The reverse, however, is not true.

Returning to the load-hit-store scenario, the preference is to speculatively mutate the store since it satisfies all three criteria for mutation. Stores, like all memory access instructions, have a relatively large footprint. Furthermore, the store is part of the load-hit-store scenario and has both collision and order constraints with its corresponding load. Finally, the store is ordered before the load in the scenario specification.

Once all the instructions are ranked, TPA performs a weighted random selection to determine the next instruction to move to the speculative path. The higher an instruction ranking, the more likely it will be chosen. This process of eliminating illegal candidates and selecting a next instruction based upon its computed ranking continues until the desired number of instructions has been speculatively mutated.

5   Experimental Results

To validate the utility of quasi-events in general, and our speculation mutation approach specifically, we performed an experiment that measured the ability of TPA to reach more interesting events when speculation mutation is used. We performed the experiments on a multi-threaded, out-of-order, superscalar IBM Power processor core.

The target of the experiment was creating potential collisions in buffers in the load store unit of the processor. More specifically, we targeted the load-hit-store (LHS) and store-hit-load (SHL) collisions in the store reorder queue (SRQ) and load reorder queue (LRQ) described in Section 2. The coverage model we used to measure the collisions was a cross-product, functional coverage model that looks at the type of the colliding instructions (load or store), whether they executed speculatively, whether they accessed the same memory address, whether the instructions appeared in the same thread, whether they were executed out of order, and the difference in cycles between their issue times. The size of the coverage space is 384 events of which 240 events are legal. Note that the coverage model looks for potential collisions because if the processor works correctly, we do not expect collisions between speculative and non-speculative instructions to actually occur. Still, these potential collisions are important quasi-events because they can expose bugs in the clean-up of the buffers from speculative instructions.

To cover this coverage model and trigger the requested collisions, we used a test template that contained 50 instances of LSUCollisions scenario of Figure 1. That is, each test case generated from the template contained 50 RAW collisions on the SRQ and 50 RAW collisions on the LRQ. The ordering and placement testing knowledge of TPA splits the requested instructions between the threads and interleaves the instructions of the various collisions, while maintaining order and distance requirements of each collision. This allows TPA to generate many variants of the requested collisions.

To validate the utility of the speculation mutation approach, we compared the coverage obtained when running TPA with the test template described above in the following three modes:

Random Speculative Path. In this mode, TPA generated random instructions in the speculative path, with bias for load and store instructions. Collisions between instructions in the speculative and normal paths are generated using the generic testing knowledge used in TPA.

Speculation Mutation (Random Transfer). This mode used the speculation mutation approach described in Section 4. The instructions that were transferred from the normal path to the speculative path were selected randomly.

Speculation Mutation (Heuristic Transfer). This mode is similar to the previous mode, except that speculative instructions are chosen from the scenario according to the heuristic criteria described in Section 4.3.

We generated and simulated 400 test cases in each mode. In all the modes the generation parameters were set such that on average, each test case included ten branch instructions and on average, two load or store instructions were in the speculative path. That is, two random load or store instructions were generated in the random speculative path mode and two load or store instructions were moved to the speculative path in the speculation mutation modes. This resulted in roughly five millions simulation cycles per mode.

Figure 4 shows coverage progress as a function of simulation cycles for each of the modes. We observe that the coverage obtained with speculation mutation is higher than the coverage when random speculative path is used. This is because speculation mutation maintains the collision properties of instructions that are moved to the speculative path, while the random speculative path relies on the generic testing knowledge that is less targeted toward such collisions. Moreover, the heuristic for transferring instructions provides faster coverage progress than the random transfer because it is able to maintain more collision relations between the speculative and normal paths. However, eventually both modes reach the same coverage because even the random transfer is able to create enough collisions between speculative and normal paths.

Table 1 shows a deeper look at the speculation collisions data. It confirms the observations from Figure 4. The first two rows (below the title row) compare the number of load/store instructions executed in the normal and speculative paths in each mode. The results in these rows are close. The speculation mutations modes executed more speculative load/store instructions, but the 15% percent difference does not explain the difference in the collisions in the bottom rows of the table. The third row in the table shows that the random speculative path has more than 10% more collisions between instructions in the normal path than the speculation mutations modes. The reason for this is that in the

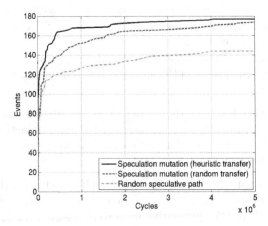

Fig. 4. Coverage progress for speculation events

speculation mutations modes colliding instructions are moved from the normal to the speculative path.

The last row in the table shows the number of collisions between instructions executed on the speculative and normal paths. These collisions correspond to the quasi-events which we hoped to reach. We see that many more of these collisions occurred when speculation mutations were used, which explain the difference in coverage between these modes and the random speculation mode. Moreover, when comparing between the two speculation mutations modes, the transfer heuristics increased the number of collisions between speculative and normal instructions, causing the faster coverage progress.

Table 1. Speculative collisions data

Mode	Random Speculative	Speculation mutations Random	Heuristic
Normal LS	100298	98839	98584
Speculative LS	5868	6639	6568
Normal Collisions	44565	39568	38895
Speculative collisions	105	3191	3643

6   Conclusions

In this paper, we defined quasi-events and described the importance of these events in enhancing the quality of scenario verification. We also introduced scenario mutations as a technique for reaching quasi-events. The advantage of scenario mutations over previous methods is that it increases the probability of hitting quasi-events without significantly sacrificing the ability to reach the intended targeted events of the scenario. Furthermore, scenario mutations can be automatically applied to any scenario in the verification test suite, thereby reducing the effort needed to cover quasi-events.

Speculation mutation is a type of scenario mutation where instructions from a scenario are transferred to the speculative path of a conditional branch. With speculation mutation, quasi-events that are triggered when a scenario is speculatively executed have a higher probability of being reached. We described the heuristics that we used to select instructions for speculation mutation, and presented experimental results that demonstrate the effectiveness of our approach.

Speculation mutation is just one of the many different types of mutations that can be applied to a given scenario. In the future, we plan to look at other mutation strategies, and investigate how different types of mutations can be combined to improve verification plan coverage.

References

1. Adir, A., Almog, E., Fournier, L., Marcus, E., Rimon, M., Vinov, M., Ziv, A.: Genesys-Pro: Innovations in test program generation for functional processor verification. IEEE Design and Test of Computers 21(2), 84–93 (2004)
2. Bin, E., Emek, R., Shurek, G., Ziv, A.: Using a constraint satisfaction formulation and solution techniques for random test program generation. IBM Systems Journal 41(3), 386–402 (2002)
3. Bose, M., Shin, J., Rudnick, E.M., Dukes, T., Abadir, M.: A genetic approach to automatic bias generation for biased random instruction generation. In: Proceedings of the 2001 Congress on Evolutionary Computation, CEC 2001, pp. 442–448 (May 2001)
4. Gutkovich, B., Moss, A.: CP with architectural state lookup for functional test generation. In: Proceedings of the High-Level Design Validation and Test Workshop, pp. 111–118 (2006)
5. Hennenhoefer, E., Typaldos, M.: The evolution of processor test generation technology, http://www.obsidiansoft.com/pdf/evolution.pdf
6. Ioannides, C., Barrett, G., Eder, K.: Feedback-based coverage directed test generation: An industrial evaluation. In: Barner, S., Harris, I., Kroening, D., Raz, O. (eds.) HVC 2010. LNCS, vol. 6504, pp. 112–128. Springer, Heidelberg (2010)
7. Kalla, R., Sinharoy, B., Starke, W., Floyd, M.: POWER7: IBM's next-generation server processor. IEEE Micro 30(2), 7–15 (2010)
8. Katz, Y., Rimon, M., Ziv, A.: Generating instruction streams using abstract CSP. In: Proceedings of the 2012 Design, Automation and Test in Europe Conference, pp. 15–20 (March 2012)
9. Katz, Y., Rimon, M., Ziv, A.: A novel approach for implementing microarchitectural verification plans in processor designs. In: Biere, A., Nahir, A., Vos, T. (eds.) HVC 2012. LNCS, vol. 7857, pp. 148–161. Springer, Heidelberg (2013)
10. Marick, B.: The Craft of Software Testing, Subsystem Testing Including Object-Based and Object-Oriented Testing. Prentice-Hall (1985)
11. Mishra, P., Dutt, N.: Automatic functional test program generation for pipelined processors using model checking. In: Seventh Annual IEEE International Workshop on High-Level Design Validation and Test, pp. 99–103 (October 2002)
12. Patterson, D.A., Hennessy, J.L.: Computer Organization and Design: The Hardware/Software Interface. Morgan Kaufmann (1997)
13. Certitude functional qualification system,
http://www.springsoft.com/products/functional-qualification/certitude

Combined Bounded and Symbolic Model Checking for Incomplete Timed Systems*

Georges Morbé, Christian Miller, Christoph Scholl, and Bernd Becker

Department of Computer Science, University of Freiburg, Freiburg, Germany
{morbe,millerc,scholl,becker}@informatik.uni-freiburg.de

Abstract. We present a hybrid model checking algorithm for incomplete timed systems where parts of the system are unspecified (so-called black boxes). Here, we answer the question of unrealisability, i.e., "Is there a path violating a safety property regardless of the implementation of the black boxes?" Existing bounded model checking (BMC) approaches for incomplete timed systems exploit the power of modern SMT solvers, but might be too coarse as an abstraction for certain problem instances. On the other hand, symbolic model checking (SMC) for incomplete timed systems is more accurate, but may fail due to the size of the explored state space. In this work, we propose a tight integration of a backward SMC routine with a forward BMC procedure leveraging the strengths of both worlds. The symbolic model checker is hereby used to compute an enlarged target which we then try to hit using BMC. We use learning strategies to guide the SMT solver's search into the right direction and manipulate the enlarged target to improve the overall accuracy of the current verification run. Our experimental results show that the hybrid approach is able to verify incomplete timed systems which are out of the scope for BMC and can neither be solved in reasonable time using SMC. Furthermore, our approach compares favourably with UPPAAL-TIGA when considering timed games as a special case of the unrealisability problem.

1 Introduction

Real-time systems appear in many areas of life, such as time-critical communication protocols or embedded controllers for automobiles. Here, in addition to the logical result, the time when the result is produced is relevant. The correctness of timing constraints is even more important for medical devices or for safety-critical systems as they appear in the transportation domain. For this reason it is crucial to perform *formal verification* of safety-critical systems. Moreover, as these systems steadily grow in complexity, verifying their correctness becomes harder and increasingly more important. Nowadays, timed automata (TAs) [2,1], which are an extension of conventional discrete automata by real-valued clock variables, are a common model for real-time systems and have become a standard in industry.

* This work was partly supported by the German Research Council (DFG) as part of the Transregional Collaborative Research Center "Automatic Verification and Analysis of Complex Systems" (SFB/TR 14 AVACS, http://www.avacs.org/).

E. Yahav (Ed.): HVC 2014, LNCS 8855, pp. 30–47, 2014.

In this work, we focus on the verification of *incomplete* timed systems, i.e., timed systems that contain unknown components (so-called black boxes). The purpose is to add a layer of abstraction if a design is too large to verify in its entirety, or to allow to start the verification process earlier when certain components of the design are only partially completed. Here, we aim to refute the realisability of a property, that is, we tell the designer, no matter how you implement the unknown parts of the system, the property will always fail. To put it in other words, the error is already in the implemented system. More formally, we prove, given an incomplete system T and a safety property ϕ (unsafe states are not reachable), that no matter what the black box BB looks like, the parallel composition of T and BB cannot satify ϕ. If this is the case, then we call the property *unrealisable*.

The unrealisability problem generalises the controller synthesis problem [14,4,11]. Here, the system communicates with an unknown controller which is more powerful than the remaining system in the sense that it may always enforce an immediate interaction with the system. In contrast to the controller synthesis problem, our scenario defines the black box as an equitable part of the system having the same impact as the implemented components. (However, we will see later, that it is also possible to define special black boxes having the same power as the unknown controller in timed games.)

Whereas some approaches to controller synthesis look into properties like LTL [12], TCTL [13] or MTL [6], we restrict our attention to safety properties which state the unreachability of certain discrete states in a timed system (as already mentioned above).

One possible method to prove unrealisability of properties in incomplete timed systems is bounded model checking (BMC). Generally, BMC starts with the initial state, iteratively unfolds the system k times, adds the negated property, and converts the BMC instance into a satisfiability problem which is solved by an appropriate solver. If the k-th instance is satisfiable, a path of length k violating the property has been found. BMC instances for real-time systems are typically encoded into so-called SAT-Modulo-Theory (SMT) formulas, since they are augmented with continuous time constraints over real-valued variables. BMC for incomplete timed systems is studied in [16,17,15]. In this paper, we use their encoding where the verification problem is limited to those transitions which are independent of the behaviour of the black boxes. This approach still yields SMT formulas which typically are easy to solve, however, due to its approximative nature this encoding limits the class of problems which can be verified. A second option for solving the unrealisability problem is symbolic model checking (SMC) for incomplete timed systems. In general, beginning with those states directly violating the property, SMC performs a backwards traversal of the state space using adequate data structures for the symbolic representation and manipulation of the state space and the transition functions. If at some point, the so far explored states include the initial state, there exists a path leading to an unsafe state. For our work, we use the symbolic model checking algorithm presented in [19]. It verifies incomplete finite state machines with time (FSMT) [20,18], which is a formal model to represent incomplete real-time systems[1]. State sets and transition functions are represented using so-called LinAIGs [9,22,8], a data structure which can hold arbitrary Boolean combinations of Boolean variables and linear constraints over real-valued variables. SMC for incomplete FSMTs is more accurate than BMC for incomplete timed systems, however, it often fails due to the size of the state sets which are generated along the verification task.

In this paper, we adopt the idea of combining BMC and SMC for incomplete discrete systems [21] to the timed world. In the timed world the main challenge is that various (known and unknown) components of the system can influence the time evolution by enforcing and/or preventing certain discrete steps. We present a verification algorithm where we use SMC for incomplete FSMTs to compute an enlarged target which we then try to hit using BMC. This tight integration in combination with learning strategies and on-the-fly manipulations of the enlarged target makes it possible to verify incomplete timed systems, which are out of reach for BMC respectively SMC alone. In other words, our approach makes BMC for incomplete timed systems more accurate and prevents SMC for incomplete timed systems from exploring state sets which are too big to verify. To show the efficacy of our hybrid verification technique, we give preliminary experimental results using multiple parameterized timed benchmarks. Furthermore, our results show that we are able to outperform the state-of-the-art controller synthesis tool UPPAAL-TIGA, when considering timed games as a special case of the unrealisability problem.

The paper is structured as follows. In Section 2, we review incomplete networks of timed automata and BMC on the one hand, and FSMT-based SMC on the other hand. Our novel method is given in Section 3. After presenting experimental results in Section 4 we conclude the paper in Section 5.

2   Preliminaries

2.1   Timed Automata

Real-time systems are often modelled using timed automata (TAs) [1,2], an extension of conventional automata by a set X of real-valued clock variables to represent the continuous time. The set of clock constraints $\mathcal{C}(X)$ contains atomic constraints of the form $(x_i \sim d)$ and $(x_i - x_j \sim d)$ with $d \in \mathbb{Q}$, $x_i, x_j \in X$ and $\sim \in \{<, \leq, =, \geq, >\}$. We consider TAs extended with bounded integer variables. Let Int be a set of bounded integer variables each having a fixed lower and upper bound. Let $Assign\,(Int)$ be the set of assignments to integer variables. Let $\mathcal{C}(Int)$ be a set of constraints of the form $(int_i \sim d)$ and $(int_i \sim int_j)$ with $d \in \mathbb{Z}$, $\sim \in \{<, \leq, \geq, >\}$ and $int_i, int_j \in Int$. Let $\mathcal{C}_c(X, Int)$ be the set of conjunctions over clock constraints and constraints from $\mathcal{C}(Int)$. Using this information we define a timed automaton as follows:

Definition 1 (Timed Automaton). *A timed automaton (TA) is a tuple* $\langle L, l_0, X, Act, Int, lb, ub, E \rangle$ *where* L *is a finite set of locations,* $l_0 \in L$ *is an*

---

[1] Note that networks of timed automata can easily be transformed into FSMTs.

initial location, $X = \{x_1, \ldots, x_n\}$ is a finite set of real-valued clock variables, $Act = Act_{nu} \cup Act_u$ with $Act_{nu} \cap Act_u = \emptyset$, Act_{nu} is a finite set of non-urgent actions and Act_u is a finite set of urgent actions, $Int = \{int_1, \ldots, int_m\}$ is a finite set of integer variables, $lb : Int \to \mathbb{Z}$ and $ub : Int \to \mathbb{Z}$ assign lower and upper bounds to each $int_i \in Int$ with $lb(int_i) \leq ub(int_i)$ for $1 \leq i \leq m$, $E \subseteq L \times \mathcal{C}_c(X, Int) \times (Act \cup \{\epsilon_u, \epsilon_{nu}\}) \times 2^X \times 2^{Assign(Int)} \times L$ is a set of transitions with $E = E_{nu} \cup E_u$. $E_{nu} = \{(l, g_e, a, r_e, Assign_e, l') \in E \mid a \in Act_{nu} \cup \{\epsilon_{nu}\}\}$ is the set of non-urgent transitions and $E_u = \{(l, g_e, a, r_e, Assign_e, l') \in E \mid a \in Act_u \cup \{\epsilon_u\}\}$ is the set of urgent transitions. If for $e = (l, g_e, a, r_e, Assign_e, l') \in E$ it holds that $a \in Act$, then we call e a transition with an (urgent or non-urgent) synchronising action, if $a \in \{\epsilon_u, \epsilon_{nu}\}$ then we call e an (urgent or non-urgent) transition without synchronising action.

A state $s_i = \langle l_i, \nu_i, \mu_i \rangle$ of a TA is a combination of a location l_i and a valuation ν_i of the clock variables and a valuation μ_i of the integer variables. A TA may perform a continuous transition, that is, all clock variables evolve over time with the same rate and neither the location nor the values of the integer variables change. Discrete transitions describe the change of the location. A discrete transition happens instantaneously and can only be taken, if its guard is satisfied, that is, if the transition is *enabled*. We consider networks of timed automata having an interleaving semantics, however, transitions labelled with the same action have to be taken simultaneously. If several transitions without action are enabled at the same time it is chosen non-deterministically which one is taken.

A discrete transition may be declared as urgent. Whenever an urgent transition labelled by ϵ_u is enabled, the current state must be left without any time delay. Analogously, whenever in all components containing a^u-transitions with $a^u \in Act_u$ a transition labelled with a^u is enabled, then there must not be any time delay before taking any transition. In literature, location invariants are used to enforce discrete transitions. However, in [18,19] the authors showed that TAs having closed invariants can be converted into semantically equivalent TAs using urgency. The translation consists in adding a supplementary urgent transition once the upper limit of the invariant is reached. A similar technique is used in the context of timed games where "forced transitions" labelled with upper limits of invariants are added in order to prevent one player from forcing the system into a timelock [3].

2.2 Incomplete Networks of Timed Automata

In this paper, we focus on *incomplete* networks of TAs where parts of the system are not specified (black box (BB)), however, the interface to the remaining system (white box (WB)) is defined. Here, we aim to prove the *unrealisability* of a safety property. We call a property unrealisable if there exists no replacement of the BB such that the property holds for the resulting overall design.

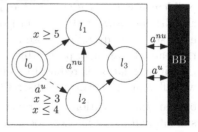

Fig. 1. Incomplete Timed System

The interface of BB components and WB components consists of non-urgent and urgent synchronisation actions. Since the behaviour of the BB is unknown it is unclear when the BB is ready to synchronise. In fact, in case of an urgent action, the BB is even able to stop time evolution of the whole system until the synchronisation takes place or until the conditions enabling the synchronising transition are not fulfilled anymore. In other words, allowing the above mentioned communication methods to define the interface of the BB, the unknown parts are able to affect the discrete behaviour of the WB and, in case of urgency, also may influence their timing behaviour. In the following, we distinguish three kinds of discrete transitions: *f-transitions* (also referred to as fixed transitions) are not labelled with any action synchronising with the BB, *nu-transitions* are labelled with a non-urgent action synchronising with the BB, and *u-transitions* are labelled with an urgent action synchronising with the BB.

Example 1. Consider the incomplete timed system shown in Fig. 1. The BB uses a non-urgent action a^{nu} and an urgent action a^u to interact with the implemented system. The nu-transition from l_2 to l_1 can only be taken if it synchronises with the BB via a^{nu}, and thus, the BB is able to influence the behaviour of the system in that way. Being in location l_0, the BB has the power to enforce the u-transition labelled with a^u leading to l_2 (dashed arrow) when $3 \leq x \leq 4$. In that case, time evolution is stopped and a discrete transition has to be taken, instantaneously. All remaining transitions in the system are f-transitions which can not be affected through the BBs behaviour.

2.3 Bounded Model Checking of Incomplete Networks of Timed Automata

Generally, the BMC procedure [5,7] starts with the initial state I^0 (superscript numeral denotes the unfolding depth), iteratively unfolds a system k times by adding a conjunction of transition relations $T^{i,i+1}$, and connects the negated property $\neg P^k$. Finally, the BMC instance is converted into a satisfiability problem. If an appropriate solver finds the k-th problem instance satisfiable, a path of length k violating the property has been found.

When proving unrealisability using BMC, the unknown behaviour of the BB needs an adequate modelling. Taking incomplete networks of TAs into account, BMC based on fixed transitions [16,17] is one option to solve the unrealisability problem as long as the system does not contain any u-transitions. The idea is that the BB can prevent the system from taking the nu-transitions on a path to an error state (by disabling those transitions). Thus, nu-transitions are omitted in the search for an error path, which does not depend on the BB behaviour, and the transition relation is reduced to f-transitions. To encode the transition relation, we differentiate between a discrete step $T^{i,i+1}_{\text{jump}}$, which describes all possibilities of changing a location via f-transitions, and a continuous step $T^{i,i+1}_{\text{flow}}$, where all subautomata stay in their locations, and time passes equally for all clocks (for a detailed description of the BMC encoding please refer to [16,17]). Finally, the

k-th BMC instance is constructed as follows

$$BMC(k) := I^0 \wedge \bigwedge_{i=0}^{k-1} \begin{cases} T_{\text{jump}}^{i,i+1} & \text{if } i \text{ is even,} \\ T_{\text{flow}}^{i,i+1} & \text{otherwise} \end{cases} \wedge \neg P^k \qquad (1)$$

using an alternation of discrete and continuous steps and then passed to an arbitrary SMT solver, which supports the theory of linear arithmetic for integers and reals. If $BMC(k)$ is satisfiable, there is a run $r = \langle s_0, s_1, \ldots, s_k \rangle$ of length k with $s_i = \langle l_i, \nu_i, \mu_i \rangle$, $0 \le i \le k$ and l_i being a location, ν_i a clock valuation, and μ_i being an integer valuation which does not depend on the BB behaviour and leads to a state s_k that violates the property P.

Whereas this encoding yields easy-to-solve SMT formulas in many cases, the model in [16] assumes that the BB may only enable and disable transitions in the WB, but never may *enforce* transitions in the WB. Thus the BB may not synchronise over urgent actions, i.e., the implemented system may not contain any u-transitions. This is a really strong restriction and limits the class of problems that can be verified.

Example 2. In this example, we show that unrealisability proofs based on f-transitions may be wrong, if u-transitions are present in the WB. We consider the incomplete timed system given in Fig. 1 and the property that the location l_1 can never be reached. The BMC procedure as defined above confines the consideration to f-transitions and it would find a path leading to l_1 (e.g. $\langle l_0, x = 0 \rangle \rightarrow \langle l_0, x = 5 \rangle \rightarrow \langle l_1, x = 5 \rangle$). However, due to the u-transition which is enabled in location l_0 once x reaches the value 3, this error path is not valid for *all* possible black box implementations, since the BB may stop time evolution and force the network to synchronise via a^u. If afterwards, the BB never synchronises via a^{nu}, then l_1 can never be reached, i.e., there is a BB-implementation which fulfills the property and unrealisability does not hold.

2.4   Symbolic Backward Model Checking Based on FSMTs

The symbolic methods we will use are based on finite state machines with time (FSMTs) [20,18] which are symbolic representations of networks of TAs well suited for fully symbolic model checking algorithms. Basically, an FSMT consists of a set of Boolean location variables Y, a set of real-valued clock variables X, a set of Boolean input variables I, a predicate *init* describing the set of initial states, and a predicate *urgent* indicating when an urgent transition is enabled. Each location variable $y_i \in Y$ is determined by a transition function δ_i, and reset conditions $reset_{x_i}$, which deterimine when each clock variable x_i is reset. A state of an FSMT is a valuation of the clock variables and the location variables. An FSMT performs a discrete step depending on the current state and the input variables. Here, the location variable y_i is set to 0 (1) iff δ_i evaluates to 0 (1) and the clock x_i is reset iff $reset_{x_i}$ evaluates to 1. In a continuous step time may pass unless the *urgent* predicate evaluates to 1. FSMTs communicate by reading each other's location variables, clock variables, and shared input variables. In [20] the authors show how to translate timed systems into FSMTs (integer communication is encoded using Boolean variables which are included into Y). In [18,19] this translation is extended to incomplete timed systems. Here, we additionally define a predicate $urgent_{BB}$, which evaluates to 1 if any u-transition is enabled.

The symbolic backward model checking algorithm for incomplete timed systems presented in [19] starts with the negation of a given safety property and computes predecessor state sets until the initial state is reached. The generated state sets contain those states from which the negated property is reachable regardless of the behaviour of the BB. Similarly to BMC, we define two kinds of predecessor operators. Starting from a state set ϕ the *discrete predecessor operator* computes a state set $Pred_d(\phi)$ containing only states from which ϕ is reachable taking a discrete transition in the WB independently from any BB behaviour. The BB can not prevent the WB from taking f-transitions and thus, only those are considered for the computation of the discrete predecessor (u-transitions and nu-transitions can be blocked when the BB is not sending the appropriate synchronisation action). The *continuous predecessor operator* computes a state set $Pre_c(\phi)$, which contains only states from which ϕ is reachable regardless of the behaviour of the BB when performing continuous transitions. A state s is added to $Pre_c(\phi)$ if it is possible to reach ϕ from s through time evolution which may not be blocked by the BB. Here we have to account for the fact that the BB is able to influence the timing behaviour of the WB by sending urgent actions and thus enabling u-transitions which stop time evolution. Consider the case that a state s_ϕ in ϕ is reachable through time evolution starting in s, but there is another state t on the way between s and s_ϕ which is the source of an enabled u-transition labelled with the urgent action a^u. Now we have to consider two cases in order to decide whether s can be included into $Pre_c(\phi)$:

(1) Assume that all enabled u-transitions labelled with a^u and starting from t lead to some state which is not in ϕ. By sending the action a^u the BB can cause time evolution to stop and it can impede the WB from reaching ϕ starting in s. Thus we may not include s into $Pre_c(\phi)$.

(2) Assume that there is some enabled u-transition that starts in t, is labelled with a^u, and leads to a state $t'' \in \phi$. In that case, the choice of the BB is irrelevant, since in both cases (synchronising via a^u gives the WB the opportunity to move to $t'' \in \phi$, not synchronising leads to ϕ through time evolution) the resulting state is included in ϕ. Thus, in this case, and if there is no other state $\tilde{t}$ on the way from s to s_ϕ fulfilling the condition of case (1), we may include s into $Pre_c(\phi)$ and, since we are only interested in the question from which states we may reach ϕ regardless of the BB behaviour (and not how), we do not need to consider stopping time evolution at t due to urgent synchronisation with the BB.

In order to know whether the WB is able to force u-transitions into some state in ϕ or not, which is crucial for the continuous predecessor operator, SMC has to be able to compute a special discrete predecessor state set of ϕ only over u-transitions (in the following named *pre-urgent (PU)* respectively $Pre_d^u(\phi)$). Put in other words, a state s is included into $Pre_d^u(\phi)$ if for all urgent actions on enabled outgoing transitions from s, there is at least one enabled u-transition in the WB synchronising over this action, which leads to ϕ. For details on the exact computation of $Pre_d(\phi)$, $Pre_c(\phi)$, and $Pre_d^u(\phi)$ we refer to [19].

Example 3. As an example consider again the incomplete timed system of Fig. 1 and a state set ϕ_1 with $\langle l_1, x \geq 0\rangle \in \phi_1$. Then the state $s_1 = \langle l_2, x \geq 0\rangle$ is no discrete predecessor of ϕ_1, $s_1 \notin Pre_d(\phi_1)$, since it is backwards reachable from ϕ_1 only over the nu-transition (l_2, l_1), which can be disabled by the BB not sending the action a^{nu}. State $s_2 = \langle l_0, x \geq 5\rangle$, reachable via the f-transition (l_0, l_1) is the only discrete predecessor of ϕ_1, $Pre_d(\phi_1) = \{s_2\}$, as it is the only state reachable over f-transitions.

Consider now another state set ϕ_2 with $\langle l_2, x \geq 0\rangle \in \phi_2$ and $\langle l_0, x \geq 5\rangle \in \phi_2$. We ask the question whether the state $s_0 = \langle l_0, x = 0\rangle$ can be included into $Pre_c(\phi_2)$. When the BB does not interfere by sending the urgent action a^u, $\langle l_0, x \geq 5\rangle$ and thus ϕ_2 is reachable from s_0 through normal time passing. By sending a^u in any state $s_3 = \langle l_0, x = c\rangle$ with $3 \leq c \leq 4$, the BB can stop time evolution. However, in that case the WB can take the enabled u-transition (l_0, l_2) leading to the state $\langle l_2, x = c\rangle$ which is in ϕ_2 (since $\langle l_2, x = c\rangle \in \phi_2$, s_3 is in pre-urgent of ϕ_2, i.e., $s_3 \in Pre_d^u(\phi_2)$). Hence state set ϕ_2 is reachable starting in s_0 independently from the BB behaviour and thus, $s_0 \in Pre_c(\phi_2)$.

3 Hybrid Verification of Incomplete Real-Time Systems

In this section we present a hybrid BMC/SMC algorithm to prove unrealisability in incomplete networks of TAs which (1) makes it possible for BMC to handle u-transitions and (2) avoids full SMC runs possibly exceeding resources.

To this end, we extend the BMC encoding given in Section 2.3 by the possibility to handle urgency. We modified the initial state and the transition relations in a way that time evolution is blocked immediately (i.e. the length of the time evolution is enforced to be 0) whenever either an urgent transition is enabled or an urgent synchronisation within WB components can take place. We call such a state where time evolution has to be blocked immediately an *urgent state*. Furthermore, time evolution started in a non-urgent state is stopped when an urgent state is reached.[2] BMC as defined above computes a path based on f-transitions without considering the timing constraints imposed by u-transitions. In that way, BMC *over-approximates* the set of possible runs leading to an error state, however, our novel approach excludes spurious error paths by using SMC methods.

The idea of the overall algorithm combining BMC and SMC is as follows: We use SMC to compute an enlarged target, that is a symbolic representation of states from which there exists a path to the negated property no matter how the BB is implemented. We then try to hit this target by searching a path via f-transitions which starts in the initial state of the incomplete network and

---

[2] Since we need a well-defined starting point in time for the urgent state, we forbid constraints with '>' instead of '≥' guarding any urgent transition.

finally ends in one of the states of the enlarged target. Whenever along this path there is a state s with an enabled u-transition, we additionally test whether for all urgent actions on enabled outgoing transitions from s, there is at least one enabled u-transition in the WB, synchronising over this action, which leads to the enlarged target. In this case we say "the WB can force the u-transitions into the enlarged target". Then the decision of the BB is irrelevant and the error state is reached in every case. If not, we have to extend the BMC problem by additional information learnt from SMC.

In the following, we describe the algorithm in general and then give a detailed description of the interaction with the enlarged target and the pre-urgent state set, respectively.

3.1   Overall Algorithm

Algorithm 1 shows the procedure to prove unrealisability of a property in an incomplete network of TAs, and consists of two steps, in the first step (lines 5 to 17) BMC is used to search for a fixed path, reaching ET, based on f-transitions, and in the second step, using SMC methods, it is checked whether the WB can force all enabled u-transitions along this error path candidate into ET (lines 20 to 31). To this end, we compute the set $Pre_d^u(ET)$ of all states which have the property that the WB can force all outgoing u-transitions into the enlarged target and check whether all states on the error path candidate, which have enabled u-transitions, are included in $Pre_d^u(ET)$. We call this test the "PU inclusion check". The enlargement of ET and the necessitated manipulations of the SMT solver are described in Algorithm 2.

We introduce a set Π_{ET} holding the conflict clauses, which are generated after an unsuccessful inclusion check of the enlarged target. Next, we store in a set Π_{PU} additional constraints resulting from the PU inclusion check, which restrict the continuous transitions of future BMC runs. Furthermore, let BMC be an SMT formula representing the current BMC instance and nr_of_fixed_paths a counter, storing the number of so far explored paths based on f-transitions. Lastly, we use a predefined number K which limits the number of BMC steps. In informal words, K defines the influence of BMC in the combined approach. As a special case consider $K = 0$ where a pure SMC run is performed.

After initialising the procedure (lines 1–2), the enlarged target (ET) is computed (line 3) by performing a predefined number (#steps$_{init}$) of continuous and discrete backward steps (Pre_c and Pre_d) as described in Section 2.4, using the negated property as a starting point. In lines 5 to 17 the algorithm searches for a path based on f-transitions. When constructing the BMC formula we omit the negated property, and thus, the pure BMC instance (i.e. the BMC instance without any additional conflict clauses) is naturally satisfiable. The state (assignment to location variables, clocks variables and integer variables) computed by the SMT solver at the end of the last unfolding is checked for inclusion in ET (line 8). If this check is successful, a path based on f-transitions has been found and we continue with the next step of the algorithm. However, in the negative case a conflict clause, which forbids the current assignment to the state variables

Algorithm 1. Hybrid Algorithm BMC–SMC

```
 1: Π_ET = ∅; Π_PU = ∅; k = 0; BMC = I^0; nr_of_fixed_paths = 0;
 2: add_transition_relation_to_BMC();
 3: compute_ET(#steps_init);
 4: while true do
 5:     fixed_path_found = false;
 6:     while !fixed_path_found do
 7:         if SMT_solve(BMC) == SAT then
 8:             if is_in_ET(state_vars(k)) then
 9:                 fixed_path_found := true; nr_of_fixed_paths++;
10:             else
11:                 π = generate_ET_cc; Π_ET = Π_ET ∪ π; add_to_solver(π, k);
12:         else
13:             k = k + 1;
14:             if k < K then
15:                 add_transition_relation_to_BMC();
16:                 remove_from_solver(Π_ET, k − 1); add_to_solver(Π_ET, k);
17:                 if k is continuous transition then add_to_solver(Π_PU, k);
18:             else
19:                 enlarge_ET_and_reset(#steps);
20:     fixed_path_valid = true;
21:     while fixed_path_valid && untested continuous transition s^i → s^{i+1} exists
       along fixed path do
22:         if !check_PU(s^i, s^{i+1}) then
23:             fixed_path_valid = false;
24:             if nr_of_fixed_paths < max_fixed_paths then
25:                 π = generate_PU_constraint;
26:                 for j=0...k do
27:                     if j is continuous transition then
28:                         add_to_solver(π, j);
29:                 Π_PU = Π_PU ∪ π;
30:             else
31:                 enlarge_ET_and_reset(#steps);
32:     if fixed_path_valid then return Unrealisability proven
```

at the end of the last unfolding is generated, added to the BMC problem and thus, prevents the solver to explore the same path of length k again (see Section 3.2 for details). The solver is invoked again and the new solution for the state variables of the last unfolding is tested, etc.. This procedure is repeated until either a path of length k leading into ET has been found, or the BMC instance including all generated conflict clauses gets unsatisfiable. In the latter case, there exists no path of length k into ET and we continue the search for $k + 1$. The generated conflict clauses exclude states which are not part of ET, and thus, they contain valuable information for future unfolding depths. Since the index of the last unfolding has increased by 1, prior to the new search, we

---

Algorithm 2. enlarge_ET_and_reset(#steps)

1: enlarge_ET(#steps);
2: **if** $I \cap ET \neq \emptyset$ **then return** Unrealisability proven
3: **else if** fixed_point(ET) **then return** Unrealisability not proven
4: reduce_k = min(#steps − 1, k); $k = k −$ reduce_k;
5: remove_transition_relations(reduce_k);
6: update_ET_cc(Π_{ET}); add_to_solver(Π_{ET}, k);
7: remove_PU_constraints_from_solver(); $\Pi_{PU} = \emptyset$;
8: nr_of_fixed_paths=0;

---

remove all conflict clauses having time index k and add them again with the incremented time index $k + 1$ (line 16).

If it is not possible to find a fixed path within K steps (line 18), the enlarged target is further extended by '#steps' backward steps and the combined procedure is reset (see line 19 and Algorithm 2).

Once a fixed path leading to ET is found (line 9), Algorithm 1 continues to check whether the BB is able to force the implemented system to leave that path by sending urgent actions (lines 20 to 31). That is, for each continuous transition along the path, we test whether there is any u-transition enabled during this time step, and – in a positive case – whether the WB can force all enabled u-transitions into ET (see Section 3.3 for details on the interaction with this state set). If this test is successful for all continuous transitions, the current fixed error path is valid and unrealisability of the system has been proven. Once this test fails for some continuous transition (line 22), the BB is able to enforce a transition leaving the current fixed error path. To avoid this situation in the future, a constraint is generated and added to Π_{PU} (lines 25 to 29). Since the current fixed error path is not valid, the algorithm starts searching for a new fixed path taking all conflict clauses included in Π_{ET} and all constraints in Π_{PU} into account.

It may be the case that the current ET is too small to lead to a result (if the BB is able to enforce transitions leaving the current fixed error path into states not in ET). Therefore from time to time (when a predefined amount of fixed paths using the same ET has been explored) we enlarge the target further (line 31). In that case, the overall accuracy is increased by expanding the ET which in turn necessitates a restart of the procedure.

Algorithm 2 performs a target enlargement (line 1) followed by necessary manipulations of the BMC instance. After the target enlargement we check in line 2 whether the new ET already contains some initial states which proves unrealisability (line 2). A fixed point check determines whether new states could be added to the enlarged target. If not, it is clear that we will never be able to prove unrealisability (line 3). However, in case new states could be added, the algorithm is restarted using the new ET as a basis after removing the last #*steps* − 1 transition relations from the BMC problem in lines 4–5 (since it has been proven that there exists no fixed paths at previous unfolding depths). In order to keep as much learnt information as possible for the next search of a fixed path, we update Π_{ET} in update_ET_cc() as follows: For each conflict clause in Π_{ET} (which describes a state set not belonging to the old ET) we test whether it still describes a state set not belonging to the extended ET. If the outcome of the test is negative, we have to remove the conflict clause from Π_{ET}. At the end, the updated ET conflict clauses again describe state sets which should be excluded from the solvers search and the conflict clauses are added to the last time frame k (line 6). In contrast, the so far generated PU constraints limit the timing behaviour of continuous transitions in BMC based on the old ET and thus, they might prevent the solver from finding valid error paths in future runs (after extending ET). Hence, we remove all PU constraints from the solver and set $\Pi_{PU} = \emptyset$ (line 7).

3.2   Enlarged Target Inclusion Check and Conflict Clause Generation

One connection point of BMC and SMC is a test whether a state $s_k = \langle l_k, \nu_k, \mu_k \rangle$ of the last BMC unfolding is included in ET (line 8 of Algorithm 1). If the test fails, a conflict clause is generated and passed to the SMT solver to prevent the search from exploring the same branch again. The inclusion check and the conflict clause generation is performed in three steps: First, we test whether there exists any state in ET having location l_k. This can be reduced to an SMT check fixing in ET the location variables $y_1, \ldots, y_l$ to the valuation ξ_k, which represents l_k. If not, it is clear that s_k cannot be part of ET as well and another possible error path has to be found. As a conflict clause, it would be sufficient to exclude only ξ_k, however, we can exclude a larger part of the search space when lifting the location variables $y_1, \ldots, y_l$: A location variable y_i can be removed from the conflict clause if the assignment to y_i is irrelevant for the SMT check. As a result, the conflict clause contains only those location variables which are essential to exclude l_k and additionally excludes further states which are not part of ET. However, if ET contains states having the location l_k, the second step tests for the integer valuation μ_k. In a negative case, the conflict clause forbids $\langle l_k, \mu_k \rangle$. Otherwise, a third test includes the valuation ν_k of the clock variables. If this SMT check succeeds as well, s_k is part of ET and a fixed error path hitting ET has been found. If not, instead of s_k, we can exclude $\langle l_k, Z, \mu_k \rangle \notin ET$ with Z being a clock zone which contains ν_k. We obtain Z by a conjunction of all linear clock constraints of ET which are satisfied by ν_k and the negations of all clock constraints which are not satisfied by ν_k.

3.3   Pre-Urgent Inclusion Check and Conflict Constraint Generation

In contrast to the ET inclusion check, where one specific state $s_k = \langle l_k, \nu_k, \mu_k \rangle$ was considered, the check whether a *u-transition* leads to ET needs to be performed for *all* states in which a u-transition is enabled. The PU inclusion check takes as an input a complete continuous BMC step of length λ from the state

$s^i = \langle l, \nu, \mu \rangle$ to its successor state $s^{i+1} = \langle l, \nu + \lambda, \mu \rangle$ along the current path based on f-transitions. Using the $urgent_{BB}$ predicate of the incomplete FSMT, SMC computes the set of states ϕ^u in which a u-transition is enabled along this continuous transition. If ϕ^u is empty, the BB is not able to enforce the WB to leave this path, and the procedure simply returns $true$. If not, the procedure checks whether ϕ^u is completely included in $Pre^u_d(ET)$, that is, the WB is able to force all u-transitions emerging from states in ϕ^u into ET. In a positive case the procedure returns $true$ and continues with the succeeding continuous transition of the candidate error path. However, if there is some

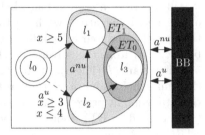

Fig. 2. Example

state s in ϕ^u, such that the WB is *not* able to force the u-transitions starting in s into ET, we generate a constraint which prevents the SMT solver to take the same continuous transition in future BMC runs. To this purpose, through SMT solving, we pick one single state $\tilde{s} \in \phi^u \setminus Pre^u_d(ET)$, and similarly to the ET conflict clause generation, we compute a state set $\tilde{\phi}$ with $\tilde{\phi} \cap Pre^u_d(ET) = \emptyset$, and furthermore restrict this set to states which are source of a u-transition by using the $urgent_{BB}$ predicate again. In this way, we obtain a *critical state set* $\langle l, \bigwedge_{i=1}^{n} (a_i \leq x_i \leq b_i), \mu \rangle$ which must be avoided in future *continuous* steps. To avoid the critical state set, we add to each continuous time frame of the BMC problem a constraint which is a conjunction of the following two conditions:

(a) If we are in location l with integer valuation μ and the valuation of at least one clock variable x_j of the starting point of a continuous transition is lower than a_j, then time passing has to be stopped before all clock variables x_k obtain valuations greater than a_k. In this way, reaching the critical state set through time evolution is prevented.

$$\left[(s^i = l) \wedge (int^i = \mu) \wedge \left(\bigvee_{j=1}^{n} (x_j^i < a_j) \right) \right] \implies \left(\bigvee_{j=1}^{n} (x_j^{i+1} \leq a_j) \right)$$

(b) It might be possible that a state of the critical state set is reached through a *discrete transition. In this case, we have to ensure that time must not proceed, that is, another discrete transition must be taken immediately.*

$$\left[(s^i = l) \wedge (int^i = \mu) \wedge \left(\bigwedge_{j=1}^{n} (a_j \leq x_j^i \leq b_j) \right) \right] \implies \left(\bigwedge_{j=1}^{n} (x_j^{i+1} = x_j^i) \right)$$

We consider the example shown in Figure 2 and the property that location l_3 can never be reached. Assume that initially the enlarged target (ET_0) contains only the location l_3. Next, BMC finds a path based on f-transitions leading into ET_0 as follows:

$$p_0^{\text{fix}} = \langle l_0, x = 0 \rangle \rightarrow \langle l_0, x = 5 \rangle \rightarrow \langle l_1, x = 5 \rangle \rightarrow ET_0$$

During the time step, the BB may enforce the u-transition e^u from l_0 to l_2 when x has a value between 3 and 4. To check whether p_0^{fix} is still valid in this situation we perform the PU inclusion check for the time step $\langle l_0, x = 0 \rangle \rightarrow \langle l_0, x = 5 \rangle$ which tests whether $\langle l_0, 3 \leq x \leq 4 \rangle$ is included in $Pre_d^u(\text{ET}_0) = \emptyset$. Obviously, this is not the case. To prevent time steps from touching $\langle l_0, 3 \leq x \leq 4 \rangle$, we add the constraint

$$\left[(s^i = l_0) \wedge (x^i < 3) \implies (x^{i+1} \leq 3) \right] \wedge \left[(s^i = l_0) \wedge (3 \leq x^i \leq 4) \implies (x^{i+1} = x^i) \right]$$

to the time step of any BMC unfolding depth. However, using these constraints, BMC is not able to find another fixed path leading to ET_0 and thus, the procedure is rerun using the expanded enlarged target ET_1, containing l_1, l_2, and l_3. The new fixed path found by the SMT-solver is

$$p_1^{\text{fix}} = \langle l_0, x = 0 \rangle \rightarrow \langle l_0, x = 5 \rangle \rightarrow \text{ET}_1$$

Again, being in location l_0 with $x = 3$ there is a u-transition e^u which the BB can enforce to be taken. However, using ET_1, the pre-urgent inclusion check succeeds since $\langle l_0, 3 \leq x \leq 4 \rangle$ is included in $Pre_d^u(\text{ET}_1) = \{\langle l_0, 3 \leq x \leq 4 \rangle\}$. To put it in words, no matter whether the BB synchronises on a^u or not, the enlarged target can always be reached either using p_1^{fix} or e^u and, as a consequence, the unrealisability has been proven.

Theorem 1. *An error path π found by Algorithm 1 is valid for all possible BB implementations.*

Proof (sketch). π is based on fixed transitions and each u-transition along π is leading to ET. Assume that the SMC methods are correct [19], then ET contains only states which lead to states violating the property for all implementations of the BB. The BB cannot influence fixed transitions, and thus, the only way the BB can enforce the system to leave π is by synchronising over u-transitions. However, since the WB can force all u-transitions which are enabled along π into ET, a state violating the property is reached regardless of the behaviour of the BB, and thus, the property is unrealisable.

Thrm. 1 proves the soundness of the approach. Note that Algorithm 1 is only complete, if we assume that (1) the safety property does not contain disjunctions and (2) the BB has the ability to make different decisions depending on the state of the WB. For this the BB has to be able to read the state of the WB or to infer the state of the WB (e.g. by reading synchronization actions which are internal to the WB). (This assumption is implicitly made in classical controller synthesis approaches as well [4,11].)

4   Experiments

To evaluate our hybrid approach for the unrealisability proof in incomplete timed systems we combined the BMC tool `timemachine` [16,15] which uses Yices [10] as underlying SMT solver and the SMC tool fsmtMC [20,19] which is based on LinAIGs [9,22,8] as the core data structure. We extended timemachine by the encoding of urgency and implemented the ET and PU routines using the methods provided by fsmtMC.

We use extended versions of the parameterizable *arbiter* [20,19] and *cpp* [19] benchmarks. The *arbiter* benchmark models n processes which try to access a shared resource and are controlled by an erroneous distributed arbiter and one counter module yielding $2n + 1$ components in total. We model all but two processes as a BB and prove the unrealisability of the property that the two processes cannot access the shared resource at the same time. The *cpp* benchmark models a ring of n parallel processes where each component communicates with its neighbours. We model $\frac{1}{2}n$ successive components as a BB and prove the unrealisability of the property that the first two components never enter an unsafe location at the same time.

We compare our hybrid approach with pure SMC. Since all tested benchmarks use urgent synchronisation *in their BB interface*, timemachine was not able to prove the unrealisability of any benchmark instance. It is neither possible to solve the unrealisability problem of our benchmark set using controller synthesis methods, since timed games are a special case of our scenario where the unknown controller has more power than the remaining components. However, we are able to modify the arbiter benchmark (by

Table 1. Results

	fsmtMC		*hyVer*			
TA	time	time	BMC	SMC	ET/CC	PU/C
orig. Arbiter 5	161.0	53.9	3	10	34/28	5/5
10	2064.5	55.3	3	10	42/36	5/5
12	5932.3	26.6	7	8	33/28	5/4
13	-	32.0	7	8	32/27	5/4
15	-	28.3	7	8	32/27	5/4
25	-	75.4	3	10	40/34	5/5
30	-	87.9	3	10	39/33	5/5
CPP 4	3.0	1.3	5	2	7/5	1/1
5	-	2.4	5	2	7/5	1/1
6	232.6	3.5	5	2	7/5	1/1
7	-	5.5	5	2	7/5	1/1
23	-	156.8	5	2	7/5	1/1
24	-	372.1	5	2	6/4	1/1

changing the power of the individual components within the network) making it possible to construct a semantically equivalent timed game. Using this modified benchmark, we are able to compare the results of our combined method to those obtained using the state-of-the-art controller synthesis tool UPPAAL-TIGA.

To test our prototype implementation we used an AMD Opteron processor running on 2.3 GHz and having 64 GB RAM. We put a time limit of 2 CPU hours and a memory limit of 2 GB.

Table 1 compares the runtime of pure SMC (fsmtMC) with our hybrid approach (hyVer). The number of instantiated components of the respective benchmark is given in Column 1 (TA) followed by the runtime of fsmtMC in Column 2. Additionally to the runtime of hyVer (time), we report the number of forward steps (BMC) and backward steps (SMC) in order to successfully find an error path which proves the unrealisability. Furthermore, the table gives the number of ET inclusion checks and the resulting conflict clauses (ET/CC), analogously we give the number of PU inclusion checks and resulting constraints (PU/C).

The hybrid approach outperforms pure SMC for both the *orig. arbiter* and the *cpp* benchmark sets. Using SMC methods, the *arbiter* benchmark ran into timeouts for 13 processes and beyond, however hyVer was able to complete the verification task for up to 30 processes in a reasonable amount of time. A similar picture is valid for the *cpp* benchmark set. Here, SMC fails to prove unrealisability for instances having more than 6 processes whereas hyVer is able to complete the task within the given timeout for up to 24 processes.

In this setting, we used the negated property as the initial ET (that is, $\#steps_{init} = 0$). Later on, ET is always expanded by one discrete symbolic step followed by one continuous symbolic step ($\#steps = 2$). max_fixed_paths is set to 1. We pick out three examples to explain the detailed results of our combined approach. First, consider the arbiter benchmark with 5 instantiated components. For this example, 5 fixed paths are discarded, since a continuous transition on the fixed path passes through a state in which a u-transition not leading to ET is enabled. The sixth candidate path is a valid error path, since it does not contain any state which is the source of a u-transition. In total, 28 ET conflict clauses are needed to find the candidate paths (6 ET inclusion checks are successful). The length of the valid path is the sum of the number of BMC steps and the number of SMC steps (in this example the length is 13). For the original arbiter benchmark having 12 instantiated components, the algorithm discards only 4 fixed paths and the fifth PU inclusion check is successful. In this case the final path contains a state which is the source of a u-transition, but using SMC it is proved that this transition leads into the ET.

For the cpp benchmark all paths found by BMC do not contain any states which are sources of a u-transition, i.e., the effect of u-transitions is handled by SMC only. Two additional SMC backward steps (discrete and continuous) are enough to find a valid fixed error path.

Table 2 shows the results of the modified arbiter benchmark when using fsmtMC, TIGA, and hyVer. Again, TA denotes the number of instantiated components, however, in this setting we vary the number of black boxed components (BB). Column TIGA reports the runtime of UPPAAL-TIGA, the remaining columns of the table are structured as before. We slightly changed the setting for this set of experiments.

Table 2. Modified Arbiter Benchmark

TA	BB	fsmtMC time	TIGA time	hyVer time	BMC	SMC	ET/CC	PU/C
5	3	1052.1	0.1	1.0	0	12	1/0	0/0
5	2	-	0.2	1.4	3	8	2/1	0/0
5	1	-	4.1	2.8	3	12	2/1	0/0
6	4	1707.6	0.1	1.3	0	14	1/0	0/0
6	3	-	0.2	1.5	3	8	2/1	0/0
6	2	-	4.3	4.7	0	20	1/0	0/0
6	1	-	761.3	7.4	0	20	1/0	0/0
7	5	1502.9	0.1	2.5	0	22	1/0	0/0
7	4	-	0.2	2.2	0	16	1/0	0/0
7	3	-	4.4	2.4	5	10	11/10	0/0
7	2	-	901.9	25.5	5	8	28/26	1/1
7	1	-	-	149.6	5	10	12/12	1/1
8	6	2952.9	0.1	2.1	6	22	12/11	1/0
8	5	-	0.2	2.9	0	22	1/0	0/0
8	4	-	4.6	2.6	5	10	11/10	0/0
8	3	-	1010.1	41.9	7	8	194/192	1/1
8	2	-	-	127.7	3	10	125/123	1/1
8	1	-	-	1280.1	15	10	234/231	2/2

In particular, as a further optimisation in the initial target enlargement procedure, we only perform continuous steps, if performing discrete steps does not add new states to ET. In that way, for many instances the paths found by BMC do not contain any states which are sources of a u-transition. fsmtMC is only able to solve benchmarks where the maximum number of components (that is, all but 2) is abstracted. TIGA can solve more benchmarks than fsmtMC, however, the runtime increases dramatically for more than 4 WB components. hyVer is the only tool which is able to solve the whole benchmark set within the given timeout. It also completes the verification task in significant less time than TIGA for benchmarks which are solvable by both tools.

We also implemented a version of `hyVer` where ET is converted into an SMT formula and then directly connected to the BMC formula to avoid possibly multiple inclusion checks in order to generate one fixed error path. However, this version was not competitive compared to the procedure depicted in Algorithm 1 and justifies to perform inclusion checks and the usage of conflict clauses.

5   Conclusion

We presented a hybrid model checking algorithm to prove unrealisability for incomplete real-time systems. We use backward SMC methods to compute an enlarged target which we then try to hit using SMT-based forward BMC procedures. In order to accelerate the verification process we apply learning strategies and manipulate the enlarged target along the verification run to improve the overall accuracy. Our combined approach makes it possible to verify incomplete timed systems, which can neither be solved using pure BMC due to its inaccuracy nor using pure SMC due to the state space explosion problem. Finally, we showed the efficacy using parameterized incomplete timed benchmark sets. Our results show advantages compared to UPPAAL-TIGA when we consider timed games as a special case of the unrealisability problem.

References

1. Alur, R.: Timed automata. Theoretical Computer Science (1999)
2. Alur, R., Dill, D.L.: A theory of timed automata. Theoretical Computer Science (1994)
3. Behrmann, G., Cougnard, A., David, R., Fleury, E., Larsen, K.G., Lime, D.: Uppaal tiga user-manual
4. Behrmann, G., Cougnard, A., David, A., Fleury, E., Larsen, K.G., Lime, D.: UPPAAL-tiga: Time for playing games! In: Damm, W., Hermanns, H. (eds.) CAV 2007. LNCS, vol. 4590, pp. 121–125. Springer, Heidelberg (2007)
5. Biere, A., Cimatti, A., Clarke, E., Zhu, Y.: Symbolic model checking without bDDs. In: Cleaveland, W.R. (ed.) TACAS 1999. LNCS, vol. 1579, pp. 193–207. Springer, Heidelberg (1999)
6. Bouyer, P., Bozzelli, L., Chevalier, F.: Controller synthesis for MTL specifications. In: Baier, C., Hermanns, H. (eds.) CONCUR 2006. LNCS, vol. 4137, pp. 450–464. Springer, Heidelberg (2006)

7. Clarke, E., Biere, A., Raimi, R., Zhu, Y.: Bounded model checking using satisfiability solving. Form. Methods Syst. Des (2001)
8. Damm, W., Dierks, H., Disch, S., Hagemann, W., Pigorsch, F., Scholl, C., Waldmann, U., Wirtz, B.: Exact and fully symbolic verification of linear hybrid automata with large discrete state spaces. Sci. Comput. Program. (2012)
9. Damm, W., Disch, S., Hungar, H., Jacobs, S., Pang, J., Pigorsch, F., Scholl, C., Waldmann, U., Wirtz, B.: Exact state set representations in the verification of linear hybrid systems with large discrete state space. In: Namjoshi, K.S., Yoneda, T., Higashino, T., Okamura, Y. (eds.) ATVA 2007. LNCS, vol. 4762, pp. 425–440. Springer, Heidelberg (2007)
10. Dutertre, B., de Moura, L.: The YICES SMT solver. Tech. rep., Computer Science Laboratory, SRI International (2006)
11. Ehlers, R., Mattmüller, R., Peter, H.-J.: Combining symbolic representations for solving timed games. In: Chatterjee, K., Henzinger, T.A. (eds.) FORMATS 2010. LNCS, vol. 6246, pp. 107–121. Springer, Heidelberg (2010)
12. Faella, M., La Torre, S., Murano, A.: Automata-theoretic decision of timed games. In: Cortesi, A. (ed.) VMCAI 2002. LNCS, vol. 2294, pp. 94–108. Springer, Heidelberg (2002)
13. Faella, M., La Torre, S., Murano, A.: Dense real-time games. In: LICS (2002)
14. Maler, O., Pnueli, A., Sifakis, J.: On the synthesis of discrete controllers for timed systems (an extended abstract). In: Mayr, E.W., Puech, C. (eds.) STACS 1995. LNCS, vol. 900, pp. 229–242. Springer, Heidelberg (1995)
15. Miller, C., Gitina, K., Becker, B.: Bounded model checking of incomplete real-time systems using quantified smt formulas. In: Proc. of MTV (2011)
16. Miller, C., Gitina, K., Scholl, C., Becker, B.: Bounded model checking of incomplete networks of timed automata. In: Proc. of MTV (2010)
17. Miller, C., Scholl, C., Becker, B.: Verifying incomplete networks of timed automata. In: Proc. of MBMV (2011)
18. Morbé, G., Scholl, C.: Fully symbolic tctl model checking for incomplete timed automata. In: Proc. of AVOCS (2013)
19. Morbé, G., Scholl, C.: Fully symbolic TCTL model checking for complete and incomplete real-time systems. Reports of SFB/TR 14 AVACS 104, SFB/TR 14 AVACS (September 2014), http://www.avacs.org
20. Morbé, G., Pigorsch, F., Scholl, C.: Fully symbolic model checking for timed automata. In: Gopalakrishnan, G., Qadeer, S. (eds.) CAV 2011. LNCS, vol. 6806, pp. 616–632. Springer, Heidelberg (2011)
21. Nopper, T., Miller, C., Lewis, M.D.T., Becker, B., Scholl, C.: Sat modulo bdd – a combined verification approach for incomplete designs. In: MBMV (2010)
22. Scholl, C., Disch, S., Pigorsch, F., Kupferschmid, S.: Computing optimized representations for non-convex polyhedra by detection and removal of redundant linear constraints. In: Kowalewski, S., Philippou, A. (eds.) TACAS 2009. LNCS, vol. 5505, pp. 383–397. Springer, Heidelberg (2009)

DynaMate: Dynamically Inferring Loop Invariants for Automatic Full Functional Verification

Juan Pablo Galeotti[1], Carlo A. Furia[2], Eva May[1], Gordon Fraser[3], and Andreas Zeller[1]

[1] Software Engineering Chair, Saarland University, Saarbrücken, Germany
lastname@cs.uni-saarland.de
[2] Chair of Software Engineering, Department of Computer Science, ETH Zurich, Switzerland
caf@inf.ethz.ch
[3] Department of Computer Science, University of Sheffield, UK
gordon.fraser@sheffield.ac.uk

Abstract. DYNAMATE is a tool that automatically infers loop invariants and uses them to prove Java programs correct with respect to a given JML functional specification. DYNAMATE improves the flexibility of loop invariant inference by integrating static (proving) and dynamic (testing) techniques with the goal of combining their complementary strengths. In an experimental evaluation involving 26 Java methods of java.util annotated with JML pre- and postconditions, it automatically discharged over 97% of all proof obligations, resulting in automatic complete correctness proofs of 23 out of the 26 methods.

1 The Challenge of Automating Program Verification

Full automation still eludes generic program verification techniques. The neologism *auto-active*—a portmanteau of *automatic* and *interactive*—has been introduced [11] to characterize some state-of-the-art tools for the formal verification of arbitrary functional properties of code. SMT-based verifiers such as ESC/Java2 [2], Dafny [10], and VCC [3] do not depend on a step-by-step interaction with the user, and hence are not purely interactive tools; but they still require substantially more input than just a program and its functional specification (typically given in the form of pre- and postcondition). For programs with loops, *loop invariants* are a crucial ingredient of any formal correctness proof; but the support to automatically infer loop invariants is generally limited and rarely available as part of the same tools used to perform verification. The general expectation is that users will provide detailed additional annotations (including loop invariants) whenever the tool needs them. DYNAMATE aims at providing more automation in these situations.

How DYNAMATE Works. The DYNAMATE tool presented in this paper combines different techniques with the overall goal of providing *fully automatic* verification of programs with loops. The only required input to DYNAMATE is a Java program (method) annotated with a JML functional specification (pre- and postcondition). DYNAMATE will try to construct a correctness proof of the program with respect to the specification; to this end it will infer necessary loop invariants. Even in the cases where it fails to find all required loop invariants, DYNAMATE still may find *some* useful invariants and use them to discard some proof obligations, thus providing *partial* verification.

E. Yahav (Ed.): HVC 2014, LNCS 8855, pp. 48–53, 2014.

We presented the details of how DYNAMATE works in a companion paper [8]. Figure 1 highlights its components and their high-level interactions: the program and its JML specification (center) are first fed into a test generator (left, EVOSUITE [6] in the current implementation), which generates executions covering possible behavior. Two dynamic invariant detector techniques (top) suggest possible loop invariants, based both on fixed patterns (DAIKON [5]) and on postconditions (GIN-DYN, a component designed as part of DYNAMATE). The candidates not invalidated by the generated runs are then fed into a static program verifier (right, ESC/Java2 [2] invoked with the -loopsafe option for sound verification of unbounded loops). When the verifier cannot produce a program proof (bottom), the test generator initiates another iteration where it tries to produce new tests that falsify candidates unproven as of yet.

While any test case generator could work with DYNAMATE, our prototype integrates the search-based test generator EVOSUITE. Besides being a fully automated tool, a specific advantage of EVOSUITE is that its genetic algorithm evolves test suites towards covering all program branches at the same time, and hence infeasible branch conditions (common in the presence of candidates that are in fact loop invariants, and hence won't be falsified) do not ultimately limit search effectiveness. A directed search is also useful to guide the successive iterations searching for new tests that specifically try to exercise unproven candidates under new conditions.

Advantages of DYNAMATE. The integration of techniques and tools in DYNAMATE compensates for individual shortcomings and achieves a greater whole in terms of flexibility and degree of automation. Dynamic techniques are capable of conclusively invalidating large amounts of loop invariant candidates, thus winnowing a smaller set of *candidate* invariants that hold in all executions, and can test candidates in isolation (dependencies are not an issue). This leaves the static verifier with a more manageable task in terms of number of candidates to check at once. The GIN-DYN component is an original contribution of DYNAMATE. Based on the observation that loop invariants can often be seen as weakened forms postconditions [7], GIN-DYN derives loop invariant candidates by mutating postconditions. This enables inferring loop invariants that are not limited to predefined templates but stem from the annotated Java program

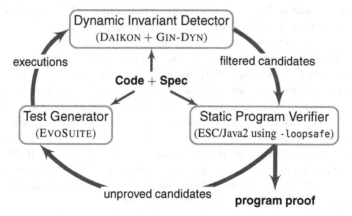

Fig. 1. How DYNAMATE works

under analysis. DYNAMATE still avails of the advantages of static techniques in terms of soundness: the static verification module scrutinizes the output of the dynamic parts until it can verify it (and uses verified invariants to construct a correctness proof).

2   Using DYNAMATE

We briefly present DYNAMATE in action on the implementation of binary search available in class java.util.Arrays from Java's JDK. [1]

```
1 /*@ requires a ≠ null
2   @ requires TArrays.within(a, fromIndex, toIndex)
3   @ requires TArrays.sorted(a, fromIndex, toIndex);
4   @ ensures \result ≥ 0 ⟹ a[\result] = key;
5   @ ensures \result < 0 ⟹ ¬TArrays.has(a, fromIndex, toIndex, key);     @*/
6   private static int binarySearch0(int[] a, int fromIndex, int toIndex, int key)
```

Fig. 2. JML specification of the binary search method from java.util. The specification includes a precondition (**requires**) and two postconditions (**ensures**)

The input to DYNAMATE consists of the method binarySearch0 annotated with the JML specification of Figure 2. Note that predicate has is a shorthand for a quantification over [fromIndex..toIndex); dealing with quantified invariants is a challenges for fully automatic verification. When it starts, DYNAMATE opens an HTML report, which shows the program and specification with all elements (statements or annotations) that trigger an ESC/Java2 warning highlighted in yellow. Clicking on a highlighted element displays its current status, including ESC/Java2's warning messages.

After each iteration of its main loop (Figure 1), DYNAMATE updates the report: elements for which all associated ESC/Java2 warnings have been discharged are highlighted in green. In addition, users can inspect the generated loop invariants by clicking on any loop header. By default only verified loop invariants are shown (in green). Candidate invariants can be viewed (in yellow) by de-selecting a check-box. These candidates have not been falsified by a test, nor have they been verified by ESC/Java2.

Figure 3 shows a report after the first iteration on binarySearch0: DYNAMATE has proven several simple scalar invariants for the selected loop. These simple invariants come from predefined templates; they are sufficient to prove the first postcondition (line 4 in Figure 2) and to show that array accesses are within bounds.

As DYNAMATE continues its search, it uses the postconditions as a basis for more complex invariants. In the example, the postcondition on line 5 in Figure 2 (corresponding to when the search returns unsuccessfully) mentions predicate ¬has(a,fromIndex, toIndex, key); DYNAMATE mutates its arguments and checks if any of the mutations are loop invariants. Among many mutations, ¬has(a, fromIndex, low, key) and ¬has(a, high + 1, toIndex, key) are valid loop invariants, essential to establishing the postcondition. DYNAMATE finds them during iteration #9, validates them, and uses them to prove the second postcondition. This concludes DYNAMATE's run, which terminates successfully having achieved full verification. Upon terminating, the tool reports all inferred loop invariants—including those listed in Figure 4—which include both scalar invariants and quantified ones (obtained by mutating postconditions).

---

[1] DYNAMATE's output report for this example is available at http://goo.gl/7TxE9d.

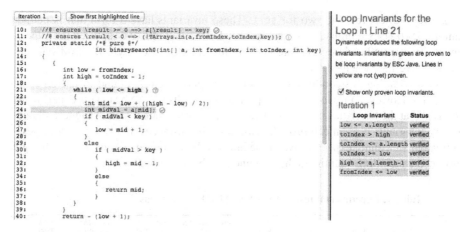

Fig. 3. DYNAMATE's report after iteration # 1 on `binarySearch0`. Verified statements and annotations (first and last highlighted element) are shown in green, unverified ones in yellow. Loop headers are highlighted in light blue. The right frame shows the proven loop invariants for the selected loop.

In spite of its brevity in lines of code, automatically verifying `binarySearch0` without extra input in the form of loop invariants or other annotations is a task that challenges most fully-automatic verifiers. In fact, we tried to verify the same method against the specification in Figure 2 using the state-of-the-art automatic tools INVGEN [9], BLAST [1], and ccheck [4]. None of them could complete a correctness proof of `binarySearch0` against its full functional specification.

7   fromIndex $\leq$ low $\wedge$ low $\leq$ high + 1 $\wedge$ high $<$ toIndex

8   ¬TArrays.has(a,fromIndex,low,key)

9   ¬TArrays.has(a,high+1,toIndex,key)

Fig. 4. Loop invariants inferred by DYNAMATE

3   Empirical Evaluation

We evaluated DYNAMATE on 26 methods with loops from the `java.util` standard package of Java, including algorithms operating on data structures such as arrays, lists, deques, and vectors. To account for the randomized algorithm used by EVOSUITE's test-case generator, we ran each example 30 times; column *success rate* in Table 1 reports the percentage of those runs that found a full correctness proof. The other columns report means over the 30 runs: the percentage of proven proof obligations[2]; the number of iterations of the DYNAMATE algorithm; the number of proven invariants; and the total running time.

DYNAMATE was never successful only with methods `merge0`, `quicksortPartition`, and `sort`, for a total of 4 missing necessary invariants, one for each of `merge0` and

---

[2] These include pre- and postcondition checks, class invariant checks, and implicit checks for out-of-bound array accesses and **null** dereferencing.

quicksortPartition and two for sort. These invariants have a form that is neither among DAIKON's templates nor among GIN-DYN's mutants. We repeated the experiments by manually adding the four missing invariants; as expected, DYNAMATE successfully verified the methods.

Since mutating postconditions is a heuristic approach, it is bound to fail on *some* examples. However, previous analysis [7] and the results of DYNAMATE's experiments suggest that the heuristics if *often* applicable—and even when it cannot suggest all necessary invariants it often can provide partial, useful instances. In all, we gain in flexibility, but we cannot expect to overcome intrinsic limitations due to dealing with logic fragments including quantifiers that are undecidable in general.

Table 1. Experimental results for DYNAMATE on methods from `java.util`.

CLASS	METHOD	SUCCESS RATE	OBLIGATIONS PROVEN	DYNAMATE ITERATIONS	INVARIANTS PROVEN	TOTAL TIME
ArrayDeque	contains	57 %	98 %	7	14	2158 s
ArrayDeque	removeFirstOccurrence	53 %	98 %	7	14	2180 s
ArrayDeque	removeLastOccurrence	87 %	99 %	9	43	3281 s
ArrayList	clear	70 %	95 %	6	9	1524 s
ArrayList	indexOf	23 %	91 %	7	16	1914 s
ArrayList	lastIndexOf	20 %	93 %	6	14	1574 s
ArrayList	remove0	23 %	93 %	7	16	2065 s
Arrays	binarySearch0	100 %	100 %	11	30	4200 s
Arrays	equals0	100 %	100 %	7	7	2240 s
Arrays	fill0	100 %	100 %	6	5	1391 s
Arrays	fill1	100 %	100 %	7	15	1880 s
Arrays	fillInteger0	100 %	100 %	6	7	1375 s
Arrays	fillInteger1	100 %	100 %	7	18	1857 s
Arrays	hashCode0	100 %	100 %	2	4	389 s
Arrays	hashCodeInteger	100 %	100 %	2	4	343 s
Arrays	insertionSort1	100 %	100 %	11	73	4512 s
Arrays	merge0	0 %	90 %	11	78	8034 s
Arrays	quicksortPartition	0 %	94 %	9	57	5657 s
Arrays	vecswap	100 %	100 %	8	18	2698 s
Collections	replaceAll	77 %	97 %	6	16	1801 s
Collections	sort	0 %	73 %	9	17	3933 s
Vector	indexOf1	100 %	100 %	6	24	1698 s
Vector	lastIndexOf1	90 %	99 %	7	19	1859 s
Vector	removeAllElements	100 %	100 %	5	12	1218 s
Vector	removeRange0	63 %	96 %	7	17	2574 s
Vector	setSize	100 %	100 %	7	31	2003 s
	AVERAGE	72 %	97 %	7	22	2475 s

Many more details on the experiments, as well as a detailed comparison of DYNAMATE against state-of-the-art tools are presented in a companion paper [8].

4   Conclusions

DYNAMATE's prototype is currently quite limited in terms of scalability, as it takes a considerable amount of time even on structurally simple methods. However, over 65% of the total time is taken up by testing. Even if dynamic techniques are generally slower than purely static ones, there are significant margins to improve the implementation for speed by customizing the test generator (which is currently used as black box) to cater to DYNAMATE's special requirements.

These details should not, however, distract us from assessing DYNAMATE's specific contributions with the right poise: fully automated program verification features an intrinsic formidable complexity; and even the shortest algorithms (in terms of lines of code) may require complex invariants [12]. DYNAMATE worked successfully on real code annotated with non-trivial (often complete) functional correctness specifications. It automatically built correctness proofs for 23 out of 26 subjects[3]; and discharged over 97% of all proof obligations on average. These results demonstrate the benefits of integrating static and dynamic verification techniques with complementary strengths and shortcomings, and improve over the state of the art in terms of complete automation and flexibility.

Availability: The current prototype of DYNAMATE is available for download at `http://www.st.cs.uni-saarland.de/dynamate-tool/`. The download page includes a virtual-machine image with all dependencies as well as scripts to run the examples mentioned in Section 3.

Acknowledgments. This work was funded by the European Research Council (ERC) Advanced Grant "SPECMATE – Specification Mining and Testing". The second author was partially funded by the Swiss SNF Grant ASII 200021-134976.

References

1. Beyer, D., Henzinger, T.A., Jhala, R., Majumdar, R.: The software model checker Blast. STTT 9(5-6), 505–525 (2007)
2. Chalin, P., Kiniry, J.R., Leavens, G.T., Poll, E.: Beyond assertions: Advanced specification and verification with JML and eSC/Java2. In: de Boer, F.S., Bonsangue, M.M., Graf, S., de Roever, W.-P. (eds.) FMCO 2005. LNCS, vol. 4111, pp. 342–363. Springer, Heidelberg (2006)
3. Cohen, E., Dahlweid, M., Hillebrand, M., Leinenbach, D., Moskal, M., Santen, T., Schulte, W., Tobies, S.: VCC: A practical system for verifying concurrent C. In: Berghofer, S., Nipkow, T., Urban, C., Wenzel, M. (eds.) TPHOLs 2009. LNCS, vol. 5674, pp. 23–42. Springer, Heidelberg (2009)
4. Cousot, P., Cousot, R., Logozzo, F.: A parametric segmentation functor for fully automatic and scalable array content analysis. In: POPL, pp. 105–118. ACM (2011)
5. Ernst, M.D., Cockrell, J., Griswold, W.G., Notkin, D.: Dynamically discovering likely program invariants to support program evolution. IEEE TSE 27(2), 99–123 (2001)
6. Fraser, G., Arcuri, A.: Evolutionary generation of whole test suites. In: QSIC, pp. 31–40. IEEE Computer Society (2011)
7. Furia, C.A., Meyer, B., Velder, S.: Loop invariants: Analysis, classification, and examples. ACM Comp. Sur. 46(3) (2014)
8. Galeotti, J.P., Furia, C.A., May, E., Fraser, G., Zeller, A.: Automating full functional verification of programs with loops (submitted, July 2014), `http://arxiv.org/abs/1407.5286`
9. Gupta, A., Rybalchenko, A.: InvGen: An efficient invariant generator. In: Bouajjani, A., Maler, O. (eds.) CAV 2009. LNCS, vol. 5643, pp. 634–640. Springer, Heidelberg (2009)
10. Leino, K.R.M.: Dafny: An automatic program verifier for functional correctness. In: Clarke, E.M., Voronkov, A. (eds.) LPAR-16 2010. LNCS, vol. 6355, pp. 348–370. Springer, Heidelberg (2010)
11. Leino, K.R.M., Moskal, M.: Usable auto-active verification. In: Usable Verification Workshop (2010), `http://fm.csl.sri.com/UV10/`
12. Zee, K., Kuncak, V., Rinard, M.C.: Full functional verification of linked data structures. In: PLDI, pp. 349–361. ACM (2008)

---

[3] The average success rate is below $23/26 = 88\%$ because not all repeated runs succeeded.

Generating Modulo-2 Linear Invariants for Hardware Model Checking

Gadi Aleksandrowicz[1], Alexander Ivrii[1], Oded Margalit[1], and Dan Rasin[2]

[1] IBM Research – Haifa, Israel
[2] Technion, Israel

Abstract. We present an algorithm to automatically extract inductive modulo-2 linear invariants from a design. This algorithm makes use of basic linear algebra and is realized on top of an incremental SAT solver. The experimental results demonstrate that a large number of designs possess linear invariants that can be efficiently found by our method. We study how these invariants can be helpful in the contexts of model checking and synthesis.

1 Introduction

Automatically extracting and exploiting invariants (Boolean functions that are constant on all reachable states) is one of the central themes in model checking [CNQ07, CMB07]. In this paper we are interested in mod-2 linear invariants

$$\sum_{i=1}^{n} a_i x_i = b \;(\text{mod } 2), \; a_i, b \in \{0, 1\}.$$

This class of linear invariants naturally generalizes the class of constant invariants (invariants of the form $x_i = b$) and the class of equivalences and anti-equivalences (invariants of the form x_i xor $x_j = b$).

The main contribution of this work is a method to find the smallest *inductive* linear over-approximation of the set of reachable states in the design, that is, the smallest linear subspace that includes all the initial states and is closed under transitions. We also show that the orthogonal complement of this subspace can be naturally identified with the maximal set of mutually inductive linear invariants that hold on all reachable states. Our algorithm is based on basic linear algebra and makes use of an incremental SAT solver. We show that this approach works reasonably well in practice, and we discuss a series of optimizations to improve it further.

We have evaluated the algorithm on HWMCC'11 and HWMCC'13 benchmarks, and we show that a large number of designs possess many linear invariants, even after most of the constants and equivalences have been filtered out by alternative methods. In addition, every linear invariant directly allows to express one of its variables as a linear combination of the remaining variables, thus allowing to reduce the total number of state variables in the design. We compare

E. Yahav (Ed.): HVC 2014, LNCS 8855, pp. 54–67, 2014.
© Springer International Publishing Switzerland 2014

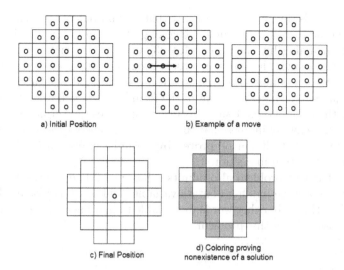

a) Initial Position   b) Example of a move

c) Final Position

d) Coloring proving
nonexistence of a solution

Fig. 1. European peg solitaire game and the proof that it is unsolvable

the runtimes of IC3 [Bra11] on the original and the simplified designs, and show that (non-surprisingly) such a reduction has a positive impact on verification.

The rest of this paper is organized as follows. In Section 2 we describe an easy-to-understand verification example which demonstrates the usefulness of large linear invariants (and which has in fact motivated this paper). Section 3 is the core of the paper containing full algorithms and implementation details. In Section 4 we present experimental results, discussing both the numbers of linear invariants and their impact on verification. In Section 5 we discuss related work, and Section 6 concludes the paper.

2 Toy Verification Example

The *European peg solitaire* is a single-player game played on a grid board shown in Figure 1a. Initially each cell of the board except for the middle square contains a peg. A legal move consists of choosing a peg and jumping it either horizontally or vertically over an adjacent peg into an empty cell two squares away. Afterwards, the jumped-over peg is removed. Figure 1b shows how such a move is performed. The goal is to find a sequence of moves which ends up with a single peg in the middle of the board, as in Figure 1c. It is well known that this version of peg solitaire has no solution. A classical proof of this fact is to color the board as shown in Figure 1d, to observe that for every legal move the number modulo 2 of colored squares containing pegs remains constant, and that this number evaluates to 0 on the board in Figure 1a and to 1 on the board in Figure 1c.

Peg solitaire can be easily described as a verification problem by introducing a state variable x_i for each cell of the board, with the interpretation that $x_i = 1$ iff there is a peg in this cell. Compared to most industrial designs, the size of this toy problem is tiny, and yet deducing that it is unsolvable proved to be very difficult even for very powerful model-checking algorithms either BDD-based or SAT-based (including Interpolation [McM03] and IC3 [Bra11]).

On the other hand, the previous observation that the number modulo 2 of colored squares containing pegs remains 0 on all forward reachable states directly translates to a single invariant of the form $\sum_{i \in C} x_i = 0 \pmod 2$, where C enumerates the colored cells. Using this invariant makes the verification problem trivial as it immediately implies that the final position is not reachable. Furthermore, the invariant itself can be proved by a simple induction (and so will be found by our algorithm in Section 3).

We note that this problem also admits other mod-2 linear invariants but all of them involve a large number of state variables and so cannot be easily found by classical methods. In other words, being able to find linear invariants of large size is a key for solving this problem.

3   Algorithms

3.1   Preliminaries

We represent a finite state system $\mathcal{T}$ as a tuple $\langle i, x, I(x), T(i, x, x') \rangle$, which consists of primary inputs i, state variables x, predicate $I(x)$ defining the initial states, and predicate $T(i, x, x')$ defining the transition relation. Next-state variables are denoted as x'. We also denote by $T(x, x')$ the predicate $\exists i : T(i, x, x')$.

We say that a state x is *reachable* if there is a sequence $x^0, \ldots, x^m$ of states such that $x^0 \in I$, $(x^i, x^{i+1}) \in T$ for $i = 0, \ldots, m-1$, and $x^m = x$. We denote the set of all reachable states by *Reach*. A Boolean function F is an *invariant* if it holds on all the reachable states (*Reach* $\Rightarrow F$), and a Boolean function F is *inductive* if it contains the initial states ($I \Rightarrow F$) and is closed under transitions ($F(x) \land T(x, x') \Rightarrow F(x')$). An inductive function is an invariant but not necessarily vice versa.

We use standard notations from linear algebra. If $a, b \in \mathbb{Z}_2^n$ we denote their scalar product by $a \cdot b = \sum_{i=1}^n a_i b_i \pmod 2$. Given any set $D \subseteq \mathbb{Z}_2^n$ we denote by $\mathsf{span}(D) = \{d \in \mathbb{Z}_2^n \mid \exists d_1, \ldots, d_k \in D, \exists a_1, \ldots, a_k \in \mathbb{Z}_2 : d = a_1 d_1 + \cdots + a_k d_k\}$ the space of all linear combinations of elements of D, and by $D^\perp = \{r \in \mathbb{Z}_2^n \mid \forall d \in D : r \cdot d = 0\}$ the orthogonal complement of D. A *canonical basis* for $\mathbb{Z}_2^n$ is the set $\{e_1, \ldots, e_n\}$, where e_i is the vector $(0, \ldots, 1, \ldots, 0)$ with the unique 1 at the i'th position. We denote by $\mathbf{0}$ the zero element in $\mathbb{Z}_2^n$.

For simplicity we limit the analysis to state variables in the design. We say that an expression of the form $\{(\bigoplus_{j \in J} x_j) = b\}$ is *xor* (or mod-2 *linear*) invariant (where $J \subseteq \{1, \ldots, n\}$ and $b \in \{0, 1\}$) if the function $1 \oplus b \oplus \bigoplus_{j \in J} x_j$ is an invariant, or in other words if *Reach* $\Rightarrow (\bigoplus_{j \in J} x_j = b)$.

3.2 Overview

For simplicity of description we first assume that $I = \{\mathbf{0}\}$, that is the initial states consist of a single all-zero element. We will extend the ideas to general initial states at the very end of this section. The proofs of the propositions appear in [AIMR].

We denote by n the number of state variables in the design, and by $V = \mathbb{Z}_2^n$ the set of all states. By the assumption on I, the state $\mathbf{0}$ is reachable, and so we only need to look for linear invariants of the form $\{\sum_{i=1}^n a_i x_i = 0\}$.

We can identify each linear invariant $\{\sum_{i=1}^n a_i x_i = 0\}$ with a point $(a_1, \ldots, a_n)$ $\in V$ and note that the set of all linear invariants forms a linear subspace of V (for example, if both $\{\sum_{i=1}^n a_i x_i = 0\}$ and $\{\sum_{i=1}^n b_i x_i = 0\}$ hold on $Reach$, then so also does $\{\sum_{i=1}^n (a_i + b_i) x_i = 0\}$). We denote this vector subspace by Inv.

We also look at a *dual* problem of finding a vector subspace of V containing all reachable states. To this end we define a *displacement set* $D_S = \{d \in V \mid \exists x, x' : T(x, x') \wedge (d = x' \oplus x)\}$ and a *displacement vector space* $D = \text{span}(D_S)$. In other words, an element in D_S describes a possible change in the state under one transition step, and an element of D represents a linear combination of such changes. We define R to be the orthogonal complement of D.

Proposition 1. *Reach* $\subseteq D$ *and* $R \subseteq Inv$.

Example 1. Suppose that $n = 3$ and the only transitions are as follows: $000 \to 011 \to 101 \to 000$ (and each state not explicitly mentioned has a single transition back to itself). Then $D_S = \{000, 011, 110, 101\}$ (for example, the transition $011 \to 101$ results in the displacement $011 \oplus 101 = 110$), $D \triangleq \text{span}(D_S) = \text{span}(\{011, 110\})$, and $R \triangleq D^\perp = \text{span}(\{111\}) = \{000, 111\}$. The element $111 \in R$ represents the xor-invariant $x_1 \oplus x_2 \oplus x_3 = 0$ that holds on all reachable states. $Reach = \{000, 011, 101\}$ is a proper subset of D, and $Inv = R$ (i.e. there are no other xor-invariants).

In Section 3.3 we describe an efficient algorithm to compute (the bases of) D and R. This algorithm is based on linear algebra over $\mathbb{Z}_2$ and makes n queries to a SAT solver. By proposition 1, every element of R is a xor-invariant.

Unfortunately R does not necessarily equal Inv, due to transitions from non-reachable states (in particular, D is not necessarily the smallest vector subspace of V containing $Reach$). We illustrate this by the following example.

Example 2. Suppose that $n = 3$ and the only transitions are as follows: $000 \to 011 \to 101 \to 000$, $100 \to 000$ (and each state not explicitly mentioned has a single transition back to itself). Then $D = \text{span}(\{000, 011, 110, 101, 100\}) = V$, $R = \{000\}$, while $Inv = \text{span}(\{111\})$ as before. Note that the "problem" results from considering the displacement from the unreachable state 100.

In Section 3.4 we remedy the situation to a large extent (albeit not perfectly) by describing an efficient algorithm to compute (the basis of) the smallest *inductive* linear subspace D_I containing $Reach$. For the previous example,

$D_I = \mathsf{span}(\{011, 110\})$, and $R_I \triangleq D_I^\perp = \mathsf{span}(\{111\}) = Inv$. This new algorithm makes at most n^2 queries to a SAT solver (and much fewer in practice).

In Sections 3.5-3.6 we describe various optimizations, implementation issues, and the extension to general initial states.

Finally, in Section 3.7 we show that linear invariants can be effectively used as a reparameterization technique for reducing the total number of state variables in the design.

3.3 Computing Displacements and Invariants

Recall that the displacement vector space D is defined as $\mathsf{span}\{d \in V \mid \exists x, x' : T(x, x') \wedge (d = x' \oplus x)\}$. The algorithm $\texttt{ComputeDI}$ (Algorithm 1) accepts the transition relation $T(x, x')$, and returns a basis δ for D and a basis ρ for $R = D^\perp$.

Algorithm 1. ComputeDI
(Compute Displacements and Invariants)

Input: $T(x, x')$
Output: a basis δ for D, and a basis ρ for $R = D^\perp$

1: $\delta \leftarrow \emptyset$, $\rho \leftarrow \emptyset$, $\gamma \leftarrow \{e_1, \ldots, e_n\}$
2: **while** $\gamma \neq \emptyset$ **do**
3:     Pick a vector $t \in \gamma$ and remove it from γ
4:     **if** $\exists x, x', d : (d = x' \oplus x) \wedge T(x, x') \wedge (t \cdot d = 1)$ **then**
5:         $\delta \leftarrow \delta \cup \{d\}$
6:         **for all** $v \in \gamma$ **do**
7:             If $v \cdot d = 0$, leave v unchanged
8:             If $v \cdot d = 1$, replace v by $v + t$ in γ
9:         **end for**
10:    **else**
11:        $\rho \leftarrow \rho \cup \{t\}$
12:    **end if**
13: **end while**

The bases δ and ρ are computed incrementally. We initialize them to empty sets, we also initialize γ to the canonical basis of V (line 1). On each iteration of the algorithm (lines 2-13) we pick an element $t \in \gamma$ and check if $t \cdot D = 0$. More precisely, we make a SAT query shown on line 4, checking whether there exist a state x and a state x' reachable from x in one transition step so that the corresponding displacement $d = x \oplus x'$ satisfies $t \cdot d = 1$. If this query is unsatisfiable (and thus $t \cdot D = 0$), then $t \in D^\perp$ and we add t to the basis ρ of R (line 11). Otherwise we have found a new displacement vector d which we add to the basis δ of D (line 5). In addition, we update the remaining elements of γ by projecting them to $D^\perp$ (lines 6-9). Note that since the size of γ decreases each time by one, the algorithm stops after exactly n iterations and hence makes exactly n calls to a SAT solver. The following proposition summarizes the correctness of the algorithm.

Proposition 2. *When* `ComputeDI` *terminates, δ is a basis for D and ρ is a basis for $D^\perp$.*

3.4 Computing the Smallest Inductive Subspace

We define the *smallest inductive subspace* $D_I \subseteq V$ as the smallest linear subspace of V which contains *Reach* and which is inductive with respect to the transition relation. Note that the use of the word *smallest* is justified: if D_1 and D_2 are both linear and inductive subspaces containing *Reach*, then so also is their intersection $D_1 \cap D_2$. We define $R_I = D_I^\perp$. The following proposition shows that R_I in general computes a larger set of invariants than given by Proposition 1.

Proposition 3. *Reach $\subseteq D_I \subseteq D$ and $R \subseteq R_I \subseteq Inv$.*

Before presenting an algorithm to compute D_I and R_I, we need a modification `ComputeRDI` of `ComputeDI` that only finds displacements starting from a restricted set of states specified by a Boolean function $J(x)$. More precisely, `ComputeRDI` accepts $J(x)$ and $T(x, x')$ as input, and replaces the SAT query on line 4 by the query

$$\exists x, x', d : (d = x' \oplus x) \wedge J(x) \wedge T(x, x') \wedge (t \cdot d = 1).$$

The output of `ComputeRDI` is a basis δ for the vector space of displacements starting from J, and a basis ρ for the orthogonal complement of this space. Because the set of considered displacements is restricted, the elements of ρ are not necessarily invariants.

The following algorithm `ComputeInductiveInvariants` to compute the smallest inductive subspace (Algorithm 2) is in the spirit of Interpolation [McM03], in the sense that it constructs linear over-approximations of states reachable in at most k steps from $\{0\}$, and stops when a fixpoint is reached.

Algorithm 2. `ComputeInductiveInvariants`
(Computes the Smallest Inductive Subspace)

Input: $I(x) = \{0\}$, $T(x, x')$
Output: a basis δ for D_I, and a basis ρ for $R_I = D_I^\perp$

1: $\delta_0 \leftarrow \{\}$
2: **for** k in $1, 2, 3, \ldots$ **do**
3:     $(\delta_k, \rho_k) \leftarrow$ `ComputeRDI`$(\mathrm{span}(\delta_{k-1}), T)$
4:     **if** $|\delta_k| = |\delta_{k-1}|$ **then**
5:         **return** (δ_k, ρ_k)
6:     **end if**
7: **end for**

We set δ_0 to the empty set (line 1), and we let $D_0 = \mathrm{span}(\delta_0) = I = \{0\}$. In the main loop of the algorithm (lines 2-7) we call `ComputeRDI` to compute the basis δ_k of the set of displacements starting from $D_{k-1} = \text{span}(\delta_{k-1})$. In this way each D_k represents a linear over-approximation of the set of states reachable from D_{k-1} in one transition step, and in particular a linear over-approximation of the set of states reachable in k steps from the initial states. The algorithm terminates when $D_k = D_{k-1}$, at this stage D_k represents an inductive linear over-approximation of reachable states (and as the following proposition shows, the *smallest* inductive linear over-approximation). Also note that since $I = \{0\}$, we have that $D_{k-1} \subseteq D_k$ for all k, and in particular the fixpoint condition can be checked just by comparing the sizes of bases for D_k (line 4).

Proposition 4. *When* `ComputeInductiveInvariants` *terminates, δ is a basis for D_I and ρ is a basis for R_I.*

We note that `ComputeInductiveInvariants` makes at most n^2 calls to a SAT solver: the loop of the algorithm can be executed at most n times, and each invocation of `ComputeRDI` makes n SAT queries. In the next section we describe several important optimizations which significantly reduces the number of SAT queries in practice.

3.5   Implementation Details and Optimizations

Non-surprisingly, in `ComputeDI` and `ComputeInductiveInvariants` most of the time is spent on SAT-solving, and thus it is important to optimize the total number of SAT calls and the time spent on each individual call.

Optimizing the Number of SAT Calls. We can modify `ComputeDI` and `ComputeRDI` by taking the set of already known displacements into account. In this case, instead of choosing a vector $t \in \gamma$ and making a SAT call to find a displacement d with $t \cdot d = 1$, we can first check the pool of known displacements to see if such d is known already. Even better, we can first look for pairs $\{t, d\}$ with $t \cdot d = 1$ (for $t \in \gamma$ and d in the known displacement set) and process such t's first (and only when no such pairs are present resort to SAT queries). In particular, we can reuse the sets δ_k found from one invocation of `ComputeRDI` for the next iteration – this is legitimate since $D_{k-1} \subseteq D_k$ and so the space of displacements starting from D_{k-1} is a subspace of displacements starting from D_k. In addition, we can run upfront simulation to compute the starting set of displacements D_0 which can be used both in `ComputeRDI` and as a starting point for `ComputeInductiveInvariants` (by initializing δ_0 to the basis of D_0 instead of an empty set).

Optimizing SAT Calls. An undoubtedly one of the most useful (and well-known) optimizations is to use an *incremental* SAT solver (that supports the MiniSat-like "solve under assumptions" mechanism [ES03]). We can implement the main SAT query "$\exists x, x', d : (d = x' \oplus x) \wedge T(x, x') \wedge (t \cdot d = 1)$" (line 4 of `ComputeDI`) as follows. Given a CNF representing the transition relation (and in particular involving variables $x_1, \ldots, x_n$ and $x'_1, \ldots, x'_n$), create additional variables $d_1, \ldots d_n$, and add clauses describing $d_i = x_i \oplus x'_i$. Create additional variables $t_1, \ldots, t_n$ and "partial sum" variables $s_1, \ldots, s_n$, and add clauses describing $s_1 = 0$, $s_n = 1$, and $s_i = s_{i-1} \oplus (t_i \wedge d_i)$ for $i = 2, \ldots, n$. Now each SAT query can be realized by passing the corresponding vector t via *assumptions*. This allows to keep a single copy of the SAT solver for all queries in ComputeDI and hence to automatically reuse all learned clauses from one SAT call to the next. As an alternative to the "partial sums" technique, we can encode an expression $t \cdot d = 1$ directly using XOR-clauses if the underlying SAT solver can handle such clauses natively (as for example CryptoMiniSat [Cryt2]). More precisely, to encode $t_1 d_1 + \cdots + t_n d_n = 1 \pmod 2$, we can introduce auxiliary variables $y_1, \ldots, y_n$, encode $y_i = t_i \wedge d_i$ (for each i), and add a single XOR-clause $(y_1 \oplus \cdots \oplus y_n)$. When we call the procedure ComputeRDI from ComputeInductiveInvariants, we need to create a CNF expression for the constraint $x \in J$, where $J = \text{span}(\delta_{k-1})$. Suppose that δ_{k-1} is given as $\{d^1, \ldots, d^m\}$. A direct way to encode $x \in \text{span}\{d^1, \ldots, d^k\}$ would be to create auxiliary variables $a_1, \ldots, a_k$ and to encode $x_i = a_1 d_i^1 + \cdots + a_k d_i^k$ for all i. We have found that in general it is better to encode $x \cdot J^\perp = 0$. In other words, if $J^\perp = \text{span}\{r^1, \ldots, r^{n-k}\}$, then we need to add constraints for $x \cdot r^i = 0$. Note that since each r^i is given explicitly, each such constraint translates to a single XOR-clause.

Improving Memory Consumption. In general the vectors considered in the algorithms have very few 1s, and as such storing only the positions of 1's (rather than the full vectors) keeps the memory consumption significantly lower.

3.6 Extension to General Initial States

We note that there are simple design transformations mapping a general design to a design with a single initial state, and this allows to immediately extend all of the methods to general initial states. However, such transformations might introduce additional displacements between pairs of initial states, which were not present in the design initially, and so we outline an alternative approach which is useful on designs with many initial states.

We construct a set of states S of the form $S = I + D$, where $I(x)$ denotes the initial states and D is a linear subspace, satisfying the following conditions:

1. $Reach \subseteq S(x)$,
2. $S(x)$ is inductive (i.e. $S(x) \wedge T(x, x') \Rightarrow S(x')$), and
3. $S(x)$ is a minimal set of states of the form $I + D$ that satisfies (1) and (2).

In the above, $I + D$ denotes the Minkowski sum of I and D, that is $I + D = \{c = a + b \mid a \in I, b \in D\}$. Strictly speaking, S itself is not linear, but rather it is a linear space D "shifted" by all possible initial states values.

The only change to ComputeInductiveInvariants (see Algorithm 3) consists of iteratively computing displacements from $I + \text{span}(\delta_{k-1})$.

Algorithm 3. ComputeInductiveInvariants
(Extension to General Initial States)

Input: $I(x)$, $T(x, x')$
Output: a basis δ for D, and a basis ρ for $D^{\perp}$

1: $\delta_0 \leftarrow \{\}$
2: **for** k in $1, 2, 3, \ldots$ **do**
3:    $(\delta_k, \rho_k) \leftarrow$ ComputeRDI$(I(x) + \mathsf{span}(\delta_{k-1}), T)$
4:    **if** $|\delta_k| = |\delta_{k-1}|$ **then**
5:       **return** (δ_k, ρ_k)
6:    **end if**
7: **end for**

Suppose that ComputeInductiveInvariants returns a basis δ for D, and a basis ρ for $D^{\perp}$, and that $(a_1, \ldots, a_n) \in \mathsf{span}(\rho)$. It follows that the value of the linear combination $\sum_i a_i x_i$ remains constant on every path in the design that starts in an initial state, although this value may differ for different paths. However, if this value is the same for all initial states (as can be checked with a SAT solver), then we indeed find a linear invariant of the form $\sum_i a_i x_i = b$ that holds on all reachable states.

3.7 State Variables Reduction

Given any linear independent set of invariants of the form $\{\sum_i a_{ij} x_i = b_i\}_{j=1}^k$ (as for example computed by ComputeInductiveInvariants), we can apply Gaussian Elimination to express exactly k of the variables in terms of the remaining variables. In other words, linear inductive invariants have an immediate application as a reparameterization technique (see for example [CCK04]) that reduces the total number of state variables in a design. We will study the effect of this reduction in Section 4.

4 Experimental Evaluation

All experiments were performed on a 2.0Ghz Linux-based machine with Intel Xeon E7540 processor and 4GB of RAM, using the techniques presented in this paper as implemented in the IBM verification tool *Rulebase-Sixthsense* [MBP+04].

4.1 Effect on Reduction Size

In the first set of experiments, we investigate the numbers of mod 2 linear invariants as would be witnessed in a typical verification flow. We consider 633 designs from the single-property HWMCC'11 and HWMCC'13 benchmark sets [Har11, Har13]. On each of these designs we apply a round of standard logic optimization (to reduce the design size), followed by combinatorial and

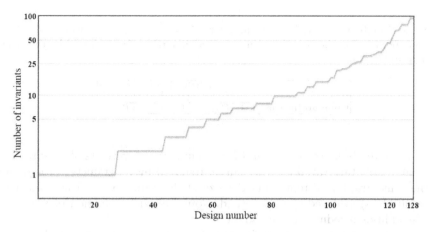

Fig. 2. Absolute numbers of invariants (for each of the designs)

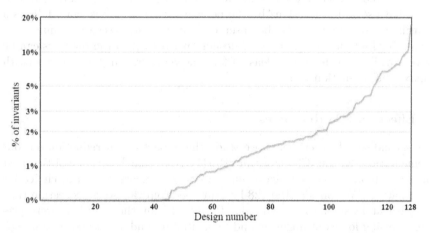

Fig. 3. Relative numbers of invariants (for each of the designs)

sequential redundancy removal [MBMB09] (to identify and merge sequentially equivalent registers), followed by another round of logic optimization. In particular, in the 532 designs that were not solved by the preprocessing alone, there are no constant, equivalent, or anti-equivalent registers that can be detected either via SAT-sweeping or induction.

Our algorithm ComputeInductiveinvariants is successful in finding at least one linear invariant on 128 of the designs (that is, in 24% of the cases). In Figure 2 we present the detailed data on the number of invariants for each of these designs. Note that the designs are sorted by the increasing number of invariants, and that the y-axis follows a logarithmic scale. It can be readily observed that in cases the number of invariants can be substantial: for example, the designs starting from 81 possess at least 10 linear invariants, while the designs starting from 121 possess at least 50 linear invariants.

Table 1. Numbers of solved benchmarks for IC3 and for ComputeInvariants + IC3. The number in parenthesis is the number of benchmarks uniquely solved by the given configuration.

	reachable	unreachable
IC3	2 (0)	41 (1)
ComputeInvariants + IC3	3 (1)	43 (3)

As we have observed in Section 3.7, the number of invariants also represents the number of state variables that can be removed by reparameterization, and so the same graph also represents the size of the reduction (in the number of state variables) achieved by our method. Note that such reduction may in turn enable additional reductions and so on.

It might be also interesting to look at the percentage of state variables that can be removed in each of the designs, and we present a plot in Figure 3. In this case we have sorted the designs by the percentages. The y-axis again follows a logarithmic scale. Again, it can be observed that in many cases the numbers are considerably high: for example, in 22 designs at least 3% of the registers can be removed, while in 4 designs at least 9% of the registers can be removed (with the maximum reduction of 17%).

4.2   Effect on IC3 Resources

In the second set of experiments, we study the impact of our reduction on (our implementation of) the IC3 algorithm [Bra11]. Note that IC3 is one of the most competitive model checking algorithms and thus presents a natural choice for the evaluation. We consider the 128 benchmarks from the previous section (i.e., those with at least one invariant found). Recall that these designs were pre-processed using logic optimization and sequential redundancy removal. For each of these designs we have run **(1)** IC3; **(2)** Our algorithm to compute mod 2 linear invariants and to express some of the state variables as functions of the remaining variables using Gaussian Elimination, followed by a quick round of logic optimization, followed by IC3 (note that including an extra round of logic optimization is natural in a typical verification flow, and that the additional optimizations, if any, are only made possible by our reduction). We refer to the latter configuration as "ComputeInvariants + IC3". In both cases the total time limit was set to 3 hours.

As presented in Table 1, the standalone IC3 was successful for 2 reachable properties and for 41 unreachable properties, while ComputeInvariants + IC3 was successful for 3 reachable properties and 43 unreachable properties. We can see that the number of solved instances is higher for IC3 on the reduced designs, both for reachable and for unreachable properties.

For a more detailed comparison between the two flows (IC3 vs. ComputeInvariants + IC3), we consider the scatter plot shown in Figure 4, representing the 47 testcases where at least one of the two strategies was successful. Both

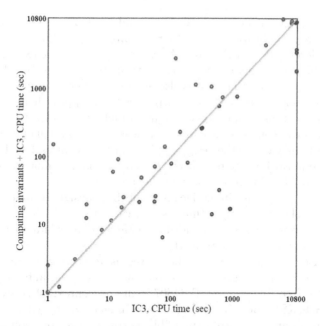

Fig. 4. CPU time comparison between IC3 and ComputeInvariants + IC3 (in seconds) on the designs with at least one linear invariant

axis follow a logarithmic scale. The points below the diagonal represent the testcases in which computing linear invariants helps to reduce the total runtime, and the points above the diagonal – where it does not. It should be noted that in general the behavior of IC3 is heavily influenced even by the smallest changes to the design, which explains the spread of the data. However, ComputeInvariants + IC3 does perform slightly better on average, and we have computed this improvement to be approximately 20%. We also note that the actual time to compute linear invariants is reasonably small in most of the cases cases, and so this improvement also corresponds to the reduction in the IC3 runtime due to the reduction in the number of state variables. This effect is by no means surprising: it is widely believed that a reduction in the number of state variables is in general helpful for model checking – and we have simply confirmed this in the context of IC3.

Finally, we note that from the 46 testcases solved by IC3 with reparameterization, 1 testcase was actually solved *before* passing the problem to IC3. In this example the property is unreachable, and the reparameterization together with logic optimization is sufficient to detect that.

5   Related and Future Work

First of all, the class of mod 2 linear invariants naturally generalizes the class of constants and (anti)equivalences. From this point of view, [vE00] describes a technique to extract equivalences, and [CMB06] and [CNQ07] extract both equivalences and binary implications. A further optimized algorithm for signal correspondence is described in [MBMB09]. As we have shown in the experiments, detecting and exploiting general mod 2 linear invariants has practical value even after signal correspondence. In fact, it is also possible to use our approach instead of signal correspondence, however at the current state the approach in [MBMB09] is significantly more scalable for larger designs. An interesting direction for further research would be to combine the two sets of ideas. We are also planning to extend our algorithm to all gates in the design (and not just state-variables). In addition, there might be linear invariants that are not part of the maximal inductive subspace, and it would be interesting to find them as well.

Other works on extracting inductive invariants from designs include IC3 [Bra11] and related model checking algorithms as they can directly produce inductive invariants in the form of clauses. In addition, [FH09] extracts inductive invariants from the bounded proofs of the property.

To some extent our algorithm can be viewed as an instance of abstract interpretation, with existing approaches to compute linear invariants between program variables (see for example [MOS07]). In the context of software model checking, [KS08, KS10] describe a similar (and in fact a more general) algorithm on inferring invariants that are expressible as congruence equations. In particular, it would be interesting to see whether such more general linear invariants could be useful in the context of hardware model checking. In fact, it is easy to generalize our algorithm to detect all inductive mod-p linear invariants, however we have found that for the preprocessed HWMCC benchmarks there are significantly fewer mod-p invariants than mod-2 invariants (when $p \neq 2$). Incidentally, this also shows that most of the mod-2 linear invariants detected by our algorithm do not correspond to one-hot constraints.

We are also planning to investigate the applicability of linear invariants towards detection of higher-level structures present in the designs. One immediate example of this is parity logic (a set of gates, where one of the gates represents a parity computation of the remaining gates). As another example, suppose that the design possesses a group of variables $x_1, \ldots, x_m$ such that on every reachable state exactly k out of $\{x_1, \ldots, x_m\}$ are true (as for example in the case of one-hot constraints), in which case $x_1 \oplus \cdots \oplus x_m$ represents a linear invariant which can be found by our method.

6   Conclusion

We have presented an efficient SAT-based method to extract all inductive mod 2 linear invariants from a design. We have demonstrated that a large number of designs possess linear invariants which are not just constants or (anti)equivalences, and that the reductions entailed by these linear invariants have a positive impact on verification.

Acknowledgements. We would like to thank the anonymous reviewers for their constructive comments.

References

[AIMR]   Aleksandrowicz, G., Ivrii, A., Margalit, O., Rasin, D.: Generating modulo-2 linear invariants for hardware model checking. Full version with appendix, available at
http://researcher.watson.ibm.com/researcher/files/il-ALEXI/xor.pdf

[Bra11]   Bradley, A.R.: SAT-based model checking without unrolling. In: Jhala, R., Schmidt, D. (eds.) VMCAI 2011. LNCS, vol. 6538, pp. 70–87. Springer, Heidelberg (2011)

[CCK04]   Chauhan, P., Clarke, E.M., Kroening, D.: A sat-based algorithm for reparameterization in symbolic simulation. In: DAC, pp. 524–529 (2004)

[CMB06]   Case, M.L., Mishchenko, A., Brayton, R.K.: Inductively finding a reachable state space over-approximation. In: IWLS (2006)

[CMB07]   Case, M.L., Mishchenko, A., Brayton, R.K.: Automated extraction of inductive invariants to aid model checking. In: FMCAD, pp. 165–172 (2007)

[CNQ07]   Cabodi, G., Nocco, S., Quer, S.: Boosting the role of inductive invariants in model checking. In: DATE, pp. 1319–1324 (2007)

[Cryt2]   CryptoMiniSat, http://www.msoos.org/cryptominisat2/

[ES03]   Eén, N., Sörensson, N.: An extensible SAT-solver. In: Giunchiglia, E., Tacchella, A. (eds.) SAT 2003. LNCS, vol. 2919, pp. 502–518. Springer, Heidelberg (2004)

[FH09]   Fuhrmann, O., Hoory, S.: On extending bounded proofs to inductive proofs. In: Bouajjani, A., Maler, O. (eds.) CAV 2009. LNCS, vol. 5643, pp. 278–290. Springer, Heidelberg (2009)

[Har11]   Hardware Model Checking Competition (2011),
http://fmv.jku.at/hwmcc11

[Har13]   Hardware Model Checking Competition (2013),
http://fmv.jku.at/hwmcc13

[KS08]   King, A., Søndergaard, H.: Inferring congruence equations using SAT. In: Gupta, A., Malik, S. (eds.) CAV 2008. LNCS, vol. 5123, pp. 281–293. Springer, Heidelberg (2008)

[KS10]   King, A., Søndergaard, H.: Automatic abstraction for congruences. In: Barthe, G., Hermenegildo, M. (eds.) VMCAI 2010. LNCS, vol. 5944, pp. 197–213. Springer, Heidelberg (2010)

[MBMB09]   Mony, H., Baumgartner, J., Mishchenko, A., Brayton, R.K.: Speculative reduction-based scalable redundancy identification. In: DATE, pp. 1674–1679 (2009)

[MBP+04]   Mony, H., Baumgartner, J., Paruthi, V., Kanzelman, R., Kuehlmann, A.: Scalable automated verification via expert-system guided transformations. In: Hu, A.J., Martin, A.K. (eds.) FMCAD 2004. LNCS, vol. 3312, pp. 159–173. Springer, Heidelberg (2004)

[McM03]   McMillan, K.L.: Interpolation and SAT-based model checking. In: Hunt Jr., W.A., Somenzi, F. (eds.) CAV 2003. LNCS, vol. 2725, pp. 1–13. Springer, Heidelberg (2003)

[MOS07]   Müller-Olm, M., Seidl, H.: Analysis of modular arithmetic. ACM Trans. Program. Lang. Syst. 29(5) (2007)

[vE00]   van Eijk, C.A.J.: Sequential equivalence checking based on structural similarities. IEEE Trans. on CAD of Integrated Circuits and Systems 19(7), 814–819 (2000)

Suraq — A Controller Synthesis Tool Using Uninterpreted Functions*

Georg Hofferek[1] and Ashutosh Gupta[2]

[1]Graz University of Technology, Austria
[2]IST, Austria

Abstract. Boolean controllers for systems with complex datapaths are often very difficult to implement correctly, in particular when concurrency is involved. Yet, in many instances it is easy to formally specify correctness. For example, the specification for the controller of a pipelined processor only has to state that the pipelined processor gives the same results as a non-pipelined reference design. This makes such controllers a good target for automated synthesis. However, an efficient abstraction for the complex datapath elements is needed, as a bit-precise description is often infeasible. We present SURAQ, the first controller synthesis tool which uses uninterpreted functions for the abstraction. Quantified first-order formulas (with specific quantifier structure) serve as the specification language from which SURAQ synthesizes Boolean controllers. SURAQ transforms the specification into an unsatisfiable SMT formula, and uses Craig interpolation to compute its results. Using SURAQ, we were able to synthesize a controller (consisting of two Boolean signals) for a five-stage pipelined DLX processor in roughly one hour and 15 minutes.

1 Introduction

When developing a complex digital system, some parts are more difficult to implement correctly than others. For example, creating a combinational circuit that multiplies two 64-bit integers is easier than implementing the stall and forwarding logic of a pipelined microprocessor. On the other hand, some system parts are also easier to formally specify than others. For the pipeline controller, the specification simply states that the execution of any program on the pipelined processor should output the same results as executing the same program on a non-pipelined reference processor. This notion has been introduced by Burch and Dill [5], who used this paradigm for verification of pipelined processors. Another key feature of their work was the use of uninterpreted functions for abstraction of complex datapath elements. A bit-precise description of, e.g., a multiplier would have been exponentially — and thus prohibitively — large. Hofferek and Bloem [12] have shown how to turn this verification setting into a synthesis

---

* The work presented in this paper was supported in part by the European Research Council (ERC) under grant agreement 267989 (QUAREM) and the Austrian Science Fund (FWF) through projects RiSE (S11406-N23) and QUAINT (I774-N23).

E. Yahav (Ed.): HVC 2014, LNCS 8855, pp. 68–74, 2014.

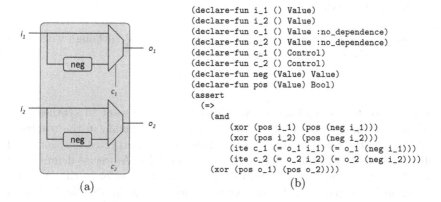

```
(declare-fun i_1 () Value)
(declare-fun i_2 () Value)
(declare-fun o_1 () Value :no_dependence)
(declare-fun o_2 () Value :no_dependence)
(declare-fun c_1 () Control)
(declare-fun c_2 () Control)
(declare-fun neg (Value) Value)
(declare-fun pos (Value) Bool)
(assert
  (=>
    (and
      (xor (pos i_1) (pos (neg i_1)))
      (xor (pos i_2) (pos (neg i_2)))
      (ite c_1 (= o_1 i_1) (= o_1 (neg i_1)))
      (ite c_2 (= o_2 i_2) (= o_2 (neg i_2))))
    (xor (pos o_1) (pos o_2))))
```

(a)   (b)

Fig. 1. (a) A controller synthesis example with missing controllers of signals c_1 and c_2. The specification for the controllers states that the outputs always have opposite signs. (b) The corresponding sythesis query to SURAQ in SMTLIB-like format.

setting. They introduced specifications that are quantified first-order formulas which state that *for all inputs/states, there exist values for Boolean control signals such that (for all values of auxiliary variables) a correctness criterion Φ holds.* The formula Φ can be a Burch-Dill style verification condition, or — for different applications — another first-order formula that states correctness of the system in question. The *certificates* for the existentially quantified Boolean control signals is a correct-by-construction implementation of the controller. One way to compute such certificates — which is based on (a generalization of) Craig interpolation [6] — has been introduced in [13].

In this paper, we present SURAQ [1], an open source tool that implements the synthesis approach of [13]. The most impressive result we achieved with SURAQ so far is the synthesis of two Boolean control signals for a five-stage pipelined DLX processor [10]. The required time for this synthesis is roughly one hour and 15 minutes. More details on SURAQ can be found in [11].

Related Work. Research on automated synthesis has flourished over the last years. A lot of work (e.g. [14,17,7,18,16,8]) is concerned with *synthesis of reactive systems from temporal specifications.* However, the specification languages used by these approaches are bit-precise. Thus, they are not suitable for the controller synthesis problems we consider. Our approach is closer to *program sketching* [19], a mixed imperative/declarative paradigm where parts of a program are implemented manually and some missing (constant) expressions are synthesized automatically. *Functional synthesis* [15] by Kuncak et al. is orthogonal to our work. Whereas we assume that data operations are already implemented, they focus on synthesizing data-oriented functions from specifications about their input-output behavior.

2   Synthesis Method

SURAQ implements the synthesis method presented in [13], although with some improvements. We start from a formula of the form

$$\forall \bar{x} . \exists \bar{c} . \forall \bar{x}' . \Phi, \tag{1}$$

where $\bar{c}$ is a vector of Boolean control signals which we want to synthesize, $\bar{x}$ and $\bar{x}'$ are vectors of first-order variables, and Φ is a formula in the combination of the quantifier-free fragment of the theory of uninterpreted functions and equality ("QF_UF"), and the array property fragment [4]. A precise definition of this combination of theories is given in [12]. SURAQ first performs the *index set construction* [4] to reduce Φ to an equivalent formula in QF_UF. Next, SURAQ instantiates the existential quantifier, renames the universally quantified $\bar{x}'$ variables in each of the resulting $2^{|\bar{c}|}$ instantiations, and negates the whole formula. This yields an unsatisfiable SMT formula in QF_UF. SURAQ uses the VERIT SMT solver [3] to obtain a refutation proof.

Based on this refutation proof, SURAQ supports two modes. In *iterative mode*, SURAQ first computes a solution for one control signal, using the interpolation method of Fuchs et al. [9]. This solution is then resubstituted into the original formula, before performing the aforementioned reduction, expansion (now yielding only $2^{|\bar{c}|-1}$ instantiations), and transformation again. From the resulting SMT instance, the solution for the next control signal is computed. This is repeated until solutions for all control signals have been obtained.

In contrast to this, in *n-interpolation mode*, SURAQ computes all control signals from the first refutation proof. To perform this so-called *n*-interpolation, the proof must be made *colorable* and *local-first* [13]. To obtain these properties, we follow the proof transformations outlined in [13], with one significant improvement: We do not perform the transformation to remove non-colorable literals from the proof. Instead, when parsing the proof, we immediately discard the subproofs of any proof nodes that are solely derived from theory lemmata. This way, the proofs never contain any non-colorable literals. Splitting of non-colorable theory lemmata is done in parallel. SURAQ provides a command-line parameter to specify how many threads should be used for splitting.

2.1   Using Suraq

As an input, SURAQ requires a specification in form of a formula as shown in Equation 1. The formula Φ should be given in SMTLIB-like [2] format. The quantifier prefix is implicitly given by the variable declarations. Variables declared with sort Control are bound by the existential quantifier (and thus, certificates for them should be synthesized). Variables declared with a :no_dependence attribute are bound by the inner universal quantifier. Thus, these are auxiliary variables that the synthesized functions cannot depend on. All other variables are bound by the outer universal quantifier. An example is shown in Figure 1.

Table 1. Runtime Results (n-Interpolation Mode). Column 1 names the benchmark. Column 2 gives the time for the formula reductions, that is, the total time required for reading the specification, performing the formula reductions, and creating an input file for VERIT. Column 3 gives the time required by VERIT to produce a proof. Column 4 gives the (wall clock) time taken to split all non-colorable theory lemmata, using 24 parallel threads. Column 5 gives the time taken by VERIT for propositional SAT solving with the stronger theory lemmata obtained from splitting. Column 6 gives the time for reorder the proof to make it local-first. Column 7 gives the time spent on proof parsing, including splitting of multi-resolution nodes. This combines the time for parsing the SMT proof and the propositional SAT proof. Column 8 gives the total time of synthesis. All times are given in seconds, and rounded to integers.

1	2	3	4	5	6	7	8
Name	Formula Reduction	SMT Solving	Splitting Leaves	SAT Solving	Re-ordering	Proof Parsing	Total
simple_pipeline	<1	<1	<1	<1	<1	<1	1
illus_02	<1	<1	<1	<1	<1	<1	<1
illus_03	<1	<1	<1	<1	<1	<1	1
illus_04	1	<1	<1	<1	<1	<1	2
illus_05	2	<1	<1	<1	<1	<1	3
illus_06	4	<1	<1	<1	<1	<1	5
illus_07	7	<1	<1	<1	<1	<1	11
illus_08	14	1	<1	<1	<1	<1	17
illus_09	28	3	<1	<1	<1	<1	34
simple_processor	<1	<1	<1	<1	<1	<1	4
dlx_stall_f-a-ex	6	1718	6	7	n/a	442	n/a

As its output, SURAQ also produces a file in SMTLIB format, where the solution for each control signal is given as an expression of the form (assert (= c_i <expr.>)). Moreover, the declarations and main formula from the input file is copied, in a slightly modified way: The sort Control is replaced by Boolean, all :no_dependence attributes are removed, and the main formula is negated. This way, the output file can directly be used for third-party verification of the synthesis result. One simply has to give the file to an SMT solver, which will return unsat if the result is correct.

3 Experimental Results

We have evaluated SURAQ with several benchmarks. First, we used the simple pipeline example from [12]. Furthermore, we used several instances of the scalable, illustrative example from [13] (see also Fig. 1). We also tried the simple, two-stage pipelined processor from [13]. Finally, to demonstrate the applicability of our approach to real-world problems, we synthesized a controller for a

Table 2. Proof Sizes. The Col. 1 gives the name of the benchmark. Col. 2 states the size of the proof, as obtained from VERIT, however with subproofs of theory lemmata already removed. Col. 3 gives the number of leaves that are non-colorable and need to be split, and Col. 4 gives the total number of leaves. Col. 5 gives the size of the proof obtained by calling a SAT solver on the skeleton of the original formula, together with the colorable theory lemmata and the (stronger) theory lemmata obtained from splitting. This is the proof that is given to the reordering procedure. The size of the proof after reordering is given in Col. 6. Col. 7 gives the size of the proof that is used for n-interpolation, that is, the reordered proof with local subproofs removed. All proof sizes are given as the number of nodes in the DAG.

1	2	3	4	5	6	7
Name	Original Proof	# Leaves to split	# Leaves (total)	Before Reordering	After Reordering	w/o Local Subproofs
simple_pipeline	506	2	178	496	494	12
illus_02	102	2	44	106	106	12
illus_03	179	3	77	198	218	26
illus_04	390	7	133	356	428	46
illus_05	408	9	165	700	971	115
illus_06	669	4	176	758	1 576	320
illus_07	1 006	11	219	916	2 823	785
illus_08	1 101	6	242	2 214	8 082	1 347
illus_09	1 101	7	269	1 388	5 364	1 293
simple_processor	9 576	123	1 503	6 853	7 899	73
dlx_stall_f-a-ex	856 121	2 748	21 349	333 260	n/a	n/a

five-stage pipelined DLX processor [10]. We have created several variants of the DLX benchmark, where we synthesize different control signals (while the other are implemented manually); in the dlx_stall_f-a-ex benchmark, we even synthesize 2 signals simultaneously.

In Table 1, we present runtime results for n-interpolation mode. Note that the reordering of the resolution proof times out for the dlx_stall_f-a-ex benchmark. In Table 2, we give sizes of the proofs (in various stages of transformation). Table 3 gives results (runtimes and proof sizes) for the iterative mode.

From this data, we can see that neither iterative mode, nor n-interpolation mode is clearly superior over the other. Instead, it depends on the characteristics of the benchmark which approach performs better. While for some benchmarks n-interpolation clearly outperforms iterative interpolation, in other instances the need for proof reordering makes n-interpolation inapplicable.

Table 3. Iterative Mode. The 8 columns after the name give the SMT solving time (in seconds) and the proof size per iteration, in the format "time; size". Columns not required are left empty. The last column gives the total synthesis time.

Name	1	2	3	4	5	6	7	8	9	Total Time
simple_pipeline	<1; 506									<1
illus_02	<1; 102	<1; 166								1
illus_03	<1; 179	<1; 493	<1; 508							2
illus_04	<1; 390	<1; 680	<1; 724	<1; 1 251						3
illus_05	<1; 408	<1; 2 133	<1; 3 608	<1; 3 298	<1; 3 361					6
illus_06	<1; 669	<1; 2 521	<1; 1 799	<1; 3 906	<1; 9 043	<1; 10 088				12
illus_07	<1; 1 006	<1; 6 430	<1; 7 210	1; 26 072	<1; 23 941	<1; 26 543	<1; 32 009			31
illus_08	1; 1 101	<1; 7 352	<1; 3 332	1; 16 312	2; 32 087	2; 52 782	2; 60 822	1; 73 887		66
illus_09	3; 1 101	5; 27 210	22; 60 002	45; 165 636	24; 117 535	23; 243 332	10; 231 789	9; 391 277	6; 281 313	485
simple_processor	<1; 9 576	<1; 8 682								4
dlx_stall	267; 898 345									537
dlx_f-a-ex	573; 1 490 028									1 358
dlx_f-b-wb	590; 2 271 288									2 174
dlx_stall_f-a-ex	1711; 856 121	923; 1 460 582								4 528

4   Conclusion

SURAQ is a controller synthesis tool based on the method presented in [13]. SURAQ has successfully synthesized a controller for a five-stage pipelined DLX processor [10]. Since the DLX benchmark is of realistic size and complexity, our experiments suggest that the approach is scalable enough for real-world problems.

References

1. SURAQ — Synthesizer using Uninterpreted functions, aRrays and eQuality (2014), http://www.iaik.tugraz.at/content/research/design_verification/suraq/
2. Barrett, C., Stump, A., Tinelli, C.: The SMT-LIB Standard: Version 2.0. In: Proc. of the 8th Int. Workshop on Satisfiability Modulo Theories (2010)
3. Bouton, T., de Oliveira, D.C.B., Déharbe, D., Fontaine, P.: veriT: An open, trustable and efficient SMT-solver. In: Schmidt, R.A. (ed.) CADE 2009. LNCS, vol. 5663, pp. 151–156. Springer, Heidelberg (2009)
4. Bradley, A.R., Manna, Z., Sipma, H.B.: What's decidable about arrays? In: Emerson, E.A., Namjoshi, K.S. (eds.) VMCAI 2006. LNCS, vol. 3855, pp. 427–442. Springer, Heidelberg (2006)

5. Burch, J.R., Dill, D.L.: Automatic verification of pipelined microprocessor control. In: Dill, D.L. (ed.) CAV 1994. LNCS, vol. 818, pp. 68–80. Springer, Heidelberg (1994)
6. Craig, W.: Three uses of the Herbrand-Gentzen theorem in relating model theory and proof theory. The Journal of Symbolic Logic 22(3), 269–285 (1957)
7. Filiot, E., Jin, N., Raskin, J.-F.: An antichain algorithm for LTL realizability. In: Bouajjani, A., Maler, O. (eds.) CAV 2009. LNCS, vol. 5643, pp. 263–277. Springer, Heidelberg (2009)
8. Finkbeiner, B., Jacobs, S.: Lazy synthesis. In: Kuncak, V., Rybalchenko, A. (eds.) VMCAI 2012. LNCS, vol. 7148, pp. 219–234. Springer, Heidelberg (2012)
9. Fuchs, A., Goel, A., Grundy, J., Krstic, S., Tinelli, C.: Ground interpolation for the theory of equality. Logical Methods in Computer Science 8(1) (2012)
10. Hennessy, J.L., Patterson, D.A.: Computer Architecture: A Quantitative Approach, 2nd edn. Morgan Kaufmann (1996)
11. Hofferek, G.: Controller Synthesis with Uninterpreted Functions. Ph.D. thesis, Graz University of Technology (July 2014)
12. Hofferek, G., Bloem, R.: Controller synthesis for pipelined circuits using uninterpreted functions. In: MEMOCODE (2011)
13. Hofferek, G., Gupta, A., Könighofer, B., Jiang, J., Bloem, R.: Synthesizing multiple boolean functions using interpolation on a single proof. In: FMCAD (2013)
14. Jobstmann, B., Galler, S., Weiglhofer, M., Bloem, R.: Anzu: A tool for property synthesis. In: Damm, W., Hermanns, H. (eds.) CAV 2007. LNCS, vol. 4590, pp. 258–262. Springer, Heidelberg (2007)
15. Kuncak, V., Mayer, M., Piskac, R., Suter, P.: Functional synthesis for linear arithmetic and sets. STTT 15(5-6) (2013)
16. Morgenstern, A., Schneider, K.: Exploiting the temporal logic hierarchy and the non-confluence property for efficient LTL synthesis. GANDALF (2010)
17. Schewe, S., Finkbeiner, B.: Bounded synthesis. In: Namjoshi, K.S., Yoneda, T., Higashino, T., Okamura, Y. (eds.) ATVA 2007. LNCS, vol. 4762, pp. 474–488. Springer, Heidelberg (2007)
18. Sohail, S., Somenzi, F.: Safety first: a two-stage algorithm for the synthesis of reactive systems. STTT 15(5-6) (2013)
19. Solar-Lezama, A.: Program sketching. STTT 15(5-6) (2013)

Synthesizing Finite-State Protocols
from Scenarios and Requirements*

Rajeev Alur[1], Milo Martin[1], Mukund Raghothaman[1],
Christos Stergiou[1,2], Stavros Tripakis[2,3], and Abhishek Udupa[1]

[1] University of Pennsylvania
[2] University of California, Berkeley
[3] Aalto University

Abstract. Scenarios, or Message Sequence Charts, offer an intuitive way of describing the desired behaviors of a distributed protocol. In this paper we propose a new way of specifying and synthesizing finite-state protocols using scenarios: we show that it is possible to automatically derive a distributed implementation from a set of scenarios augmented with a set of safety and liveness requirements, provided the given scenarios adequately *cover* all the states of the desired implementation. We first derive incomplete state machines from the given scenarios, and then synthesis corresponds to completing the transition relation of individual processes so that the global product meets the specified requirements. This completion problem, in general, has the same complexity, PSPACE, as the verification problem, but unlike the verification problem, is still hard (NP-complete) even for a constant number of processes. We present an algorithm for solving the completion problem, based on counterexample-guided inductive synthesis. We evaluate the proposed methodology for protocol specification and the effectiveness of the synthesis algorithm using the classical alternating-bit protocol, the VI cache-coherence protocol, and a consensus protocol.

1 Introduction

In formal verification, a system model is checked against correctness requirements to find bugs. Sustained research in improving verification tools over the last few decades has resulted in powerful heuristics for coping with the computational intractability of problems such as Boolean satisfiability and search through the state-space of concurrent processes. The advances in these analysis tools now offer an opportunity to develop new methodologies for system design that allow a programmer to specify a system in more intuitive ways. In this paper, we focus on distributed protocols: the multitude of behaviors arising due

* This work was partially supported by the Academy of Finland and by the NSF via projects *COSMOI: Compositional System Modeling with Interfaces* and *ExCAPE: Expeditions in Computer Augmented Program Engineering*. This work was also partially supported by IBM and United Technologies Corporation (UTC) via the iCyPhy consortium.

E. Yahav (Ed.): HVC 2014, LNCS 8855, pp. 75–91, 2014.

to asynchronous concurrency makes the design of such protocols difficult, and the benefits of using model checkers to debug such protocols have been clearly demonstrated. Traditionally, a distributed protocol is described using communicating finite-state machines (FSMs). The goal of this paper is to develop a methodology aimed at simplifying the task of designing them.

An intuitive way of specifying the desired behaviors of a protocol is by *scenarios*, where each scenario describes an expected sequence of message exchanges among participating processes. Such scenarios are used in textbooks and classrooms to describe the protocol and can be specified using the intuitive visual notation of Message Sequence Charts. In fact, the MSC notation is standardized by IEEE [1], and it is supported by some system development environments as design supplements. These observations raise the question: is it plausible to ask the designer to provide enough scenarios so that the protocol implementation can be automatically synthesized? Although one cannot expect a designer to provide scenarios that include all the possible behaviors, our key observation is that even a *representative* set of scenarios *covers* all the states of the desired implementation. The (local) states of a process are obtained from a scenario — using the explicit state-labels that appear as annotations as well as from the histories of events in which the process participates. If we consider all the states and the input/output transitions out of these states for a given process that appear in the given set of scenarios, we obtain a *skeleton* of the desired FSM implementation of that process. The synthesis problem now corresponds to *completing* this skeleton by adding transitions. This requires the synthesizer to infer, for instance, how to respond to a particular input event in a particular state even when this information is missing from the specified scenarios. The more such completions that the synthesizer can learn successfully, the lower the burden on the designer to specify details of each and every case. To rule out incorrect completions, we ask the designer to provide a model of the environment and correctness requirements. Some requirements such as absence of deadlocks can be generic to all the protocols, whereas other requirements can be specific to the coordination problem being solved by the protocol and given as finite-state monitors for safety and liveness properties in the form commonly used in model checkers. Note that scenarios and correctness requirements are used as under- and over-approximations of the behaviors of the protocol, respectively.

The synthesis problem then maps to the following *protocol completion* problem: given (1) a set of FSMs with incomplete transition functions, (2) a model of the environment, and (3) a set of safety/liveness requirements, find a completion of the FSMs such that the composition satisfies all the requirements. We show this problem, similar to the model checking problem, to be PSPACE-complete, but, unlike the model checking problem, to be NP-hard even for just one process. We present an algorithm for solving the protocol completion problem. The algorithm is an example of counterexample-guided synthesis [2]: candidates from the search space of completions are evaluated with respect to requirements and violations of the correctness requirements are used to prune the space.

To evaluate our methodology, we first consider the Alternating Bit Protocol (ABP), a classical solution to provide reliable transmission over unreliable channels. The canonical description of the protocol uses four scenarios to explain its behavior [3]. It turns out that the first scenario corresponding to the typical behavior contains a representative of each local state of both the sender and receiver processes. Our algorithm for protocol completion is able to find a correct implementation from just one scenario, and thus, automatically learn how to cope with message losses and message duplications. We vary the input, both in terms of the set of scenarios and the set of correctness requirements, and study how it affects the computational requirements and the ability to learn the correct protocol. We also evaluate the effectiveness of scenarios on two other protocols: a cache coherence protocol and a distributed consensus protocol. In both cases, as in ABP, the scenarios produce automata that cover all the states of a desired implementation and our algorithm is able to synthesize the missing behaviors in a reasonable amount of time.

Related Work

Our work builds on techniques and tools for model checking [4] and also on the rich literature for formal modeling and verification of distributed protocols [5].

The problem of deriving finite-state implementations from formal requirements specified, for instance, in temporal logic, is called *reactive synthesis*, and has been studied extensively [6–8]. When the implementation is required to be distributed, the problem is known to be undecidable [9–12]. In *bounded synthesis*, one fixes a bound on the number of states of the implementation, and this allows algorithmic solutions to distributed synthesis [13]. Another approach uses *genetic programming* combined with model checking, to search through protocol implementations to find a correct one, which has been shown to be effective in synthesizing protocols such as leader election [14, 15].

Specifying a reactive system using example scenarios has also a long tradition. In particular, the problem of deriving an implementation that exhibits at least the behaviors specified by a given set of scenarios is well-studied (see, for instance, [16–18]). A particularly well-developed approach is *behavioral programming* [19] that builds on the work on an extension of message sequence charts, called *live sequence charts* [20], and has been shown to be effective for specifying the behavior of a single controller reacting with its environment. The work in [21] generalizes Angluin's learning algorithm to synthesize automata from MSCs but does not allow for the specification of requirements and relies on the programmer to answer classification and equivalence queries. More recently, scenarios — in the form of "flows" — have been used in the modular verification of cache coherence protocols [22].

Our approach of using both the scenarios and the requirements in an integrated manner and using scenarios to derive incomplete state machines offers a conceptually new methodology compared to the existing work. We are inspired by recent work on program sketching [2, 23] and on protocol specification [24]. PSKETCH [2] uses similar techniques but targets concurrent data structures and is limited to safety properties. Compared to TRANSIT [24] in this paper we limit ourselves to finite-state protocols but consider both safety and liveness requirements and provide a fully automatic synthesis procedure.

The protocol completion problem itself has conceptual similarities to problems such as *program repair* studied in the literature [25], but differs in technical details.

2   Methodology

We explain our methodology by illustrating it on an example, the well-known Alternating Bit Protocol (ABP). The ABP protocol ensures reliable message transmission over unreliable channels which can duplicate or lose messages. As input to the synthesis tool the user provides the following:

- The *protocol skeleton*: this is a set of processes which are to be synthesized, and for each process, the *interface* of that process, i.e., its inputs and outputs.
- The *environment*: this is a set of processes which are known and fixed, that is, are not to be synthesized nor modified in any way by the synthesizer. The environment processes interact with the protocol processes and the product of all these processes forms a *closed* system, which can be model-checked against a formal specification.
- A *specification*: this is a set of formal requirements. These can be expressed in different ways, e.g., as temporal logic formulas, safety or liveness (e.g., Büchi) monitors, or "hardwired" properties such as absence of deadlock.
- A set of *scenarios*: these are example behaviors of the system. In our framework, a scenario is a type of *message sequence chart* (MSC).

In the case of the ABP example, the above inputs are as follows. The overall system is shown in Figure 1. The protocol skeleton consists of the two unknown processes *ABP Sender* and *ABP Receiver*. Their interfaces are shown in the figure, e.g., ABP Sender has inputs a'_0, a'_1, and *timeout* and outputs *send*, p_0, and p_1. The environment processes are: *Forward Channel* (FC) (from ABP Sender to ABP Receiver, duplicating and lossy), *Backward Channel* (BC) (from ABP Receiver to ABP Sender, also duplicating and lossy), *Timer* (sends *timeout* messages to ABP Sender), *Safety Monitor*, and a set of *Liveness Monitors*.

As specification for ABP we will use the following requirements: (1) deadlock-freedom, i.e., absence of reachable global deadlock states (in the product system) (2) safety, captured using safety monitors, which guarantee that send and deliver messages alternate (3) Büchi liveness monitors, which accept incorrect infinite executions in which either a send message is not followed by a deliver, a deliver is not followed by a send, or a send never appears, provided that the channels are fair and that the processes do not indefinitely ignore input messages.

We will use the four message sequence charts shown in Figure 2 to describe the behavior of the ABP protocol. They come from a textbook on computer networking [3]. The first scenario describes the behavior of the protocol when no packets or acknowledgments are lost or duplicated. The second and the third

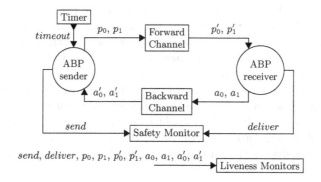

Fig. 1. ABP system architecture

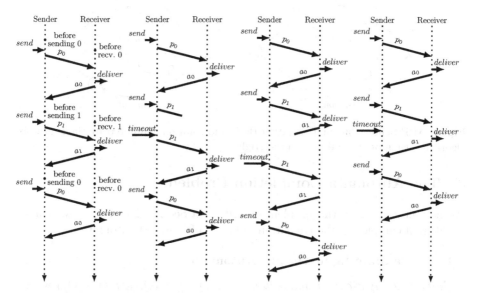

Fig. 2. Four scenarios for the alternating-bit protocol. From left to right: No loss, Lost packet, Lost ACK, Premature timeout/duplication.

scenarios correspond to the expected behaviors of the protocol in the event of the loss of a packet and in the event of the loss of an acknowledgment respectively. Finally, the fourth scenario describes the behavior of ABP on premature timeouts and/or packet duplication.

A candidate solution to the ABP synthesis problem is a pair of processes, one for the ABP Sender and one for the ABP Receiver. Such a candidate is a valid solution if: (a) the two processes respect their I/O interface and satisfy some additional requirements such as determinism (these are defined formally in Section 3.1), (b) the overall ABP system (product of all processes) may exhibit each of the input scenarios, and (c) it satisfies all correctness requirements.

Figure 3 shows for the ABP sender automaton, on the left, a manually constructed solution, and on the right, the output of the synthesis algorithm, when invoked with the requirements mentioned above and only the first scenario from Figure 2. It can be checked that the two instances of the ABP sender automaton are "similar" in the sense that they satisfy the same intuitive properties that one expects from the ABP protocol. In particular, the computed solution differs from the manual one in that it eagerly re-transmits p_0 when an unexpected acknowledgment a_1' is received. This might incur additional traffic but satisfies all the safety and liveness properties for the ABP protocol. The computed solution for the ABP Receiver is the same as the manually constructed automaton.

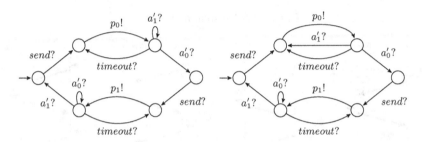

Fig. 3. ABP Sender "manual" solution (left) and solution computed by the synthesis algorithm using only the first scenario (right)

3   The Automata Completion Problem

We now describe how the problem described in Section 2 can be viewed as a problem of completing the transition relations of finite IO automata.

3.1   Finite-State Input-Output Automata

A *finite-state input-output automaton* is a tuple $A = (Q, q_0, I, O, T, O_f)$ where Q is a finite set of states, $q_0 \in Q$ is the initial state, I is a finite (possibly empty) set of inputs, O is a finite (possibly empty) set of outputs, with $I \cap O = \emptyset$, $T \subseteq Q \times (I \cup O) \times Q$ is a finite set of transitions,[1] and $O_f \subseteq O$ is a (possibly empty) set of outputs representing a fairness constraint.

We write a transition $(q, x, q') \in T$ as $q \xrightarrow{x?} q'$ when $x \in I$, and as $q \xrightarrow{x!} q'$ when $x \in O$. We write $q \to q'$ if there exists x such that $(q, x, q') \in T$. A transition labeled with $x \in I$ (respectively, $x \in O$) is called an *input transition* (respectively, an *output transition*).

A state $q \in Q$ is called a *deadlock* if it has no outgoing transitions. q is called an *input state* if it has at least one outgoing transition, and all outgoing transitions from q are input transitions. q is called an *output state* if it has a single outgoing transition, which is an output transition.

---

[1] The framework and synthesis algorithms can easily be extended to handle internal transitions as well, but we suppress this detail for simplicity of presentation.

Automaton A is called *deterministic* if for every state $q \in Q$, if there are multiple outgoing transitions from q, then all these transitions must be labeled with distinct inputs. Determinism implies that every state $q \in Q$ is a deadlock, an input state, or an output state. Automaton A is called *closed* if $I = \emptyset$.

A *safety monitor* is an automaton equipped with a set of *error states* Q_e, $A = (Q, q_0, I, O, T, O_f, Q_e)$. A *liveness monitor* is an automaton equipped with a set of *accepting states* Q_a, $A = (Q, q_0, I, O, T, O_f, Q_a)$. A monitor could be both safety and liveness, in which case it is a tuple $A = (Q, q_0, I, O, T, O_f, Q_e, Q_a)$.

A *run* of an automaton A is a finite or infinite sequence of transitions starting from the initial state: $q_0 \rightarrow q_1 \rightarrow q_2 \rightarrow \cdots$. A state q is called *reachable* if there exists a finite run reaching that state: $q_0 \rightarrow q_1 \rightarrow \cdots \rightarrow q$. A safety monitor is called *safe* if it has no reachable error states. An infinite run of a liveness monitor is called *accepting* if it visits accepting states infinitely often. An infinite run is called *fair*, if for every $o \in O_f$, if it infinitely often visits some state q such that $o \in \{x \mid (q, x, q') \in T\}$ (o is "enabled" at q), then it makes a transition with output o infinitely often.[2] A liveness monitor is called *empty* if it has no infinite accepting fair runs.

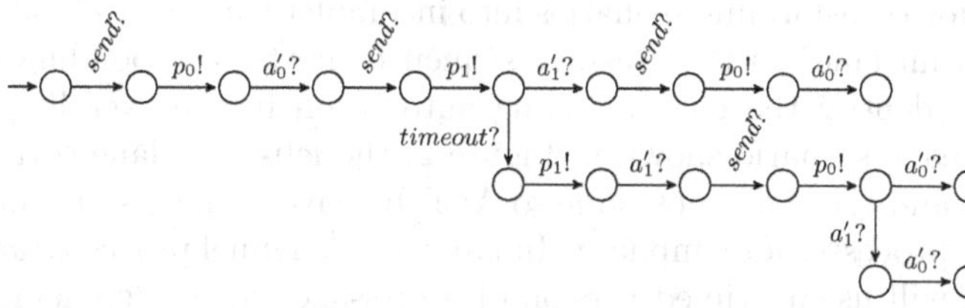

Fig. 4. Incomplete protocol automaton for ABP Sender using all scenarios from Figure 2, without using symmetric scenarios or labels.

3.2 Composition

We define an asynchronous (interleaving-based) parallel composition operator with rendezvous synchronization. Given two automata $A_1 = (Q_1, q_{0,1}, I_1, O_1, T_1, O_{f,1})$ and $A_2 = (Q_2, q_{0,2}, I_2, O_2, T_2, O_{f,2})$, the composition of A_1 and A_2, denoted $A_1 \| A_2$, is defined, provided $O_1 \cap O_2 = \emptyset$, as the automaton

$$A_1 \| A_2 \triangleq (Q_1 \times Q_2, (q_{0,1}, q_{0,2}), (I_1 \cup I_2) \setminus (O_1 \cup O_2), O_1 \cup O_2, T, O_{f,1} \cup O_{f,2})$$

where $((q_1, q_2), x, (q_1', q_2')) \in T$ iff one of the following holds:

- $x \in O_1$ and $q_1 \xrightarrow{x!} q_1'$ and either $x \in I_2$ and $q_2 \xrightarrow{x?} q_2'$ or $x \notin I_2$ and $q_2' = q_2$.
- $x \in O_2$ and $q_2 \xrightarrow{x!} q_2'$ and either $x \in I_1$ and $q_1 \xrightarrow{x?} q_1'$ or $x \notin I_1$ and $q_1' = q_1$.

---

[2] Of the many notions of fairness which are discussed in literature, we have chosen one notion of fairness that is adequate for the case studies in this paper. Our approach can be extended to more general forms of fairness assumptions.

– $x \in (I_1 \cup I_2) \setminus (O_1 \cup O_2)$ and at least one of the following holds: (1) $x \in I_1 \setminus I_2$ and $q_1 \overset{x?}{\rightarrow} q_1'$ and $q_2' = q_2$, (2) $x \in I_2 \setminus I_1$ and $q_2 \overset{x?}{\rightarrow} q_2'$ and $q_1' = q_1$, (3) $x \in I_1 \cap I_2$ and $q_1 \overset{x?}{\rightarrow} q_1'$ and $q_2 \overset{x?}{\rightarrow} q_2'$.

During composition, the product automaton $A_1 \| A_2$ "inherits" the safety and liveness properties of each of its components. Specifically, a product state (q_1, q_2) is an error state if either q_1 or q_2 are error states. A product state (q_1, q_2) is an accepting state if either q_1 or q_2 is an accepting state.

Note that $\|$ is commutative and associative. So we can write $A_1 \| A_2 \| \cdots \| A_n$ without parentheses, for a set of n automata.

3.3   From Scenarios to Incomplete Automata

The first step in our synthesis method is to automatically generate from the set of input scenarios an *incomplete automaton* for each protocol process. The second step is then to complete these incomplete automata to derive a complete protocol. In the sections that follow, we formalize and study the automata completion problem. In this section, we illustrate the first step of going from scenarios to incomplete automata, by means of the ABP example.

The idea for transforming scenarios into incomplete automata is simple. First, for every "swim lane" in the message sequence chart corresponding to a given scenario, we identify the corresponding automaton in the overall system. For example, in each scenario shown in Figure 2, the left-most lane corresponds to ABP Sender and the right-most lane to ABP Receiver. These scenarios omit the environment processes for simplicity. In particular channel processes are omitted, however, we will use a primed version of a message when referencing it on the process that receives it.

Second, for every protocol process P, we generate an incomplete automaton A_P as follows. For every message *history* ρ (ρ is a finite sequence of messages received or sent by the process) specified in some scenario in the lane for P, we create a state s_ρ in A_P. If $\rho' = \rho \cdot x$ is an extension of history ρ by one message x, then there is a transition $s_\rho \overset{x}{\rightarrow} s_{\rho'}$ in A_P. At this point, we check that the inputs and outputs of A_P are included in the interface of P in the protocol skeleton and that A_P is deterministic. Applying this procedure to the scenarios in Figure 2, we obtain the incomplete automaton shown in Figure 4 for the ABP Sender.

Third, scenarios are annotated with labels. As shown in the first scenario of Figure 2, labels appear between messages on swim lanes. These are used to merge the states that correspond to message histories that are followed by the same label. Merging occurs for states of a single scenario as well as across multiple ones if the same label is used in different scenarios. If consistent labels are given to the initial and final positions in all swim lanes of the scenarios the resulting incomplete automata can be made cyclic. Furthermore, labels are essential for specifying recurring behaviors in scenarios and the structure of the incomplete automaton depends on the number and positions of labels used.

Finally, it is often the case that different behaviors of a system are equivalent up to simple replacement of messages. For example, all the ABP scenarios express

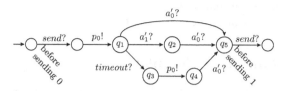

Fig. 5. Incomplete protocol automaton for ABP Sender from all scenarios of Figure 2 and their symmetric and after merging labeled states. (Only one half of the automaton is shown, the rest is the symmetric case for packet 1.)

valid behaviors if p_0 and a_0 messages are consistently replaced with p_1 and a_1 messages respectively and vice-versa. Thus, our framework allows for scenarios to be characterized as "symmetric".

We annotate the swim lanes of the ABP Sender scenarios of Figure 2 with "before sending 0" and "before sending 1" labels, and the swim lanes of the ABP Receiver with "before receiving 0" and "before receiving 1" labels. We also add the symmetric scenarios by switching 0 messages with 1 messages. The resulting incomplete automaton for ABP Sender is shown in Figure 5.

3.4 Automata Completion

Having transformed the input scenarios into incomplete automata, the next step is to *complete* those automata by adding the appropriate transitions, so as to synthesize a complete and correct protocol. In this section we formalize this completion problem. We define two versions of the problem: a special version with only a single incomplete automaton and a general version. In Section 4.1 we show that these problems are combinatorially hard.

Consider an automaton $A = (Q, q_0, I, O, T)$. Given a set of transitions $T' \subseteq Q \times (I \cup O) \times Q$, the *completion of A with T'* is the new automaton $A' = (Q, q_0, I, O, T \cup T')$.

Problem 1. Given automaton E (the *environment*) and deterministic automaton P (the *process*) such that $E \| P$ is defined, find a set of transitions T such that, if P' is the completion of P with T, then P' is deterministic and $E \| P'$ has no reachable deadlock states.

Note that if $E \| P$ is defined then $E \| P'$ is also defined, because, by definition, completion does not modify the interface (inputs and outputs) of an automaton.

Problem 2. Given a set of *environment automata* $E_1, ..., E_m$ (some of which can be safety or liveness monitors), and a set of deterministic *process automata* $P_1, ..., P_n$ such that $E_1 \| \cdots \| E_m \| P_1 \| \cdots \| P_n$ is defined, find sets of transitions $T_1, ..., T_n$ such that, if P'_i is the completion of P_i with T_i, then for $i = 1, ..., n$,

- P'_i is deterministic, for $i = 1, ..., n$,
- if the product automaton $\Pi := E_1 \| \cdots \| E_m \| P'_1 \| \cdots \| P'_n$ is a safety automaton then it is safe,

- if Π is a liveness automaton then it is empty,
- and, Π has no reachable deadlock states.

4 Solving Automata Completion

In this section, we first show that Problems 1 and 2 are NP-complete and PSPACE-complete respectively. We then present a synthesis algorithm to solve the automata completion problem.

4.1 Complexity

It can be shown that Problem 2 is PSPACE-complete. Note that this is not surprising, as the verification problem itself is PSPACE-complete, for safety properties of distributed protocols. However, in the special case of one process and one environment automaton, while verification can be performed in polynomial time, a reduction from 3-SAT shows that the corresponding completion Problem 1 is NP-complete. The proofs are omitted due to lack of space, and can be found in [26].

Theorem 1. *Problem 1 is NP-complete and Problem 2 is PSPACE-complete.*

4.2 Synthesis Algorithm

We propose an algorithm for solving the automata completion problem that can be viewed as an instance of counter-example guided inductive synthesis [2]. At a high-level the algorithm works by maintaining a set of constraints on correct completions. The algorithm repeatedly chooses a candidate completion such that it satisfies these constraints. If this candidate completion satisfies the correctness requirements, the algorithm terminates. Otherwise, the information from the violation of the requirements is used to create more constraints on the set of correct completions and prune the search space.

We associate a Boolean variable with every candidate transition that can be added to the individual automata. The constraints maintained by the algorithm are propositional formulas over these transition variables. We initialize the constraint set with determinism and deadlock constraints. The first enforce that the protocol automata are deterministic, as described in subsection 3.1. For the second, we explore the reachable state space of the product of the environment and incomplete process automata; for every deadlock state, we add constraints that guarantee that at least one transition will be enabled out of that state. In the remainder of this section we will use t_i to refer both to transitions and their corresponding Boolean variables.

At the beginning of every iteration, a constraint solver — an ILP solver in our implementation — produces an assignment to the transition variables such the assignment satisfies the constraints. If the constraints are unsatisfiable, the algorithm concludes that no solution is possible and terminates. Otherwise, we translate the assignment to a set of transitions T, such that for every transition variable that the assignment sets to true, the corresponding transition is in T. Let $T = \{t_1, \ldots, t_n\}$. We complete the process automata with T, form their product with the environment automata, and monitors, and we check the absence of deadlocks, safety, and liveness violations using a model checker. The following cases are possible:

1. No violations are found. In this case, T is a correct completion, and the algorithm terminates.
2. A safety violation is found. This case means that the candidate solution T is incorrect. Moreover, any candidate T' obtained by adding extra transitions to T, i.e., $T' \supseteq T$, will also be incorrect, because adding extra local transitions can only add, but not remove, global transitions. This in turn implies that any reachable error state with T will also be a reachable error state with T', so any safety violation with T will also be a safety violation with T'. To enforce that no superset of T is included in any future candidate set, we add the formula $\neg(t_1 \wedge t_2 \wedge \ldots \wedge t_n)$ to the constraint set.
3. A liveness violation is found. This case also means that the candidate solution T is incorrect. A liveness violation, according to the definition of the problem 2, corresponds to a fair infinite accepting run, represented by a reachable cycle, that contains an accepting state of a liveness monitor. Although adding more transitions cannot eliminate the cycle, it is possible that additional transitions can render a fair run unfair: if a particular output $o \in O_f$ was not enabled in the cycle, then adding local transitions can cause o to become enabled. Let $T' = \{t'_1, \ldots, t'_m\}$ be the set of transitions that, if added, would make the infinite run unfair.[3] We add as a constraint the formula $\neg(t_1 \wedge t_2 \wedge \ldots \wedge t_n) \vee (t'_1 \vee t'_2 \vee \ldots \vee t'_m)$. The constraint guarantees that in all future candidate sets, the cycle will be unreachable, broken, or not fair.
4. A deadlock state is found. In this case, T is also incorrect, but could potentially be made correct by adding more transitions. Let $T' = \{t'_1, \ldots, t'_m\}$ be the set of candidate transitions such that, if any transition in T' is added, a transition is enabled out of the deadlock state. We add the constraint $(t_1 \wedge \ldots \wedge t_n) \rightarrow (t'_1 \vee \ldots \vee t'_m)$.

In every iteration, either a correct completion is found or the search space is pruned. We use an ILP solver to generate candidate sets from the constraints with an objective function that minimizes the size of the candidate set. In that way, in each iteration, we examine the smallest set of transitions that satisfies the constraints. This keeps the size of the product of the automata small and allows for faster checking of the properties.

We employ the following heuristic to prune the search space faster. Assume that a candidate set $T = \{t_1, \ldots, t_n\}$ is tested in an iteration of the algorithm and a safety violation is discovered. As described so far, the algorithm will remove

---

[3] For simplicity, we assume that process automata only communicate with environment automata. The constraint for the general case is more complicated but conceptually similar.

all supersets of T from the search space by adding the constraint $\neg(t_1 \wedge \ldots \wedge t_n)$. However, if the safety violation is reachable by using only a subset of T, T'', then it is safe to also remove all supersets of T'' from the search space. Ideally, one would find all minimal subsets of T that alone can lead to a violation and remove all supersets of them. We approximate this by finding a minimal path to a safety violation using breadth-first search. If the path contains a subset of the transitions in T, we remove all supersets of that subset from the search space.

5   Evaluation

In this section we evaluate the effectiveness of scenarios and our methodology for specifying finite-state protocols. We use three benchmarks: the ABP protocol, a cache coherence protocol, and a consensus protocol. We first check whether the corresponding scenarios result in incomplete automata that cover all the states of a desired implementation. We then evaluate our synthesis algorithm on those benchmarks and investigate the effectiveness of scenarios in reducing the empirical complexity of the automata completion problem. Lastly, we discuss the interaction between the number of scenarios used to construct the initial incomplete automata and the number of requirements that are necessary to synthesize a correct protocol. A quantitative summary of our experiments can be found in Table 1. Each row corresponds to a combination of benchmark and set of input scenarios used for that benchmark, column "time" shows the total time that the synthesis algorithm took to find a correct completion, column "# iterations" shows the number of iterations of the algorithm, i.e., the number of candidate sets of transitions tested, and "# candidate transitions" is the total number of candidate transitions for all process automata. Note that this last number, n, represents individual local transitions and not number of candidate completions. The size of the space of all possible completions is the number of subsets of the set of candidate transitions, i.e., 2^n.

5.1   Benchmarks

ABP. This protocol was described in Section 2. We use different sets of input scenarios to create three versions of this benchmark. ABP1 used only the first scenario of Figure 2 to construct the incomplete automata, ABP2 used the second scenario, while ABP1-4 used all four scenarios.

We also construct a variation of the protocol that allows the clients to send different types of messages. In the protocol described in Section 2, only one type of message can be sent and received. In experiments ABPcolored1, ABPcolored2, and ABPcolored1-4, there are two types of messages that can be sent and received representing the different data that messages could carry.

VI Protocol. The VI protocol is a protocol for maintaining coherence among the private caches of a multi-processor system. The coherence requirement is that the value *read* by any processor is the same as the *last* value *written* to that location by any processor in the system. The scenarios shown in Figure 6

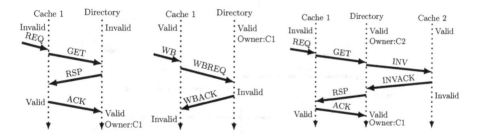

Fig. 6. Scenarios for the VI protocol

describe the working of the protocol. In the first scenario, Cache 1 acquires permissions to read or write to the cache block from the directory when no other processor in the system has permissions on the block. The second scenario demonstrates how a directory invalidates a cache that already has permissions on a block to fulfill the request of another cache for the block. These scenarios do not describe the behavior of the protocol when the second and third scenarios are interleaved, i.e., Cache 1 relinquishing permissions while Cache 2 attempts to acquire permissions.

We examine two variations of the VI protocol: one where there is a unique value for the data, in which case the protocol reduces to a distributed locking protocol (VI-no-data), and one where the data can take values 0 or 1, which captures the essence of the VI cache coherence protocol (VI).

Consensus. In this problem we specify a protocol that describes how two processes can reach consensus on one value. Each process chooses initially a preferred value and then they coordinate using shared memory to decide which of the two values to choose. The properties that the protocol has to satisfy are agreement (the two decisions must be the same), validity (the common decision must equal one of the preferred values), and wait-freedom (at any point, if only one process makes progress it will be able to make a decision). It has been shown that wait-freedom can be achieved only if a test-and-set register is used. The test-and-set register allows a process to write a value to it and read its previous value as an atomic operation

Figure 7 shows the scenario used for the consensus protocol. Both processes begin by non-deterministically choosing a value, messages "Prefer0" and "Prefer1", then write their choices in shared registers, "Register1" and "Register2", and then compete on setting the common test-and-set register which is initialized with 0. In this case, Process1 succeeds, the return value of the test-and-set operation is 0, and Process1 decides on its preferred value with message "decide0". On the other hand, Process2 fails, the test-and-set register returns 1, and Process2 reads the value chosen by Process1, and decides on that with messages "read0" and "decide0". We first attempt to synthesize the protocol starting from the incomplete automata constructed from the "success path", i.e., Process 1 lane of the scenario, and the "fail path", i.e., Process 2 lane. These two experiments

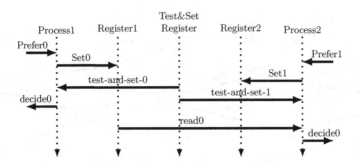

Fig. 7. Scenarios for the consensus protocol

correspond to rows "Consensus-success" and "Consensus-fail" of the Table 1. Finally, we implement a consensus protocol that does not use a test-and-set register, row "Consensus-no-test-and-set".

5.2   State Coverage

We first observe that in all our experiments, except for "Consensus-success" and "Consensus-no-test-and-set", the states of the incomplete automata constructed by the scenarios cover all states of the protocols. In the "Consensus-success" experiment, the incomplete automaton is constructed using only the successful path of the protocol. A large part of the protocol's logic is missing from the input scenario, leaving the automaton with not enough states. The synthesis algorithm terminates and thus proves that no successful completion is possible. When we add an extra state in the incomplete automata without any edges to or from the rest of the states, the synthesis algorithm returns a completion that uses the extra state to implement the missing behavior. Row "Consensus-success+1" corresponds to that experiment.

5.3   Generalization and Inference of Unspecified Behaviors

In all cases where the given scenarios covered all the states of the desired implementation the synthesis algorithm terminated with a correct completion. For the case of ABP with just one scenario specified, the algorithm successfully performs the generalization required to obtain a correct completion. The generalization performed is non-obvious: the correct protocol behaviors on packet loss, loss of acknowledgments and message duplication are inferred, even though the scenario does not describe what needs to happen in these situations. As can be seen in Figure 8, the incomplete automata constructed from the scenario describe only the protocol behavior over lossless channels. The algorithms are guided solely by the liveness and safety specifications to infer the correct behavior. In contrast, when all four scenarios are used, the scenarios already contain information about the behavior of the protocol when a single packet loss or a single message duplication occurs. The algorithm thus needs to only generalize this behavior to handle an arbitrary number of losses and duplications.

Table 1. Quantitative summary of experiments

Benchmark	time (s)	# iterations	# candidate transitions
ABP1	2.8	44	84
ABP2	9.9	87	172
ABP1-4	11.5	59	240
ABPcolored1	63.8	197	260
ABPcolored2	168.9	273	652
ABPcolored1-4	409.4	293	1012
VI-no-data	28.6	208	1170
VI	183.7	215	4538
Consensus-fail	0.3	5	264
Consensus-success	13.8	162	112
Consensus-success+1	21.4	163	216
Consensus-no-test-and-set	11.2	156	88

The same is true about the generalizations made by the algorithm in the other benchmarks. Specifically, in the case of VI, the synthesis algorithm correctly infers that in a complete protocol write-back and invalidate messages should be treated in the same way both from the caches and from the directory. Note that this behavior cannot be inferred by looking at caches and directory independently: they both have to implement it for the result to be correct.

5.4   Scalability

To validate our hypothesis that scenarios make the synthesis problem easier, we attempted to synthesize the ABP protocol with no scenarios specified, but with bounds on the number of states of the processes. These bounds were set to be equal to the corresponding number of states in the manually constructed version of the ABP protocol. We required that the protocol satisfy all the properties discussed in Section 2. The synthesis algorithm ran out of time with no correct completion with a timeout of thirty minutes.

5.5   Scenarios and Requirements

We observed that when fewer scenarios were used we needed to specify more properties — some of which were non-obvious — so that the algorithms could converge to a correct completion. For instance, when only one scenario was specified, we needed to include the liveness property that every deliver message was

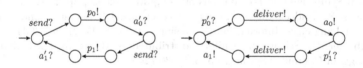

Fig. 8. Incomplete automata constructed from the first scenario of Figure 2

eventually followed by a send message. Owing to the structure of the incomplete automata, this property was not necessary to obtain a correct completion when all four scenarios were specified. Another property which was necessary to reject trivial completions when no scenarios were specified was that there has to be at least one send message in every run. Therefore, in some cases, using scenarios can compensate for the lack of detailed formal specifications.

6   Conclusions

The main contribution of this paper is a new methodology, supported by an automatic synthesis technique, for specifying finite-state distributed protocols using a mix of representative behaviors and correctness requirements. The synthesizer derives a skeleton of the state machine for each process using the states that appear in the scenarios and then finds a completion that satisfies the requirements. The promise of the proposed method is demonstrated by the ability of the synthesis algorithm to learn the correct ABP protocol from just a single scenario corresponding to the typical case. We would like to look at protocols that are best described using *extended* FSM with variables, such as more advanced cache-coherence protocols. In such cases, it will be necessary to synthesize symbolic guards and updates for each transition, see for example [24].

References

1. ITU Telecommunication Standardization Sector: ITU-R recommendation Z.120, Message Sequence Charts (MSC 1996) (May 1996)
2. Solar-Lezama, A., Jones, C.G., Bodik, R.: Sketching concurrent data structures. In: Proceedings of the 2008 ACM SIGPLAN Conference on Programming Language Design and Implementation (PLDI 2008) (2008)
3. Kurose, J.F., Ross, K.W.: Computer Networking: A Top-Down Approach, 5th edn. Addison-Wesley Publishing Company, USA (2009)
4. Clarke, E.M., Grumberg, O., Peled, D.A.: Model checking. MIT Press (2000)
5. Lynch, N.A.: Distributed algorithms. Morgan Kaufmann (1996)
6. Ramadge, P., Wonham, W.: The control of discrete event systems. IEEE Transactions on Control Theory 77, 81–98 (1989)
7. Pnueli, A., Rosner, R.: On the synthesis of a reactive module. In: Proceedings of the 16th ACM Symposium on Principles of Programming Languages (1989)
8. Bloem, R., Jobstmann, B., Piterman, N., Pnueli, A., Sa'ar, Y.: Synthesis of reactive(1) designs. J. Comput. Syst. Sci. 78(3) (2012)
9. Pnueli, A., Rosner, R.: Distributed reactive systems are hard to synthesize. In: 31st Annual Symposium on Foundations of Computer Science, pp. 746–757 (1990)
10. Tripakis, S.: Undecidable Problems of Decentralized Observation and Control on Regular Languages. Information Processing Letters 90(1), 21–28 (2004)
11. Finkbeiner, B., Schewe, S.: Uniform distributed synthesis. In: IEEE Symposium on Logic in Computer Science, pp. 321–330 (2005)
12. Lamouchi, H., Thistle, J.: Effective control synthesis for DES under partial observations. In: 39th IEEE Conference on Decision and Control, pp. 22–28 (2000)

13. Finkbeiner, B., Schewe, S.: Bounded synthesis. Software Tools for Tchnology Transfer 15(5-6), 519–539 (2013)
14. Katz, G., Peled, D.: Model checking-based genetic programming with an application to mutual exclusion. In: Ramakrishnan, C.R., Rehof, J. (eds.) TACAS 2008. LNCS, vol. 4963, pp. 141–156. Springer, Heidelberg (2008)
15. Katz, G., Peled, D.: Synthesizing solutions to the leader election problem using model checking and genetic programming. In: Namjoshi, K., Zeller, A., Ziv, A. (eds.) HVC 2009. LNCS, vol. 6405, pp. 117–132. Springer, Heidelberg (2011)
16. Alur, R., Etessami, K., Yannakakis, M.: Inference of message sequence charts. IEEE Transactions on Software Engineering 29(7) (2003)
17. Uchitel, S., Kramer, J., Magee, J.: Synthesis of behavioral models from scenarios. IEEE Trans. Softw. Eng. 29(2) (2003)
18. Basu, S., Bultan, T., Ouederni, M.: Deciding choreography realizability. In: Proceedings of the 39th Annual ACM SIGPLAN-SIGACT Symposium on Principles of Programming Languages (2012)
19. Harel, D., Marron, A., Weiss, G.: Behavioral programming. Commun. ACM 55(7), 90–100 (2012)
20. Damm, W., Harel, D.: LSCs: Breathing life into message sequence charts. Formal Methods in System Design 19(1) (2001)
21. Bollig, B., Katoen, J., Kern, C., Leucker, M.: Learning Communicating Automata from MSCs. IEEE Transactions on Software Engineering 36(3), 390–408 (2010)
22. O'Leary, J., Talupur, M., Tuttle, M.R.: Protocol verification using flows: An industrial experience. In: Formal Methods in Computer-Aided Design, FMCAD 2009, pp. 172–179 (November 2009)
23. Solar-Lezama, A., Rabbah, R., Bodik, R., Ebcioglu, K.: Programming by sketching for bit-streaming programs. In: Proceedings of the 2005 ACM Conference on Programming Language Design and Implementation (2005)
24. Udupa, A., Raghavan, A., Deshmukh, J.V., Mador-Haim, S., Martin, M.M.K., Alur, R.: TRANSIT: specifying protocols with concolic snippets. In: Proceedings of the 34th ACM SIGPLAN Conference on Programming Language Design and Implementation, PLDI 2013, pp. 287–296 (2013)
25. Jobstmann, B., Griesmayer, A., Bloem, R.: Program repair as a game. In: Etessami, K., Rajamani, S.K. (eds.) CAV 2005. LNCS, vol. 3576, pp. 226–238. Springer, Heidelberg (2005)
26. Alur, R., Martin, M.M.K., Raghothaman, M., Stergiou, C., Tripakis, S., Udupa, A.: Synthesizing finite-state protocols from scenarios and requirements. CoRR abs/1402.7150 (2014)

Automatic Error Localization for Software Using Deductive Verification*

Robert Könighofer, Ronald Toegl, and Roderick Bloem

IAIK, Graz University of Technology, Austria

Abstract. Even competent programmers make mistakes. Automatic verification can detect errors, but leaves the frustrating task of finding the erroneous line of code to the user. This paper presents an automatic approach for identifying potential error locations in software. It is based on a deductive verification engine, which detects errors in functions annotated with pre- and post-conditions. Using an automatic theorem prover, our approach finds expressions in the code that can be modified such that the program satisfies its specification. Scalability is achieved by analyzing each function in isolation. We have implemented our approach in the widely used Frama-C framework and present first experimental results.

1 Introduction

Formal verification attempts to detect mismatches between a program and its specification automatically. However, the time-consuming work of locating and fixing detected bugs is usually performed manually. At the same time, the diagnostic information provided by the tools is often limited. While model checkers commonly provide counterexamples, deductive software verification engines usually only give yes/no (or worse: only yes/maybe) answers. Analyzing a proof or witness given by the underlying theorem prover is usually not a viable option.

In this work, we strive to lessen this usability defect in the context of deductive software verification [2]. This approach assumes that source code is annotated with pre- and post-conditions. It computes a set of *proof obligations*, i.e., formulas that need to be proven to attest correctness. These formulas are then discharged by an automatic theorem prover. Scalability is achieved by analyzing functions in isolation. We extend this verification flow such that the tool does not only report the existence of an error, but also pinpoints its location.

Our solution assumes that some code expression is faulty. This fault model is fine-grained and quite general. If verification of a function fails, we iterate over each expression in this function and analyze if it can be modified such that the function satisfies its contract for all inputs. If so, we report this expression as potential error location. Expressions that cannot be modified such that the error goes away do not have to be analyzed by the developer when trying to fix the

---

* This work was supported by the European Commission through project STANCE (31775) and the Austrian Science Fund (FWF) through project RiSE (S11406-N23).

E. Yahav (Ed.): HVC 2014, LNCS 8855, pp. 92–98, 2014.

error. We have implemented a proof-of-concept in Frama-C [2], and provide first experimental results comparing our approach to FoREnSiC [1] and Bug-Assist [6].

Related Work. Our fault model has been successfully applied before [7,1]: This approach also checks repairability of expressions, but only for fixed inputs. It uses assertions as specification, and SMT solvers as reasoning engines. [4] is similar but uses a model checker. In [6] a MAX-SAT engine is used. Our work resolves many drawbacks of these existing works: pre- and post-conditions are more powerful than assertions, we check repairability for *all* inputs, and we achieve scalability by analyzing functions in isolation. Model-based diagnosis [10] has already been applied in many settings (cf. [7]). Our approach is similar (we also check repairability), but focuses on single-fault diagnoses to avoid floods of diagnoses. Dynamic methods [5] rely on the quality of available test cases. In contrast, our method is purely formal. An extended version [8] of this paper contains an additional appendix with more detailed experimental results.

2 Automatic Error Localization

2.1 Fault Models

Intuitively, a fault model defines what can go wrong in a program, thereby inducing a set of candidate error locations. An error localization algorithm can then decide which of these candidates can actually be responsible for the detected problem. A good fault model needs to balance conflicting objectives: it should cover many errors, be fine-grained, allow for efficient error localization and not yield too many spurious error locations. Existing approaches include fault patterns [9] specifying common bugs, mutation-based fault models [3] assuming that the error is a small syntactic change, and faulty expressions [4,7] assuming that the control structure is correct but some code expression may be wrong. In this work we use faulty expressions because this fault model is fine-grained, more generic than mutation-based models, more automatic than fault patterns, and still allows for efficient error localization, as shown below.

2.2 Basic Idea for Error Localization

Our approach is inspired by [4,7]: An expression in the source code is a potential error location if it can be replaced such that the detected error is resolved.

Example 1. The program on the right is supposed to compute the maximum of a and b, but contains a bug in line 5. The postcondition \result >= b is incomplete but sufficient to detect the bug: it is violated if $b > a$. Our fault model (incorrect expressions) identifies 4 candidate error locations: Candidate C_1 is the expression "a" in line 3, C_2 is "b > a" in line 4, C_3 is the "a" in line 5,

```
1 /*@ensures \result >= b;@*/
2 int max(int a, int b) {
3     int r = a;
4     if(b > a)
5         r = a; //correct: r = b
6     return r; }
```

and C_4 is the "r" in line 6. Neither C_1 nor C_2 are error locations. C_1 cannot be changed to satisfy the post-condition because r is overwritten with the incorrect value "a" if $b > a$. If we change only C_2, \result will always be "a", which is incorrect if $b > a$. C_3 and C_4 are possible error locations, because these expressions can be replaced by "b" to make the program satisfy its specification.   □

2.3   Realization with Deductive Verification

We now discuss how to answer such repairability questions automatically. From a high-level perspective, most formal verification tools compute a correctness condition $\mathsf{correct}(\bar{\imath})$ in some logic, where $\bar{\imath}$ is the vector of input variables of the program. Next, a solver checks if $\forall \bar{\imath} : \mathsf{correct}(\bar{\imath})$ holds. If not, an error has been detected. Deductive verification tools like the WP plug-in of Frama-C [2] follow this pattern by defining correct as implication: if the pre-condition of a function holds, then the function must satisfy its post-condition. Loops are handled with user-provided invariants, and a theorem prover checks $\forall \bar{\imath} : \mathsf{correct}(\bar{\imath})$. In practice, correct may be composed of parts that can be solved independently.

If a function is incorrect, we compute if a certain expression C is a potential error location as follows. First, we replace C by a placeholder c for a new expression. Next, we compute the correctness condition $\mathsf{correct}(\bar{\imath}, c)$, which depends now also on c. Finally, C is a potential error location if $\forall \bar{\imath} : \exists c : \mathsf{correct}(\bar{\imath}, c)$. This formula asks if expression C can, in principle, be replaced such that the function satisfies its contract. For every input $\bar{\imath}$, there must exist a value c to which the replacement of C evaluates such that the function behaves as specified. Note that this approach can, in principle, also compute a repair if the underlying theorem prover can produce a witness in form of a Skolem function for the c variable. However, this feature is not supported by our current implementation.

Example 2. We continue Example 1. We check if expression C_1 is a potential error location by replacing it with a placeholder c_1, as shown on the right. Next, we compute $\mathsf{correct}(a, b, c_1) = (b \leq a) \wedge (c_1 \geq b)$ using deductive verification. C_1 is not an error location because $\forall a, b : \exists c_1 : \mathsf{correct}(a, b, c_1)$ is false.

```
1 /*@ensures \result >= b;@*/
2 int max(int a, int b) {
3     int r = c1;
4     if(b > a)
5         r = a; //correct: r = b
6     return r; }
```

When replacing C_3 we get $\mathsf{correct}(a, b, c_3) = (b \leq a) \vee (c_3 \geq b)$. We have that $\forall a, b : \exists c_3 : (b \leq a) \vee (c_3 \geq b)$, so C_3 is a potential error location — as expected.   □

2.4   Implementation in Frama-C

We implemented our error localization approach as a proof of concept in the WP plug-in of the widely used software verification framework Frama-C [2]. We discuss implementation challenges and reasons for imperfect diagnostic resolution.

Instrumentation. Frama-C normalizes the source code while parsing it into an Abstract Syntax Tree (AST). For instance, it decomposes complicated statements using auxiliary variables. Our instrumentation, replacing candidate expressions by a placeholder c, operates on this normalized AST. This makes it robust when handling complicated constructions. The disadvantage is that our approach may report error locations that are only present in the normalization. However, we do not consider this a severe usability issue, because the line number in the original code is available, and Frama-C presents the normalized source code and how it links to the original source code in its GUI.

Computation of correct$(\bar{i}, c)$. Internally, the WP plug-in of Frama-C performs simplifications that may rewrite or eliminate our newly introduced placeholder c, and thus, we cannot use WP a black-box to compute the correctness formula correct$(\bar{i}, c)$ after instrumentation. We solve this issue by extending Frama-C's memory model such that the placeholder c is not touched by simplifications.

Quantification. Once we have correct$(\bar{i}, c)$, we need to add the quantifier prefix $\forall \bar{i} : \exists c$. Unfortunately, correct may also contain auxiliary variables $\bar{t}$ that express values of variables at specific program points. Intuitively, c should not depend on variables that are assigned later in the program. This would violate the causality and lead to false-positives. Hence, we need to separate the variables of correct to construct the formula $\forall \bar{i} : \exists c : \forall \bar{t} : \text{correct}(\bar{i}, \bar{t}, c)$. This is done by computing the input variables (parameters and globals) of the function under analysis and linking them to the corresponding variables in the formula.

Axiomatization. WP uses axiomatized functions and predicates in correct. For instance, for $a < b$ it writes zlt(a, b), where the predicate zlt $: \mathbb{Z} \times \mathbb{Z} \to \mathbb{B}$ is axiomatized as $\forall x, y : (zlt(x, y) \to x < y) \wedge (\neg zlt(x, y) \to x \geq y)$. In our experiments we observed cases where the automatic theorem prover (AltErgo) could not decide formulas when using the axiomatization, but had no difficulty when the axiomatized predicates and functions are replaced by the corresponding native operators. Hence, we modified the interface to the theorem prover such that formulas do not contain axiomatized functions and predicates, where possible.

Diagnostic Resolution. Our implementation is neither guaranteed to be sound (it may produce spurious error locations) nor complete (it may miss potential error locations). The reasons are:

- The theorem prover may time-out or return "Unknown" if it could neither prove nor disprove the formula. We treat such verdicts as if the program was incorrect (a choice justified by experience), which results in incompleteness.
- Instead of one monolithic formula correct, WP may compute multiple formulas that are checked independently. In error localization, we also check each formula in isolation. This is weaker than checking the conjunction, i.e., can result in spurious error locations, but increases efficiency.
- Incomplete specifications can result in spurious error locations.
- The bug may not match our fault model. E.g., code may be missing or the control flow may be incorrect. This results in missed error locations.

3   First Experimental Results

Despite the potential imprecisions discussed in the last section, our implementation produces meaningful results. We evaluated our proof-of-concept implementation[1] on the widely used TCAS benchmark [11], which implements an aircraft traffic collision avoidance system in 180 lines of C code. It comes in 41 faulty versions that model realistic bugs. We annotated all functions with contracts.

3.1 Performance Evaluation

We compare the execution time and effectiveness of our approach with that of FoREnSiC [7,1] and Bug-Assist [6] on an ordinary laptop.[2] For our new approach, the error localization time (at most 129 [s], 37 [s] on average) is acceptable for all TCAS instances. For 37% of the cases, the execution time increases by only <40% when going from error detection to localization. FoREnSiC is slightly faster on average (17 [s]) but the median runtime is on par (16 vs. 18 [s]). With 7 [s] on average, Bug-Assist is even faster. Although only 66% of the benchmarks match our fault model, errors were successfully located in 90.2%. While FoREnSiC and Bug-Assist reported 15 error locations on average, our approach reported only 3.5. Thus, in our experiments, our tool provides much higher accuracy with only slightly longer runtime. The user has to examine only a few expressions in the code, which can speed-up debugging significantly.

3.2 Examples

This section investigates the reported error locations for a few TCAS versions.

Version 7. A constant is changed from 500 to 550 in an initialization function. Our tool reports exactly this constant 550 as the only possible error location. This takes 6 seconds, whereof 5.1 seconds are spent on error detection.

Version 9. This version contains the following function:

The correct program has a ">" instead of the ">=" in line 121. Our tool reports two potential er-

```
119 bool NonCrossBiasedDescend() {
120   bool r;
121   if (InhibitBiasedClimb() >= DwnSep) {
122     r = OwnBlTh() && VerSep >= MSEP && DwnSep >= ALIM();
123   } else {
124     r = !(OwnAbTh()) || (OwnAbTh() && UpSep >= ALIM());
125   }
126   return r; }
```

ror locations: tmp_6 >= DwnSep in line 121, and tmp_1 in line 122. This output looks cryptic because the code has been normalized by Frama-C. tmp_6 is an auxiliary variable that stands for InhibitBiasedClimb(). This is shown in the GUI. Hence, the first error location is just what we expect. tmp_1 holds the value for r in line 122. This value can be changed to satisfy the specification for all inputs as well. Hence, it is also reported. NonCrossBiasedDescend() is not long, but contains complex logic. Analyzing this logic to locate a bug can be cumbersome. The diagnostic information provided by our approach helps.

---

[1] See www.iaik.tugraz.at/content/research/design_verification/others/

[2] Table 1 in the Appendix of [8] gives more details to our performance results.

Version 14 changes `MAXDIFF` (a preprocessor macro) from 600 to 600+50. Our tool reports two possible error locations: `VerSep > 600+50` in line 167 and `OtherCap == 1` in line 168 of function `altSepTest`, which is shown below. The first one pinpoints exactly the problem. Note that `altSepTest()` is all but trivial.

If verification fails, tracking down this bug can be a very time-consuming and frustrating task. By checking only the reported locations, we can significantly reduce the manual work to fix the bug. Thus, the reported error locations are usually both meaningful and helpful.

```
165 int altSepTest() {
166   bool en, eq, intentNotKnown, needUpRA, needDwnRA;
167   en = HConf && OwnTrAlt <= OLEV && VerSep > MAXDIFF;
168   eq = OtherCap == TCAS_TA;
169   intentNotKnown = TwoRepValid && OtherRAC == NO_INT;
170   int altSep = UNRESOLVED;
171   if (en && ((eq && intentNotKnown) || !eq)) {
172     needUpRA = NonCrossBiasedClimb() && OwnBlTh();
173     needDwnRA = NonCrossBiasedDescend() && OwnAbTh();
174     if(needUpRA && needDwnRA) altSep = UNRESOLVED;
175     else if (needUpRA)        altSep = UPWARD_RA;
176     else if (needDwnRA)       altSep = DOWNWARD_RA;
177     else                      altSep = UNRESOLVED;
178   }
179   return altSep; }
```

4 Conclusions

Tracking down a subtle program error in large source code is — like finding a needle in a haystack — a tedious task. We have extended a widely used deductive software verification engine so that it can report expressions that may be responsible for incorrectness. We evaluated our proof-of-concept implementation on a few examples and conclude that our approach is viable and gives fast and clear guidance to developers on the location of program defects.

Acknowledgment. We thank Loïc Correnson and the Frama-C team for their support with our proof-of-concept implementation.

References

1. Bloem, R., Drechsler, R., Fey, G., Finder, A., Hofferek, G., Könighofer, R., Raik, J., Repinski, U., Sülflow, A.: foRenSiC– an automatic debugging environment for C programs. In: Biere, A., Nahir, A., Vos, T. (eds.) HVC 2012. LNCS, vol. 7857, pp. 260–265. Springer, Heidelberg (2013)
2. Cuoq, P., Kirchner, F., Kosmatov, N., Prevosto, V., Signoles, J., Yakobowski, B.: Frama-C - A software analysis perspective. In: Eleftherakis, G., Hinchey, M., Holcombe, M. (eds.) SEFM 2012. LNCS, vol. 7504, pp. 233–247. Springer, Heidelberg (2012)
3. Debroy, V., Wong, W.E.: Using mutation to automatically suggest fixes for faulty programs. In: ICST 2010. IEEE (2010)
4. Griesmayer, A., Staber, S., Bloem, R.: Automated fault localization for C programs. Electr. Notes Theor. Comput. Sci. 174(4), 95–111 (2007)
5. Jones, J.A., Harrold, M.J.: Empirical evaluation of the tarantula automatic fault-localization technique. In: ASE 2005. ACM (2005)

6. Jose, M., Majumdar, R.: Cause clue clauses: error localization using maximum satisfiability. In: PLDI 2011, pp. 437–446. ACM (2011)
7. Könighofer, R., Bloem, R.: Automated error localization and correction for imperative programs. In: FMCAD 2011, IEEE (2011)
8. Könighofer, R., Toegl, R., Bloem, R.: Automatic error localization for software using deductive verification. CoRR, abs/1409.4637 (2014)
9. Larus, J.R., Ball, T., Das, M., DeLine, R., Fähndrich, M., Pincus, J.D., Rajamani, S.K., Venkatapathy, R.: Righting software. IEEE Softw. 21(3), 92–100 (2004)
10. Reiter, R.: A theory of diagnosis from first principles. Art. Int. 32(1), 57–95 (1987)
11. Siemens benchmark suite,
    http://pleuma.cc.gatech.edu/aristotle/Tools/subjects

Generating JML Specifications
from Alloy Expressions*

Daniel Grunwald, Christoph Gladisch, Tianhai Liu, Mana Taghdiri,
and Shmuel Tyszberowicz

Karlsruhe Institute of Technology, Germany
{christoph.gladisch,tianhai.liu,mana.taghdiri}@kit.edu,tyshbe@tau.ac.il

Abstract. Java Modeling Language (JML) is a specification language
for Java programs, that follows the design by contract paradigm. However, it is not always easy to use JML, for example when specifying properties of linked data structures. Alloy, on the other hand, is a relational
specification language with a built-in transitive closure operator, which
makes it particularly suitable for writing concise specifications of linked
data structures. This paper presents Alloy2JML, a tool that generates
JML specifications from Alloy expression, in order to support both Alloy
and JML specifications in the KeY verification engine. This translation
allows Java programs with Alloy specifications to be fully verified for
correctness. Moreover, Alloy2JML lets Alloy specifications be employed
in a variety of tools that accept only JML as their specification language.
Supporting Alloy has the additional advantage that users can validate
the specifications beforehand using the Alloy Analyzer.

Keywords: JML, Alloy, Java, Theorem proving, KeY, Relational logic.

1 Introduction

The ability to write concise and readable specifications highly affects the efficiency of program verification. Providing correct formal specifications can be
as difficult as implementing the code correctly. A suitable formalism for specifying program properties not only makes the task of providing specifications
easier, but also reduces the likelihood of making mistakes. However, no single
specification language is optimal for specifying all possible properties.

JML [21] is a behavioral interface specification language for Java, that adds
first-order logic constructs to Java expressions. JML integrates seamlessly into
Java and is supported by a wide range of tools for specification type-checking,
runtime debugging, static analysis, and verification [4]. JML provides a rich set of
specification facilities, yet JML specifications tend to be close to the implementation. Specifying and verifying operations on linked data structures are difficult
in JML. Such operations have been specified in JML, e.g. in [1, 24], but no deductive verification of them has been reported. To enable verification, extensions
of JML have been used [3].

---

* This work has been partially supported by GIF (grant No. 1131-9.6/2011).

E. Yahav (Ed.): HVC 2014, LNCS 8855, pp. 99–115, 2014.
© Springer International Publishing Switzerland 2014

To our knowledge, in [15] we provided the first specification of list operations in *standard* JML that was deductively verified. The approach is to use recursively defined queries (also called observer methods) in specifications to express reachability in linked lists. Consider, for example, a method add that inserts the data d into a singly linked list starting from the entry this.head. Using the approach in [15] we would write the following JML formula to specify that every data x in the resulting list is either d or was already in the original list:

```
(\forall Data x;
       (\exists Entry a, int i; i>0 && hasNext(this.head,i,a) && a.data==x)
    <==> (x==d || (\exists Entry b, int j;
                   j>0 && \old(hasNext(this.head,j,b)) && \old(b.data==x))))  (1)
```

The query hasNext expresses that an object a can be reached from the object head in i steps (by traversing the field next). This specification approach has the following advantages: (a) it uses a basic subset of JML which enables compatibility with various tools (e.g., [6,8,22]); (b) it allows automatic construction of proofs by induction over the integer provided to the query as the second argument (here i and j); (c) it does not require ghost-states or ghost-fields, thus makes the specification easier to understand; and (d) the specifications can be used both for deductive verification and for testing[1]. The query is similar to the JML reach clause, yet it provides more flexibility; some tools do not support the reach clause (e.g. [23,26]), and those that do support it interpret it differently (e.g., [8,22]). However, writing such JML specifications is error-prone as they contain technical details. For set-based specifications, it would be easier to use a notation that hides those details and focuses only on the abstract properties.

Alloy [18] is a lightweight declarative specification language for expressing structure-rich software systems. It is based on first-order relational logic, and has built-in operators for transitive closure, set cardinality, integer arithmetic, and set comprehension. Several tools (e.g., [7,25]) support Alloy as a specification language for Java programs. The transitive closure operator enables users to write concise specifications of linked data structures. The relational override operator allows compact specification of frame conditions. Furthermore, when appropriate, relational specifications let users easily abstract away from the exact order and connection of elements in a data structure by viewing it as a set. The above example can be concisely expressed in Alloy as follows:

$$\texttt{this.head'.\^{}next'.data' = this.head.\^{}next.data + d;} \qquad (2)$$

where ^next denotes the transitive closure over the field next (i.e., all nodes reachable by traversing next), + denotes set union, and unprimed and primed symbols refer to the pre- and post-state of the method, respectively. With this notation we provide a succinct and intuitive representation of set-based specifications. This notation is shorter, easier to understand, and less error-prone than its JML counterpart.

---

[1] When used for testing the quantifiers have to be bound.

Fig. 1. Alloy2JML

JML and Alloy offer complementary views. JML allows to provide detailed Java-specific annotations and to utilize Java for that. It is also suitable for specifying arithmetic properties, and certain properties of data structures where the position of elements is important. Other properties, e.g. those that constrain the set of all the elements of a linked data structure, are easier to express in Alloy.

This paper describes Alloy2JML, a tool that translates Alloy specifications of Java programs into JML. The automatic translation is particularly beneficial for properties that are difficult or error-prone to express in JML directly. It takes programs in which each property is specified in either JML or Alloy, and translates Alloy specifications to JML to yield uniform JML specifications. The translation lets Java programs with Alloy specifications be fully verified for correctness using the KeY verification engine [2]. Alloy2JML's output conforms to the format suggested in [15], thus offers all the advantages listed above. For example, it generates the JML specification (1) from the Alloy formula (2). The output is essentially in standard JML—minor differences exist to support KeY, which can be eliminated by simple syntactic changes. We have proved the correctness of our translation [16] for a subset of Alloy using Isabelle/HOL [20].

We aim at producing JML formulas that are both usable for verification and human-readable. Readability is particularly important when using interactive verification tools such as KeY. It is not only necessary for debugging failed proof attempts, but also for providing additional lemmas in the proof process. To generate readable specifications, we use a translation function that tries to minimize the syntactic scope of quantifiers by delaying the introduction of quantification guards. A subsequent simplification step eliminates most of the redundant quantifiers.

In [15] we showed only specification examples and did not provide a *systematic* way of defining the queries and how to write the specifications. Its applicability to trees was also an open question. Here, we generalize and extend that work. The translation provides a systematic way of deriving JML specifications for arbitrary linked data structures from the more abstract Alloy specifications and it eliminates the error-prone task of manually defining of queries. The queries can be applied not only over a single field but also over an arbitrary relation denoted by an Alloy expression.

As shown in Fig. 1, the input to Alloy2JML is a Java program annotated with both JML and Alloy specifications, and the output is a Java program annotated with JML specifications only. Alloy2JML also outputs an Alloy model that declares Alloy signatures for the classes in the input program and Alloy predicates for methods' specifications (see [16]). Using this model, the Alloy Analyzer [18]—

```
exp ::= id | id' | freshType          form ::= exp in exp | exp = exp
| none | exp + exp| exp & exp          | exp (> | >= | < | <=) exp
| exp - exp | exp . exp                | form (and | or | implies | iff) form
| exp -> exp | exp ++ exp | ~exp       | not form | (no | some | lone) exp
| ^exp | {[id: expr]+ | form}          | (all | some) [id : exp]+ | form
| number | #exp | (sum id: exp | exp)
```

Fig. 2. Abstract syntax for translated Alloy expressions (exp) and formulas (form)

an automatic tool that checks Alloy models within bounded domains—can be used to sanity-check the Alloy specifications prior to performing the full (possibly interactive) verification. For example, it can help detect under-specification and errors by visualizing instances that satisfy the specifications, and detect over-specification by showing the unsatisfiable core. This makes Alloy a particularly attractive specification language compared to other languages that support sets and relations.

2   Background

2.1   Alloy

Alloy is a specification language based on first-order logic [18]. Every Alloy expression evaluates to a relation. Unary relations are declared as signatures, and represent sets of atoms. Relations with higher arities are declared as fields and represent sets of tuples. The constant **none** denotes the empty set. Set operations union, intersection, and difference are denoted by +, &, and -, respectively. For relations r and s, the relational join and Cartesian product are denoted by r.s and r->s, respectively. The relational override r++s contains all tuples of s, and those tuples of r whose first element does not appear as the first element of any tuple in s. The expression ~r denotes the transpose of r, and the transitive closure ^r defines the smallest transitive relation that contains r. Set comprehensions make relations with all tuples for which a certain formula holds. The Alloy integer type, Int, represents the set of integer atoms. All integers (including numbers, the result of the set cardinality operator #, and the sum quantifier) are treated as sets of integer atoms (Alloy 4.2). Arithmetic operators are defined as functions in the Alloy integer library (add[a,b] and sub[a,b]). The expression (sum x: S | e) computes the sum of the values that the integer expression e can take for all distinct bindings of the variable x in S.

Basic formulas are constructed using the operators in (subset), = (equality), and integer comparators. They are combined using the standard logical operators. The multiplicity formulas no r, some r, and lone r constrain r to have zero, at least one, and at most one tuple, respectively. The quantifiers all and some denote the universal and existential quantifiers. It should be noted that the Alloy Analyzer supports higher-order quantification when the quantifier can be eliminated through skolemization. We, however, do not support higher-order quantifications at all as they cannot be translated to JML.

We let Java programs be annotated with legal Alloy formulas. We provide special translation rules for the Alloy constructs of Fig. 2, and desugar all others to this subset. Figure 2 slightly deviates from Alloy by introducing extra identifiers that have special meanings in our translation: a primed identifier refers to the post-state of a method, whereas an unprimed one refers to its pre-state. freshT denotes the set of objects of type T that are allocated in the post-state, but not in the pre-state[2].

2.2   JML

Java Modeling Language (JML) [21] is a first-order, behavioral interface specification language for Java. Side-effect free Java expressions, standard logical operators, universal and existential quantifiers are allowed in JML annotations. JML also supports various clauses and keywords for better specifications. The ones used by our translation are described below.

The **requires** clause denotes a method's precondition, evaluated in the pre-state of the method call. If a method terminates normally, i.e. without throwing an exception, then the normal post-condition—given in the **ensures** clause—must hold in the post-state. The **normal_behavior** clause specifies that if a method's precondition holds, the method must return normally. The **invariant** clause denotes an object invariant that must hold at the end of each constructor's execution, and at the beginning and end of all non-static methods that are not marked as **helper**. The memory locations (represented by a set of fields) that are listed in the **modifies** clause are the only pre-state locations that can be modified by a method. The **measured_by** e clause is used in a termination argument for a recursive specification, where the integer expression e decreases on each iteration and evaluates to zero when the method terminates.

Java expressions used in pre- and post-conditions are evaluated in the heap's pre-state and the post-state, respectively. To access the initial (pre-state) value of an expression e in the post-condition, the expression \old(e) is used. The keyword \result refers to the value returned by a non-void method. The \fresh(o) operator constrains the object o not to exist in the pre-state and to be non-null in the post-state. Member fields, formal parameters, and return values are considered to be non-null by default. The **nullable** modifier specifies that the null value is also acceptable. The modifier **pure** denotes that a method has no side-effects and thus can be used in the annotations. The **model** modifier denotes those fields and methods that can be used only in the annotations.

KeY [2] accepts JML*, a modified version of JML, as the specification language for Java programs. JML* implements most, but not all, JML features and adds a few more. Most relevant to our work is a semantic difference in the interpretation of quantifiers. The range of JML quantifiers extends over all objects of the given type, including those that are not yet created [21]. In JML*, on the other hand, the quantifier ranges over only those objects that have been created in the current

---

[2] Fresh objects could be specified by T' - T, but then the translation could not distinguish other set differences from fresh objects (for which it generates \fresh clauses).

```
1   class Entry {
2     /*@nullable*/ Entry next;
3     /*@nullable*/ Data data;
4
5     //$ensures this.data' = d;
6     //$ensures no this.next';
7     //$modifies this.data,this.next;
8     Entry(/*@nullable*/Data d)
9     { this.data = d; }
10  }
11  class LinkedList {
12    Entry head;
13    int length;
14
15    //$ensures this.head'.^next'.data'
16    //$ = this.head.^next.data + d;
17    //$ensures this.length'=add[this.length,1];
18    //$modifies this.head.next, this.length;
19    void add(Data d) {
20      Entry newEntry = new Entry(d);
21      newEntry.next = head.next;
22      head.next = newEntry;
23      length++;
24    }
25  }
26  class Data { .. }
```

(a)

```
1   class Entry {
2     /*@nullable*/ Entry next;
3     /*@nullable*/ Data data;
4
5     //@ensures this.data == d;
6     //@ensures this.next == null;
7     //@modifies this.data,this.next;
8     Entry(/*@nullable*/Data d){ .. }
9   }
10  class LinkedList {
11    Entry head;
12    int length;
13
14    //@ensures (\forall Data x;
15    //@  (\exists Entry a, int i;
16    //@   a.data == x && i > 0 &&
17    //@   hasNext(this.head,i,a))
18    //@  <==> (\exists Entry b, int j;
19    //@   \old(b.data == x) && j > 0 &&
20    //@   \old(hasNext(this.head,j,b)))
21    //@  || d == x);
22    //@ensures this.length ==
23    //@        \old(this.length)+1;
24    //@modifies this.head.next, this.length;
25    void add(Data d) { ... }
26  }
27  class Data { .. }
```

(b)

Fig. 3. Example: (a) original, (b) translated

heap state. It is possible to obtain the JML* quantifier semantics in JML by introducing predicates that explicitly distinguish between created and uncreated objects. Furthermore, the JML* construct \infinite_union(C o; o.f), where C is a class and f is a field, gives the set of memory locations o.f for all objects o of class C. The construct can be replaced using the model type JMLDataGroup in standard JML (cf. [15]) (not included in JML*).

3   Motivating Example

We assume that the Alloy specifications of Java programs are written at the concrete representation level of the code, and follow a *relational view of the heap* [25]. That is, Java types are viewed as Alloy signatures, fields as binary relations, and local variables and parameters as singleton sets.

Figure 3 elaborates the example of Section 1, showing our translation of Alloy to JML. Figure 3(a) gives an implementation of a singly linked list where the head and the length fields (Lines 12-13) denote the first entry and the number of entries of the list, respectively. The list's first entry is dummy; it does not contain any data, and exists even for an empty list. The length field ensures that the list is finite, which is necessary for proving termination of methods that traverse the list. The add method (Lines 19-24) inserts the given data d at the beginning of the receiver list.

Alloy and JML annotations are marked by //$ and //@ respectively. The post-conditions of the Entry constructor ensure that the given data d is stored in the data field of the created entry (Fig. 3(a), Line 5), and that the next field of this entry is set to null (Line 6). We assume that Alloy specifications model the Java null object as an empty set. The first post-condition of the add method specifies that the set of data stored in this list in the post-state equals that set in the pre-state, augmented with the added data d (Lines 15-16). This example demonstrates that specifications can be arbitrarily partial. This post-condition, for example, does not specify that the given data is inserted at the *beginning* of the list. The second post-condition (Line 17) specifies that length is updated properly. The invariants of the LinkedList class are omitted for space reasons.

JML specifications produced by Alloy2JML are shown in Fig. 3(b). To handle Alloy's transitive closure operator, we introduce pure Java methods that can be used in JML annotations. For a field f of type T declared in a class S, we define a pure Java method hasF(C x, int i, C y) that returns true if x is non-null and y is reachable from x by i times following the field f, and false otherwise. The type C is the first common type of S and T in the type hierarchy of the analyzed method. In addition to simple relational joins which are translated to field dereferences, the post-condition of add (Fig. 3(a), Lines 15-17) contains set equality, set union, and transitive closure operators. Set equality is translated using its definition: any object in the right-hand-side set must be in the left-hand-side one, and vice versa. Set union is handled using disjunction. An expression containing the transitive closure some o.^next is translated using (\exists Entry e, int i; hasNext(o, i, e)), where the integer i can be any positive number. The resulting JML specification is shown in Lines 14-23 of Fig. 3(b).

As shown by this example, we translate Alloy annotations into a basic variant of JML. Alloy annotations are particularly concise and readable when specifications involve reachability and set semantics. More examples can be found in [16].

4 Translation from Alloy to JML

4.1 The Translation Function

We have experimented with several translations and evaluated the applicability and readability of the resulting JML specifications for verification using KeY. In the following, we describe two preliminary approaches (Approach 1, Approach 2) to motivate and explain our solution (Approach 3). For brevity we often use the term *relation* to refer to sets and relations.

Approach 1: Since Alloy expressions evaluate to relations, a direct translation of Alloy to JML requires the notion of relations in JML. Such a translation could be done using a translation function $\mathcal{E}(r) \to e$ that maps an Alloy expression r to a JML expression e of a container (or array) type in Java. The translation of a union operation, for instance, would then become $\mathcal{E}(\mathbf{r} + \mathbf{s}) = \mathtt{union}(\mathcal{E}(\mathbf{r}), \mathcal{E}(\mathbf{s}))$ where $\mathtt{union}$ is a Java method that operates on containers. KeY expands method invocations to their contracts. Expanding complex expressions, however, leads to very complex verification conditions which we found impractical.

Approach 2: The explicit representation of sets and relations in Java/JML can be omitted by expanding relational operators to their semantic definitions during the translation. For this, we modify the translation function to $\mathcal{E}(\mathbf{r}\|t_1, \ldots, t_n) \rightarrow e$ which now maps an Alloy expression $\mathbf{r}$ along with JML expressions $t_1, \ldots, t_n$ to a boolean JML expression e, such that e is true iff $<t_1, \ldots, t_n>$ corresponds to a tuple in $\mathbf{r}$. The double bars $\|$ are a visual aid separating the translated expression (left-hand side) from the expressions that form the tuple (right-hand side). For example, the translation of the union operation can be expressed as $\mathcal{E}(\mathbf{u}+\mathbf{v}\|obj) := \mathcal{E}(\mathbf{u}\|obj) \,|\, \mathcal{E}(\mathbf{v}\|obj)$, where, for simplicity, $\mathbf{u}$ and $\mathbf{v}$ are unary relations denoting program variables. In isolation, this expression cannot be further resolved to a JML expression as the meta variable obj needs to be instantiated. However, it can be resolved in the context of the formula in which it is used. For this, we introduce another translation function, $\mathcal{B}$, which maps Alloy formulas to boolean JML expressions. Consider, for example, the following translation rules:

$$\mathcal{B}(\mathtt{no}\ \mathbf{r}) \quad := \mathtt{!(\backslash exists\ Object\ x;\ } \mathcal{E}(\mathbf{r}\|\mathbf{x}))$$
$$\mathcal{E}(\mathbf{v}\|val) \quad := \mathbf{v}_c\ \mathtt{==}\ val \qquad\qquad v_c\ \textit{denotes name resolution}$$
$$\mathcal{E}(\mathbf{r} + \mathbf{s}\|objs) := \mathcal{E}(\mathbf{r}\|objs)\ \texttt{||}\ \mathcal{E}(\mathbf{s}\|objs)$$
$$\mathcal{E}(\char94\mathbf{r}\|obj_1, obj_2) := \mathtt{(\backslash exists\ int\ i;\ } 0\ \mathtt{<=}\ \mathtt{i;\ hasR}(obj_1,\ \mathtt{i},\ obj_2))$$

Using the first three rules, the expression $\mathtt{no}$ $\mathtt{u+v}$ will be translated to the JML expression $\mathtt{!(\backslash exists\ Object\ x;\ u{==}x\ ||\ v{==}x)}$ without explicitly using Java containers. The last rule shows our basic idea for translating transitive closure. We express the reachability of obj_2 from obj_1 via the relational expression $\mathbf{r}$, i.e. $(obj_1, obj_2) \in \char94 r$, using a boolean query method $\mathtt{hasR}$. The integer $\mathtt{i}$ stands for the number of times that $\mathbf{r}$ is traversed in order to reach obj_2 when starting from obj_1. This is used as the induction variable in induction proofs. However, to generate $\mathtt{hasR}$ from $\mathbf{r}$, the translation function $\mathcal{E}$ has to be generalized further.

Approach 3: In [15] we have described how a user can manually write a query (such as $\mathtt{hasR}$) for a list data structure. Here we describe a general method to automatically translate the transitive closure of an arbitrary expression $\mathbf{r}$ into a recursive definition of the query. Rather than introducing another translation function for this purpose, we generalize the function $\mathcal{E}$ to the form $\mathcal{E}(\mathbf{r}\|p_1, \ldots, p_n)_c$ where $\mathbf{r}$ is the Alloy relational expression to be translated; $p_1, \ldots, p_n$ is a list of translation predicates applicable to JML expressions; and c is a translation context capturing various information. The context provides a mapping from Alloy types, relations, and variables to their corresponding symbols in JML, and tells whether the expression is evaluated in the pre- or post-state (the latter generates expressions embedded in $\mathtt{\backslash old(...)}$). The number of predicates (n) must match the arity of the relation $\mathbf{r}$, and the predicates must be well-formed. The semantics of the translation function is defined by:

$$\mathcal{E}(\mathbf{r}\|p_1, .., p_n)_c \text{ evaluates to } \mathtt{true} \iff \exists(\mathbf{t}_1, .., \mathbf{t}_n) \in \mathbf{r}\colon\ p_1(c(\mathbf{t}_1)) \wedge .. \wedge p_n(c(\mathbf{t}_n))$$

Table 1. The translation functions $\mathcal{E}$ and $\mathcal{B}$, and simplification rules $R_{29} - R_{34}$. v is an Alloy variable, T is a type signature, **member** is an Alloy relation for a Java field, n is an integer literal, r, s are relational Alloy expressions, i, j are integer Alloy expressions, F, G are Alloy formulas, $\mathcal{T}_i$ gives the JML type corresponding to the type of the ith column of the given relation, the translation contexts $c_i, c', c*$ are extensions of c with the mappings from the Alloy variables to the JML variables.

R₁: $\mathcal{E}(\text{v}\|p_1)_c$ $:= p_1(c(\text{v}))$

R₂: $\mathcal{E}(\text{T}\|p_1)_c$ $:= (\backslash\texttt{exists } c(\text{T}) \texttt{ obj}; p_1(\texttt{obj}))$

R₃: $\mathcal{E}(\text{member}\|p_1, p_2)_c$ $:= (\backslash\texttt{exists } \mathcal{T}_1[\text{member}] \texttt{ obj}; p_1(\texttt{obj}) \texttt{ \&\& } p_2(\texttt{obj}.c(\text{member})))$

R₄: $\mathcal{E}(\text{none}\|p_1)_c$ $:= \texttt{false}$

R₅: $\mathcal{E}(\text{n}\|p_1)_c$ $:= p_1(\text{n})$

R₆: $\mathcal{E}(\text{r.s}\|p_1, ..., p_{n+m})_c := (\backslash\texttt{exists } \mathcal{T}_1[\text{s}] \texttt{ obj}; \mathcal{E}(\text{r}\|p_1, ..., p_n, \mathit{lift}(\texttt{obj}))_c$
                       $\texttt{\&\& } \mathcal{E}(\text{s}\|\mathit{lift}(\texttt{obj}), p_{n+1}, ..., p_{n+m})_c)$
               where $n = arity(\text{r}) - 1$ and $m = arity(\text{s}) - 1$

R₇: $\mathcal{E}(\text{r + s}\|p_1, ..., p_n)_c$ $:= (\mathcal{E}(\text{r}\|p_1, ..., p_n)_c \texttt{ || } \mathcal{E}(\text{s}\|p_1, ..., p_n)_c)$

R₈: $\mathcal{E}(\text{r \& s}\|p_1, ..., p_n)_c$ $:= (\backslash\texttt{exists } \mathcal{T}_1[\text{r\&s}] \text{o}_1, ..., \mathcal{T}_n[\text{r\&s}] \text{o}_n; p_1(\text{o}_1) \texttt{ \&\&} ... \texttt{\&\& } p_n(\text{o}_n) \texttt{ \&\&}$
                $\texttt{\&\& } \mathcal{E}(\text{r}\|\mathit{lift}(\text{o}_1), ..., \mathit{lift}(\text{o}_n))_c \texttt{ \&\& } \mathcal{E}(\text{s}\|\mathit{lift}(\text{o}_1), ..., \mathit{lift}(\text{o}_n))_c)$

R₉: $\mathcal{E}(\text{r - s}\|p_1, ..., p_n)_c$ $:= (\backslash\texttt{exists } \mathcal{T}_1[\text{r-s}] \text{o}_1, ..., \mathcal{T}_n[\text{r-s}] \text{o}_n; p_1(\text{o}_1) \texttt{ \&\&} ... \texttt{\&\& } p_n(\text{o}_n) \texttt{ \&\&}$
                $\mathcal{E}(\text{r}\|\mathit{lift}(\text{o}_1), ..., \mathit{lift}(\text{o}_n))_c \texttt{ \&\& } !\mathcal{E}(\text{s}\|\mathit{lift}(\text{o}_1), ..., \mathit{lift}(\text{o}_n))_c)$

R₁₀: $\mathcal{E}(\text{r ++ s}\|p_1, ..., p_n)_c$ $:= (\backslash\texttt{exists } \mathcal{T}_1[\text{r++s}] \texttt{ obj}; p_1(\texttt{obj}) \texttt{ \&\& } (\mathcal{E}(\text{b}\|\mathit{lift}(\texttt{obj}), p_2, ..., p_n)_c \texttt{ ||}$
              $(\mathcal{E}(\text{r}\|\mathit{lift}(\texttt{obj}), p_2, ..., p_n)_c \texttt{ \&\& } !\mathcal{E}(\text{s}\|\mathit{lift}(\texttt{obj}), \underline{nonnull}, ...)_c)))$
                                             $n - 1$ times

R₁₁: $\mathcal{E}(\text{r -> s}\|p_1, ..., p_{n+m})_c := (\mathcal{E}(\text{r}\|p_1, ..., p_n)_c \texttt{ \&\& } \mathcal{E}(\text{s}\|p_{n+1}, ..., p_{n+m})_c)$
               where $n = arity(\text{r})$ and $m = arity(\text{s})$

R₁₂: $\mathcal{E}(\tilde{}\text{r}\|p_1, ..., p_n)_c$ $:= \mathcal{E}(\text{r}\|p_n, ..., p_1)_c$

R₁₃: $\mathcal{E}(\{\text{v}_1 : \text{r}_1, ..., \text{v}_n : \text{r}_n \mid \text{F} \}\|p_1, ..., p_n)_c :=$
     $(\backslash\texttt{exists } \mathcal{T}_1[\text{v}_1] \text{o}_1, ..., \mathcal{T}_1[\text{v}_n] \text{o}_n; p_1(\text{o}_1) \texttt{ \&\& } ... \texttt{\&\& } p_n(\text{o}_n)$
     $\texttt{\&\& } \mathcal{E}(\text{r}_1\|\mathit{lift}(\text{o}_1))_{c_1} \texttt{ \&\& } ... \texttt{\&\& } \mathcal{E}(\text{r}_n\|\mathit{lift}(\text{o}_n))_{c_n} \texttt{ \&\& } \mathcal{B}(\text{F})_{c_{n+1}})$

R₁₄: $\mathcal{E}(\#\text{r}\|p_1)_c := p_1(\backslash\texttt{num\_of } \mathcal{T}_1[\text{r}] \text{o}_1, ..., \mathcal{T}_n[\text{r}] \text{o}_n; \mathcal{E}(\text{r}\|\mathit{lift}(\text{o}_1), ..., \mathit{lift}(\text{o}_n))_c)$

R₁₅: $\mathcal{E}(\texttt{sum v: r | i}\|p_1)_c := p_1(\backslash\texttt{sum } \mathcal{T}_1[\text{r}] \texttt{ obj}; \mathcal{E}(\text{r}\|\mathit{lift}(\texttt{obj}))_c; \mathcal{I}(\text{i})_{c'})$

R₁₆: $\mathcal{B}(\text{F and G})_c := (\mathcal{B}(\text{F})_c \texttt{ \&\& } \mathcal{B}(\text{G})_c)$ **R₁₇:** $\mathcal{B}(\text{F or G})_c := (\mathcal{B}(\text{F})_c \texttt{ || } \mathcal{B}(\text{G})_c)$

R₁₈: $\mathcal{B}(!\text{F})_c := (!\mathcal{B}(\text{F})_c)$ **R₁₉:** $\mathcal{B}(\text{F iff G})_c := (\mathcal{B}(\text{F})_c \texttt{ <==> } \mathcal{B}(\text{G})_c)$

R₂₀: $\mathcal{B}(\text{F implies G})_c := (\mathcal{B}(\text{F})_c \texttt{ ==> } \mathcal{B}(\text{G})_c)$

R₂₁: $\mathcal{B}(\text{i } op \text{ j})_c := (\mathcal{I}(\text{i})_c \text{ } op \text{ } \mathcal{I}(\text{j})_c)$ where $op \in \{<, >, <=, >=\}$

R₂₂: $\mathcal{B}(\text{r in s})_c := (\backslash\texttt{forall } \mathcal{T}_1[\text{r+s}] \text{o}_1, ..., \mathcal{T}_n[\text{r+s}] \text{o}_n;$
               $\mathcal{E}(\text{r}\|\mathit{lift}(\text{o}_1), ..., \mathit{lift}(\text{o}_n))_c \texttt{ ==> } \mathcal{E}(\text{s}\|\mathit{lift}(\text{o}_1), ..., \mathit{lift}(\text{o}_n))_c)$

R₂₃: $\mathcal{B}(\text{r = s})_c := (\backslash\texttt{forall } \mathcal{T}_1[\text{r+s}] \text{o}_1, ..., \mathcal{T}_n[\text{r+s}] \text{o}_n;$
               $\mathcal{E}(\text{r}\|\mathit{lift}(\text{o}_1), ..., \mathit{lift}(\text{o}_n))_c \texttt{ <==> } \mathcal{E}(\text{s}\|\mathit{lift}(\text{o}_1), ..., \mathit{lift}(\text{o}_n))_c)$

R₂₄: $\mathcal{B}(\text{no r})_c := (!\mathcal{E}(\text{r}\| \underline{nonnull})_c)$ **R₂₅:** $\mathcal{B}(\text{some r})_c := \mathcal{E}(\text{r}\| \underline{nonnull})_c$
                      $arity(\text{r})$ times $arity(\text{r})$ times

R₂₆: $\mathcal{B}(\text{lone r})_c := (\backslash\texttt{forall } \mathcal{T}_1[\text{r}] \text{o}_1, ..., \mathcal{T}_n[\text{r}] \text{o}_n, \mathcal{T}_1[\text{r}] \text{w}_1, ..., \mathcal{T}_n[\text{r}] \text{w}_n;$
               $(\mathcal{E}(\text{r}\|\mathit{lift}(\text{o}_1), ..., \mathit{lift}(\text{o}_n))_c \texttt{ \&\& } \mathcal{E}(\text{r}\|\mathit{lift}(\text{w}_1), ..., \mathit{lift}(\text{w}_n))_c)$
               $\texttt{==> } (\text{o}_1 == \text{w}_1 \texttt{ \&\& } ... \texttt{\&\& } \text{o}_n == \text{w}_n))$

R₂₇: $\mathcal{B}(\text{all v : r | F})_c := (\backslash\texttt{forall } \mathcal{T}_1[\text{r}] \texttt{ obj}; \mathcal{E}(\text{r}\|\mathit{lift}(\texttt{obj}))_c \texttt{ ==> } \mathcal{B}(\text{F})_{c*})$

R₂₈: $\mathcal{B}(\text{some v : r | F})_c := (\backslash\texttt{exists } \mathcal{T}_1[\text{r}] \texttt{ obj}; \mathcal{E}(\text{r}\|\mathit{lift}(\texttt{obj}))_c \texttt{ \&\& } \mathcal{B}(\text{F})_{c*})$

Table 1. (Continued)

R_{29}: (\exists T obj; f_1 && x==obj && f_2(obj))	$\hookrightarrow$ (f_1 && x instanceof T && f_2((T)x))
R_{30}: (\forall T obj; f_1 && x==obj ==> f_2(obj))	$\hookrightarrow$ (f_1 && x instanceof T ==> f_2((T)x))
R_{31}: (\forall T obj; f_1 && x==obj <==> f_2 && y==obj) $\hookrightarrow$ ((f_1 ? x : null) == (f_2 ? y : null))
R_{32}: (x instanceof T) $\hookrightarrow$ (x != null) if the type of x is a subtype of T
R_{33}: ((T)x) $\hookrightarrow$ (x) if the type of x is equal to T
R_{34}: (x != null) $\hookrightarrow$ true if x is statically known to be non-null

The predicates are a generalization of the terms $t_1, ..., t_n$ described in Approach 2. While a term can represent only one element, a predicate can represent a set of elements. This generalization allows a concise and unified translation of simple expressions as well as expressions with transitive closure. It also improves the readability of the resulting JML expressions, because the predicates are used as quantification guards and are propagated to subexpressions where they are needed, thus quantifiers can be introduced locally near the subexpression. The translation uses the predicates $lift(\texttt{obj})$, $nonnull$, $headrec_r$, and $tailrec_r$. The latter two are used for transitive closure, and are defined recursively over r as described in Section 4.2. The semantics of the former predicates is defined by:

$$R_{35}: lift(\texttt{obj})(e) := e\texttt{==obj} \qquad\qquad R_{36}: nonnull(e) := e\texttt{!=null}$$

For relations of arity 1, using the $lift(\texttt{obj})$ predicate with the $\mathcal{E}$ function corresponds to membership semantics[3]: $\mathcal{E}(\texttt{r}\|lift(\texttt{obj}))_c \iff \exists e \in \texttt{r}: lift(\texttt{obj})(e) \iff \exists e \in \texttt{r}: (e\texttt{==obj}) \iff \texttt{obj} \in \texttt{r}$. The usage of the $nonnull$ predicate with the $\mathcal{E}$ function checks whether an Alloy relation is non-empty: $\mathcal{E}(\texttt{r}\|nonnull)_c \iff \exists e \in \texttt{r}: nonnull(e) \iff \exists e \in \texttt{r}: (e! = null) \iff \texttt{r} \neq \emptyset$. Note that if the value of a dereferenced field, say o.f, is non-null, then o.f represents a singleton set containing this value. However, if o.f is null, we treat o.f as the empty set (as in [25]), rather than a set containing null as an element (as in [27]). Using null as a *marker* for empty sets is convenient since it is the only value that can be assigned to any field of any reference type.

The first two sections of Table 1 define $\mathcal{E}$, for relational expressions, and $\mathcal{B}$, for formulas. An additional third function $\mathcal{I}$ is used for integer expressions. Due to space issues, some rules are omitted. We have proved the correctness of the rules with respect to the semantics of the $\mathcal{E}$ function as given above using Isabelle/HOL [20]. These proofs allowed us to discover and fix subtle problems related to Java heap-states and handling of null references. The complete list of rules, correctness proofs, and further details can be found in [16].

To illustrate the details of the translation rules, consider the translation of the expression "no this.next" (using the declarations from Fig. 3).

---

[3] The application of the context c is omitted to improve readability.

$\mathcal{B}(\text{no this.next})_c \overset{R_{24}}{=} (!\mathcal{E}(\text{this.next}\|nonnull)_c)$

$\overset{R_6}{=}$ $(!(\text{\exists Entry t; } \mathcal{E}(\text{this}\|lift(\text{t}))_c \text{ \&\& } \mathcal{E}(\text{next}\|lift(\text{t}), nonnull)_c))$

$\overset{R_1,R_3}{=}$ $(!(\text{\exists Entry t; } lift(\text{t})(\text{this})$
$\text{\&\& } (\text{\exists Entry obj; } lift(\text{t})(\text{obj}) \text{ \&\& } nonnull(\text{obj.next}))))$

$\overset{R_{35},R_{36}}{=}$ $(!(\text{\exists Entry t; this == t}$
$\text{\&\& } (\text{\exists Entry obj; obj == t \&\& obj.next != null})))$

Both quantifiers are redundant due to the equalities this==t and obj==t. The translation is followed by a simplification step. The third section of Table 1 shows a subset of our simplification rules (cf. [16] for complete details). This step dramatically increases the readability and analyzability of the resulting JML formulas. Applying the simplifications to the example yields:

$\mathcal{B}(\text{no this.next})_c \overset{R_{29}}{=} (!(\text{\exists Entry t; this == t}$
$\overset{R_{32},R_{33}}{=}$ $\text{\&\& (t instanceof Entry \&\& ((Entry)t).next != null)))}$
$(!(\text{\exists Entry t; this == t}$
$\text{\&\& (t != null \&\& t.next != null)))}$

$\overset{R_{34}}{=}$ $(!(\text{\exists Entry t; this == t \&\& t.next != null}))$

$\overset{R_{29}}{=}$ $(!(\text{this instanceof Entry \&\& ((Entry)this).next != null}))$

$\overset{R_{32},R_{33}}{=}$ $!(\text{this != null \&\& this.next != null})$

$\overset{R_{34}}{=}$ this.next == null

Note that although Java null value is assumed to be represented as empty set in Alloy specifications, an empty set in Alloy specifications does not always represent null. E.g., our rules translate the formula "no left & right" to:

$(\text{\forall Tree obj; obj.left != null ==> obj.right != obj.left})$

where left and right denote the two pointers of a binary tree.

4.2   Transitive Closure

In [15] we have explored how to specify methods of a linked list using a query (i.e., an observer method) getNext(o,i) that returns the i'th element of the list starting from o. Here we generalize that approach to arbitrary data structures, and support the use of complex Alloy expressions with the transitive closure operator. Given an Alloy relational expression r, we define the query method hasR such that it evaluates to true iff a given object **node** is reachable from object **root** via the relation r in **steps** number of steps:[4]

---

[4] R is always a unique name for r, e.g. left + right gets the name LeftUnionRight.

```
/*@ public normal_behavior
ensures steps < 0 ==> \result == false;
ensures steps == 0 ==> (\result <==> root==node && root != null);
ensures steps > 0 ==> (\result <==> root!=null && E(r‖lift(root), headrecᵣ)c);
ensures steps > 0 ==> (\result <==> node!=null && E(r‖tailrecᵣ, lift(node))c);
measured_by steps;
static model helper pure
boolean hasR(nullable T root, int steps, nullable T node); */
```

In this definition, $T \times T$ is the JML type corresponding to the type of `^r` as determined by Alloy's type inference. The translation predicates $headrec_r$ and $tailrec_r$ recursively call the method hasR and are defined as:

$$headrec_r(e) := (e \ \texttt{instanceof} \ T \ \&\& \ \texttt{hasR}((T)e, \ \texttt{steps-1}, \ \texttt{node}))$$

$$tailrec_r(e) := (e \ \texttt{instanceof} \ T \ \&\& \ \texttt{hasR}(\texttt{root}, \ \texttt{steps-1}, \ (T)e))$$

In the head-recursive **ensures** clause, the $\mathcal{E}$ function is used to produce a JML expression that evaluates to **true** if the relation r contains a pair (root, e), i.e. e is reachable from root in one step, and node is reachable from e in steps-1 steps. Similarly, the tail-recursive postcondition uses $\mathcal{E}$ to produce a JML expression that evaluates to **true** if the relation r contains a pair (e, node) and e is reachable from root in steps-1 steps. For specification, it is sufficient to use either head- or tail-recursion, but having both sometimes simplifies the verification. Using the hasR query definition, we can translate the transitive closure as follows:

R$_{37}$: $\mathcal{E}(\texttt{^r}\|p_1, p_2)_c :=$ (\exists $\mathcal{T}_1$[^r] obj1, obj2; p_1(obj1) && p_2(obj2) &&
(\exists int steps; steps>0; hasR(obj1, steps, obj2)))

The query method, as declared above, does not have access to the variables in the context of its call. To solve this problem, we pass such variables to the query method as additional parameters. For example, consider the expression `^(left + right + (a->b))`, where left and right are fields of a binary tree, and a->b denotes an added edge from node a to b (both program variables). When translated to JML, the parameters list of the query becomes: `Tree root, int steps, Tree node, Tree a, Tree b`.

We disallow taking the transitive closure of a relation that accesses both the pre- and post-state. This is because it is impossible to pass heap states to a JML model method. If the transitive closure relation accesses only the pre-state, we use the \old operator around the call to the query (see Fig. 3). Reflexive transitive closure is translated similarly and is described in [16]. Our Isabelle/HOL proofs do not cover rule R$_{37}$ because, unlike the rules of Table 1, R$_{37}$ requires a more elaborated formalization of JML and Java in order to express the semantics of the query method. Such a formalization could not be done as part of this work. Correctness of this rule has been manually validated instead.

4.3   The Modifies Clause

Each location in a **modifies** clause is given by the syntax r.member, where r is an Alloy expression that specifies the set of objects whose **member** field may

─────── (a) Alloy ───────

```
1    /*$ensures this.*(left' + right').value' = (this.*(left + right).value) + v;
2         ensures (this.*(left' + right') - this.*(left + right)) in freshTree;
3         modifies this.*(left+right).left, this.*(left+right).right; */
```

─────── (b) JML Translation ───────

```
1    /*@ensures (\forall int o1;(\exists Tree o2,int i; i>=0 && hasLR(this,i,o2) && o2.value==o1)
2              <==> \old((\exists Tree o3,int j; j>=0 && hasLR(this,j,o3) && o3.value==o1)) || v == o1);
3    ensures (\forall Tree o1; (\exists int i; i>=0 && hasLR(this,i,o1)) &&
4              (\fresh(o1) || (\forall int j; j>=0 ==> !\old(hasLR(this,j,o1)))) ==> \fresh(o1));
5    ensures (\forall Tree o,int i;!\fresh(o)&&(i>=0==>!\old(hasLR(this,i,o)))==>o.left==\old(o.left));
6    ensures (\forall Tree o,int i;!\fresh(o)&&(i>=0==>!\old(hasLR(this,i,o)))==>o.right==\old(o.right));
7    modifies \infinite_union(Tree o;o.left), \infinite_union(Tree o;o.right); */
```

Fig. 4. Specification of the add method

be modified. Simple expressions (e.g. "`this.length`") can be directly translated into JML. In general, however, the object set cannot be expressed as a JML expression. In this case, Alloy2JML will generate a less specific JML modifies clause which allows modification of the member field of *all* objects rather than the ones specified by the expression r. In JML*, this is done using \infinite_union:

//@ modifies \infinite_union(*Type* obj; obj.*member*);

Furthermore, the translation generates an Alloy post-condition which specifies that the **member** field of any object not included in r remains unchanged:

//$ ensures all v:*Type* - *freshType* - r | v.member'=v.member

This post-condition is translated to JML as usual using the $\mathcal{B}$ function.

5   Evaluation

As a proof of concept that the generated JML specifications indeed are amendable to verification, we have applied Alloy2JML to 6 methods of two Java data structures: `constructor`, `add`, and `removeAt` of `LinkedList` and `constructor`, `contains`, and `add` of `BinarySearchTree`. We have manually written the Alloy specifications, then automatically translated them to JML using Alloy2JML, and proved the resulting JML specifications using the KeY verification engine. The complete experiments are explained in [16] and can be found in http://asa.iti.kit.edu/402.php.

As an example, Fig. 4 shows the specifications of the add method of the class `BinarySearchTree`[5]. The method adds a node to a tree which is defined using its `left`, `right`, and `value` fields. `BinarySearchTree` also includes invariants to preserve sortedness and acyclicity of the tree. These invariants are omitted here due to lack of space. Given a value v, **add** recursively traverses the receiver tree, and inserts a new tree node containing v to the appropriate place if v is not already stored in the tree. The Alloy expression `this.*(left+right)` provides the set of all nodes reachable from the current node. Alloy's relational logic allows us to elegantly express the addition to the set of values in the tree nodes. In Fig. 4(a), Line 1 specifies that the values of the tree nodes in the post-state are

─────────

[5]   In the interest of space, `BinarySearchTree` is named `Tree` in the figure.

the union of the nodes' values in the pre-state and the input argument v; Line 2 specifies that the nodes added to the tree are newly allocated objects. These two lines are translated respectively to Lines 1–2 and 3–4 of Fig. 4(b). Line 3 of Fig. 4(a) indicates that the memory locations referred to by the left and right fields (hereafter *locs*) of any node of the current tree can be changed by the method. Various translations of this modifies clause are possible. Alloy2JML translates this to Lines 5–7 of Fig. 4(b), which we found more amenable to verification. Lines 5–6 specify that the locs of any node that is not in the current tree stay unchanged. Line 7 specifies that the locs of any tree node can be changed by the method.

We used an experimental KeY version that has improved support for recursively specified query methods (e.g. hasLR). The query expansion and quantifier instantiation can be performed automatically in KeY. However, KeY may not always automatically find proofs. For any incomplete branch of the proof, we transformed the problem into first-order SMT logic that contains unbounded integers, uninterpreted functions and quantifiers, and tried to prove it using the Z3 SMT solver. If neither KeY nor Z3 could find an automatic proof, we manually performed explicit instantiations or query expansions, and provided several lemmas to assist KeY. In the case of add, the proof required 75 interactive steps, around 31000 automatic steps, and 40 subgoals were closed by Z3 invocations.

For the data structures that we analyzed, the Alloy specifications are concise (e.g. reachability via arbitrary combinations of fields is expressed easily, and frame conditions are implied elegantly). The generated JML specifications are readable, which is crucial for providing additional lemmas, and are provable using KeY.

To our knowledge, this is the first successful deductive verification of the operations on a tree data structure specified in standard JML. In [3], for example, a much bigger subset of JML* (including abstract data types and other features) is used to verify a remove operation of a tree. This subset, however, cannot be reduced to standard JML.

In order to check the compatibility of our generated JML specifications with JML tools other than KeY, we translated some of our JML* specifications to standard JML as explained in Section 2.2. All of our target JML tools, namely ESC/Java2 [6], JMLForge [8], InspectJ [22], TACO [12], and Krakatoa [10], accepted the resulting JML specifications.

6   Related Work

Several approaches, e.g. [5,17,19], translate the specification languages containing relations into JML. B2JML [5] presents a translation from B machines to JML specifications; in [19] a translation strategy from VDM-SL to JML is presented; and [17] provides a translation technique between OCL and JML. Unlike our approach, these approaches translate the relations of the source language to JML mathematical collections and the relational operators to JML model methods of those collections. We, on the other hand, translate relations to a basic variant of JML which can generally be used in other contexts after making the minor modifications described in Section 2.

JKelloy [14] translates Java programs annotated with Alloy specifications into the first order logic of KeY by defining a special relational theory in KeY. Similar to our approach, it enables full verification of Alloy specifications for Java programs. Alloy2JML, however, does not require any special background theory in the underlying verification engine, but provides a translation that can be used in other contexts as well.

TACO [11] and JMLForge [8] provide fully automated, bounded analysis of JML-annotated Java programs. These tools perform the reverse translation of what we do: they translate JML to a variant of Alloy by introducing the concept of method behavior of JML into Alloy. The resulting Alloy formula is then translated to a SAT problem, and solved using an off-the-shelf SAT solver.

A model transformation from a subset of Alloy to UML class diagrams annotated with OCL is presented in [13]. Their translation and simplifications have ideas common with ours, but their target domain is very different. In [9], we proposed a translation of Alloy to an SMT first-order logic by translating Alloy relations to membership predicates with set semantics. Here, on the other hand, we target Alloy expressions used as specifications of Java programs, and produce well-defined JML expressions (e.g. no null pointer dereferences) that respect the semantics of Java heap. Moreover, specializing the translation enables us to substantially improve the readability of the resulting JML expressions.

In [15], the JML query method `Node getNext(Node o, int n)` is manually specified to verify linked list data structure. The query provides access to the n'th node of the list starting from node o, following the field `next`. It complements the JML `reach` clause by additionally identifying the position of list nodes. Here we generalize that work by automatically generating the query method `hasR` (Section 4.2), which allows us to reason about arbitrary data structures.

7   Conclusion

JML is a popular specification language. Yet, manually specifying certain properties, e.g. those of linked data structures, can be complicated and error-prone when using a basic subset that is supported by most JML tools. On the other hand, Alloy operators (e.g., relational join, transitive closure, set comprehension, and set cardinality) let users concisely specify such properties. Hence we have built Alloy2JML, a tool that translates Alloy specifications to a basic subset of JML without the use of mathematical sets and containers. In most cases, we convert relational operators into JML first-order logic by quantifying over the elements of relations. For the transitive closure, we introduce recursively specified model methods. The outcome of the translation is suitable for verification and enabled us, among others, to verify methods of a tree class. Using Isabelle/HOL, we proved that our translation is correct for a subset of Alloy.

Alloy2JML also provides an Alloy model as output, thus the Alloy specifications of the code can also be validated using the Alloy Analyzer. Moreover, translating Alloy specifications into JML enables the use of Alloy specifications in a larger set of tools that accept only JML specifications.

Alloy2JML allows both Alloy and JML annotations to be used together, thus enabling to specify each property in the more appropriate language. Each annotation, however, must be written completely either in Alloy or in JML. We plan to design a uniform language that allows Alloy and JML subexpressions to be mixed in a wellformed manner. Such a combination has the potential to bring together the best of both paradigms. We also plan to add support for loop invariants, so that those too can be specified using the Alloy language.

References

1. Becker, K., Leavens, G.T.: Class LinkedList,
   http://www.eecs.ucf.edu/ leavens/JML-release/javadocs/java/util/
   LinkedList.html
2. Beckert, B., Hähnle, R., Schmitt, P.H. (eds.): Verification of Object-Oriented Software. LNCS (LNAI), vol. 4334. Springer, Heidelberg (2007)
3. Bruns, D., Mostowski, W., Ulbrich, M.: Implementation-level verification of algorithms with KeY. STTT, 1–16 (2013)
4. Burdy, L., Cheon, Y., Cok, D., Ernst, M., Kiniry, J., Leavens, G., Leino, R., Poll, E.: An overview of JML tools and applications. STTT 7(3), 212–232 (2005)
5. Cataño, N., Wahls, T., Rueda, C., Rivera, V., Yu, D.: Translating B Machines to JML Specifications. In: 27th ACM Symp. on App. Comp., pp. 1271–1277 (2012)
6. Cok, D.R., Kiniry, J.R.: ESC/Java2: Uniting eSC/Java and JML. In: Barthe, G., Burdy, L., Huisman, M., Lanet, J.-L., Muntean, T. (eds.) CASSIS 2004. LNCS, vol. 3362, pp. 108–128. Springer, Heidelberg (2005)
7. Dennis, G., Chang, F.S.-H., Jackson, D.: Modular verification of code with SAT. In: ISSTA, pp. 109–120. ACM (2006)
8. Dennis, G., Yessenov, K., Jackson, D.: Bounded verification of voting software. In: Shankar, N., Woodcock, J. (eds.) VSTTE 2008. LNCS, vol. 5295, pp. 130–145. Springer, Heidelberg (2008)
9. El Ghazi, A.A., Taghdiri, M.: Relational reasoning via SMT solving. In: Butler, M., Schulte, W. (eds.) FM 2011. LNCS, vol. 6664, pp. 133–148. Springer, Heidelberg (2011)
10. Filliâtre, J.-C., Marché, C.: The why/Krakatoa/Caduceus platform for deductive program verification. In: Damm, W., Hermanns, H. (eds.) CAV 2007. LNCS, vol. 4590, pp. 173–177. Springer, Heidelberg (2007)
11. Galeotti, J.P., Rosner, N., Pombo, C.L., Frias, M.: Analysis of invariants for efficient bounded verification. In: ISSTA, pp. 25–36. ACM (2010)
12. Galeotti, J.P., Rosner, N., Pombo, C.G.L., Frias, M.F.: TACO: Efficient SAT-based bounded verification using symmetry breaking and tight bounds. IEEE Transactions on Software Engineering 39(9), 1283–1307 (2013)
13. Garis, A.G., Cunha, A., Riesco, D.: Translating Alloy specifications to UML class diagrams annotated with OCL. SoSyM, 1–21 (2013)
14. El Ghazi, A.A., Ulbrich, M., Gladisch, C., Tyszberowicz, S., Taghdiri, M.: JKelloy: A proof assistant for relational specifications of java programs. In: Badger, J.M., Rozier, K.Y. (eds.) NFM 2014. LNCS, vol. 8430, pp. 173–187. Springer, Heidelberg (2014)

15. Gladisch, C., Tyszberowicz, S.: Specifying a linked data structure in JML for formal verification and runtime checking. In: Iyoda, J., de Moura, L. (eds.) SBMF 2013. LNCS, vol. 8195, pp. 99–114. Springer, Heidelberg (2013)

16. Grunwald, D.: Translating Alloy specifications to JML. Master's thesis, Karlsruhe Institute of Technology (December 2013), http://asa.iti.kit.edu/410.php

17. Hanada, K., et al.: Implementation of a prototype bi-directional translation tool between OCL and JML. J. Informatics Society 5(2), 89–95 (2013)

18. Jackson, D.: Software Abstractions (revised edition). MIT Press (2012)

19. Jin, D., Yang, Z.: Strategies of Modeling from VDM-SL to JML. In: Advanced Language Processing and Web Information Technology, pp. 320–323 (2008)

20. Klein, G., Nipkow, T.: A machine-checked model for a Java-like language, virtual machine, and compiler. ACM Trans. Program. Lang. Syst, 619–695 (2006)

21. Leavens, G.T., et al.: JML Reference Manual (draft, revision 1.235) (June 2008), http://www.jmlspecs.org/

22. Liu, T., Nagel, M., Taghdiri, M.: Bounded program verification using an SMT solver: A case study. In: ICST, pp. 101–110 (April 2012)

23. Marché, C., et al.: The KRAKATOA tool for certification of JAVA/JAVACARD programs annotated in JML. J. Log. Algebr. Program. 58(1-2), 89–106 (2004)

24. Müller, P., et al.: Modular specification of frame properties in JML. Concurrency and Computation: Practice and Experience 15(2), 117–154 (2003)

25. Vaziri, M.: Finding Bugs in Software with a Constraint Solver. PhD thesis, Massachusetts Institute of Technology (2004)

26. Weiß, B.: Deductive Verification of Object-Oriented Software. PhD thesis, Karlsruhe Institute of Technology (2011)

27. Yessenov, K.T.: A Lightweight Specification Language for Bounded Program Verification. Master's thesis, Massachusetts Institute of Technology (2009)

Assume-Guarantee Abstraction Refinement Meets Hybrid Systems

Sergiy Bogomolov[1], Goran Frehse[2], Marius Greitschus[1], Radu Grosu[3], Corina Pasareanu[4], Andreas Podelski[1], and Thomas Strump[1]

[1] University of Freiburg, Germany
{bogom,greitsch,podelski,strumpt}@informatik.uni-freiburg.de
[2] Université Joseph Fourier Grenoble 1 – Verimag, France
goran.frehse@imag.fr
[3] Vienna University of Technology, Austria
radu.grosu@tuwien.ac.at
[4] NASA Ames Research Center, USA
Corina.S.Pasareanu@nasa.gov

Abstract. Compositional verification techniques in the assume-guarantee style have been successfully applied to transition systems to efficiently reduce the search space by leveraging the compositional nature of the systems under consideration. We adapt these techniques to the domain of hybrid systems with affine dynamics. To build assumptions we introduce an abstraction based on location merging. We integrate the assume-guarantee style analysis with automatic abstraction refinement. We have implemented our approach in the symbolic hybrid model checker SpaceEx. The evaluation shows its practical potential. To the best of our knowledge, this is the first work combining assume-guarantee reasoning with automatic abstraction-refinement in the context of hybrid automata.

1 Introduction

Assume-guarantee (AG) reasoning [14] is a well-known methodology for the verification of large systems. The idea behind is to decompose the verification of a system into the verification of its components, which are smaller and therefore easier to verify. A typical example of such systems would be a system comprised of a controller and a plant. In this work, we mainly concentrate on hybrid systems [1] with *stratified* controllers, i.e., controllers consisting of multiple strata (layers), where each of them is responsible for some particular plant parameter. Assume-guarantee reasoning can be performed using the following rule, ASYM, where P is a safety property and $\mathcal{H}_1 \parallel \mathcal{H}_2$ denotes the parallel composition of components $\mathcal{H}_1$ and $\mathcal{H}_2$, where $\mathcal{H}_1$ is a plant and $\mathcal{H}_2$ is a controller.

$$\frac{1 : \mathcal{H}_1 \parallel A \models P \qquad 2 : \mathcal{H}_2 \models A}{\mathcal{H}_1 \parallel \mathcal{H}_2 \models P}$$

Rule ASYM

E. Yahav (Ed.): HVC 2014, LNCS 8855, pp. 116–131, 2014.

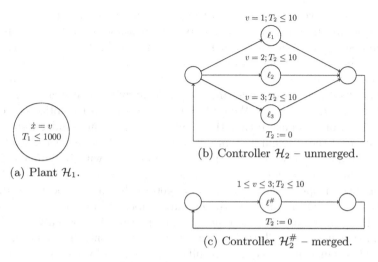

$v = 1; T_2 \leq 10$

ℓ_1

$v = 2; T_2 \leq 10$

ℓ_2

$v = 3; T_2 \leq 10$

ℓ_3

$T_2 := 0$

(b) Controller $\mathcal{H}_2$ – unmerged.

$\dot{x} = v$
$T_1 \leq 1000$

(a) Plant $\mathcal{H}_1$.

$1 \leq v \leq 3; T_2 \leq 10$

$\ell^{\#}$

$T_2 := 0$

(c) Controller $\mathcal{H}_2^{\#}$ – merged.

Fig. 1. A motivating example

In this rule, A denotes an *assumption* about the controller of $\mathcal{H}_1$. Premise 1 ensures that when $\mathcal{H}_1$ is a part of a system that satisfies A, the system also guarantees P. Premise 2 ensures that any system that contains $\mathcal{H}_2$ satisfies A. Together the two premises imply the conclusion of the rule. The rule ASYM is applicable if the assumption A is more abstract than $\mathcal{H}_2$, but still reflects $\mathcal{H}_2$'s behavior. Additionally, an appropriate assumption for the rule needs to be strong enough for $\mathcal{H}_1$ to satisfy P in premise 1.

The most challenging part of applying assume-guarantee reasoning is to come up with appropriate assumptions to use in the application of the assume-guarantee rules. Several learning and abstraction-refinement techniques [5,13] have been proposed for automating the generation of assumptions for the verification of transition systems.

In this paper, we focus on the automated generation of assumptions in the context of hybrid systems. Similar to the work by Bobaru et al. [5] we use abstraction-refinement techniques to iteratively build the assumptions for the rule ASYM. In our case, $\mathcal{H}_2$, i.e., the controller of $\mathcal{H}_1$, is abstracted. The use of over-approximations guarantees that the assumption describes the component correctly and hence premise 2 holds by construction. However, it is possible that premise 1 does not hold, in which case a counterexample is provided. The counterexample is analyzed to see if it is spurious, in which case the abstraction of $\mathcal{H}_2$ is refined to eliminate it. If the counterexample is real, then $\mathcal{H}_1 \parallel \mathcal{H}_2$ violates P.

We present a framework which can efficiently handle the class of affine hybrid systems. Due to the mixed discrete-continuous nature of hybrid systems, we need to pay special attention on the abstraction of continuous dynamics. We illustrate the idea of our compositional analysis on a toy example. Fig. 1 shows a simple hybrid automaton consisting of the plant $\mathcal{H}_1$ in Fig. 1a and controller $\mathcal{H}_2$ in Fig. 1b. We observe that the derivative of variable x in plant $\mathcal{H}_1$ depends on the value of v governed by the controller $\mathcal{H}_2$. Furthermore, we see that the controller operates in iterations of length 10. The possible controller options are grouped in a stratum. While analyzing this system, a hybrid model checker will consider all the three options on every controller iteration which results in 3^n branches for n iterations. By noting that for some properties only the minimal and maximal values of v are of relevance, we come up with an abstracted version of the automaton $\mathcal{H}_2$ in Fig. 1c. We replace the three alternative options by only one *coarser* option. To ensure that the resulting automaton is indeed an over-approximation of the original system, we use $1 \leq v \leq 3$ as an invariant of the merged location $\ell^\#$, i.e., we replace the exact values of v with its bounds. This abstraction will be especially useful to prove, e.g., that within the first 1000 seconds of system operation the state $x = 4000$ will still not be reached. In the abstraction we will reduce an exponential number of branchings to a linear one. Note that this kind of location-merging abstractions is especially useful for the class of stratified controllers. The reason is that the controller structure can be exploited to efficiently generate an initial abstraction by merging locations belonging to the same stratum. Intuitively, this step allows us to adjust the precision level at which the system parameters are taken into account. If the resulting abstraction is too coarse, a finer-grained abstraction is generated in the refinement step.

The lesson we learn from this example is that merging of locations is a promising approach to generate abstractions in scope of the assume-guarantee reasoning paradigm. To ensure the conservativeness of the resulting abstraction, we compute the invariants as a convex hull of the original locations. Note that the computation of minimal and maximal values of v shown above represents a simple case of a general convex hull computation. Given the continuous, affine dynamics of the form $\dot{x}(t) = Ax(t) + u(t)$, the merged locations are computed by first eliminating the (unprimed) state variables and consequently computing the convex hull of the resulting polytopes over the derivatives. As outlined above, sometimes we might end up with *spurious* counterexamples. To overcome this issue we proceed to the phase of spuriousness checking. If the found path is indeed spurious, we refine the system by splitting one or multiple locations and continue with the analysis of this new system. Note that the assume-guarantee reasoning methodology is a variant of the CEGAR approach [6]. The essential difference of AGAR compared to CEGAR is the compositional handling of the system. We develop our approach along these lines by ensuring that the proposed algorithms work in the compositional fashion, e.g., we only abstract a part of the system and the refinement algorithm considers a projection of the found counterexample on the abstracted component. Our implementation in SpaceEx [9] shows the practical potential.

The remainder of the paper is organized as follows. We introduce the necessary preliminary notions in Sec. 2. In Sec. 3, we introduce our compositional framework. This is followed by a discussion about related work in Sec. 4. Afterwards, we present our experimental evaluation in Sec. 5. Finally, we conclude the paper in Sec. 6.

2   Preliminaries

Hybrid automata [11] provide an expressive formalism suitable for modeling complex real-world systems.

Definition 1 (Affine Hybrid Automaton). *An affine hybrid automaton is a tuple $\mathcal{H} = (Loc, Var, Init, Flow, Trans, I)$, where Loc is a finite set of locations, $Var = \{x_1, \ldots, x_n\}$ is a set of real-valued variables, $Init(\ell) \subseteq \mathbb{R}^n$ is the convex set of initial values for $x_1, \ldots, x_n$ for all locations $\ell \in Loc$. For each $\ell \in Loc$, $Flow(\ell)$ is a relation over the variables in Var and their derivatives*

$$\dot{x}(t) = Ax(t) + u(t), u(t) \in \mathcal{U},$$

where $x(t) \in \mathbb{R}^n$, A is a real-valued $n \times n$ matrix and $\mathcal{U} \subseteq \mathbb{R}^n$ is a closed and bounded convex set. Trans is a set of discrete transitions (ℓ, g, ξ, ℓ'), where ℓ and ℓ' are the source and the target locations, g is the guard (given as a linear constraint), and ξ is the update (given by an affine mapping). $I(\ell) \subseteq \mathbb{R}^n$ is the convex invariant for all locations $\ell \in Loc$.

The semantics of hybrid automata is defined as follows. A *state* of $\mathcal{H}$ is a tuple $(\ell, \mathbf{x})$ consisting of a location $\ell \in Loc$ and a point $\mathbf{x} \in \mathbb{R}^n$. More formally, $\mathbf{x}$ is a valuation of the continuous variables in *Var*. Let $T = [0, \Delta]$ be a time interval for some $\Delta \geq 0$. A *trajectory* of $\mathcal{H}$ from state $s = (\ell, \mathbf{x})$ to state $s' = (\ell', \mathbf{x}')$ is defined by a tuple $\rho = (L, \mathbf{X})$, where $L : T \to Loc$ and $\mathbf{X} : T \to \mathbb{R}^n$ are functions that define for each time point in T the location and values of the continuous variables, respectively. The trajectory ρ starts in $(\ell, \mathbf{x})$, ends in $(\ell', \mathbf{x}')$, and obeys the following constraints:

- The sequence of time points in ρ, where the location is changed (according to L) increases strictly monotonically, starts with time point 0, and ends with time point Δ.
- There are no location changes which are not defined by L (i. e., locations are not changed during the continuous evolution).
- For all $t \in T$, the continuous variable evolution is consistent with the differential equation and invariant of $L(t)$.

We define $traj(\mathcal{H})$ as a set of all trajectories ρ for $\Delta \geq 0$. The *length* of the trajectory $|\rho|$ is equal to the number of different locations on it. The initial set of states $S_{init}(\mathcal{H})$ of $\mathcal{H}$ is defined as $\bigcup_{\ell}(\ell, Init(\ell))$. We say that s' is *reachable* from s if a trajectory from s to s' exists. The reachable state space $\mathcal{R}(\mathcal{H})$ of $\mathcal{H}$ is defined as the set of states such that a state s is reachable from $S_{init}(\mathcal{H})$. In this paper, we also refer to *symbolic states*. A symbolic state $s = (\ell, R)$ is defined as a tuple, where $\ell \in Loc$, and R is a convex set consisting of points $\mathbf{x} \in \mathbb{R}^n$. The continuous part R of a symbolic state is also called *region*. The symbolic state space of $\mathcal{H}$ is called the *region space*. The *convex hull* of two regions R_1 and R_2 is denoted by $\mathcal{CH}(R_1 \cup R_2)$. The *path* in the region space is a sequence of symbolic states $\pi = s_0, \ldots, s_{n-1}$. The *length* of the path $|\pi| = n$ is equal to the number of symbolic states on it. We assume without loss of generality that there is a single bad location ℓ_{bad} with unrestricted invariant and flow. Our goal is to find a trajectory from $S_{init}(\mathcal{H})$ to the bad location. A trajectory that starts in a state s and leads to a bad location is called an *error trajectory* $\rho_e(s)$.

Composition of hybrid automata. A *product automaton* $\mathcal{N} = \mathcal{H}_1 || \ldots || \mathcal{H}_m$ denotes a set of interacting hybrid automata. The semantics of $\mathcal{N}$ is defined based on the semantics of a single hybrid automaton, with the following extensions. Every automaton in $\mathcal{N}$ is associated with a finite set of *synchronization labels*, including a special label τ in all label sets. The discrete component of a *state* s of $\mathcal{N}$ is defined as a *vector* of locations that denotes the current locations of every component in $\mathcal{N}$. Similarly, in addition to single automata, a *trajectory* of $\mathcal{N}$ maps time points to vectors of locations of each automaton. For a time point t, changes in the location vectors in a trajectory can either be caused by a single transition labeled with τ of one automaton in $\mathcal{N}$ ("interleaving transition"), or there are several automata in $\mathcal{N}$ that simultaneously fire transitions with equal synchronization labels other than τ ("synchronized transition"). We refer to the work by Donzé et al. [7] for more details.

3   Compositional Framework for Hybrid Systems

In this section, we introduce the main ingredients of our compositional framework: the abstraction of a hybrid system, an algorithm for spuriousness check, and a refinement algorithm.

3.1   Abstraction Algorithm

We construct our abstraction by partially merging system locations. To formally define the abstraction, we introduce a location abstraction function α and a location concretization function α^{-1} as follows.

Definition 2 (Location Abstraction Function). *Location abstraction function* $\alpha : Loc \rightarrow Loc^{\#}$ *provides a mapping from every concrete location in Loc to its abstract counterpart. Furthermore, we require* $|Loc^{\#}| \leq |Loc|$, *i.e., the abstract system should have at most the same number of locations as the original one.*

Definition 3 (Location Concretization Function). *Location concretization function* $\alpha^{-1} : Loc^{\#} \rightarrow 2^{Loc}$ *provides a mapping from every abstract location in* $Loc^{\#}$ *to the set of concrete locations which were merged into it.*

If $\ell \in \alpha^{-1}(\ell^{\#})$, then ℓ is a *corresponding* location to the abstract location $\ell^{\#}$. Furthermore, we abuse the notation and apply a concretization function not only to abstract locations, but also to abstract symbolic states and abstract symbolic paths. We define an abstract hybrid automaton $\mathcal{H}^{\#}$ induced by the location abstraction function α and concrete hybrid automaton $\mathcal{H}$ as follows:

Definition 4 (Location-Merging Abstraction). *Let $\mathcal{H} = (Loc, Var, Init,$ $Flow, Trans, I)$ be a hybrid automaton and $\alpha \; : \; Loc \; \rightarrow \; Loc'$ be a location abstraction function. The abstract automaton $\mathcal{H}^{\#} \; = \; (Loc^{\#}, Var^{\#}, Init^{\#}, Flow^{\#}, Trans^{\#}, I^{\#})$ induced by the location-merging abstraction with respect to the location function α is defined as follows:*

- *$Loc^{\#} = Loc'$, i.e., the location abstraction function provides which locations of $\mathcal{H}$ are to be merged. We assume that α keeps the bad location ℓ_{bad} as a singleton.*
- *$Var^{\#} = Var$, i.e., the abstraction preserves the continuous variables of the original system.*
- *$\forall \ell^{\#} \in Loc^{\#} : Init^{\#}(\ell^{\#}) = \mathcal{CH}(\bigcup_{\ell \in \alpha^{-1}(\ell^{\#})} Init(\ell))$, i.e., the regions describing the initial values in concrete locations are first merged into one (possibly non-convex) set and afterwards are over-approximated by a convex hull. Note that if an abstract location is a singleton, the application of the convex hull operator will result in the original set as we consider only hybrid automata with $Init(\ell)$ being a convex set (see Def. 1).*
- *$\forall \ell^{\#} \in Loc^{\#} :*

$$Flow^{\#}(\ell^{\#})(x, \dot{x}) = \begin{cases} \mathcal{CH}(\bigcup_{\ell \in \alpha^{-1}(\ell^{\#})} F_{\ell}), & |\alpha^{-1}(\ell^{\#})| > 1 \\ Flow(\alpha^{-1}(\ell^{\#}))(x, \dot{x}), & |\alpha^{-1}(\ell^{\#})| = 1 \end{cases}$$

where $F_{\ell} = \exists x : (Flow(\ell)(x, \dot{x}) \wedge I(\ell)(x))$.
- *$Trans^{\#} = \{(\ell^{\#}, g, \xi, \hat{\ell}^{\#}) | \exists \ell \in \alpha^{-1}(\ell^{\#}), \hat{\ell} \in \alpha^{-1}(\hat{\ell}^{\#})$ s.t. $(\ell, g, \xi, \hat{\ell}) \in Trans\}$, i.e., an abstract transition between $\ell^{\#}$ and $\hat{\ell}^{\#}$ is added when a transition in the concrete state space connecting the corresponding locations exists.*
- *$\forall \ell^{\#} \in Loc^{\#} : I^{\#}(\ell^{\#}) = \mathcal{CH}(\bigcup_{\ell \in \alpha^{-1}(\ell^{\#})} I(\ell))$, i.e., similarly to the initial regions, the invariants are merged and over-approximated by a convex hull.*

In other words, we merge the dynamics of multiple locations in two steps. We first over-approximate the original dynamics in every concrete location by quantifying away unprimed variables, i.e., we obtain a constraint reasoning only about derivatives (see Fig. 2). Secondly, we define abstract dynamics by constructing a convex hull of the constraints computed in the first step. If an abstract location is a singleton, i.e., $|\alpha^{-1}(\ell^{\#})| = 1$, we just keep its original dynamics.

We observe that by construction the set of reachable states of the abstract automaton $\mathcal{H}^{\#}$ leads to an over-approximation compared to the states reachable by the concrete automaton $\mathcal{H}$. Therefore, the following proposition holds:

Proposition 1. *Let $\mathcal{H}^{\#}$ be a location-merging abstraction of the concrete hybrid automaton $\mathcal{H}$. Then the non-reachability of the bad location ℓ_{bad} in $\mathcal{H}^{\#}$ implies its non-reachability also in the concrete automaton $\mathcal{H}$.*

3.2 Compositional Analysis

Our compositional analysis is illustrated in Algorithm 1. In order to simplify the presentation we consider a case of a system consisting of two components

Dynamics:
$\dot{x} = 2x + 3y$
$\dot{y} = 4x - 5y$

Dynamics:
$\dot{x} = -x + 3y + 5$
$\dot{y} =\ \ x + 2y$

Invariant:
$\ \ 0 \le x \le 1$
$\wedge\ 0 \le y \le 1$

Invariant:
$\ \ 1 \le x \le 3$
$\wedge\ -1 \le y \le 0.3$

F_1:
$\ \ -5\dot{x} - 3\dot{y} \le 0$
$\wedge\ -22 + 5\dot{x} + 3\dot{y} \le 0$
$\wedge\ -2\dot{x} + \dot{y} \le 0$
$\wedge\ -11 + 2\dot{x} - \dot{y} \le 0$

F_2:
$\ \ -5 + 2\dot{x} - 3\dot{y} \le 0$
$\wedge\ -5 - 2\dot{x} + 3\dot{y} \le 0$
$\wedge\ -\dot{x} - \dot{y} \le 0$
$\wedge\ -6.5 + \dot{x} + \dot{y} \le 0$

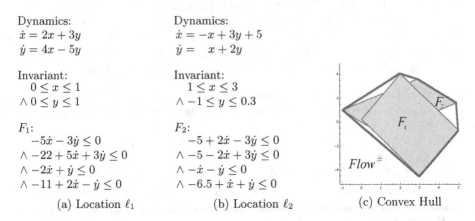

(a) Location ℓ_1 (b) Location ℓ_2 (c) Convex Hull

Fig. 2. Elimination of unprimed variables before merging of the locations

$\mathcal{H}_1$ and $\mathcal{H}_2$, where $\mathcal{H}_1$ is a plant and $\mathcal{H}_2$ is a controller. However, the scheme is applicable to systems with more than two components [5].

In the following we provide a conceptual description of the algorithm. The algorithm checks whether the bad state S_{bad} can be reached by the system $\mathcal{H}_1 || \mathcal{H}_2$. The algorithm starts by computing an abstraction of $\mathcal{H}_2$ in the function CONSTRUCTABSTRACTION (line 1). For more details on the abstraction construction see Sec. 3.1. The algorithm iteratively refines the original abstraction (lines 2–14). Note that in the worst case we will end up with the original system. However, in many cases we will need to refine only a part of the system (see Sec. 5 for the detailed discussion). In every refinement iteration the algorithm proceeds as follows. First, the state space of the abstract system $\mathcal{H}_1 || \mathcal{H}_2^{\#}$ is analyzed in the function ANALYSIS (line 3). This function returns an abstract bad path or "empty" if no such path has been found. If no abstract bad path has been found, we can conclude that also the original system is safe as we consider only over-approximations (line 5). Otherwise, the algorithm proceeds in the function SPURIOUSNESSANALYSIS (line 7) with the spuriousness analysis of the found abstract bad path $\pi^{\#}$. The function SPURIOUSNESSANALYSIS returns the information on how to refine $\mathcal{H}_2^{\#}$ or "empty" if the abstract path $\pi^{\#}$ can be concretized. In the latter case, we exit with status "System is unsafe" (line 9). Otherwise, $\mathcal{H}_2^{\#}$ is refined in the function REFINEMENT based on the structure of the abstract bad path gained during the spuriousness analysis.

3.3   Spuriousness Check

In this section, we consider the function SPURIOUSNESSANALYSIS (see Algorithm 2) in more detail. Given an abstract bad path $\pi^{\#} = s_0^{\#}, \ldots, s_{m-1}^{\#}$, the function enumerates concrete paths corresponding to $\pi^{\#}$ and looks for the ones which end up in a bad state. The enumeration of concrete paths of the composed automaton

---

Algorithm 1. Compositional analysis of $\mathcal{H}_1 \| \mathcal{H}_2$

Input: Hybrid automata $\mathcal{H}_1$ and $\mathcal{H}_2$
Output: Is the composed system $\mathcal{H}_1 \| \mathcal{H}_2$ safe?
1: $\mathcal{H}_2^\# := \text{ConstructAbstraction} (\mathcal{H}_2)$
2: **while** *true* **do**
3:    $\pi^\# := \text{Analysis} (\mathcal{H}_1 \| \mathcal{H}_2^\#)$
4:    **if** $\pi^\#$ is empty **then**
5:       **return** "System is safe"
6:    **else**
7:       $\mathcal{SP} := \text{SpuriousnessAnalysis} (\mathcal{H}_1, \mathcal{H}_2, \mathcal{H}_2^\#, \pi^\#)$
8:       **if** $\mathcal{SP}$ is empty **then**
9:          **return** "System is unsafe"
10:      **else**
11:         $\mathcal{H}_2^\# := \text{Refinement} (\mathcal{H}_2^\#, \mathcal{SP})$
12:      **end if**
13:   **end if**
14: **end while**

$\mathcal{H}_1 \| \mathcal{H}_2$ along the abstract path $\pi^\#$ is organized in a breadth-first fashion. In particular, we make use of two lists: $\mathcal{L}_{waiting}$ and $\mathcal{L}_{passed}$. $\mathcal{L}_{waiting}$ stores symbolic states which still have to be considered and $\mathcal{L}_{passed}$ stores symbolic states which have already been considered and thus do not have to be visited again. The data structure $\mathcal{SP}$ stores information relevant for the refinement step. In particular, tuples $(\pi^\#, \pi)$, where π is a path in the concrete state space which does not belong to $\alpha^{-1}(\pi^\#)$, are kept in $\mathcal{SP}$. In other words, in the last symbolic state $s_{|\pi|-1}$ of π we cannot take any discrete transition which would lead to some concrete state represented by an abstract state $s_{|\pi|}^\#$. Therefore, a tuple $(\pi^\#, \pi)$ essentially provides a possible *reason* for the spuriousness of π with respect to $\pi^\#$. We will use this information to refine the abstract component $\mathcal{H}_2^\#$ (see Sec. 3.4).

The algorithm starts by pushing the concrete initial states which correspond to the first abstract symbolic state $s_0^\#$ in $\mathcal{L}_{waiting}$ (line 2). It is important to mention that α^{-1} concretizes only the part of the symbolic state relevant to $\mathcal{H}_2^\#$. This property also holds for the algorithm described in Sec. 3.4. Note that we furthermore store the position of the abstract state which corresponds to the considered concrete symbolic state in the waiting list (we start with $s_0^\#$ and thus the position is 0). We will consequently use this information to compute the discrete symbolic successors of a given symbolic state which correspond to the analyzed bad path $\pi^\#$. In lines 3–20 the concrete state space is iteratively explored in a breadth-first manner. Every iteration consists of the following steps. First, the next tuple (s_{curr}, i) is picked from the waiting list $\mathcal{L}_{waiting}$ (line 4), where s_{curr} is a symbolic state and i shows its position with respect to the abstract path. Afterwards, the continuous successor, i.e., a symbolic state reflecting the states reachable according to the continuous dynamics, is computed and added to the passed list $\mathcal{L}_{passed}$ (lines 5–6). If the end of the abstract path

---

Algorithm 2. Spuriousness analysis

Input: Concrete automaton $\mathcal{H}_1$, concrete automaton $\mathcal{H}_2$ and its abstract version $\mathcal{H}_2^{\#}$
and abstract bad path $\pi^{\#} = s_0^{\#}, \ldots, s_{m-1}^{\#}$ in the state space of $\mathcal{H}_1 \| \mathcal{H}_2^{\#}$.

Output: Information about the possible splitting points store or empty set if the
abstract bad path $\pi^{\#}$ is concretizable

1: $\mathcal{SP} := \emptyset$
2: PUSH $(\mathcal{L}_{waiting}, (\alpha^{-1}(s_0^{\#}) \cap S_{init}(\mathcal{H}_1 \| \mathcal{H}_2), 0))$
3: **while** $\mathcal{L}_{waiting} \neq \emptyset$ **do**
4:     $(s_{curr}, i) := $ GETNEXT $(\mathcal{L}_{waiting})$
5:     $s'_{curr} := $ CONTSUCCESSORS (s_{curr})
6:     PUSH $(\mathcal{L}_{passed}, s'_{curr})$
7:     **if** $i = m - 1$ **then**
8:         **if** s'_{curr} is a symbolic error state **then**
9:             **return** empty set, i.e., concrete bad state found
10:         **else**
11:             Store the abstract bad path $\pi^{\#}$ and the corresponding concrete path π
                ending in s'_{curr} into $\mathcal{SP}$
12:         **end if**
13:     **end if**
14:     $S' := $ DISCRETESUCCESSORS $(s'_{curr}) \cap \alpha^{-1}(s_{i+1}^{\#})$
15:     **if** S' is empty **then**
16:         Store the abstract bad path $\pi^{\#}$ and the corresponding concrete path π ending
            in s'_{curr} into $\mathcal{SP}$
17:     **else**
18:         PUSH $(\mathcal{L}_{waiting}, S' \setminus \mathcal{L}_{passed}, i + 1)$
19:     **end if**
20: **end while**
21: **return** $\mathcal{SP}$

---

is reached then the intersection with the bad state is checked (lines 8–10). If the
end of the abstract path is reached, but no intersection with the bad state is
detected, we store both the abstract and concrete paths in $\mathcal{SP}$ in order to use
this information in the refinement step. If the algorithm is still in the middle of
the abstract bad path, it moves on to the computation of the concrete symbolic
states which correspond to the abstract bad path (line 14). We achieve this by
computing discrete successors and intersecting them with the concrete states
represented by the next symbolic state on the abstract path. Note that the
position i allows the algorithm to easily find the next abstract symbolic state on
the path with respect to the currently considered concrete state.

If the set of discrete successors is empty, we say that a possible *splitting point*
has been found. In other words, we could refine the abstract location $\ell_i^{\#}$ of
$s_i^{\#} = (\ell_i^{\#}, R_i^{\#})$ by splitting it (see Sec. 3.4). We store the abstract bad path and
the concrete path we have considered up to now into $\mathcal{SP}$ (line 16). Otherwise,
we add the discrete state into the waiting list $\mathcal{L}_{waiting}$ (line 18). After having
analyzed all concrete paths corresponding to $\pi^{\#}$, the function SPURIOUSNESS-
ANALYSIS returns $\mathcal{SP}$. It is only possible to report that the considered abstract

bad path is not concretizable after having considered all possible concrete paths corresponding to it. Thus, the algorithm does not stop after discovering a particular splitting point, but just stores it for the later reuse during the refinement.

While mapping an abstract bad path to a concrete one, Algorithm 2 refers to the functions CONTSUCCESSORS and DISCRETESUCCESSORS which are applied to concrete symbolic states. Thus, if the function SPURIOUSNESSANALYSIS declares some abstract bad path $\pi^{\#}$ to be genuine by finding its concrete counterpart π, then we can automatically conclude that the standard SpaceEx reachability algorithm would also have reported π to be a bad path. Therefore, our framework provides the same level of precision as the standard SpaceEx reachability algorithm. Finally, we note that the full concretization of a symbolic path is known to be a highly nontrivial problem. Once a concrete symbolic bad path is found with our approach, further concretization to hybrid automaton trajectories can be achieved using techniques from optimal control such as the one proposed in the work by Zutshi et al. [17].

3.4   Refinement Algorithm

The refinement algorithm REFINEMENT uses $\mathcal{SP}$ in order to appropriately refine the abstraction $\mathcal{H}_2^{\#}$ in a compositional way. The data structure $\mathcal{SP}$ contains information about multiple possible splitting points. For the refinement we choose a tuple $(\pi^{\#}, \pi_{max}) \in \mathcal{SP}$ which *maximizes* the length of the concrete path π over all the elements of $\mathcal{SP}$. Intuitively, by choosing a tuple with this property, we ensure that π_{max} cannot be extended for all concrete paths which correspond to $\pi^{\#}$. Let the abstract bad path $\pi^{\#} = s_0^{\#}, \ldots, s_i^{\#}, \ldots, s_n^{\#}$ and the concrete path $\pi_{max} = s_0, \ldots, s_i, \ldots, s_m$ $(m \leq n)$, where $s_i = (\ell_i, R_i)$ and $s_i^{\#} = (\ell_i^{\#}, R_i^{\#})$. Furthermore, $\ell_i = (\ell_i^{(1)}, \ell_i^{(2)})$, where $\ell_i^{(1)}$ and $\ell_i^{(2)}$ are locations of $\mathcal{H}_1$ and $\mathcal{H}_2$, respectively. The location of the abstracted composed automaton $\mathcal{H}_1 || \mathcal{H}_2^{\#}$ is given by the tuple $\ell_i^{\#} = (\ell_i^{(1)}, \ell_i^{\#(2)})$. Depending on the location partitioning of $\mathcal{H}_2^{\#}$ the refinement algorithm distinguishes three cases:

1. $|\alpha^{-1}(\ell_m^{\#(2)})| > 1$, i.e., the abstract location corresponding to the last concrete location can be split:

   The refinement algorithm proceeds by splitting the abstract location $\ell_m^{\#(2)}$ of $\mathcal{H}_2^{\#}$ into two locations: $\alpha^{-1}(\ell_m^{\#(2)}) \setminus \ell_m^{(2)}$ and $\ell_m^{(2)}$, where $\ell_m^{(2)}$ is a location of $\mathcal{H}_2$ corresponding to the concrete symbolic state $s_m = ((\ell_m^{(1)}, \ell_m^{(2)}), R_m)$.

2. $|\alpha^{-1}(\ell_m^{\#(2)})| = 1$ and $|\alpha^{-1}(\ell_{m+1}^{\#(2)})| > 1$, i.e., the abstract location of $\mathcal{H}_2^{\#}$ corresponding the last concrete location cannot be split, whereas the successor abstract location still comprises multiple locations:

   The refinement algorithm splits $\ell_{m+1}^{\#(2)}$ into $\alpha^{-1}(\ell_{m+1}^{\#(2)}) \setminus \ell'$ and ℓ', where $\ell' = \{\ell | \ell \in \ell_{m+1}^{\#(2)}$ and ℓ is a target location of discrete transition from $\ell_m^{\#(2)} \}$. In other words, we look for locations in $\ell_{m+1}^{\#(2)}$ which have incoming transitions from $\ell_m^{\#(2)}$ and split them apart. Note that in this case we do not look at the transition guard and any other continuous artifacts.

3. $|\alpha^{-1}(\ell_m^{\#(2)})| = 1$ and $|\alpha^{-1}(\ell_{m+1}^{\#(2)})| = 1$, i.e., neither the abstract location corresponding to the last concrete location nor its successor can be split: The algorithm iterates over the abstract path and looks for a abstract state in $\mathcal{H}_2^{\#}$ with a location which still can be split, i.e., we look for i s.t. $i < m \wedge |\alpha^{-1}(\ell_i^{\#(2)})| > 1$. The location $\ell_i^{\#(2)}$ is split into locations $\alpha^{-1}(\ell_i^{\#(2)}) \setminus \ell_i^{(2)}$ and $\ell_i^{(2)}$, where $\ell_i^{(2)}$ is a location of $\mathcal{H}_2$ corresponding to $s_i = ((\ell_i^{(1)}, \ell_i^{(2)}), R_i)$.

Therefore, during the refinement process, we only refer to the locations of the abstracted component $\mathcal{H}_2^{\#}$, i.e., we consider the projection of the found path to $\mathcal{H}_2^{\#}$. The refinement algorithm as described above also has a progress property:

Proposition 2 (Progress Property). *The size of the location partitioning increases by one location after every application of the refinement algorithm over cases 1–3.*

Proof. By construction, the number of locations in $\mathcal{H}_2^{\#}$ increases by one in cases 1 and 2 after every refinement iteration. In case 3 the refinement can be only done under the assumption that there exists an index i s.t. $i < m \wedge |\alpha^{-1}(\ell_i^{\#(2)})| > 1$ holds. This statement is true as the opposite would mean that the whole abstract bad path $\pi^{\#}$ only consists of *concrete* states. This in turn would lead to the fact that $\pi^{\#}$ is already a concrete path to the bad state. The function RE-FINEMENT is, however, called only for abstract bad paths which were found to be spurious.   □

This proposition lets us conclude that Algorithm 1 terminates after a finite number of iterations after having considered the original system in the worst case. By combining this result with Proposition 1 and rule ASYM, we can derive the following soundness and relative completeness results:

Theorem 1 (Soundness). *If our compositional framework is able to prove that $\mathcal{H}_1 \| A$ cannot reach the (abstract) error states, then the composition $\mathcal{H}_1 \| \mathcal{H}_2$ is safe, that is, it cannot reach the (concrete) error states.*

Theorem 2 (Relative Completeness). *If our compositional framework is able to find a symbolic error path in $\mathcal{H}_1 \| A$ which is not spurious, then there exists a concrete symbolic error path in the composition $\mathcal{H}_1 \| \mathcal{H}_2$, too.*

The existence of a symbolic error path does not necessarily imply the existence of an error trajectory (due to the undecidability of the reachability problem for affine hybrid automata). This is why we call the above result (for symbolic paths) relative completeness.

4   Related Work

The framework developed by Pasareanu et al. [13] enables automated compositional verification using rule ASYM. In that work, both assumptions and properties are expressed as finite state automata. The framework uses the L* [4] automata-learning algorithm to iteratively compute assumptions in the form of deterministic finite-state automata. Other learning-based approaches for automating assumption generation for rule ASYM have been suggested as well [3]. All these approaches were done in the context of transition systems, not for hybrid systems as we do here.

Several ways to compute abstractions of hybrid automata have been proposed. Alur et al. [2] propose to use a variant of predicate abstraction to construct a hybrid automaton abstraction. In a slightly different setting, Tiwari [16] suggests to use Lie derivatives to generate useful predicates. Both mentioned approaches essentially reduce the analysis of a hybrid automaton to the level of a discrete transition system. Jha et al. [12] partially eliminate continuous variables in the system under consideration. Prabhakar et al. [15] propose the use of CEGAR for initialized rectangular automata (IRA), where the abstractions reduce the complexity of both the continuous and the discrete dynamics. In this paper, we use a similar idea, but apply it to the more general class of affine hybrid automata, and even more importantly, we extend it to a compositional verification framework. Finally, Doyen et al. [8] take an affine automaton, and, through hybridization, obtain its abstraction in the form of a rectangular automaton with larger discrete space. We do the opposite: we take an affine automaton, and construct a much smaller linear hybrid automaton.

5   Evaluation

5.1   Benchmarks

For the evaluation of our approach we have extended the switched buffer network benchmark [10]. The system under consideration consists of multiple tanks connected by channels. The channels are used to transport the liquid stored in the tanks. There are two special tanks: the liquid enters the network through the *initial* tank and is transported towards the *sink* tank. We consider properties reasoning about the fill level of the sink tank.

The rate of change of the fill level f_T of a tank T, depends on the rates of inflow $v_{in\,i}$ and the rates of outflow $v_{out\,j}$ of the liquid, where $v_{in\,i}$ is the velocity at which the liquid flows into the tank of the i-th input channel, and $v_{out\,j}$ is the velocity at which the liquid flows out of the tank for the j-th output channel. Therefore, the evolution of the fill level of the tank T is described by the differential equation $\dot{f}_T = \sum_i v_{in\,i} - \sum_j v_{out\,j}$, where i and j range over incoming and outgoing channels of T, respectively. Note that due to fine-granular modelling of tanks and channels this benchmark class exhibits a large number of continuous variables. In particular, in our benchmark suite the number of continuous variables is in the range from 17 to 21 for the buffer networks with up to 4 tanks, whereas it is well-known that the analysis complexity of hybrid automata rapidly grows with the number of variables in the system under consideration.

We extend the switched buffer network [10] by the model of a complex *stratified* controller. The controller is organized in a number of phases of some given length, where multiple options (governing the modes of particular channels) are available in every phase. After having finished the last phase the controller returns to the first one. The controller can open/close channels and adjust the throughput values at every step. We consider the following modes of controller operations:

1. Throughput provided by an interval ("No Dynamics"): when the channel is activated, its throughput v is constrained by the inequality $v_{min} \le v \le v_{max}$.
2. Throughput evolving at a constant rate ("Constant Dynamics"): the throughput is defined by the differential equation of the form $\dot{v} = c$ for some constant c.
3. Throughput evolving according to affine dynamics $\dot{v} = c(v_{target} - v)$ ("Affine Dynamics"): the controller provides a target throughput velocity v_{target} and some constant factor c. According to this dynamics the channel opens gradually with the opening speed decaying towards the target velocity.

5.2   Experiments

We have implemented our approach in SpaceEx [9]. The implementation and the benchmarks are available at http://swt.informatik.uni-freiburg.de/tool/spaceex/agar. The experiments were conducted on a machine with an Intel Core i7 3.4 GHz processor and with 16 GB of memory. In the following, we report the results for our compositional analysis implemented in SpaceEx. We compare the analysis results of the original concrete system and the compositional analysis. For both settings, we compare the number of iterations of SpaceEx and the whole analysis run-time in seconds (see Table 1). The best results are highlighted in bold. We analyze 12 structurally different benchmark instances. For each of them we vary forbidden states and in this way end up with 36 different benchmark settings. We also vary controller dynamics. In particular, we provide 12 instances for each of the modes "No Dynamics", "Constant Dynamics" and "Affine Dynamics". The number of continuous variables varies in the considered benchmark instances from 17 to 21 variables. The initial abstraction is generated by merging some of the strata in the controller.

We observe that our compositional reasoning algorithm generally boosts the run time compared to the analysis of the original system. For example, in instance 4 (system is safe) the analysis of the concrete system takes around 609 seconds compared to around 158 seconds with the compositional analysis. The speed-up is justified by the smaller branching factor due to location merging. In Fig. 3a and Fig. 3b the fill level of sink tank vs. time for the original system and the initial abstraction are plotted. Fig. 3b particularly shows that multiple "thin" flow-pipes are merged into a couple of "thick" ones, i.e., the system stops differentiating between some options in the controller.

Table 1. Experimental results for the switched buffer benchmark. Abbreviations: #: benchmark instance number, Res.: result of the system analysis, i.e., whether the bad state can be reached, Tanks: number of tanks in the instance, Vars.: number of continuous variables in the system, Phases: number of phases in the controller and number of options in every phase, Refs.: number of refinement steps, It. (u): number of SpaceEx iterations when analyzing the concrete (unmerged) system, It. (m): number of SpaceEx iterations in scope of the compositional analysis, Time (u): total time in seconds of the analysis of the concrete system, Time (m): total time in seconds of the compositional analysis.

#	Res.	Tanks	Vars.	Phases	Refs.	It. (u)	It. (m)	Time (u)	Time (m)
				No Dynamics					
1	safe	3	17	2 (5,1)	0	4640	**253**	779.754	**14.692**
2	unsafe	3	17	2 (5,1)	0	2555	**191**	299.437	**35.370**
3	safe	3	17	2 (5,1)	1	4640	**1744**	796.218	**191.841**
4	safe	3	17	4 (6,1,2,1)	0	3242	**1115**	608.796	**157.924**
5	unsafe	3	17	4 (6,1,2,1)	0	2410	**756**	196.461	**66.740**
6	safe	3	17	4 (6,1,2,1)	2	3242	**1648**	639.838	**254.653**
7	safe	4	21	2 (5,1)	0	2345	**690**	2162.273	**621.137**
8	unsafe	4	21	2 (5,1)	0	1348	**483**	1139.365	**479.811**
9	safe	4	21	2 (5,1)	1	2345	**1001**	2164.069	**937.064**
10	safe	4	21	4 (4,1,2,1)	0	1361	**394**	1327.062	**406.592**
11	unsafe	4	21	4 (4,1,2,1)	0	1070	**316**	502.992	**303.988**
12	safe	4	21	4 (4,1,2,1)	1	1361	**684**	1174.735	**700.072**
				Constant Dynamics					
13	safe	3	17	4 (2,1,5,1)	0	1386	**424**	90.457	**21.484**
14	unsafe	3	17	4 (2,1,5,1)	0	461	**232**	18.773	**10.807**
15	safe	3	17	4 (2,1,5,1)	2	1386	**1261**	81.076	**77.938**
16	safe	3	17	6 (2,1,6,1,2,1)	0	1989	**1027**	146.726	**63.878**
17	unsafe	3	17	6 (2,1,6,1,2,1)	0	809	**352**	32.961	**14.279**
18	safe	3	17	6 (2,1,6,1,2,1)	2	**1989**	2041	**142.385**	250.451
19	safe	4	21	4 (2,1,4,1)	0	1293	**787**	1350.973	1318.623
20	unsafe	4	21	4 (2,1,4,1)	0	1080	**682**	1429.120	1298.147
21	safe	4	21	4 (2,1,4,1)	1	1293	**814**	1579.792	1197.098
22	safe	4	21	6 (2,1,4,1,2,1)	0	903	**563**	1255.978	1140.114
23	unsafe	4	21	6 (2,1,4,1,2,1)	0	798	**510**	1230.193	1141.791
24	safe	4	21	6 (2,1,4,1,2,1)	1	903	**581**	1365.629	1318.049
				Affine Dynamics					
25	safe	3	17	4 (2,1,5,1)	0	7747	**1168**	1544.363	**86.046**
26	unsafe	3	17	4 (2,1,5,1)	0	5103	**1042**	939.430	**100.871**
27	safe	3	17	4 (2,1,5,1)	1	7747	**6214**	1669.268	1240.215
28	safe	3	17	6 (2,1,6,1,2,1)	0	6129	**2760**	717.462	**231.727**
29	unsafe	3	17	6 (2,1,6,1,2,1)	0	5382	**2397**	639.342	**203.143**
30	safe	3	17	6 (2,1,6,1,2,1)	7	**6129**	15068	**706.960**	2158.671
31	safe	4	21	4 (2,1,4,1)	0	1718	**1451**	3603.238	3125.016
32	unsafe	4	21	4 (2,1,4,1)	0	1692	**1392**	3776.840	3247.464
33	safe	4	21	4 (2,1,4,1)	1	**1718**	2559	4372.284	3805.045
34	safe	4	21	6 (2,1,4,1,2,1)	0	983	**642**	1382.567	1078.893
35	unsafe	4	21	6 (2,1,4,1,2,1)	0	922	**611**	1206.011	1213.798
36	safe	4	21	6 (2,1,4,1,2,1)	1	983	**755**	1442.506	1321.658

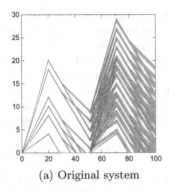 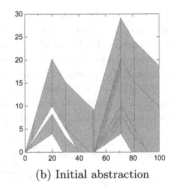

(a) Original system   (b) Initial abstraction

Fig. 3. Fill level of the sink tank for instance 4 vs. time

Furthermore, we remark that our compositional algorithm shows promising results also in the falsification setting, i.e., when the bad state is reachable. In instance 5, our approach reduces the run-time from around 196 seconds for the concrete system to only 67 seconds in scope of the compositional framework.

The necessity to refine the abstraction, in case a spurious abstract bad path has been discovered, can generally be handled efficiently by our framework, e.g., in instance 6 our approach takes around 254 seconds (including two refinement steps) compared to 640 seconds for the concrete system. However, due to an unfortunate choice of the abstract bad path, we might need to refine an excessive number of times (instance 30) which in turn decreases the overall performance.

6   Conclusion

In this paper, we have adapted the idea of compositional analysis to the domain of hybrid systems. We have presented an abstraction based on location merging. The abstract location invariant is computed by taking a convex hull of the concrete locations to be merged. The abstract continuous dynamics are computed by eliminating the state variables and computing a convex hull.

Acknowledgments. This work was partly supported by the German Research Foundation (DFG) as part of the Transregional Collaborative Research Center "Automatic Verification and Analysis of Complex Systems" (SFB/TR 14 AVACS, http://www.avacs.org/). We thank Jannik Rebmann and Simon Ganz for their help with the benchmark suite preparation.

References

1. Alur, R., Courcoubetis, C., Halbwachs, N., Henzinger, T., Ho, P., Nicolin, X., Olivero, A., Sifakis, J., Yovine, S.: The algorithmic analysis of hybrid systems. Theoretical Computer Science 138, 3–34 (1995)
2. Alur, R., Dang, T., Ivančić, F.: Reachability analysis of hybrid systems via predicate abstraction. In: Tomlin, C.J., Greenstreet, M.R. (eds.) HSCC 2002. LNCS, vol. 2289, pp. 35–48. Springer, Heidelberg (2002)
3. Alur, R., Madhusudan, P., Nam, W.: Symbolic compositional verification by learning assumptions. In: Etessami, K., Rajamani, S.K. (eds.) CAV 2005. LNCS, vol. 3576, pp. 548–562. Springer, Heidelberg (2005)
4. Angluin, D.: Learning regular sets from queries and counterexamples. Inf. Comput. 75(2), 87–106 (1987)
5. Gheorghiu Bobaru, M., Păsăreanu, C.S., Giannakopoulou, D.: Automated assume-guarantee reasoning by abstraction refinement. In: Gupta, A., Malik, S. (eds.) CAV 2008. LNCS, vol. 5123, pp. 135–148. Springer, Heidelberg (2008)
6. Clarke, E., Grumberg, O., Jha, S., Lu, Y., Veith, H.: Counterexample-guided abstraction refinement. In: Emerson, E.A., Sistla, A.P. (eds.) CAV 2000. LNCS, vol. 1855, pp. 154–169. Springer, Heidelberg (2000)
7. Donzé, A., Frehse, G.: Modular, hierarchical models of control systems in SpaceEx. In: European Control Conference (ECC) (2013)
8. Doyen, L., Henzinger, T.A., Raskin, J.-F.: Automatic rectangular refinement of affine hybrid systems. In: Pettersson, P., Yi, W. (eds.) FORMATS 2005. LNCS, vol. 3829, pp. 144–161. Springer, Heidelberg (2005)
9. Frehse, G., Le Guernic, C., Donzé, A., Cotton, S., Ray, R., Lebeltel, O., Ripado, R., Girard, A., Dang, T., Maler, O.: SpaceEx: Scalable verification of hybrid systems. In: Gopalakrishnan, G., Qadeer, S. (eds.) CAV 2011. LNCS, vol. 6806, pp. 379–395. Springer, Heidelberg (2011)
10. Frehse, G., Maler, O.: Reachability analysis of a switched buffer network. In: Bemporad, A., Bicchi, A., Buttazzo, G. (eds.) HSCC 2007. LNCS, vol. 4416, pp. 698–701. Springer, Heidelberg (2007)
11. Henzinger, T.A.: The theory of hybrid automata. In: LICS, pp. 278–292 (1996)
12. Jha, S.K., Krogh, B.H., Weimer, J.E., Clarke, E.M.: Reachability for linear hybrid automata using iterative relaxation abstraction. In: Bemporad, A., Bicchi, A., Buttazzo, G. (eds.) HSCC 2007. LNCS, vol. 4416, pp. 287–300. Springer, Heidelberg (2007)
13. Pasareanu, C.S., Giannakopoulou, D., Bobaru, M.G., Cobleigh, J.M., Barringer, H.: Learning to divide and conquer: applying the L* algorithm to automate assume-guarantee reasoning. Formal Methods in System Design (FMSD) 32(3), 175–205 (2008)
14. Pnueli, A.: In transition from global to modular temporal reasoning about programs. In: Logics and Models of Concurrent Systems. NATO ASI Series (1985)
15. Prabhakar, P., Duggirala, P.S., Mitra, S., Viswanathan, M.: Hybrid automata-based CEGAR for rectangular hybrid systems. In: Giacobazzi, R., Berdine, J., Mastroeni, I. (eds.) VMCAI 2013. LNCS, vol. 7737, pp. 48–67. Springer, Heidelberg (2013)
16. Tiwari, A.: Abstractions for hybrid systems. Formal Methods in System Design (FMSD) 32(1), 57–83 (2008)
17. Zutshi, A., Sankaranarayanan, S., Deshmukh, J., Kapinski, J.: A trajectory splicing approach to concretizing counterexamples for hybrid systems. In: Conference on Decision and Control (CDC), pp. 3918–3925 (2013)

Handling TSO in Mechanized Linearizability Proofs

Oleg Travkin and Heike Wehrheim

Universität Paderborn, Institut für Informatik,
33098 Paderborn, Germany
{oleg82,wehrheim}@uni-paderborn.de

Abstract. Linearizability is the key correctness criterion for concurrent data structures. In recent years, numerous verification techniques for linearizability have been developed, ranging from model checking to mechanized proving. Today, these verification techniques are challenged by the fact that concurrent software is most likely to be run on multi-core processors equipped with a weak memory semantics (like total store order, TSO), making standard techniques unsound. While for model checking and static analysis techniques, approaches for handling weak memory in verification have already emerged, this is lacking for theorem-prover supported, mechanized correctness proofs.

In this paper, we present the very first approaches to handling TSO semantics in mechanized proofs of linearizability. More precisely, we introduce two approaches, one explicitly modelling store buffers and a second avoiding this modelling by instead reordering program operations. We exemplify and discuss our approach on two case studies, Burns mutual exclusion algorithm and a work stealing dequeue of Arora et al., both of which require additional memory barriers when executed on TSO.

Keywords: Linearizability, weak memory models, verification, TSO, KIV.

1 Introduction

With the advent of multi-core processors and the consequently rising increase in concurrent software, high performance concurrent data structures have come into the focus of algorithm designers. Concurrent data structures allow for a concurrent access to standard data structures like lists, queues or stacks. High performance is achieved by (mostly) avoiding locks, and instead relying on very fine-grained atomicity. Due to the subtlety of lock-free algorithms, their proof of correctness can be exceptionally complex. The quasi-standard correctness criterion for concurrent data structures is *linearizability* [18]. Many techniques for the verification of linearizability emerged in the past, ranging from manual proofs (usually done by the algorithm designers themselves), to model checking [29] and theorem proving [25,28].

A large number of existing verification techniques, both for concurrent software in general and more specifically for linearizability, assume a sequentially

E. Yahav (Ed.): HVC 2014, LNCS 8855, pp. 132–147, 2014.

consistent memory model (SC) [21], i.e., assume statements in a sequential program to be executed in program order and concurrent programs to be an interleaving of components. However, multicore processors like x86, SPARC or POWER provide weaker execution semantics than SC and allow executions to deviate from program order [2]. The reason behind these out-of-order execution is (mainly) the use of *store buffers* attached to processor cores. Store buffers can delay write instructions while later instructions w.r.t. program order are further processed. As a consequence, an execution may appear as though out-of-order. Verification techniques coping with weak memory can so far be classified into two strands. The first strand aims at reusing verification technique for sequential consistency. This starts with techniques for detecting non-sequentially consistent behaviour (monitoring, testing, robustness checking [10,11,8]) which can then be eliminated by fence insertion (e.g. using techniques of [1,20]), or finding program structures which guarantee SC behaviour even for relaxed memory models (like data race freedom or triangular race freedom [22]). The other strand of research takes weak memory behaviour into account, either by explicitly modelling store buffers [9] or by rewriting the program in such a way that an SC-based verification becomes sound [6,3,14]. None of these approaches have, however, proposed techniques for handling weak memory within mechanized proofs of linearizability. The advantage of a mechanized proof is the establishment of correctness for *arbitrary uses* of the data structure, i.e. arbitrary method invocations by an *arbitrary number* of processes. Compared to model checking or testing approaches, mechanized proofs are not limited to specific usage scenarios.

In this paper, we propose two approaches for handling weak memory semantics in mechanized correctness proofs of linearizability. The first approach builds on an explicit modelling of store buffers and delayed writes. Unlike model checking approaches, we need not (but could) assume bounds on the buffer size in our models. The second approach employs an explicit reordering of program statements as to mimic the behaviour of store buffers. It turns out that the second approach is more convenient for mechanized proving as it keeps us from having to define and reason about invariants on the store buffer contents. In our definition of linearizability we follow [17,7] in that we compare the implementations of concurrent data structures run on TSO against sequential specifications interpreted in an SC way (TSO-to-SC linearizability). Our general proof principle proceeds by showing a *simulation* relation to exist between implementation and specification, and follows established simulation-based proof techniques for linearizability on SC [15,25].

We discuss and exemplify our approach(es) on two case studies, a variant of Burns mutual exclusion algorithm [12] and a work-stealing double-ended queue of Arora et al. [5]. While the first example is rather small and mainly used for demonstration purposes, the second example realistically reflects the size of modern concurrent data structures. Both examples are non-linearizable when executed on a TSO architecture in their original form and need additional memory barriers for soundness. We were able to prove linearizability of the fenced versions for both examples, using the theorem prover KIV [24].

2   Background

TSO Architecture. Nowadays, one of the most wide-spread multicore processor architecture is the x86 [19,4], which provides the TSO memory model. Figure 1 illustrates the architecture of a modern multicore processor providing a TSO memory model. Each processor has a write buffer to store its writes before they are (later) flushed to shared memory. Reading of variables either takes place from the buffer (if there is a pending write of this variable in the store buffer) or from shared memory. Memory barriers (or *fence* operations) can be used to block program execution until the store buffer is completely flushed.

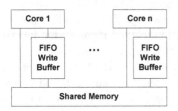

$$Initially : x = 0 \wedge y = 0$$

Process 1	Process 2
$write(x, 1);$	$write(y, 1);$
$read(y, r1);$	$read(x, r2);$

$$r1 = 0 \wedge r2 = 0$$

Fig. 1. TSO architecture as common for x86-based multicore processors.

Fig. 2. Test program for detection of *Write* → *Read* reordering, also known as litmus test

As a consequence of this architecture, TSO exhibits two relaxations of program order compared to SC. First, writes may appear as if they were executed after a later read, i.e., the order *Write* → *Read* is relaxed. This can happen when write and read access different memory locations. Figure 2 shows a test program for detection of this behavior. Initially both shared variables x and y hold the value 0. The test detects reordering if both registers have values $r1 = 0 \wedge r2 = 0$ at the end of its execution and hence at least one process must have had its instructions reordered. Simple interleaving, as in an SC setting, does not allow this outcome. A second relaxation allows processes to read their own writes early. If a write buffer contains a pending write to an address requested by a read, the value from the buffer is read. This behavior is called *early-read* [2] or *Intra-Process-Forwarding* [19], because a reading processor is allowed to see its own writes before they are committed to the memory and hence before other processes can see them.

Burns Algorithm. Our objective is to show (a certain form of) correctness of algorithms executed on weak memory models. The correctness proofs thus will need to take the unusual non-SC semantics into account. We will exemplify our approach on the following mutual exclusion algorithm of [12]. Originally, the algorithm was defined with a loop for each process, in which it tries to enter and leave a critical section. We modified the algorithm slightly (as to be able

```
bool *flag0 = 0, *flag1 = 0;

//process0:                          //process1:
void acquire0{                       void acquire1{
    *flag0 = 1;               retry: while (*flag0 != 0) {
    /*need fence here*/                  /*wait*/
    while (*flag1 != 0) {             }
        /*wait*/                     *flag1 = 1;
    }                                /*need fence here*/
}                                    if(*flag0 != 0) {
                                         *flag1 = 0;
void release0() {                        goto retry;
    *flag0 = 0;                       }
}                                    }

                                     void release1() {
                                         *flag1 = 0;
                                     }
```

Fig. 3. Mutual exclusion algorithm for two processes (based on [12])

to view it as a concurrent data structure) by explicitly defining two operations — *acquire* and *release* — which can then be repeatedly called (in turn). The Burns algorithm (see Fig. 3) uses a flag for each process to indicate its intention of a process to enter the critical section. Both flags are initially 0 and set to 1, when a process tries to enter. It is an asymmetric algorithm in the sense that processes are ordered in terms of priority. Process $p0$ (highest priority) sets its flag to $flag0 = 1$ and waits until it observes $flag1 = 0$. In this case, process $p1$ is not trying to enter the critical section and will not enter until $p0$ has left it. In contrast to $p0$, $p1$ checks the flag of $p0$ before setting its own flag and checks $flag0$ again after having set $flag1$ to 1. If $flag0$ changes in the meantime, $p1$ resets its flag to 0 (allowing $p0$ to enter and finish) and retries. Otherwise, $p1$ finishes by entering the critical section. Both processes release their ownership by setting their flag to 0.

In order to determine possible effects of weak memory on the execution of this algorithm, we first of all need to explicitly see the low-level reads and writes. To this end, we first compile a C program into an intermediate representation, here using the LLVM[1] compiler framework with intermediate representation LLVM IR. On this, we can see the atomic reads and writes. Figure 4 shows the compiled code for the operation acquire0. The code defines a function which is structured into labeled blocks (entry, cond, body and end). Global variables (here, the two flags) are prefixed with @. Local registers are prefixed with %. The local variables %tobool, %conv and %cmp are just used to store values of type conversions (the first two) and the value of a comparison. We thus will not explicitly model these later. The br instruction is either a simple jump (e.g., in block entry) or a conditional jump (e.g., in block cond with variable %cmp being the boolean condition). Instruction load (resp. store) corresponds to a read (resp. write) of a global variable. When determining the semantics of this LLVM-IR code on TSO, we thus need to assign these statements a non-standard semantics.

---

[1] www.llvm.org

```
define void @_Z5acquire0() nounwind {
entry:
  store i8 1, i8* @flag0
; ---- need fence here ----
  br label %cond

cond:
  %0 = load i8* @flag1
  %tobool = trunc i8 %0 to i1
  %conv = zext i1 %tobool to i32
  %cmp = icmp ne i32 %conv, 0
  br i1 %cmp, label %cond, label %end

end:
  ret void
}
```

$$COP_1 \mathrel{\hat=} ls.pc = A1_0 \ \wedge \ ls'.pc = A2_0$$
$$\wedge \ write((flag0, 1), ls, mem, ls', mem')$$
$$COP_2 \mathrel{\hat=} ls.pc = A2_0 \ \wedge \ ls'.pc = A3_0$$
$$\wedge \ fence(ls, mem, ls', mem')$$
$$COP_3 \mathrel{\hat=} ls.pc = A3_0 \ \wedge \ ls'.pc = A4_0$$
$$\wedge \ read((flag1, f1), ls, mem, ls', mem')$$
$$COP_{4a} \mathrel{\hat=} ls.pc = A4_0 \ \wedge \ ls.f1 \neq 0 \ \wedge \ ls'.pc = A3_0$$
$$COP_{4b} \mathrel{\hat=} ls.pc = A4_0 \ \wedge \ ls.f1 = 0 \ \wedge \ ls'.pc = A5_0$$
$$COP_{flush} \mathrel{\hat=} flush(ls, mem, ls', mem')$$

Fig. 4. LLVM IR code for method acquire0 after compilation

Fig. 5. Encoding of program behavior for method acquire0. Parameters (mem, ls, mem', ls') of each COP predicate were omitted for brevity.

3 TSO model

We are ultimately interested in a mechanized proof of correctness of algorithms. To this end, we first need a precise formal model of TSO on top of which we can then define the semantics of programs. We model shared memory as a function $mem : \mathbb{N} \to (\mathbb{N} \cup null)$, where we use $\mathbb{N}$ as the memory address space and allow $\mathbb{N}$ or $null$ to be the result of a memory access. The following three axioms define memory access (written as $mem[n]$) and modification ($mem[n, a]$ modifying memory mem at address n to become a):

$$\vdash \ mem = mem0 \ \Leftrightarrow \ \forall n \bullet mem[n] = mem0[n] \tag{1}$$
$$\vdash \ mem[n, a][n] = a \tag{2}$$
$$\vdash \ n \neq n0 \ \Rightarrow \ mem[n0, a][n] = mem[n] \tag{3}$$

(1) defines the identity of two memory functions, (2) states that access to the address n will yield the last value written to it, and (3) states that modifying one address will not change the value of another address.

In order to fix the semantics of programs on TSO, we first define an instruction set for the interaction with the memory and store buffer (similar to [26]). Instructions affecting store buffer and memory are *write*, *read* and *fence* explicitly appearing as operations in programs plus *flush* which is occasionally executed as to flush the store buffer. We let P be the set of all process identifiers, and write ls to describe the *local state* of a process $p \in P$. The local state comprises the process identifier $ls.p \in P$, the store buffer $ls.buf \in (\mathbb{N} \times (\mathbb{N} \cup null))^*$, values of local registers $ls.r$ from some set of registers Reg and a program counter $ls.pc$ from some set PC. We use LS to denote the set of local states. The instructions modify the state as follows (where $+$ is concatenation and primed variables are used to describe the after state):

$$write((n, a), ls, mem, ls', mem') \Leftrightarrow ls'.buf = ls.buf + (n, a)$$
$$\wedge \, mem' = mem \qquad (4)$$
$$flush(ls, mem, ls', mem') \Leftrightarrow ls.buf = (n, a) + ls'.buf$$
$$\wedge \, mem' = mem[n, a] \qquad (5)$$

For the definition of a read, we need a helper function $latest(n, buf)$ (not given here) to determine the latest entry for the requested address in the buffer.

$$read((n, r), ls, mem, ls', mem') \; \Leftrightarrow ls'.buf = ls.buf \, \wedge \, mem' = mem \, \wedge$$
$$\textbf{if } n \in ls.buf \textbf{ then } ls'.r = latest(n, ls.buf)$$
$$\textbf{else } ls'.r = mem[n] \qquad (6)$$

A read either obtains the latest value from the store buffer, if there is one, or it obtains the value directly from the memory. The buffer and memory remain unmodified. Finally, fences in the program code block program execution until the store buffer is emptied. To this end, the fence is only enabled when $ls.buf = \langle \rangle$ and blocks execution otherwise.

$$fence(ls, mem, ls', mem') \Leftrightarrow ls.buf = \langle \rangle \wedge ls'.buf = ls.buf \wedge mem' = mem \quad (7)$$

It is in the semantics of these instructions (and thus of the load and store in LLVM) where the difference to SC semantics can be found. For modelling the behavior of a given program we next proceed as follows. For the Burns algorithm, we fix the set Reg of registers and assign the register %0 used in acquire0 a name (here, $f1$ because it stores the value of $flag1$). For the memory, we use the global variable names $flag0$ and $flag1$ as constants 0 and 1 to access mem.

Figure 5 shows the encoding for the method acquire0 in Figure 4. In principle, we define one operation per program instruction. However, as LLVM-IR contains a lot of operations which need not be modelled in the theorem prover we use (e.g., type conversions), we get more compact operations in our model. All operations are modelled as predicates. By specifying the change of the program counter, we define the control flow of the method. After invocation, the program counter is at $A1_0$. The first instruction (store) changes the program counter to $A2_0$ and attempts to write value 1 into address flag1. Note that the write does not modify the memory directly, but enqueues the address value pair to the store buffer. We ignore the following br instruction since it is just a jump to next instruction in program order. Operation COP_2 is a fence instruction which we will need further on, but which first of all is not part of the operations. Please note that local instructions, e.g., the four instructions after the load in Figure 4, can be composed to a single one, because they are invisible to other processes and hence, their atomicity is irrelevant for the correctness of the algorithm. The predicate COP_{flush} models the non-deterministic flushes of the store buffer. It is not restricted to any particular program location and can be performed repeatedly.

4   Proving Linearizability

Our main interest is in proving linearizability of concurrent data structures. Linearizability is a correctness condition for concurrent data structures which states that — when used concurrently — the data structure acts as though used sequentially. To prove this, we need to find an "equivalent" sequential execution for every concurrent run. An execution, or *history*, consists of a sequence of invocations and responses of methods, e.g. of the acquire and release of Burns algorithm. Every concurrent history, i.e., history in which more than one method might run at a time, has to have a matching sequential history preserving the order of operations from the concurrent history. For a formal definition see [18]. Linearizability is often explained in terms of *linearization points* (LPs) which are points within methods where the real effect of the methods seems to take place atomically. The acquire methods of Burns algorithm pass their linearization point when they observe the flag of the other process to be zero. The release methods have their LPs, when the write to their flag becomes visible.

There are a number of different ways of formally proving linearizability for a given data structure. Here, we intend to prove linearizability by showing that the algorithm's implementation *simulates* a sequential specification of the data structure (following approaches in [15,25]). In the sequential specification all operations are executed atomically, and thus the sequential specification only has sequential histories. The proof needs to build up a *simulation relation* between our behavior model of the algorithm and another sequential model. We also call this the *concrete* and the *abstract* model. The concrete model has concrete operations (called $COP_{...}$), which we have already seen, and the abstract model has abstract operations. For the Burns algorithm, we have an abstract state space simply consisting of one variable $mtx \in (\{none\} \cup P)$ and operations acquire and release for each process.

$$AOP_{acquire0} \;\widehat{=}\; (mtx = none \land mtx' = 0)$$
$$AOP_{acquire1} \;\widehat{=}\; (mtx = none \land mtx' = 1)$$
$$AOP_{release0} \;\widehat{=}\; (mtx = 0 \land mtx' = none)$$
$$AOP_{release1} \;\widehat{=}\; (mtx = 1 \land mtx' = none)$$

Thus, in the abstract model, we have atomic operations corresponding to methods, and, in the concrete model, these are implemented by lots of concrete operations, some of which are LPs. Formally, we thus have a non-atomic refinement between abstract and concrete model which we intend to prove via a forward simulation. For showing the existence of a forward simulation, we first need to define an abstraction relation *Abs* between the state space of the abstract model (here, variable mtx) and that of the concrete model (here, global variable mem plus all local states ls of processes). In our case, the abstraction relation will be a *function* from concrete to abstract. Second, we need to define the linearization points of methods[2]. All concrete steps COP which are not LPs have to be shown

---

[2] In general, simulation proofs can also be done when LPs are not fixed, but for the algorithms in this paper this is not necessary.

to simulate abstract skip steps (empty operations) while the LP steps have to simulate the corresponding abstract operation. In case of the method acquire0, the LP is at COP_3, but only if the method observes $flag1 = 0$. Hence, COP_3 observing $flag1 = 0$ has to simulate $AOP_{acquire0}(mtx, mtx')$. All other acquire0 operations have to simulate skip steps. Our proof technique then proceeds by locally reasoning about processes.

The main idea behind the local proof obligations (LPO) (see [15]) is to prove linearizability for two processes, where one process p is explicit and the other process q a symbolic representation of all other processes. Both processes operate on the shared global state $gs \in GS$, which in our case studies is the memory function mem. The local states of both processes p and q are $lsp, lsq \in LS$. In addition, we need to define and establish an *invariant INV* on global and local states. The following is one of a number of proof obligations which need to be shown for simulation.

$$\forall\, gs, gs' : GS, lsp, lsq, lsp' : LS \bullet$$
$$INV(gs, lsp) \wedge INV(gs, lsq) \wedge COP(gs, lsp, gs', lsp')$$
$$\Rightarrow$$
$$INV(gs', lsp') \wedge INV(gs', lsq) \wedge AOP_{pq}(Abs(gs, lsp, lsq), Abs(gs', lsp', lsq))$$

This proof obligation states the following condition: if the invariant holds both for process p and the other process q, and p executes operation COP thereby changing the global state and its local state, then the invariant still holds for p and q afterwards and a corresponding abstract operation can be executed on the corresponding abstract states[3]. If a particular COP-transition is a linearization point (LP), then AOP_{pq} must be the corresponding abstract operation, and a skip step, otherwise. Depending on which process passes its linearization point, AOP_{pq} can be an abstract operation performed by either process p or q or both. The latter two cases can occur by process p helping other processes to finish their operation or by p passing its own linearization point and by doing this causing the other process to linearize as well.

Next, we apply this technique to our running example. However, the first observation (found by using the model checking approach [27]) is that the acquire methods of the Burns algorithm both need a fence (see Fig. 3). Otherwise, the initial write could be still pending while the flag of the other process is read within the loop. Hence, both processes would be able to enter the critical section at the same time by observing the other flag value to be zero while the write to the own flag is still pending. In particular, the following history of invokes and returns would be possible:

$$\langle inv_0(acquire0), inv_1(acquire1), ret_0(acquire0), ret_1(acquire1) \rangle$$

which corresponds to one of the sequences:

$$AOP_{acquire0};\ AOP_{acquire1} \text{ or } AOP_{acquire1};\ AOP_{acquire0}$$

---

[3] In principle, Abs is only defined on gs. If information about local states is needed for the definition of Abs, these have to moved into the global state via auxiliary variables.

Both sequences violate the corresponding AOP definitions, because both require $mtx = none$, but modify its value. Hence, the second AOP must not finish until a release method linearizes. We place a fence at COP_2 in acquire0 in order to ensure the write is no longer pending during observation of the other flag. Thereby, we disable executions as the one mentioned above. We modify acquire1 similarly.

Now that we fixed the implementation by ruling out non-linearizable executions, we can define the invariant, which is defined as properties holding at a particular program location. In case of the Burns algorithm, we are interested in the values of the flags. However, the flag values depend on the state of the store buffer, i.e., whether a write to the flag was flushed or not. Thus, we have to specify two kinds of properties in our invariant: First, the invariant has to establish the possible states of the store buffer at particular program locations. Second, the possible flag values depending on the store buffer state and the program have to be specified. For the method acquire0 the invariant is defined as:

$$
\begin{aligned}
INV(mem, ls) \mathrel{\hat{=}} ((ls.pc \in \{A1_0, A3_0, A4_0, A5_0\} &\Rightarrow ls.buf = \langle\rangle) \\
\wedge\ (ls.pc = A2_0 &\Rightarrow ls.buf = \langle\rangle \vee ls.buf = \langle(flag0, 1)\rangle) \\
\wedge\ (ls.pc = A1_0 &\Rightarrow mem[flag0] = 0) \\
\wedge\ (ls.pc = A2_0 \wedge ls.buf = \langle\rangle &\Rightarrow mem[flag0] = 1) \\
\wedge\ (ls.pc = A2_0 \wedge ls.buf = \langle(flag0, 1)\rangle &\Rightarrow mem[flag0] = 0) \\
\wedge\ ((ls.pc \in \{A3_0, A4_0, A5_0\} &\Rightarrow mem[flag0] = 1) \\
\wedge\ (ls.pc = A5_0 &\Rightarrow ls.f1 = 0)
\end{aligned}
$$

where program location $A2_0$ is the one with a potentially pending write to $flag0$ and thus having two possible states of the store buffer, which determine the value of $mem[flag0]$. Note that the value of $mem[flag0]$ at the other program locations ($A1_0, A3_0, A4_0, A5_0$) can only be stated without referring to the store buffer state, because we know that the store buffer is empty. Otherwise, a similar distinction to the one at location $A2_0$ would be necessary.

Finally, we provide an abstraction function Abs that maps each concrete state to an abstract state. Throughout all executions, $flag0 = 1$ (resp. $flag1 = 1$) means that process 0 (resp. 1) is either the owner of the mutex or it tries to acquire it. We distinguish the two cases by taking the progress of local states into account. We use the two range predicates $observed_0(mem[flag1] = 0)$ in order to define the range after process 0 observed $flag1 = 0$ and $observed_1(mem[flag0] = 0)$ for process 1, respectively. The abstraction function is then defined as a case distinction over the three cases:

$$
\begin{aligned}
Abs(lsp, lsq, mem) \mathrel{\hat{=}} \mathbf{if}\ & mem[flag0] = 1 \wedge observed_0(mem[flag1] = 0) \\
& \mathbf{then}\ mtx = 0 \\
& \mathbf{else\ if}\ mem[flag1] = 1 \wedge observed_1(mem[flag0] = 0) \\
& \mathbf{then}\ mtx = 1 \\
& \mathbf{else}\ mtx = none
\end{aligned}
$$

Given the above abstraction function and invariant, we were able to show all proof obligations for the fenced Burns algorithm, thereby establishing linearizability with respect to the given sequential specification.

5   Avoiding Store Buffers

In the last section, we have seen how to prove linearizability using an explicit modelling of store buffers to encode the TSO behavior. However, keeping store buffers as part of the state has a huge drawback. Mechanized proofs reveal many impossible cases of executions which thus need to be ruled out by the invariant (unless they are harmless). Hence, the invariant not only has to cover the properties of potential store buffer states, but also the interconnection between store buffer states and values of global and local variables. Hence, the simplicity of specification due to an operational memory model is paid by the complexity of invariants, which have a major impact on the size of correctness proofs and the time and effort that is required for the proofs.

In the following, we will therefore present an idea of how to transform our program model under TSO into an equivalent program model under SC, for which store buffers are no longer required. For the proof, we use the proof obligations from the previous section in combination with the new program model. First of all, we have to make some restrictions to the class of the programs to which our transformation applies. We restrict our transformation to programs, which are (1) in SSA-form [13], (2) do not read early (from store buffer) and (3) loops must be either non-writing or contain at least one synchronizing instruction (fence, CAS instruction, etc.) that limits the potential reordering to a finite delay. Although the three conditions seem to be a strong limitation to the applicability of our approach, they hold surprisingly often to the best of our experience: (1) is a typical intermediate representation by compilers as in case of the LLVM compiler framework, (2) is rarely relevant for concurrent algorithms that are adapted for weak memory models, because reads to previously written shared variables do usually have synchronization in between in order to ensure that the write is flushed before the read is issued. Condition (3) is the actual limitation of the class of programs, since not all loops will have memory barriers. However, our transformation still applies to a large class of algorithms, since most concurrent algorithms rely on some sort of synchronization primitives.

The transformation proceeds in two steps. The starting point of the transformation are the concrete operations COP_i of some method implementation. These are used to build a *symbolic reachability graph* in the first step. In this graph, the nodes are pairs of program location and symbolic store buffer contents. In a later step, we use this graph as basis for the construction of an equivalent program with its operations having SC semantics, and thus, without the need of store buffers.

Definition 1. *A symbolic reachability graph* $G = (N, E)$ *consists of a set of nodes* $N \subseteq PC \times (\mathbb{N} \times (\mathbb{N} \cup Reg))^*$ *and edges* $E \subseteq N \times Lab \times N$. *The labels of the edges are memory instructions or are empty.*

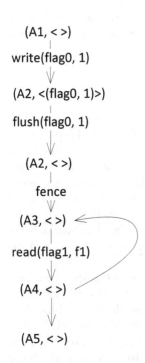

$$COP_{1asc} \hat{=} ls.pc = (A1_0, \langle \rangle)$$
$$\wedge ls'.pc = (A1_0, \langle (flag0, 1) \rangle)$$
$$\wedge mem' = mem$$
$$COP_{1bsc} \hat{=} ls.pc = A1_0, \langle (flag0, 1) \rangle$$
$$\wedge ls'.pc = (A2_0, \langle \rangle)$$
$$\wedge mem' = mem[flag0, 1]$$
$$COP_{2sc} \hat{=} ls.pc = (A2_0, \langle \rangle)$$
$$\wedge ls'.pc = (A3_0, \langle \rangle)$$
$$\wedge mem' = mem$$
$$COP_{3sc} \hat{=} ls.pc = (A3_0, \langle \rangle)$$
$$\wedge ls'.pc = (A4_0, \langle \rangle)$$
$$\wedge ls'.f1 = mem[flag1]$$
$$COP_{4asc} \hat{=} ls.pc = (A4_0, \langle \rangle)$$
$$\wedge ls.f1 = 0 \wedge ls'.pc = (A5_0, \langle \rangle)$$
$$\wedge mem' = mem$$
$$COP_{4bsc} \hat{=} ls.pc = (A4_0, \langle \rangle)$$
$$\wedge ls.f1 \neq 0 \wedge ls'.pc = (A3_0, \langle \rangle)$$
$$\wedge mem' = mem$$

Fig. 6. Abstract reachability graph of operation acquire0

Fig. 7. Encoding of program behavior for operation $acquire0$

The symbolic store buffer contents either contain pairs of memory address and register name or memory address and constant. The graph of an operation implementation is incrementally constructed as follows. The initial node consists of the initial program location and an empty store buffer. New nodes and edges are constructed as follows:

$(l, buf) \xrightarrow{lab} (l', buf')$ iff $\exists COP_i$ such that

- $COP_i = (ls.pc = l \wedge ls'.pc = l' \wedge write((n, r), ls, mem, ls', mem')$ and $buf' = buf \frown \langle (n, r) \rangle$, $lab = write(n, r)$, (ditto constants)
- $COP_i = (ls.pc = l \wedge ls'.pc = l' \wedge r_* := r \wedge write((n, r_*), ls, mem, ls', mem')$ and $buf' = buf \frown \langle (n, r_*) \rangle$, $lab = r_* := r \wedge write(n, r)$
- $COP_i = (ls.pc = l \wedge ls'.pc = l' \wedge read((n, r), ls, mem, ls', mem')$ and $buf' = buf$, $lab = read(n, r)$,
- $COP_i = (ls.pc = l \wedge ls'.pc = l' \wedge flush(ls, mem, ls', mem')$ and $\exists (n, r)$ such that $buf = \langle (n, r) \rangle \frown buf'$, $lab = flush$,
- $COP_i = (ls.pc = l \wedge ls'.pc = l' \wedge fence(ls, mem, ls', mem'))$ and $buf = buf' = \langle \rangle$, $lab = fence$,
- $COP_i \Rightarrow (ls.pc = l \wedge ls'.pc = l')$, COP_i is no memory instruction and $buf' = buf$, lab empty.

Operation predicates with more complex structure can be treated in a similar way, e.g. by first logically splitting them into one of the forms of above. Thus, what we are tracking here is just the potential contents of the store buffer, and this only symbolically in that we store which register (or constant) the value must come from. This is similar to symbolic execution [23], however, not tracking all variables. The symbolic reachability graph is finite due to the above mentioned restrictions, in particular, because we have no loops with write operations but without fences. Such a graph can be automatically constructed. For operation acquire0 the graph is given in Figure 6.

Note that in loops, the flush of a $write(x, r)$ can be delayed past the re-definition of r corresponding to the next loop iteration (i.e., synchronization between definition and write of r). Thus, the redefinition of register r also modifies the symbolic store buffer content in our reachability graph. To overcome this problem, we replace COPs with such writes $write(x, r)$ in the program by $r_* := r \wedge write(x, r_*)$ with r_* representing the value of r while the write is still pending. Such cases are the only cases in which we need a second variable instance. However, for both of our case studies this was not necessary.

The second step consists of constructing new concrete operations for the SC execution. Basically, the new operations operate on the same global and local variables, however, without $ls.buf$. Instead, we use the nodes in the symbolic reachability graph as new program locations and define one new operation for every edge in the graph according to the following procedure:

1. For edges $(l, buf) \xrightarrow{lab} (l', buf')$, the predicate of the operation has to contain $ls.pc = (l, buf) \wedge ls'.pc = (l', buf')$,
2. If $lab = write(n, r)$, we add a predicate $mem = mem'$.
3. If $lab = r_* := r \wedge write(n, r_*)$, we add a predicate $r_* := r \wedge mem = mem'$.
4. If $lab = read(n, r)$, we add a predicate $ls'.r = mem[n]$.
5. If $lab = flush$ and $buf = \langle (n, r) \rangle ^\frown buf'$, we add predicate $mem' = mem[n, r]$.
6. If $lab = fence$, we add a predicate $mem = mem'$.
7. If the label of the edge is empty, we re-use the part of the old predicate not refering to program locations.

For the symbolic reachability graph of method acquire0 given in Figure 6, we thus get the operations as depicted in Figure 7.

These two transformation steps have to be applied to every method of the algorithm, i.e., to acquire1, release0 and release1 as well. Together, they form our new concrete SC model which then has to be shown to simulate the (same) abstract model. So far, we have just shown correctness of this transformation, i.e. equivalence of old program on TSO to new program on SC, for the concrete algorithms at hand (Burns and the work-stealing deque). A general correctness proof will be one of our next steps.

6   Evaluation

We used the Burns mutual exclusion algorithm [12] as a toy example to play with our transformation idea as described in the previous section and to compare it against a proof based on an operational encoding of the TSO memory model (see Section 3). After getting the first promising results, we decided to tackle a more realistic case study, the work-stealing deque algorithm by Arora et al. [5]. In particular, we were interested in whether we would be able to prove a more realistic size of case study and therefore applied the transformation based approach to it. The algorithm is an array based queue implementation for thread scheduling and requires fences under weak memory models. The queue implementation is based on fine-grained concurrency primitives, e.g., CAS operations. The provided methods require fences in order to prevent elements from being removed twice. Compared to the 20 LOC of the Burns algorithm, the work stealing deque had 58 LOC in our implementation of it. The C/C++ and LLVM IR code for both implementations[4] and the full linearizability proofs[5] are available for download.

We used the theorem prover KIV [24] for the specification and mechanization of our linearizability proofs. KIV provides a library with the proof obligations (including fully mechanized soundness and completeness proofs) for proving linearizability that our work is based on. Furthermore, KIV allows for automation of proofs and provides strong visualization features, e.g., proof trees and specification dependencies, which are crucial for the understanding of why a proof fails. In the following, we provide our key insights about the presented approaches.

Operational vs. Transformed.   The operational encoding of the memory model allows for a straightforward translation of the program code to a program model. The simplicity stems from having no need to think about the potential contents of the store buffers during specification. However, as we figured out in our proof of Burns, the store buffer content becomes crucial anyway. A theorem prover reveals all the cases that are *impossible*, but break the property you try to prove. For instance, the store buffer of process 0 could contain pending writes to *flag1*, although process 0 never writes to *flag1*. Such cases have to be ruled out by the invariant. Thus, we specified the possible store buffer contents for each program location in the invariant. Furthermore, we had to specify whether a flag has a particular value or not as properties depending on the state of store buffer. The more states a store buffer can have, the more complex the invariant can get.

Although the transformation of the program model seemed to be more effort in the first place, it actually reduced our proof effort for several reasons. Since, we had to find out about the possible store buffer states anyway, the construction of the abstract reachability graph did not really increase our effort. The presence of the store buffer as part of the state in the operational encoding basically forced us to reason about a FIFO queue in every step, because an invariant has to be established over all steps of the program. We got rid of this burden by removing the store buffer from the local state, although this was paid by gaining more transitions and program locations in the program behavior. However, some of the transitions became empty transitions (e.g., COP_{1asc} in Fig. 7) and were removed. A second beneficial side effect of store

---

[4] http://lina-rmm-verification.googlecode.com/svn/trunk/examples
[5] http://linearizability.bplaced.de

buffer removal was a better automation of the proofs. In particular, the Burns proof based on the operational encoding required 3784 proof steps in KIV of which 201 were manual. The proof based on the transformed program model required 1536 steps of which 63 were manual. The generally lower number of proof steps was also due to the significantly smaller invariant in the transformation based proofs (approx. half the size of the former invariant). By removing store buffer properties and the corresponding case distinctions on the flag values, we got simple properties (e.g. $mem[flag0] = 1$) in certain program location ranges $(ls.pc \in \{(A2_0, \langle\rangle)\}, (A3_0, \langle\rangle), (A4_0, \langle\rangle), (A5_0, \langle\rangle))$. The difference in time effort was even bigger, but since many specifications could be reused or needed just a bit of adaption from the operational encoding, a comparison would be unfair.

Work Stealing Deque. We verified the work stealing deque by Arora et al. with the transformation based approach only, but experienced similar benefits from the approach. First, we applied the model checking approach [27] to the example in order to find out, where fences had to be placed in the program and to get an idea of how the algorithm works on a low level. Although the specification in KIV took us just a few days, we spent several weeks to find a correct invariant allowing us to prove the algorithm linearizable. The effort was mainly caused due to iterations of adding invariant properties, trying to establish them within the proof, and in case of a failing proof trying to understand why and to adapt the invariant properties again. We assume that a proof based on the operational encoding would have required more effort because of the complexity due to store buffers. The full linearizability proofs for the work stealing deque required 6923 steps of which 1100 were manual.

7 Conclusion

In this paper, we have presented two approaches for the specification of program behavior under TSO and provided first experimental results on their impact to the proof effort. Both approaches focus on the mechanization of proofs in a theorem prover. The operational encoding, a widely used approach, is modular by keeping a memory model separate from the program specification and therefore allows for straightforward program specification. Proofs based on this approach unfold the full behavior during a proof, but require reasoning about store buffer content, which makes the proof tedious and complex.

The basic principle of employing program transformations to allow for SC-based proofs afterwards has also been followed in [6], however, using different transformations. The transformation in [6] uses a bounded number of shared variable copies in order to simulate store buffer behavior. Our transformation makes reasoning about store buffer content obsolete, without adding a burden to reason about store buffer replacements. We were able to show that our approach reduces the proof effort and complexity (in our experiment by half compared to the operational approach) and also enables the reuse of SC-based techniques. The drawback of our transformation is that it is restricted to a particular class of programs (see Sec. 5).

Since the linearizability theory [15] used in our proofs assumes an SC memory model, our proofs do not cover the case of delays (of store buffer flushes) past the return statement of a method. Thus, we implicitly assume fences at invocation and return of methods in order to be sound. We plan to adapt the linearizability theory (similar to [16]) as to be able to drop this assumption.

Currently, we are working on proving correctness of the program transformation, i.e. proving that the TSO model of the original program and the new SC model of the transformed program give us equivalent (up to weak bisimulation) transition systems. Furthermore, we aim at generalizing the transformation to a larger class of programs.

References

1. Abdulla, P.A., Atig, M.F., Chen, Y.-F., Leonardsson, C., Rezine, A.: Automatic Fence Insertion in Integer Programs via Predicate abstraction. In: Miné, A., Schmidt, D. (eds.) SAS 2012. LNCS, vol. 7460, pp. 164–180. Springer, Heidelberg (2012)
2. Adve, S.V., Gharachorloo, K.: Shared Memory Consistency Models: A Tutorial. IEEE Computer 29(12), 66–76 (1996)
3. Alglave, J., Kroening, D., Nimal, V., Tautschnig, M.: Software verification for weak memory via program transformation. In: Felleisen, M., Gardner, P. (eds.) Programming Languages and Systems. LNCS, vol. 7792, pp. 512–532. Springer, Heidelberg (2013)
4. AMD. AMD64 Architecture Programmer's Manual Volume 2: System Programming (2012),
   http://support.amd.com/us/Processor_TechDocs/24593_APM_v2.pdf
5. Arora, N.S., Blumofe, R.D., Greg Plaxton, C.: Thread Scheduling for Multiprogrammed Multiprocessors. In: Proceedings of the Tenth Annual ACM Symposium on Parallel Algorithms and Architectures, SPAA 1998, pp. 119–129. ACM, New York (1998)
6. Atig, M.F., Bouajjani, A., Parlato, G.: Getting Rid of Store-Buffers in TSO Analysis. In: Gopalakrishnan, G., Qadeer, S. (eds.) CAV 2011. LNCS, vol. 6806, pp. 99–115. Springer, Heidelberg (2011)
7. Batty, M., Dodds, M., Gotsman, A.: Library abstraction for C/C++ concurrency. In: POPL, pp. 235–248 (2013)
8. Bouajjani, A., Derevenetc, E., Meyer, R.: Checking and Enforcing Robustness against TSO. In: Felleisen, M., Gardner, P. (eds.) Programming Languages and Systems. LNCS, vol. 7792, pp. 533–553. Springer, Heidelberg (2013)
9. Burckhardt, S., Gotsman, A., Musuvathi, M., Yang, H.: Concurrent Library Correctness on the TSO Memory Model. In: Seidl, H. (ed.) Programming Languages and Systems. LNCS, vol. 7211, pp. 87–107. Springer, Heidelberg (2012)
10. Burnim, J., Sen, K., Stergiou, C.: Sound and complete monitoring of sequential consistency for relaxed memory models. In: Abdulla, P.A., Leino, K.R.M. (eds.) TACAS 2011. LNCS, vol. 6605, pp. 11–25. Springer, Heidelberg (2011)
11. Burnim, J., Sen, K., Stergiou, C.: Testing concurrent programs on relaxed memory models. In: Dwyer, M.B., Tip, F. (eds.) ISSTA, pp. 122–132. ACM (2011)
12. Burns, J., Lynch, N.A.: Mutual Exclusion Using Indivisible Reads and Writes. In: Proceedings of the 18th Annual Allerton Conference on Communication, Control, and Computing, pp. 833–842 (1980)

13. Cytron, R., Ferrante, J., Rosen, B.K., Wegman, M.N., Zadeck, F.K.: Efficiently computing static single assignment form and the control dependence graph. ACM Trans. Program. Lang. Syst. 13, 451–490 (1991)
14. Dan, A.M., Meshman, Y., Vechev, M., Yahav, E.: Predicate abstraction for relaxed memory models. In: Logozzo, F., Fähndrich, M. (eds.) SAS 2013. LNCS, vol. 7935, pp. 84–104. Springer, Heidelberg (2013)
15. Derrick, J., Schellhorn, G., Wehrheim, H.: Mechanically verified proof obligations for linearizability. ACM Trans. Program. Lang. Syst. 33(1), 4 (2011)
16. Derrick, J., Smith, G., Dongol, B.: Verifying linearizability on TSO architectures. In: iFM (to appear, 2014)
17. Gotsman, A., Musuvathi, M., Yang, H.: Show no weakness: Sequentially consistent specifications of TSO libraries. In: Aguilera, M.K. (ed.) DISC 2012. LNCS, vol. 7611, pp. 31–45. Springer, Heidelberg (2012)
18. Herlihy, M.P., Wing, J.M.: Linearizability: a correctness condition for concurrent objects. ACM Trans. Program. Lang. Syst. 12(3), 463–492 (1990)
19. Intel, Santa Clara, CA, USA. Intel 64 and IA-32 Architectures Software Developer's Manual Volume 3A: System Programming Guide, Part 1 (May 2012)
20. Kuperstein, M., Vechev, M.T., Yahav, E.: Automatic Inference of Memory Fences. SIGACT News 43(2), 108–123 (2012)
21. Lamport, L.: How to Make a Multiprocessor Computer That Correctly Executes Multiprocess Programs. IEEE Trans. Computers 28(9), 690–691 (1979)
22. Owens, S.: Reasoning about the Implementation of Concurrency Abstractions on x86-TSO. In: D'Hondt, T. (ed.) ECOOP 2010. LNCS, vol. 6183, pp. 478–503. Springer, Heidelberg (2010)
23. Corina, S.: Păsăreanu and Willem Visser. A Survey of New trends in Symbolic Execution for Software Testing and Analysis. Int. J. Softw. Tools Technol. Transf. 11(4), 339–353 (2009)
24. Reif, W., Schellhorn, G., Stenzel, K., Balser, M.: Structured Specifications and Interactive Proofs with KIV. In: Automated Deduction—A Basis for Applications. Interactive Theorem Proving, vol. II, ch. 1, pp. 13–39. Kluwer (1998)
25. Schellhorn, G., Wehrheim, H., Derrick, J.: How to prove algorithms linearisable. In: Madhusudan, P., Seshia, S.A. (eds.) CAV 2012. LNCS, vol. 7358, pp. 243–259. Springer, Heidelberg (2012)
26. Sewell, P., Sarkar, S., Owens, S., Nardelli, F.Z., Myreen, M.O.: x86-TSO: a rigorous and usable programmer's model for x86 multiprocessors. Commun. ACM 53(7), 89–97 (2010)
27. Travkin, O., Mütze, A., Wehrheim, H.: SPIN as a linearizability checker under weak memory models. In: Bertacco, V., Legay, A. (eds.) HVC 2013. LNCS, vol. 8244, pp. 311–326. Springer, Heidelberg (2013)
28. Vafeiadis, V., Herlihy, M., Hoare, T., Shapiro, M.: Proving correctness of highly-concurrent linearisable objects. In: Torrellas, J., Chatterjee, S. (eds.) PPOPP, pp. 129–136 (2006)
29. Vechev, M., Yahav, E., Yorsh, G.: Experience with model checking linearizability. In: Păsăreanu, C.S. (ed.) SPIN 2009. LNCS, vol. 5578, pp. 261–278. Springer, Heidelberg (2009)

Partial Quantifier Elimination

Eugene Goldberg and Panagiotis Manolios

Northeastern University, USA
{eigold,pete}@ccs.neu.edu

Abstract. We consider the problem of Partial Quantifier Elimination (PQE). Given formula $\exists X[F(X,Y) \wedge G(X,Y)]$, where F, G are in conjunctive normal form, the PQE problem is to find a formula $F^*(Y)$ such that $F^* \wedge \exists X[G] \equiv \exists X[F \wedge G]$. We solve the PQE problem by generating and adding to F clauses over the free variables that make the clauses of F with quantified variables *redundant* in $\exists X[F \wedge G]$. The traditional Quantifier Elimination problem (QE) can be viewed as a degenerate case of PQE where G is empty so *all* clauses of the input formula with quantified variables need to be made redundant. The importance of PQE is threefold. First, in non-degenerate cases, PQE can be solved more efficiently than QE. Second, many problems are more naturally formulated in terms of PQE rather than QE. Third, an efficient PQE-algorithm will enable new methods of model checking and SAT-solving. We describe a PQE algorithm based on the machinery of dependency sequents and give experimental results showing the promise of PQE.

1 Introduction

The elimination of existential quantifiers is an important problem arising in many practical applications. We will refer to this problem as the Quantifier Elimination problem, or QE. Given a formula $\exists X[G]$ where G is a propositional formula, the **QE problem** is to find a quantifier free formula G^* such that $G^* \equiv \exists X[G]$. In this paper, we assume that all propositional formulas are represented in conjunctive normal form (CNF).

Unfortunately, the efficiency of current QE algorithms still leaves much to be desired. This is why many successful theorem proving methods such as interpolation and IC3 avoid QE and use SAT-based approaches instead. The lack of efficient QE solvers can be addressed by looking for variations of QE that are easier to solve. In this paper, we consider such a variation called Partial QE (PQE). Given formula $\exists X[F(X,Y) \wedge G(X,Y)]$, the **PQE problem** is to find a quantifier free formula $F^*(Y)$ such that $F^* \wedge \exists X[G] \equiv \exists X[F \wedge G]$. We will say that F^* is obtained by **taking F out of the scope of the quantifiers**. QE can be viewed as a degenerate case of PQE where G is empty and so the entire formula is taken out of the scope of quantifiers. In the following exposition, when contrasting PQE and QE we mean non-degenerate instances of PQE.

An important advantage of PQE over QE is that the former is "structurally sound". A prototypical QE problem is to compute the range of a circuit. Let formula $G(X,Y,Z)$ specify a combinational circuit N where X, Y, Z are sets of

E. Yahav (Ed.): HVC 2014, LNCS 8855, pp. 148–164, 2014.

input, internal and output variables respectively. Then a formula $G^*(Z)$ such that $G^* \equiv \exists W[G]$ where $W = X \cup Y$ specifies the range of N. The very definition of QE forces one to build formula G^* by *destroying* the structure of G inherited from circuit N. A prototypical PQE problem [8] is to compute reduction of range of N when one excludes the inputs of N falsifying a formula $F(X)$. Let $F^*(Z)$ be a formula such that $F^* \wedge \exists W[G] \equiv \exists W[F \wedge G]$. One can view the assignments falsifying F^* as the outputs excluded from the range of N after the inputs falsifying F are removed from consideration. So F^* describes the reduction in the range of N caused by constraining its inputs by F. Note that computation of formula F^* leaves formula G *intact*. Moreover, an intelligent PQE-solver will *exploit* the structure of G to find F^* more efficiently.

Besides our interest in PQE as being "structurally sound", our motivation for studying PQE is twofold. First, in addition to traditional QE applications, PQE brings in many new ones. In Subsection 2.1, we show that PQE can be used to compute states reachable *only* from a specified set of states, which enables a new class of model checkers. Subsection 2.3 gives an example of using PQE for SAT-solving. Second, in some cases, even if the original problem is formulated in terms of QE, it can sometimes be reduced to PQE. In Subsection 2.2, we show that this is the case for pre-image computation in backward model checking.

The relation between efficiency of solving PQE and QE can be better understood in terms of clause redundancy [7]. The PQE problem of taking F out of the scope of quantifiers in $\exists X[F \wedge G]$ reduces to finding a set of clauses F^* that makes all X-clauses of F redundant in $\exists X[F \wedge G]$. (An **X-clause** is a clause that contains a variable from X.) Then every clause of F can be either dropped as redundant or removed from the scope of the quantifiers as it contains only free variables.

One can view the process of building F^* as follows. X-clauses of F are made redundant in $\exists X[F \wedge G]$ by adding to F resolvent clauses derived from $F \wedge G$. Notice that no clause obtained by resolving *only* clauses of G needs to be made redundant. Adding resolvents to F goes on until all X-clauses of the current formula F are redundant. At this point, the X-clauses of F can be dropped and the remaining clauses of F form F^*. If F is much smaller than G, the process of solving PQE looks like wave propagation where F is the original "perturbation" and G is the "media" where this wave propagates. Such propagation can be efficient even if G is large. By contrast, when solving the QE problem for $\exists X[F \wedge G]$ one needs to make redundant the X-clauses of both F and G and *all* resolvent X-clauses including the ones obtained by resolving only clauses of G.

In this paper, we describe a PQE-algorithm called *DS-PQE* that is based on the machinery of D-Sequents [6, 7]. One needs this machinery for PQE for the same reason as for QE [6]. Every clause of $F^*(Y)$ can be obtained by resolving clauses of $F \wedge G$. However, the number of clauses that are implied by $F \wedge G$ and depend only on Y is, in general, exponential in $|Y|$. So it is crucial to identify the moment when the set of clauses derived so far that depend only on Y is sufficient to make the X-clauses of F redundant in $\exists X[F \wedge G]$. The machinery of D-sequents is used by *DS-PQE* to perform such identification.

The following exposition is structured as follows. In Section 2, we discuss some problems that can benefit from an efficient PQE-algorithm. A run of *DS-PQE* on a simple formula is described in Section 3. Sections 4 and 5 give basic definitions and recall the notion of D-Sequents. In Section 6, algorithm *DS-PQE* is described. Some background is given in Section 7. In Section 8, we experimentally compare *DS-PQE* with our QE algorithm from [7] in the context of model checking. We make conclusions in Section 9.

2   Some Applications of PQE

In this section, we describe some applications where using an efficient PQE solver can be very beneficial. More applications of PQE can be found in [8–10]. Section 2.1 shows that PQE can be used to compute the set of states reachable *only* from a specified set of states, which enables a new type of model checkers [8]. In Subsection 2.2, we describe application of PQE to the traditional method of backward model checking. Application of PQE to SAT-solving is presented in Subsection 2.3.

2.1   Enabling a New Type of Model Checkers

The basic operation of forward model checking is to compute the set of states reachable from another set of states or to find its over-approximation. In this subsection, we show that one can use PQE to compute the set of states reachable *only* from a specified set of states. This enables a new type of model checkers [8] that iteratively eliminate traces of reachable states. This elimination goes on until a counterexample is found or the set of possible behaviors is reduced to one trace consisting of good states. These new model checkers have a great potential in verification of sequential circuits e.g. they can be used to find very deep bugs.

Let $T(S, S')$ be a transition relation where S and S' specify the current and next state variables respectively. We will refer to complete assignments s and s' to variables S and S' as present and next states respectively. Let C^s be the longest clause of variables of S that is falsified by s. The set of states reachable from s in one transition is specified by formula $R^s(S')$ logically equivalent to $\exists S[\overline{C^s} \wedge T]$. That is for every state s' *satisfying* R^s there is a transition from state s.

Let formula $H(S)$ specify a set of states. Let s be one of states specified by H i.e. $H(s) = 1$. Now we show how to compute the *subset* of states specified by R^s that consists of states reachable in one transition *only* from s. More precisely, we want to exclude from R^s every state that is reachable in one transition from a state r satisfying H and different from s. Let $Q^s(S')$ be a CNF formula such that $Q^s \wedge \exists S[H \wedge T] \equiv \exists S[C^s \wedge H \wedge T]$. It is not hard to show that $Q^s(s') = 0$ iff a) s' is reachable in one transition only from state s or b) s' is not reachable from a state specified by H in one transition. The states of item b) are just "noise" i.e. Q^s remains a solution to the PQE problem above even if it is not falsified by any of such states. So, complete assignments *falsifying* Q^s specify the states reachable only from s modulo some noise. The set of states reachable only from s can be very *small* even when the set of states reachable from s is *huge*. This important fact is what enables the new type of model checkers mentioned above.

2.2   Computing Pre-image in Backward Model Checking

Let formula $F(S')$ specify a set of next-states and $H(S)$ specify the pre-image of $F(S')$. That is, a present state s satisfies H iff there exists a next state s' such that $F(s') \wedge T(s, s') = 1$. Here T is a transition relation.

Finding H comes down to building a formula logically equivalent to $\exists S'[F \wedge T]$ i.e. reduces to QE. However, one can construct the pre-image of F by PQE as follows. Let F^* be a formula such that $F^* \wedge \exists S'[T] \equiv \exists S'[F \wedge T]$ i.e., F^* is a solution to the PQE problem. Notice that $\exists S'[T] \equiv 1$ and hence can be dropped. Indeed, for every present state s there always exists some next state s' such that $T(s, s') = 1$. So $F^* \equiv \exists S'[F \wedge T]$ and therefore F^* specifies the pre-image of F. In other words, here QE reduces to PQE.

2.3   SAT-Solving by PQE

In this subsection, we give a method of using PQE for SAT-solving. Other methods of applying PQE to SAT-solving can be found in [9, 10].

Testing the satisfiability of a CNF formula $G(X)$ is equivalent to checking if formula $\exists X[G]$ is true. The latter problem can be viewed as a special instance of QE where *all* variables are quantified. In this case, every non-empty clause of G is an X-clause and needs to be proved redundant to solve the QE problem. If the clauses of G are proved redundant in $\exists X[G]$ without derivation of an empty clause, then G is satisfiable. Otherwise, it is unsatisfiable.

Let x be a complete assignment to variables of X that falsifies G. Let F be the set of clauses of G that are falsified by x. Formula $\exists X[G]$ can be represented as $\exists X[F \wedge G']$ where $G' = G \setminus F$. Let us consider the PQE problem of finding formula F^* such that $F^* \wedge \exists X[G'] \equiv \exists X[F \wedge G']$. Since $\exists X[F \wedge G']$ has no free variables, F^* is a constant. If $F^* \equiv 1$, then the clauses of F are redundant in $\exists X[F \wedge G']$. In other words, G is satisfiable iff G' is. Since x satisfies G', the original formula G is *satisfiable* as well. If $F^* \equiv 0$, then, to take F out of the scope of quantifiers, one needs to derive an empty clause from $F \wedge G'$ i.e. from G. In this case, G is obviously *unsatisfiable*. So, to check the satisfiability of G, PQE needs to prove *only* redundancy of clauses of F as opposed to proving redundancy of *all* clauses of G in QE.

The PQE algorithm we present in this paper is not powerful enough to compete with SAT-solvers yet. (One of the problems here is that D-sequents are not re-used. A brief discussion of this topic is given in Section 8). However, this may change soon.

3   Example

In this section, we describe a run of a PQE algorithm called *DS-PQE* that is described in Section 6. *DS-PQE* is based on the machinery of Dependency sequents.

The latter will be formally defined in Section 5. Recall that an X-clause is a clause that contains at least one variable from a set X of Boolean variables.

Let $F = C_1 \wedge C_2$ where $C_1 = y \vee x_1$, $C_2 = \overline{y} \vee x_3$ Let $G = C_3 \wedge C_4 \wedge C_5 \wedge C_6$ where $C_3 = \overline{x}_1 \vee x_2$, $C_4 = \overline{x}_1 \vee \overline{x}_2$, $C_5 = \overline{x}_3 \vee x_4$, $C_6 = y \vee \overline{x}_4$. Let $X = \{x_1, x_2, x_3, x_4\}$ be the set of variables quantified in formula $\exists X[F \wedge G]$. So y is the only free variable of $\exists X[F \wedge G]$.

Problem formulation. Suppose one needs to solve the PQE problem of taking F out of the scope of the quantifiers in $\exists X[F \wedge G]$. That is one needs to find $F^*(y)$ such that $F^* \wedge \exists X[G] \equiv \exists X[F \wedge G]$. Below, we describe a run of *DS-PQE* when solving this problem.

Search tree. DS-PQE is a branching algorithm. It first proves redundancy of X-clauses of F in subspaces and then merges results of different branches. When *DS-PQE* returns to the root of the search tree, all the X-clauses of F are proved redundant in $\exists X[F \wedge G]$. The search tree built by *DS-PQE* is given in Figure 1. It also shows the nodes where new clauses C_7 and C_8 were derived. *DS-PQE* assigns free variables *before* quantified. So, variable y is assigned first. At every node of the search tree specified by assignment $\boldsymbol{q}$, *DS-PQE* maintains a set of clauses denoted as $PR(\boldsymbol{q})$. Here PR stands for "clauses to Prove Redundant". We will refer to a clause of $PR(\boldsymbol{q})$ as a **PR-clause**.

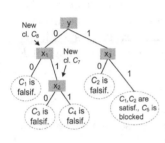

Fig. 1. The search tree built by *DS-PQE*

Adding a clause to $PR(\boldsymbol{q})$ is an *obligation* to prove redundancy of this clause in subspace $\boldsymbol{q}$. $PR(\boldsymbol{q})$ includes all X-clauses of F plus some X-clauses of G. The latter are proved redundant to make proving redundancy of X-clauses of F easier. Sets $PR(\boldsymbol{q})$ are shown in Figure 3. For every non-leaf node of the search tree, two sets of PR-clauses are shown. The set on the left side (respectively right side) of node $\boldsymbol{q}$ gives $PR(\boldsymbol{q})$ when visiting node $\boldsymbol{q}$ for the first time (respectively when backtracking to the right branch of node $\boldsymbol{q}$).

Using D-sequents. The main concern of *DS-PQE* is to prove redundancy of PR-clauses. Branching is used to reach subspaces where proving redundancy is easy. The redundancy of a PR-clause C is expressed by a Dependency Sequent (D-sequent). In short notation, a D-sequent is a record $\boldsymbol{s} \to \{C\}$ saying that clause C is redundant in formula $\exists X[F \wedge G]$ in any subspace where assignment $\boldsymbol{s}$ is made. We will refer to $\boldsymbol{s}$ as the **conditional part** of the D-sequent. The D-sequents $S_1, \ldots, S_7$ derived by *DS-PQE* are shown in Figure 2. They are numbered in the order they were generated. So-called atomic D-sequents record trivial cases of redundancy. More complex D-sequents are derived by a resolution-like operation called *join*.

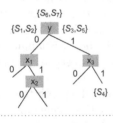

$S_1: (y=0) \to \{C_2\}$, $S_2: (y=0) \to \{C_1\}$,
$S_3: (y=1) \to \{C_1\}$, $S_4: (y=1) \to \{C_5\}$,
$S_5: (y=1) \to \{C_2\}$,
$S_6: \varnothing \to \{C_1\}$, $S_7: \varnothing \to \{C_2\}$

Fig. 2. Derived D-sequents

When *DS-PQE* returns to the root, it derives D-sequents stating the unconditional redundancy of the X-clauses of F.

Merging results of different branches. Let v be the current branching variable and $v = 0$ be the first branch explored by *DS-PQE*. After completing this branch, *DS-PQE* proves redundancy of all clauses that currently have the PR-status. (The only exception is the case when a PR-clause gets falsified in branch $v = 0$. We discuss this exception below.) Then *DS-PQE* explores branch $v = 1$ and derives D-sequents stating redundancy of clauses in this branch. Before backtracking from node v, *DS-PQE* uses operation *join* to produce D-sequents whose conditional part does not depend on v. For example, in branch $y = 0$, D-sequent S_1 equal to $(y = 0) \rightarrow \{C_2\}$ was derived. In branch $y = 1$, D-sequent S_5 equal to $(y = 1) \rightarrow \{C_2\}$ was derived. By joining S_1 and S_5 at variable y, D-sequent S_7 equal to $\emptyset \rightarrow \{C_2\}$ was produced where the conditional part did not depend on y.

Derivation of new clauses. Proving redundancy of PR-clauses in subspace $y = 0$ required derivation of clauses $C_7 = \overline{x}_1$ and $C_8 = y$. For instance, clause C_7 was generated at node $(y = 0, x_1 = 1)$ by resolving C_3 and C_4. Clause C_7 was *temporarily* added to F to make PR-clauses C_3 and C_4 redundant at the node above. However, C_7 was removed from formula F after derivation of clause C_8 because the former is subsumed by the latter in subspace $y = 0$. This is similar to conflict clause generation in SAT-solvers where the intermediate resolvents are discarded.

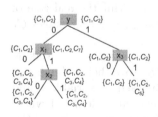

Fig. 3. Dynamics of the $PR(q)$ set

Derivation of atomic D-sequents. $S_1, \ldots, S_5$ are the atomic D-sequents derived by *DS-PQE*. They record trivial cases of redundancy. (Due to the simplicity of this example, the conditional part of all atomic D-sequents has only assignment to y *i.e.*, the free variable. In general, however, the conditional part of a D-sequent also contains assignments to quantified variables.) There are three kinds of atomic D-sequents. *D-sequents of the first kind* state redundancy of clauses satisfied in a subspace. For instance, D-sequent S_1 states redundancy of clause C_2 satisfied by assignment $y = 0$. *D-sequents of the second kind* record the fact that a clause is redundant because some other clause is falsified in the current subspace. For instance, D-sequent S_2 states that C_1 is redundant because clause $C_8 = y$ is falsified in subspace $y = 0$. *D-sequents of the third kind* record the fact that a clause is redundant in a subspace because it is blocked [15] at a variable v. That is this clause cannot be resolved on v. For example, D-sequent S_4 states redundancy of C_5 that cannot be resolved on x_4 in subspace $(y = 1, x_3 = 1)$. Clause C_5 is resolvable on x_4 only with C_6 but C_6 is satisfied by assignment $y = 1$. Atomic D-sequents are further discussed in Subsection 6.3.

Computation of the set of PR-clauses. The original set of PR-clauses is equal to the the initial set of X-clauses of F. Denote this set as PR_{init}. In our example,

$PR_{init} = \{C_1, C_2\}$. There are two situations where $PR(q)$ is extended. The first situation occurs when a parent clause of a new resolvent is in $PR(q)$ and this resolvent is an X-clause. Then this resolvent is added to $PR(q)$. An example of that is clause $C_7 = \overline{x_1}$ obtained by resolving PR-clauses C_3 and C_4.

The second situation occurs when a PR-clause becomes unit. Suppose a PR-clause C is unit at node q and v is the unassigned variable of C where $v \in X$. DS-PQE first makes the assignment falsifying C. Suppose that this is assignment $v = 0$. Note that all PR-clauses but C itself are obviously redundant at node $q \cup (v = 0)$. DS-PQE backtracks and explores the branch $v = 1$ where clause C is satisfied. At this point DS-PQE extends the set $PR(q \cup (v = 1))$ by adding *every* clause of $F \wedge G$ that a) has literal $\overline{v}$; b) is not satisfied; c) is not already in $PR(q)$. The extension of the set of PR-clauses in the second situation is done to guarantee that clause C will be proved redundant when backtracking off the node q. Depending on whether formula $F \wedge G$ is satisfiable or unsatisfiable in branch $v = 1$, the second situation splits into two cases considered below.

The first case is that formula $F \wedge G$ is *unsatisfiable* in branch $v = 1$. Then extension of the set of PR-clauses above guarantees that a clause falsified by $q \cup (v = 1)$ will be derived to make the new PR-clauses redundant. Most importantly, this clause will be resolved with C on v to produce a clause rendering C redundant in subspace q. In our example, the first case occurs at node $y = 0$ where PR-clause C_1 becomes unit. DS-PQE falsifies C_1 in branch $x_1 = 0$, backtracks and explores branch $x_1 = 1$. In this branch, clauses C_3, C_4 of G are made PR-clauses. This branch is unsatisfiable. Making C_3, C_4 PR-clauses forces DS-PQE to derive $C_7 = \overline{x_1}$ that makes C_3, C_4 redundant. But the real goal of obtaining C_7 is to resolve it with C_1 to produce clause $C_8 = y$ that makes C_1 redundant.

The second case is that formula $F \wedge G$ is *satisfiable* in branch $v = 1$. Making the clauses with literal $\overline{v}$ PR-clauses forces DS-PQE to prove their redundancy. So when backtracking to node q, clause C will be blocked at variable v and hence redundant. In our example, the second case occurs at node $y = 1$ where clause C_2 becomes unit. Clause C_2 gets falsified in branch $x_3 = 0$. Then DS-PQE backtracks and explores branch $x_3 = 1$. In this branch, C_5 of G becomes a new PR-clause as containing literal $\overline{x_3}$. This branch is satisfiable and C_5 is proved redundant without adding new clauses. Due to redundancy of C_5, clause C_2 gets blocked at node $y = 1$ and hence redundant.

Importantly, the extension of the set $PR(q)$ in the first and second situations above is *temporary*. Suppose that a clause C is added to $PR(q)$ as a result of the first situation. That is at least one of the parents of C is a PR-clause. Then C preserves its PR-status as long as its parents (see Subsection 6.7 for more details). In the second situation, the clauses that became PR-clauses at node q lose their PR-status when DS-PQE backtracks off this node.

Forming a solution to the PQE problem. The D-sequents derived by DS-PQE at a node of the search tree are *composable*. This means that the clauses that are redundant individually are also redundant together. For example, on returning to the root node, D-sequents S_6 and S_7 equal to $\emptyset \rightarrow \{C_1\}$ and $\emptyset \rightarrow \{C_2\}$

respectively are derived. The composability of S_6 and S_7 means that D-sequent $\emptyset \rightarrow \{C_1, C_2\}$ holds as well. The only new clause added to F is $C_8 = y$ (clause C_7 was added temporarily). After dropping the X-clauses C_1, C_2 from F as proved redundant one concludes that $y \wedge \exists X[G] \equiv \exists X[F \wedge G]$ and $F^* = y$ is a solution to the PQE problem.

4   Basic Definitions

In this section, we give relevant definitions.

Definition 1. *An* **∃CNF formula** *is a formula of the form* $\exists X[F]$ *where* F *is a Boolean CNF formula, and* X *is a set of Boolean variables. Let* q *be an assignment,* F *be a CNF formula, and* C *be a clause. Vars(q) denotes the variables assigned in* q*; Vars(F) denotes the set of variables of* F*; Vars(C) denotes the variables of* C*; and Vars($\exists X[F]$) = Vars(F) \ X.*

We consider *true* and *false* as a special kind of clauses.

Definition 2. *Let* C *be a clause,* H *be a CNF formula, and* q *be an assignment such that Vars(q) $\subseteq$ Vars(H). Denote by* C_q *the clause equal to true if* C *is satisfied by* q*; otherwise* C_q *is the clause obtained from* C *by removing all literals falsified by* q*. H_q denotes the formula obtained from* H *by replacing every clause* C *of* H *with* C_q*. In this paper, we assume that clause* C_q *equal to true remains in* H_q*. We treat such a clause as redundant in* H_q*.*

Let $\exists X[H]$ be an ∃CNF and y be an assignment to $Vars(H) \setminus X$. Note that in this case, $(\exists X[H])_y = \exists X[H_y]$.

Definition 3. *Let* S, Q *be ∃CNF formulas. We say that* S, Q *are* **equivalent***, written* $S \equiv Q$*, if for all assignments,* y*, such that Vars(y) $\supseteq$ (Vars(S) $\cup$ Vars(Q)), we have* $S_y = Q_y$*. Notice that* S_y *and* Q_y *have no free variables, so by* $S_y = Q_y$ *we mean semantic equivalence.*

Definition 4. *The* **Quantifier Elimination (QE) problem** *for ∃CNF formula* $\exists X[H]$ *is to find a CNF formula* H^* *such that* $H^* \equiv \exists X[H]$*. The* **Partial QE (PQE) problem** *for ∃CNF formula* $\exists X[F \wedge G]$ *is to find a CNF formula* F^* *such that* $F^* \wedge \exists X[G] \equiv \exists X[F \wedge G]$*.*

Definition 5. *Let* X *be a set of Boolean variables,* H *be a CNF formula and* R *be a subset of* X*-clauses of* H*. The clauses of* R *are* **redundant** *in CNF formula* H *if* $H \equiv (H \setminus R)$*. The clauses of* R *are* **redundant** *in ∃CNF formula* $\exists X[H]$ *if* $\exists X[H] \equiv \exists X[H \setminus R]$*. Note that* $H \equiv (H \setminus R)$ *implies* $\exists X[H] \equiv \exists X[H \setminus R]$ *but the opposite is not true.*

The notion of clause redundancy in a *quantified* formula is very powerful. For example, if formula $H(X)$ is satisfiable, *every* clause of H is redundant in $\exists X[H]$.

5   Dependency Sequents

In this section, we recall clause Dependency sequents (D-sequents) introduced in [7], operation *join* and the notion of composability. Informally, the join operation extends resolution-like reasoning to subspaces where formula is satisfiable. For example, in Definition 7, formula H can be satisfiable in subspaces s' and s''. In this paper, we will refer to clause D-sequents of [7] as just D-sequents.

Definition 6. *Let $\exists X[H]$ be an $\exists$CNF formula. Let s be an assignment to $Vars(H)$ and R be a subset of X-clauses of H. A dependency sequent (**D-sequent**) has the form $(\exists X[H], s) \rightarrow R$. It states that the clauses of R_s are redundant in $\exists X[H_s]$. Alternatively, we will say that the clauses of R are redundant in $\exists X[H]$ in subspace s (and in any other subspace q such that $s \subseteq q$).*

We will say that a D-sequent $(\exists X[H], s) \rightarrow R$ **holds**, to tell apart a correct D-sequent where clauses of R are indeed redundant in $\exists X[H]$ in subspace s from a record $(\exists X[H], s) \rightarrow R$ relating an arbitrary s with some set R of X-clauses.

Definition 7. *Let $\exists X[H]$ be an $\exists$CNF formula. Let D-sequents $(\exists X[H], s') \rightarrow R$ and $(\exists X[H], s'') \rightarrow R$ hold. We will refer to them as parent D-sequents. Let s', s'' have precisely one variable $v \in Vars(s') \cap Vars(s'')$ that is assigned differently in s' and s''. Let s be the assignment equal to $s' \cup s''$ minus assignments to variable v. We will say that D-sequent $(\exists X[H], s) \rightarrow R$ is obtained by **joining** the parent D-sequents at v. The fact that the parent D-sequents hold implies that the D-sequent obtained by joining them at v holds too [7].*

Definition 8. *Let $(\exists X[H], s') \rightarrow R'$ and $(\exists X[H], s'') \rightarrow R''$ be two D-sequents such that every assignment to variables of $Vars(s') \cap Vars(s'')$ is the same in s' and s''. We will call these D-sequents **composable** if the D-sequent $(\exists X[H], s' \cup s'') \rightarrow R' \cup R''$ holds.*

6   Algorithm

In this section, we describe a PQE algorithm called **DS-PQE** where DS stands for Dependency Sequents. *DS-PQE* algorithm is the result of a substantial modification of our QE algorithm *DCDS* described in [7]. The new features of *DS-PQE* are summarized in Subsection 6.7.

DS-PQE derives D-sequents $(\exists X[F \wedge G], s) \rightarrow \{C\}$ stating the redundancy of PR-clause C in any subspace q such that $s \subseteq q$. From now on, we will use a short notation of D-sequents writing $s \rightarrow \{C\}$ instead of $(\exists X[F \wedge G], s) \rightarrow \{C\}$. We will assume that the parameter $\exists X[F \wedge G]$ missing in $s \rightarrow \{C\}$ is the *current* $\exists$CNF formula (with all resolvents added to F). One can omit $\exists X[F \wedge G]$ from D-sequents because $(\exists X[F \wedge G], s) \rightarrow \{C\}$ holds no matter how many resolvent clauses are added to F [7]. We will call D-sequent $s \rightarrow \{C\}$ **active** in subspace q if $s \subseteq q$. The fact that $s \rightarrow \{C\}$ is active in subspace q means that C is redundant in $\exists X[F \wedge G]$ in subspace q.

6.1   Input and Output of *DS-PQE*

Recall that a PR-clause is an X-clause of $F \wedge G$ whose redundancy needs to be proved in subspace q (see Section 3). *DS-PQE* shown in Figure 4 accepts an $\exists$CNF formula $\exists X[F \wedge G]$ (denoted as Φ), an assignment q to $Vars(F)$, the set of PR-clauses (denoted as W) and a set Ω of D-sequents active in subspace q stating redundancy of *some* PR-clauses in $\exists X[F \wedge G]$ in subspace q.

// q is an assignment to $Vars(F \wedge G)$
// Ω is a set of active D-sequents
// Φ denotes $\exists X[F \wedge G]$
// W denotes $PR(q)$
// If ds_pqe returns nil (or a clause),
// $(F \wedge G)_q$ is sat. (respect. unsat.)

$ds\_pqe(\Phi,W,q,\Omega)\{$
1   if $(\exists C \in F \cup G$ is falsif. by $q)$ {
2        $\Omega := atomic\_Dseqs1(\Omega, q, C);$
3   return$(\Phi, \Omega, C);\}$
4     $\Omega := atomic\_Dseqs2(\Phi, q, \Omega);$
5*   if $(every\_PR\_clause\_redund(W, \Omega))$
6*   return$(\Phi, \Omega, nil);$
        - - - - - - - - - - - - -
7     $v := pick\_variable(F \wedge G, q, \Omega);$
8     $q_b := q \cup \{(v = b)\};$
9* $(\Phi, \Omega, C_b) := ds\_pqe(\Phi,W,q_b,\Omega);$
10    $\Omega^- := InactiveDseqs(F, \Omega, v);$
11   if $(\Omega^- = \emptyset)$ return$(\Phi, \Omega, C_b);$
12    $\Omega := \Omega \setminus \Omega^-;$
13*   if $(impl\_assgn(v, \overline{b}))$
14* $W' := newPRclauses(W, F \wedge G, \overline{b});$
15*   else $W' := \emptyset;$
16    $q_{\overline{b}} := q \cup \{(v = \overline{b})\}; W'' := W \cup W';$
17* $(\Phi, \Omega, C_{\overline{b}}) := ds\_pqe(\Phi,W'',q_{\overline{b}},\Omega);$
        - - - - - - - - - - - - -
18   if $((C_b \neq nil)$ and $(C_{\overline{b}} \neq nil))\{$
19       $C := resolve\_clauses(C_b, C_{\overline{b}}, v);$
20       $F := F \wedge C;$
21       $\Omega := atomic\_Dseqs1(\Omega, q, C);$
22*   if $((C_b \in W)$ or $(C_{\overline{b}} \in W))$
23*   if $(X\_clause(C))$
24* $W := W \cup \{C\};$
25   return$(\Phi, \Omega, C);\}$
26    $\Omega := merge(\Phi, q, v, \Omega^-, \Omega, C_b, C_{\overline{b}});$
27   return$(\Phi, \Omega, nil);\}$

Fig. 4. *DS-PQE* procedure

Similarly to Section 3, we will assume that the resolvent clauses are added to formula F while formula G remains unchanged. *DS-PQE* returns a formula $\exists X[F \wedge G]$ modified by resolvent clauses added to F (if any), a set Ω of D-sequents active in subspace q that state redundancy of *all* PR-clauses in $\exists X[F \wedge G]$ in subspace q and a clause C or nil. If $(F \wedge G)_q$ is unsatisfiable, C is a clause of $F \wedge G$ falsified by q. Otherwise, *DS-PQE* returns nil meaning that no clause implied by $F \wedge G$ is falsified by q.

The active D-sequents derived by *DS-PQE* are composable. That is if $s_1 \rightarrow \{C_1\},\dots, s_k \rightarrow \{C_k\}$ are the active D-sequents of subspace q, then the D-sequent $s^* \rightarrow \{C_1, \dots, C_k\}$ holds where $s^* = s_1 \cup \dots \cup s_k$ and $s^* \subseteq q$. Like *DCDS*, *DS-PQE* achieves composability of D-sequents by proving redundancy of PR-clauses in a particular order (that can be different for different paths). This guarantees that no circular reasoning is possible and hence the D-sequents derived at a node of the search tree are composable.

A solution to the PQE problem in subspace q is obtained by discarding the PR-clauses of subspace q (specified by W) from the CNF formula F returned by *DS-PQE*. To solve the original problem of taking F out of the scope of the quantifiers in $\exists X[F \wedge G]$, one needs to call *DS-PQE* with $q = \emptyset$, $\Omega = \emptyset$, $W = PR_{init}$. Recall that PR_{init} is the set of X-clauses of the original formula F.

6.2   The Big Picture

DS-PQE consists of three parts separated in Figure 4 by the dotted lines. In the first part (lines 1-6), *DS-PQE* builds atomic D-sequents recording trivial cases of redundancy of PR-clauses. If all the PR-clauses are proved redundant in $\exists X[F \wedge G]$ in subspace q, *DS-PQE* terminates at node q.

If some PR-clauses are not proved redundant yet, *DS-PQE* enters the second part of the code (lines 7-17). First, *DS-PQE* picks a branching variable v (line 7). Then it recursively calls itself (line 9) starting the left branch of v by adding to q assignment $v = b$, $b \in \{0,1\}$. Once the left branch is finished, *DS-PQE* explores the right branch $v = \bar{b}$ (line 17).

In the third part, *DS-PQE* merges the left and right branches (lines 18-27). This merging results in proving all PR-clauses redundant in $\exists X[F \wedge G]$ in subspace q. For every PR-clause C proved redundant in subspace q, the set Ω contains precisely one active D-sequent $s \rightarrow \{C\}$ where $s \subseteq q$. As soon as C is proved redundant, it is marked and ignored until *DS-PQE* enters a subspace q' where $s \not\subseteq q'$ i.e., a subspace where D-sequent $s \rightarrow \{C\}$ becomes inactive. Then clause C gets unmarked signaling that *DS-PQE* does not have a proof of redundancy of C in subspace q' yet.

6.3   Building Atomic D-Sequents

Procedures *atomic_Dseqs1* and *atomic_Dseqs2* are called by *DS-PQE* to compute D-sequents for trivial cases of clause redundancy listed in Section 3. We refer to such D-sequents as *atomic*. Procedure *atomic_Dseqs1* is called when a clause C of $F \wedge G$ is falsified by q. For every PR-clause C'_q of F_q that has no active D-sequent yet, *atomic_Dseq1* generates a D-sequent $s \rightarrow \{C'\}$. Here s is the shortest assignment falsifying C.

If no clause of $F \wedge G$ is falsified by q, procedure *atomic_Dseqs2* is called. It builds D-sequents for PR-clauses that became satisfied or blocked in F_q. Let C be a clause satisfied by q. Then D-sequent $s \rightarrow \{C\}$ is generated where $s = (w=b)$, $b \in \{0,1\}$ is the assignment to a variable w satisfying C.

Let clause C be blocked [15] in F_q at variable $w \in X$. Let K be the set of clauses of $F \wedge G$ that can be resolved with C on w. The fact that C is blocked in F_q means that every clause of K is either satisfied by q or is proved redundant in subspace q. In this case, *atomic_Dseqs2* generates a D-sequent $s \rightarrow \{C\}$ where s is constructed as follows. If $C' \in K$ is satisfied by q, then s contains the assignment to a variable of $Vars(q)$ that satisfies C'. If $C' \in K$ is proved redundant in subspace q and $r \rightarrow \{C'\}$ is the active D-sequent for C', then s contains r.

6.4   Selection of a Branching Variable

Let q be the assignment *DS-PQE* is called with. Let $Y = Vars(F) \setminus X$. *DS-PQE* branches on unassigned variables of X and Y. Importantly, an unassigned variable $x \in X \setminus Vars(q)$ is picked for branching *only* if a PR-clause contains x and is not proved redundant yet.

Although Boolean Constraint Propagation (BCP) is not shown explicitly in Figure 4, it is included into the *pick_variable* procedure as follows: a) preference is given to branching on variables of unit clauses of F_q (if any); b) if v is a variable of a unit clause C_q of F_q and v is picked for branching, then the value falsifying C_q is assigned first to cause immediate termination of this branch.

To simplify merging results of the left and right branches, *DS-PQE* first assigns values to variables of Y (see Subsection 6.6). This means that *pick_variable* never selects a variable $x \in X$ for branching, if there is an unassigned variable of Y. In particular, BCP does not assign values to variables of X if a variable of Y is still unassigned.

6.5   Switching from Left to Right Branch

Let $s \rightarrow \{C\}$ be a D-sequent of the set Ω computed by *DS-PQE* in the left branch $v = b$ (line 9 of Figure 4). We will call this D-sequent **symmetric in** v, if v is not assigned in s. Otherwise, this D-sequent is called **asymmetric in** v. Notice that if s is symmetric in v, then D-sequent $s \rightarrow \{C\}$ is active in the right branch $v = \bar{b}$ and so C is redundant in $\exists X[F \wedge G]$ in subspace $q \cup \{(v = \bar{b})\}$. Denote by Ω^- the subset of active D-sequents that are asymmetric in v. It is computed in line 10. Before exploring the right branch (line 17), the PR-clauses of $F \wedge G$ whose redundancy is stated by D-sequents of Ω^- become non-redundant again.

6.6   Branch Merging

Let $q_b = q \cup \{(v = b)\}$ and $q_{\bar{b}} = q \cup \{(v = \bar{b})\}$. The goal of branch merging is to use solutions of the PQE problem in subspaces q_b and $q_{\bar{b}}$ to produce a solution to the PQE problem in subspace q. If both F_{q_b} and $F_{q_{\bar{b}}}$ are unsatisfiable, this is done as described in lines 19-25 of Figure 4. Let $C_b, C_{\bar{b}}$ be clauses returned in the left and right branches respectively. Then, the empty clauses $(C_b)_{q_b}$ and $(C_{\bar{b}})_{q_{\bar{b}}}$ are solutions to the PQE in subspaces q_b and $q_{\bar{b}}$. The empty clause C_q where C is the resolvent of C_b and $C_{\bar{b}}$ added to F (line 20) is a solution to the PQE problem in subspace q. After C is added, *atomic_Dseqs1* completes Ω by generation of atomic D-sequents built due to presence of a clause falsified by q.

Suppose that F_{q_b} and/or $F_{q_{\bar{b}}}$ is satisfiable. In this case, to finish solving the QE problem in subspace q, one needs to make sure that every PR-clause is proved redundant in F_q. This means that every PR-clause should have a D-sequent active in subspace q and hence symmetric in the branching variable v. This work is done by procedure *merge* (line 26) that consists of three steps.

In the first step, *merge* takes care of D-sequents of "old" PR-clauses that is the clauses that were present in F at the time the value of v was flipped from b to $\bar{b}$. For every such PR-clause, a D-sequent was derived in the left branch $v = b$. Let S_b be a D-sequent from Ω^- (that is asymmetric in v) that states redundancy of clause C in the left branch. Let $S_{\bar{b}}$ be the D-sequent stating redundancy of C

in the right branch. These D-sequents are joined at variable v to produce a new D-sequent stating redundancy of C in subspace $\boldsymbol{q}$.

In the second step, *merge* processes new PR-clauses that is PR-clauses generated in the right branch $v = \bar{b}$. No D-sequents were derived for such clauses in the branch $v = b$. Let S be a D-sequent $\boldsymbol{s} \rightarrow \{C\}$ derived in the right branch $v = \bar{b}$ where clause C was generated. If S is symmetric in v, it simply remains in Ω untouched. Otherwise, S is updated by removing the assignment to v from $\boldsymbol{s}$.

In the third step, if, say, clause C_b mentioned above is not equal to *nil*, a D-sequent is generated for C_b if it is a PR-clause. It can be shown [7] that due the fact that free variables are assigned before quantified (see Subsection 6.4), clause C_b is always blocked at the branching variable v. So, an atomic D-sequent is built for C_b as described in Subsection 6.3.

6.7   New Features of *DS-PQE* with Respect to *DCDS*

In this subsection, we focus on the part of *DS-PQE* that is different from *DCDS*. The lines of this part are marked with an asterisk inf Figure 4.

The main difference between *DS-PQE* and *DCDS* is that at every node $\boldsymbol{q}$ of the search tree, *DS-PQE* maintains a set $PR(\boldsymbol{q})$ of PR-clauses. $PR(\boldsymbol{q})$ contains all the X-clauses of F and some X-clauses of G (if any). *DS-PQE* terminates its work at node $\boldsymbol{q}$ when all the current PR-clauses are proved redundant (lines 5-6). In contrast to *DS-PQE*, *DCDS* terminates at node $\boldsymbol{q}$, when *all* X-clauses are proved redundant. Line 9 is marked because *DS-PQE* uses an additional parameter W when recursively calling itself to start the left branch of node $\boldsymbol{q}$. Here W specifies the set of PR-clauses to prove redundant in the left branch.

Lines 13-15 show how $PR(\boldsymbol{q})$ is extended. As we discussed in Section 3, this extension takes place when assignment $v = \bar{b}$ satisfies a unit PR-clause C. In this case, the set W' of new PR-clauses is computed. It consists of all the X-clauses that a) contain the literal of v falsified by assignment $v = \bar{b}$; b) are not PR-clauses and c) are not satisfied. As we explained in Section 3, this is done to facilitate proving redundancy of clause C at node $\boldsymbol{q}$. The set W' is added to W before the right branch is explored (lines 16-17). Notice that the clauses of W' have PR-status only in the subtree rooted at node $\boldsymbol{q}$. Upon return to node $\boldsymbol{q}$ from the right branch, the clauses of W' lose their PR-status.

As we mentioned in Section 3, one more source of new PR-clauses are resolvents (lines 22-24). Let $v = b$ and $v = \bar{b}$ be unsatisfiable branches and C_b and $C_{\bar{b}}$ be the clauses returned by *DS-PQE* . If C_b or $C_{\bar{b}}$ is currently a PR-clause, and the resolvent C is an X-clause, then C becomes a new PR-clause. One can think of a PR-clause as supplied with a tag indicating the level up to which this clause preserves its PR-status. If only one of the clauses C_b and $C_{\bar{b}}$ is a PR-clause, then C inherits the tag of this clause. If both parents have the PR-status, the resolvent inherits the tag of the parent clause that preserves its PR-status longer.

6.8 Correctness of *DS-PQE*

The correctness of *DS-PQE* is proved similarly to that of *DCDS* [7]. *DS-PQE* is complete because it examines a finite search tree. Here is an informal explanation of why *DS-PQE* is sound. First, the clauses added to F are produced by resolution and so are correct in the sense they are implied by $F \wedge G$. Second, the atomic D-sequents built by *DS-PQE* are correct. Third, new D-sequents produced by operation *join* are correct. Fourth, the D-sequents of individual clauses are composable.

So when *DS-PQE* returns to the root node of the search tree, it derives the correct D-sequent $(\exists X[F \wedge G], \emptyset) \rightarrow F^X$. Here F^X denotes the set of all X-clauses of F. By removing the X-clauses from F one obtains formula F^* such that $\exists X[F^* \wedge G] \equiv \exists X[F \wedge G]$. Since F^* does not depend on variables of X it can be taken out of the scope of quantifiers.

7 Background

QE has been studied by many researchers, due to its important role in verification *e.g.*, in model checking. QE methods are typically based on BDDs [2, 3] or SAT [16, 11, 17, 13, 5, 12, 14]. At the same time, we do not know of research where the PQE problem was solved or even formulated. Of course, identification and removal of redundant clauses is often used in preprocessing procedures of QBF-algorithms and SAT-solvers [4, 1]. However, these procedures typically exploit only situations where clause redundancies are obvious.

One of the most important differences of PQE from QE is that a PQE-algorithm has to have a significant degree of "structure-awareness". This is because PQE is essentially based on the notion of redundancy of a subset of clauses in a quantified formula. So it is not clear, for example, if a BDD-based algorithm would benefit from replacing QE with PQE. This also applies to many SAT-based algorithms of QE. For instance, in [6] we presented a QE algorithm called DDS that was arguably more structure aware than its SAT-based predecessors. DDS is based on the notion of D-sequents defined in terms of redundancy of variables rather than clauses. DDS makes quantified variables redundant in subspaces and merges the results of different branches. Despite its structure-awareness, it is hard to adjust DDS to solving PQE: in PQE, one, in general, does not eliminate quantified variables (only some clauses with quantified variables are eliminated).

Interestingly, there is no trivial algorithm for solving PQE like solving QE by resolving out quantified variables one by one. For example, one cannot solve PQE by simply resolving out X-clauses of formula F in $\exists X[F \wedge G]$ because this can lead to looping [9].

8   Experimental Results

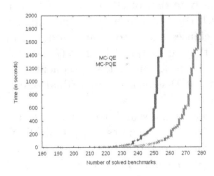

Fig. 5. Performance of model checkers on 282 examples solved by *MC-QE* or *MC-PQE*

Since we are not aware of another tool performing PQE, in the experiments we focused on contrasting PQE and QE. Namely, we compared *DS-PQE* with our QE algorithm called *DCDS* [7]. The fact that *DS-PQE* and *DCDS* are close in terms of implementation techniques is beneficial: any difference in performance should be attributed to difference in algorithms rather than implementations.

In the experiments, we used *DS-PQE* and *DCDS* for backward model checking. It is important to emphasize that, in the long run, we plan to use PQE in new types of model checkers like the ones mentioned in Section 2. However, since these model checkers are not available yet we experimented with *DS-PQE* in the context of a traditional model checker. We will refer to the two algorithms for backward model checking based on *DS-PQE* and *DCDS* as *MC-PQE* and *MC-QE* respectively. The difference between *MC-PQE* and *MC-QE* is as follows. Let $F(S')$ and $T(S, S')$ specify a set of next-states and transition relation respectively. The basic operation here is to find the pre-image $H(S)$ of F where $H \equiv \exists S'[F \wedge T]$. So H is a solution to the QE problem. As we showed in Subsection 2.2, one can also find H just by taking F out of the scope of the quantifiers in formula $\exists S'[F \wedge T]$. *MC-QE* computes H by making redundant *all* S'-clauses of $F \wedge T$ while *MC-PQE* finds H by making redundant *only* the S'-clauses of F.

The current implementations of *DCDS* and *DS-PQE* lack D-sequent re-using: the parent D-sequents are discarded after a join operation. We believe that re-using D-sequents should boost performance like clause recording in SAT-solving. However, when working on a new version of *DCDS* we found out that re-using D-sequents indiscriminately may lead to circular reasoning. We have solved this problem theoretically and resumed our work on the new version of *DCDS*. However, here we report the results of implementations that do not re-use D-sequents.

We compared *MC-PQE* and *MC-QE* on the 758 benchmarks of HWMCC-10 competition [18]. With the time limit of 2,000s, *MC-QE* and *MC-PQE* solved 258 and 279 benchmarks respectively. On the set of 253 benchmarks solved by both model checkers, *MC-PQE* was about 2 times faster (the total time is 4,652s versus 8,528s). However, on the set of 282 benchmarks solved by at least one model checker *MC-PQE* was about 6 times faster (10,652s versus 60,528s). Here we charged 2,000s, *i.e.*, the time limit, for every unsolved benchmark.

Figure 5 gives the performance of *MC-QE* and *MC-PQE* on the 282 benchmarks solved by at least one model checker in terms of the number of problems finished in a given amount of time. Model checking results on some concrete benchmarks are given in Table 1. The column *iterations* show the number of backward images computed by the algorithms before finding a bug or reaching a fixed point.

Table 1. *Model checking results on some concrete examples*

benchmark	#latches	#gates	#iterations	bug	MC-QE (s.)	MC-PQE (s.)
bj08amba3g62	32	9,825	4	no	241	**38**
kenflashp03	51	3,738	2	no	**33**	104
pdtvishuffman2	55	831	6	yes	>2,000	**296**
pdtvisvsar05	82	2,097	4	no	1,368	**7.7**
pdtvisvsa16a01	188	6,162	2	no	>2,000	**17**
texaspimainp12	239	7,987	4	no	807	**580**
texasparsesysp1	312	11,860	10	yes	39	**25**
pj2002	1,175	15,384	3	no	254	**47**
mentorbm1and	4,344	31,684	2	no	**1.4**	1.7

In [7], we compared *MC-QE* with a BDD-based model checker (MC-BDD). This comparison showed that although MC-BDD solved more benchmarks than MC-QE, there were 65 benchmarks solved by MC-QE that MC-BDD failed to solve. In addition to these 65 benchmarks, *MC-PQE* solved 7 more benchmarks that MC-BDD failed to solve (and that were not solved by *MC-QE* either).

Acknowledgment. This research was supported in part by DARPA under AFRL Cooperative Agreement No. FA8750-10-2-0233 and by NSF grants CCF-1117184 and CCF-1319580.

9 Conclusion

We introduced the Partial Quantifier Elimination problem (PQE), a generalization of the Quantifier Elimination problem (QE). We presented a PQE-algorithm based on the machinery of D-sequents and gave experimental results showing that PQE can be more efficient than QE. An efficient PQE-solver will enable new methods of solving old problems like model checking and SAT. In addition, many verification problems can be formulated and solved in terms of PQE rather than QE, a topic ripe for further exploration.

References

1. Biere, A., Lonsing, F., Seidl, M.: Blocked clause elimination for QBF. In: Bjørner, N., Sofronie-Stokkermans, V. (eds.) CADE 2011. LNCS, vol. 6803, pp. 101–115. Springer, Heidelberg (2011)
2. Bryant, R.: Graph-based algorithms for Boolean function manipulation. IEEE Transactions on Computers C-35(8), 677–691 (1986)
3. Chauhan, P., Clarke, E., Jha, S., Kukula, J., Veith, H., Wang, D.: Using combinatorial optimization methods for quantification scheduling. In: Margaria, T., Melham, T.F. (eds.) CHARME 2001. LNCS, vol. 2144, pp. 293–309. Springer, Heidelberg (2001)

4. Eén, N., Biere, A.: Effective preprocessing in SAT through variable and clause elimination. In: Bacchus, F., Walsh, T. (eds.) SAT 2005. LNCS, vol. 3569, pp. 61–75. Springer, Heidelberg (2005)
5. Goldberg, E., Manolios, P.: SAT-solving based on boundary point elimination. In: Barner, S., Harris, I., Kroening, D., Raz, O. (eds.) HVC 2010. LNCS, vol. 6504, pp. 93–111. Springer, Heidelberg (2010)
6. Goldberg, E., Manolios, P.: Quantifier elimination by dependency sequents. In: FMCAD 2012, pp. 34–44 (2012)
7. Goldberg, E., Manolios, P.: Quantifier elimination via clause redundancy. In: FMCAD 2013, pp. 85–92 (2013)
8. Goldberg, E., Manolios, P.: Bug hunting by computing range reduction. Technical Report arXiv:1408.7039 [cs.LO] (2014)
9. Goldberg, E., Manolios, P.: Partial quantifier elimination. Technical Report arXiv:1407.4835 [cs.LO] (2014)
10. Goldberg, E., Manolios, P.: Software for quantifier elimination in propositional logic. In: Hong, H., Yap, C. (eds.) ICMS 2014. LNCS, vol. 8592, pp. 291–294. Springer, Heidelberg (2014)
11. Jin, H., Somenzi, F.: Prime clauses for fast enumeration of satisfying assignments to boolean circuits. In: DAC 2005, pp. 750–753 (2005)
12. Brauer, J., King, A., Kriener, J.: Existential quantification as incremental SAT. In: Gopalakrishnan, G., Qadeer, S. (eds.) CAV 2011. LNCS, vol. 6806, pp. 191–207. Springer, Heidelberg (2011)
13. Jiang, J.-H.R.: Quantifier elimination via functional composition. In: Bouajjani, A., Maler, O. (eds.) CAV 2009. LNCS, vol. 5643, pp. 383–397. Springer, Heidelberg (2009)
14. Klieber, W., Janota, M., Marques-Silva, J., Clarke, E.: Solving QBF with free variables. In: Schulte, C. (ed.) CP 2013. LNCS, vol. 8124, pp. 415–431. Springer, Heidelberg (2013)
15. Kullmann, O.: New methods for 3-sat decision and worst-case analysis. Theor. Comput. Sci. 223(1-2), 1–72 (1999)
16. McMillan, K.L.: Applying SAT methods in unbounded symbolic model checking. In: Brinksma, E., Larsen, K.G. (eds.) CAV 2002. LNCS, vol. 2404, pp. 250–264. Springer, Heidelberg (2002)
17. Ganai, M.K., Gupta, A., Ashar, P.: Efficient sat-based unbounded symbolic model checking using circuit cofactoring. In: ICCAD 2004, pp. 510–517 (2004)
18. HWMCC-2010 benchmarks, http://fmv.jku.at/hwmcc10/benchmarks.html

Formal Verification of 800 Genetically Constructed Automata Programs: A Case Study

Mikhail Lukin, Maxim Buzdalov, and Anatoly Shalyto

ITMO University
49 Kronverkskiy prosp.
Saint-Petersburg, Russia, 197101
{lukinma,mbuzdalov}@gmail.com, shalyto@mail.ifmo.ru

Abstract. Engineering of mission critical software requires a program to be verified that it satisfies a number of properties. This is often done using model checking. However, construction of a program model to be verified and analyzing counterexamples is not an easy task. This can be made easier with the automata-based programming paradigm.

There exist some cases when there are many programs to verify and it is impossible to construct a precise enough finite-state model of the environment. We present an approach for automata program verification under such conditions. Our case study is based on 800 automata programs which solve a simple path-planning problem. As a result, we verified that at least 231 of them are provably correct.

Keywords: automata-based programming, formal verification, model checking.

1 Introduction

Engineering of mission critical software requires a program to be verified that it satisfies a number of properties. This is often done using the model checking approach [7]. However, construction of a program model to be verified and analysing counterexamples is not an easy task.

Automata-based programming [3, 8, 9] is a programming paradigm which proposes to design and implement software systems as systems of interacting automated controlled objects. Each automated controlled object consists of a controlling extended finite-state machine (EFSM) and a controlled object. One of the main advantages of automata-based programming is that automata programs can be effectively verified using the model checking approach. Automata programs are isomorphic to their own models, which automates many steps needed to verify an automata program [5, 10]. This makes automata-based programming a good tool in industry, a notable example of which is a new standard for distributed control and automation IEC 61499 [11].

In some cases, synthesis of automata programs is possible using search-based software engineering methods, such as genetic algorithms [1, 2, 10]. This may lead to existence of many programs to check, and their underlying logic can be

E. Yahav (Ed.): HVC 2014, LNCS 8855, pp. 165–170, 2014.

cumbersome. What is more, it is sometimes impossible to construct a finite-state model of the environment that is enough to verify the necessary properties.

In this paper, an approach for automata program verification, which can cope with such conditions, is presented. We illustrate this approach on a case study, which is based on 800 automata programs constructed by a genetic algorithm. We verified that 231 of them are provably correct.

2   Problem Formulation

In the paper [1] solutions to the path-planning problem were constructed in the form of finite state machines using a genetic algorithm. More precisely, the path planning problem with incomplete information was addressed: an *agent* with $O(1)$ memory and only contact sensors has to find a *target* in an unknown area with finite obstacles. In the paper [6] some algorithms (the most known are BUG-1 and BUG-2) are given which find the target or determine that the target is unreachable in finite number of steps.

The paper [1] considered a discretized version of this problem, which is more suitable to experiments with automata program synthesis. The field is an infinite square grid. Each grid cell is either free or contains an obstacle. Each eight-connected group of cells with obstacles has a finite size. One of the cells without an obstacle is declared to be a target. An agent occupies an entire cell. The position of the agent is determined by its Cartesian coordinates and direction (N, W, S or E). The next cell in this direction is said to be the *adjacent* cell. The agent has $O(1)$ additional memory which is used to store a single position of the agent. The agent's logic is encoded as an EFSM.

The agent has access to the following data: (X_t, Y_t) – the target location, (X_a, Y_a, D_a) – the agent's coordinates and direction, (X_s, Y_s, D_s) – saved coordinates and direction, (X_j, Y_j) – coordinates of the adjacent cell (which is a function of X_a, Y_a, D_a), O – is there an obstacle in the adjacent cell. These data are converted to the Boolean variables which the agent directly accesses:

- "can move forward": $x1 = \textbf{not } O$;
- "is move forward cool": $x2 = dist(X_j, Y_j, X_t, Y_t) < dist(X_a, Y_a, X_t, Y_t)$;
- "is at finish": $x3 = X_a = X_t \textbf{ and } Y_a = Y_t$;
- "is at saved": $x4 = X_a = X_s \textbf{ and } Y_a = Y_s \textbf{ and } D_a = D_s$;
- "is better than saved": $x5 = dist(X_a, Y_a, X_t, Y_t) < dist(X_s, Y_s, X_t, Y_t)$;

where $dist(X_1, Y_1, X_2, Y_2) = |X_1 - X_2| + |Y_1 - Y_2|$. The possible actions are:

- "move forward": move forward to the adjacent cell;
- "rotate positive": rotate 90 degrees clockwise;
- "rotate negative": rotate 90 degrees counter-clockwise;
- "report reached": terminate and say it has reached the target;
- "report unreachable": terminate and say the target is unreachable;
- "save position": save current coordinates and direction to memory;
- "do nothing": do nothing.

The agent may end up in one of the following ways:

1. It moves to a cell which contains an obstacle ("crashes").
2. It enters a loop in the state space.
3. It moves apart from the target forever.
4. It performs the "report reached" action and is **not** located at the target.
5. It performs the "report reached" action and is located at the target.
6. It performs the "report unreachable" action, the target is **not** unreachable.
7. It performs the "report unreachable" action, the target is unreachable and the agent has **not** visited all cells that are surrounding the eight-connected obstacle component which contains the target inside.
8. It performs the "report unreachable" action, the target is unreachable and the agent has visited all cells mentioned in the previous case.

From these ways, only the cases 5 and 8 refer to the correct termination.

In the paper [1], it was reported that 800 EFSMs were evolved using genetic programming and some rudimentary coevolution with tests. They were extensively tested and have never failed. However, a formal proof for their correctness is missing in [1].

3 Proposed Verification Approach

The correctness of an agent can follow from two statements only: "for any field with a reachable target, the agent will eventually reach the target and perform the "report reached" action" and "for any field with an unreachable target, the agent will eventually perform the "report unreachable" action". If a field were fixed, checking these statements would be possible by a partial breadth-first traversal of a graph, whose vertices are possible program states. However, the fields are not fixed, which makes the statements inexpressible in terms of states or paths in the agent's EFSM.

We suggest the following workflow:

1. Construct a hypothesis of how a series of EFSMs work.
2. Construct a (probably lossy and non-deterministic) finite-state model of an agent and the environment, and a set of LTL formulae that together can be used by a model checker to prove that a given EFSM satisfies the hypothesis.
3. Prove formally that any EFSM that satisfies the hypothesis is correct.
4. Run a model checker on available EFSMs using the model and formulae from step 2. All EFSMs that are successfully verified are correct.

In Section 4 we apply this workflow, step by step, to verification of 800 finite-state machines solving the path planning problem described in Section 2.

4 Application to the Path Planning Problem

After preliminary experiments with several agents we hypothesized that they follow the BUG-2 scheme scheme [6]. Such agents move towards the target while it is possible. When an obstacle is approached, there are two possibilities. First, if an agent can turn in such a way that it can continue moving towards the target, it may do so. Otherwise, it switches into the *obstacle detour* mode: it traverses the obstacle clockwise or counter-clockwise until it reaches a condition when it is possible to continue moving towards the target without hitting an obstacle, or to change the obstacle being detoured. During the detour process, it tracks the cell that is the closest so far to the target. If it is impossible to move towards the target from the closest possible cell, then the target is unreachable, and the agent performs the corresponding action.

4.1   The Model

The first component of the model is a finite description of the part of the field that directly influence the next move of the agent. It consists of:

- information for each of the neighboring cells if it is occupied by an obstacle;
- direction of the agent (north, south, east or west);
- the direction of the target related to the agent;
- information on how the current agent location compares to saved cell in terms of Manhattan distance to the target (closer, farther, at the same distance, cells and directions coincide, only cells coincide).

The first three parts are grouped in a structure called *profile*. The fourth part is stored in the global variable. The part of the model described so far is enough to determine the next move of an agent if the EFSM of the agent is given. All the actions except for "move forward" change the model deterministically. For the "move forward" action, the following components have to be updated non-deterministically: information about obstacles in some of the neighboring cells, the direction to the target and the relation of the saved cell to the current agent location. To reduce the number of false failures, the current profile is saved at the "save position" action, and the last two variants of the latter property can be chosen only if the current and the saved profiles match.

In addition to that, a global bit `detourWall` is used to track whether the agent is detouring an obstacle. We set or clear this bit using heuristic conditions.

The model is implemented in Promela and is verified by Spin [4]. The common part of the model is coded by hand. The part of the model which depends on the actual agent's EFSM is generated by a tool called Stater.[1]

4.2   Weaknesses of the Model

Due to the fact that the model of the agent and the field is finite-state and partially non-deterministic, it can happen that some situations may be produced by the verifier which cannot happen while running the agent on a real field. These situations include:

---

[1] Available for download at `https://yadi.sk/d/clWWtMrIYhQZJ`.

- mutable field – the visited parts of the field may effectively change;
- infinitely large obstacles;
- infinitely distant target;
- wandering target – the target may change its location;
- wandering saved cell – the location of the saved cell can change in time;
- target in a cell with an obstacle.

These situations cannot happen when evaluating an agent on a real field, so the agent may process them seemingly incorrectly (which does not imply that the agent is incorrect). In out LTL formulae we allow certain forms of incorrect behavior, but ensure it can happen only under impossible conditions.

4.3 LTL Formulae and Theorems

We think there are two possibilities for each agent under verification: it can detour each obstacle either clockwise or counter-clockwise. Technically, it should be possible to construct an agent that can perform both kinds of detours; however, it requires a larger number of states. Accordingly to this idea, we prepared two sets of formulae: the first one is for the clockwise detour, and the second one is for the counter-clockwise one.

The formulae $f0$–$f30$ for the clockwise detour, augmented with their explanation, are available at GitHub.[2] The counter-clockwise versions can be obtained by performing simple "reflective" transformations.

One lemma and four theorems were proven, from which it follows that every EFSM which satisfies the specification (the LTL formulae $f0$–$f30$) also solves the problem. The theorems and proofs are available at GitHub[3] for the sake of brevity.

4.4 Verification Results

The archive with all necessary Spin models and scripts is available for download[4] for experiment reproduction.

We constructed 1600 models for verification, namely 800 models for each EFSM from [1] using the "clockwise" LTL formula set and 800 modes for the "counter-clockwise" formula set. Verification of all these models took us approximately two days on a 32-core server with AMD Opteron^{TM} 6272 processors.

There were 231 EFSMs which satisfy either clockwise or counter-clockwise LTL formula set. No EFSM satisfied both formula sets, which was expected because any EFSM which satisfies both formula sets traverses every obstacle both clockwise and counter-clockwise. All other 569 EFSMs satisfied none of the formula sets. This does not mean that they are incorrect – they seem to implement a different algorithm (for example, one of them implements BUG-1).

---

[2] https://github.com/mbuzdalov/papers/blob/master/2014-hvc-bugs/formulae.ltl

[3] https://github.com/mbuzdalov/papers/blob/master/2014-hvc-bugs/proofs.txt

[4] https://yadi.sk/d/-orvfVKnYhRFc

5   Conclusion

We presented an approach that can be used to verify programs in the absence of a finite-state model of the program environment that is precise enough to verify the necessary properties. This approach involves creating a hypothesis about how the verified program works, an intermediate finite-state model and temporal formulae which capture this hypothesis, and finally proving that any program which satisfies the hypothesis performs as expected.

This approach is illustrated on a sample path-planning problem, where constructing a proper counterexample involves creating large unbounded structures. From a previous work [1] we inherited 800 programs in a form of extended finite-state machines which supposedly solve the problem. We were able to prove that 231 of these programs are correct. For other programs proving their correctness should be possible by constructing another hypothesis.

Acknowledgments. This work was financially supported by the Government of Russian Federation, Grant 074-U01.

References

1. Buzdalov, M., Sokolov, A.: Evolving EFSMs Solving a Path-Planning Problem by Genetic Programming. In: Proceedings of GECCO Companion, pp. 591–594 (2012)
2. Chivilikhin, D., Ulyantsev, V.: MuACOsm: A New Mutation-Based Ant Colony Optimization Algorithm for Learning Finite-State Machines. In: Proceedings of GECCO, pp. 511–518 (2013)
3. Gurov, V., Mazin, M., Narvsky, A., Shalyto, A.: Tools for support of automata-based programming. Programming and Computer Software 33(6), 343–355 (2007)
4. Holzmann, G.: The model checker SPIN. IEEE Transactions on Software Engineering 23(5), 279–295 (1997)
5. Kuzmin, E.V., Sokolov, V.A.: Modeling, specification, and verification of automaton programs. Programming and Computer Software 34(1), 27–43 (2008)
6. Lumelsky, V., Stepanov, A.: Path planning strategies for a point mobile automaton moving amidst unknown obstacles of arbitraty shape. Algorithmica 2, 403–430 (1987)
7. Pingree, P.J., Mikk, E., Holzmann, G.J., Smith, M.H., Dams, D.: Validation of mission critical software design and implementation using model checking (2002), http://spinroot.com/gerard/pdf/02-1911.pdf
8. Polikarpova, N., Shalyto, A.: Automata-based Programming, 2nd edn. Piter (2011) (in Russian)
9. Shalyto, A.: Logic control and reactive systems: Algorithmization and programming. Automation and Remote Control 62(1), 1–29 (2001)
10. Tsarev, F., Egorov, K.: Finite State Machine Induction Using Genetic Algorithm Based on Testing and Model Checking. In: Proceedings of GECCO Companion, pp. 759–762 (2011)
11. Yang, C.H., Vyatkin, V., Pang, C.: Model-driven development of control software for distributed automation: a survey and an approach. IEEE Transactions on Systems, Man and Cybernetics 44(3), 292–305 (2014)

A Framework to Synergize Partial Order Reduction with State Interpolation

Duc-Hiep Chu and Joxan Jaffar

National University of Singapore
{hiepcd,joxan}@comp.nus.edu.sg

Abstract. We address the problem of reasoning about interleavings in safety verification of concurrent programs. In the literature, there are two prominent techniques for pruning the search space. First, there are well-investigated *trace-based* methods, collectively known as "Partial Order Reduction (POR)", which operate by weakening the concept of a trace by abstracting the total order of its transitions into a partial order. Second, there is *state-based* interpolation where a collection of formulas can be generalized by taking into account the property to be verified. Our main contribution is a framework that *synergistically* combines POR with state interpolation so that the sum is more than its parts.

1 Introduction

We consider the *state explosion problem* in safety verification of concurrent programs. This is caused by the interleavings of transitions from different processes. In explicit-state model checking, a general approach to counter this explosion is Partial Order Reduction (POR) (e.g., [22,19,11]). This exploits the equivalence of interleavings of "independent" transitions: two transitions are independent if their consecutive occurrences in a trace can be swapped without changing the final state. In other words, POR-related methods prune away *redundant* process interleavings in a sense that, for each Mazurkiewicz [17][1] trace equivalence class of interleavings, if a representative has been checked, the remaining ones are regarded as redundant.

On the other hand, *symbolic execution* [16] is another method for program reasoning which recently has made increasing impact on software engineering research [4]. The main challenge for symbolic execution is the exponential number of symbolic paths. The works [14,18] tackle successfully this fundamental problem by eliminating from the concrete model, on-the-fly, those facts which are *irrelevant* or *too-specific* for proving the unreachability of the error nodes. This learning phase consists of computing *state-based interpolants* in a similar spirit to that of conflict clause learning in SAT solvers.

Now symbolic execution with state interpolation (SI) has been shown to be effective for verifying sequential programs. In SI [14,18], a node at program point

---

[1] We remark that the concept of POR goes beyond the preservation of Mazurkiewicz traces, e.g., [22]. However, from a practical perspective, it is safe to consider such form of pruning as a representative example of POR.

E. Yahav (Ed.): HVC 2014, LNCS 8855, pp. 171–187, 2014.

ℓ in the reachability tree can be pruned, if its context is subsumed by the interpolant computed earlier for the same program point ℓ. Therefore, even in the best case scenario, the number of states explored by an SI method must still be at least the number of all *distinct* program points[2]. However, in the setting of concurrent programs, exploring each distinct global program point[3] once might already be considered prohibitive. In short, symbolic execution with SI *alone* is not efficient enough for the verification of concurrent programs.

Recent work (e.g., [27]) has shown the usefulness of going *stateful* in implementing a POR method. It directly follows that SI can help to yield even better performance. In order to implement an efficient stateful algorithm, we are required to come up with an abstraction for each (concrete or symbolic) state. Unsurprisingly, SI often offers us good abstractions.

The above suggests that POR and SI can be very much *complementary* to each other. In this paper, we propose a general framework employing *symbolic execution* in the exploration of the state space, while both POR and SI are exploited for pruning. SI and POR are combined synergistically as the concept of interpolation. Interpolation is essentially a form of learning where the completed search of a *safe* subtree is then formulated as a recipe, ideally a *succinct* formula, for future pruning. The key distinction of our interpolation framework is that each recipe discovered by a node is *forced* to be conveyed back to its ancestors, which gives rise to pruning of larger subtrees.

In summary, we address the challenge: "combining classic POR methods with symbolic technique has proven to be difficult" [15], especially in the context of *software verification*. More specifically, we propose an algorithm schema to combine *synergistically* POR with state interpolation so that the sum is more than its parts. However, we first need to formalize POR wrt. a symbolic search framework with abstraction in such a way that: (1) POR can be *property driven* and (2) POR, or more precisely, the concept of persistent set, can be applicable for a set of states (rather than an individual state). While the main contribution is a theoretical framework, our experimental results also indicate a potential for the development of advanced implementations.

2   Related Work

Partial Order Reduction (POR) is a well-investigated technique in model checking of concurrent systems. Some notable early works are [22,19,11]. Later refinements of POR, Dynamic [10] and Cartesian [13] POR (DPOR and CPOR respectively) improve traditional POR techniques by detecting collisions on-the-fly. Recently, [1] has proposed the novel concept of *source sets*, optimizing the implementation

---

[2] Whereas POR-related methods do not suffer from this. Here we assume that the input concurrent program has already been preprocessed (e.g., by static slicing to remove irrelevant transitions, or by static block encodings) to reduce the size of the transition system for each process.

[3] The number of global points is the product of the numbers of local program points in all processes.

for DPOR. These methods, in general, often achieve better reduction than traditional techniques, due to the more accurate detection of independent transitions.

Traditional POR techniques [22,19,11] distinguish between liveness and safety properties. POR has also been extended for symbolic model checking [2] where a symbolic state can represent a number of concrete states. These methods, however, are not applicable to safety verification of modern concurrent programs (written in mainstream APIs such as POSIX). One important weakness of traditional POR is that it is *not sensitive* wrt. different target safety properties. In contrast, recent works have shown that property-aware reduction can be achieved by symbolic methods using a general-purpose SAT/SMT solver [26,15,24,7]. Verification is often encoded as a formula which is *satisfiable* iff there exists an interleaving execution of the programs that violates the property. Reductions happen inside the SAT solver through the addition of learned clauses derived by conflict analysis [20]. This type of reduction is somewhat similar to what we call *state interpolation*.

An important related work is [15], which is the first to consider enhancing POR with property driven pruning, via the use of an SMT solver. Subsequently, there is a follow-up work [24]. In [15], they begin with an SMT encoding of the underlying transition system, and then enhance this encoding with a concept of "monotonicity". The effect of this is that traces can be grouped into equivalence classes, and in each class, all traces which are *not monotonic* will be considered as *unsatisfiable* by the SMT solver. The idea of course is that such traces are in fact redundant. This work has demonstrated some promising results as most concurrency bugs in real applications have been found to be *shallow*. We note that [15] incidentally enjoyed some (weak) form of SI pruning, due to the similarity between conflict clause learning and state interpolation. However, there the synergy between POR and SMT is *unclear*. We later demonstrate in Sec. 7 that such synergy in [15] is indeed relatively poor.

There is a fundamental problem with scalability in [15], as mentioned in the follow-up work [24], that "It will not scale to the entire concurrent program" if we encode the whole search space as a single formula and submit it to an SMT solver.

Let us first compare [15] with our work. Essentially, the difference is twofold. First, in this paper, the theory for partial order reduction is *property driven*. In contrast, the monotonicity reduction of [15] is not. In other words, though property driven pruning is observed in [15], it is contributed mainly by the conflict clauses learned, not from the monotonicity relation. We specifically exemplify the power of property driven POR in the later sections. Second, the encoding in [15] is processed by a *black-box* SMT solver. Thus important algorithmic refinements are not possible. Some examples:

• There are different options in implementing SI. Specifically in this paper, we employ "precondition" computations. Using a black-box solver, one has to rely on its fixed interpolation methods.

• Our approach is *lazy* in a sense that our solver is only required to consider *one* symbolic path at a time; in [15] it is not the case. This matters most when the program is unsafe and finding counter-examples is relatively easy (there are many traces which violate the safety property).

• In having a (forward) symbolic execution framework, one can direct the search process. This is useful since the order in which state interpolants are generated does give rise to different reductions. Of course, such manipulation of the search process is hard, if not impossible, when using a black-box solver.

In order to remedy the scalability issue of [15], the work [24] adapted it to the setting of program testing. In particular, [24] proposed a concurrent trace program (CTP) framework which employs both concrete execution and symbolic solving to strike a balance between efficiency and scalability of an SMT-based method. However, when the input program is *safe*, i.e., absence of bugs, [24] in general suffers from the same scalability issue as in [15].

We remark that, the new direction of [24], in avoiding the blow-up of the SMT solver, is in fact preceded by the work on under-approximation widening (UW) [12]. As with CTP, UW models a subset, which will be incrementally enlarged, of all the possible interleavings as an SMT formula and submits it to an SMT solver. In UW the scheduling decisions are also encoded as constraints, so that the *unsatisfiable core* returned by the solver can then be used to further the search in probably a useful direction. This is the major contribution of UW. However, an important point is that this furthering of the search is a *repeated* call to the solver, this time with a weaker formula; which means that the problem at hand is now larger, having more traces to consider. On this repeated call, the work done for the original call is thus *duplicated*.

At first glance, it seems attractive and simple to encode the problem compactly as a set of constraints and delegate the search process to a general-purpose SMT solver. However, there are some fundamental disadvantages, and these arise mainly because it is hard to exploit the semantics of the program to direct the search inside the solver. This is in fact evidenced in the works mentioned above.

We believe, however, the foremost disadvantage of using a general-purpose solver lies in the encoding of process interleavings. For instance, even when a concurrent program has only *one* feasible execution trace, the encoding formula being fed to the solver is still of enormous size and can easily choke up the solver. More importantly, different from safety verification of sequential programs, the encoding of interleavings (e.g., [15] uses the variable *sel* to model which process is selected for executing) often hampers the normal derivations of succinct conflict clauses by means of resolution in modern SMT solvers. We empirically demonstrate the inefficiency of such approach in Sec. 7.

Another important related work is [23], developed independently[4] but follows a similar direction as in the current paper: combining POR with a standard state interpolation algorithm, which is often referred to as the IMPACT algorithm [18].

---

[4] Our work has been publicly available since 2012 in forms of a draft paper and a Ph.D. thesis.

Nevertheless, it is important to note that the theoretical framework presented in this paper subsumes [23]. While this paper proposes the novel concept of Property Driven POR before combining it with the state interpolation algorithm, [23] exploits directly the concept of "monotonicity" as in [15], thus their POR part does not give rise to property driven pruning.

3 Background

We consider a concurrent system composed of a finite number of threads or processes performing atomic operations on shared variables. Let P_i $(1 \le i \le n)$ be a process with the set $trans_i$ of transitions. For simplicity, assume that $trans_i$ contains no cycles.

We also assume all processes have disjoint sets of transitions. Let $\mathcal{T} = \cup_{i=1}^{n} trans_i$ be the set of all transitions. Let V_i be the set of local variables of process P_i, and V_{shared} the set of shared variables of the given concurrent program. Let $pc_i \in V_i$ be a special variable representing the process program counter, and the tuple $\langle pc_1, pc_2 \cdots, pc_n \rangle$ represent the global program point. Let $SymStates$ be the set of all global symbolic states of the given program where $s_0 \in SymStates$ is the initial state. A state $s \in SymStates$ comprises two parts: its *global program point* ℓ, also denoted by $\mathrm{pc}(s)$, which is a tuple of local program counters, and its *symbolic constraints* $[\![s]\!]$ over the program variables. In other words, we denote a state s by $\langle \mathrm{pc}(s), [\![s]\!] \rangle$.

We consider the *transitions* of states induced by the program. Following [11], we only pay attention to *visible* transitions. A (visible) transition $t^{\{i\}}$ pertains to some process P_i. It transfers process P_i from control location ℓ_1 to ℓ_2. In general, the application of $t^{\{i\}}$ is guarded by some condition cond (cond might be just true). At some state $s \in SymStates$, when the ith component of $\mathrm{pc}(s)$, namely $\mathrm{pc}(s)[i]$, equals ℓ_1, we say that $t^{\{i\}}$ is *schedulable*[5] at s. And when s satisfies the guard cond, denoted by $s \models$ cond, we say that $t^{\{i\}}$ is *enabled* at s. For each state s, let $Schedulable(s)$ and $Enabled(s)$ denote the set of transitions which respectively are schedulable at s and enabled at s. A state s, where $Schedulable(s) = \emptyset$, is called a *terminal state*.

Let $s \xrightarrow{t} s'$ denote transition step from s to s' via transition t. This step is possible only if t is *schedulable* at s. We assume that the effect of applying an enabled transition t on a state s to arrive at state s' is well-understood. In our symbolic execution framework, executing a schedulable but not enabled transition results in an *infeasible* state. A state s is called *infeasible* if $[\![s]\!]$ is unsatisfiable. For technical reasons needed below, we shall allow schedulable transitions emanating from an infeasible state; it follows that the destination state must also be *infeasible*.

For a sequence of transitions w (i.e., $w \in \mathcal{T}^*$), $Rng(w)$ denotes the set of transitions that appear in w. Also let $\mathcal{T}_\ell$ denote the set of all transitions which are schedulable somewhere after global program point ℓ. We note here that the

---

[5] This concept is not standard in traditional POR, we need it here since we are dealing with symbolic search.

schedulability of a transition at some state s only depends on the program point component of s, namely $\texttt{pc}(s)$. It does not depend on the constraint component of s, namely $[\![s]\!]$. Given $t_1, t_2 \in \mathcal{T}$ we say t_1 can *de-schedule* t_2 iff there exists a state s such that both t_1, t_2 are schedulable at s but t_2 is not schedulable after the execution of t_1 from s.

Following the above, $s_1 \overset{t_1 \cdots t_m}{\Longrightarrow} s_{m+1}$ denotes a sequence of state transitions, and we say that s_{m+1} is reachable from s_1. We call $s_1 \overset{t_1}{\to} s_2 \overset{t_2}{\to} \cdots \overset{t_m}{\to} s_{m+1}$ a *feasible* derivation from state s_1, iff $\forall\ 1 \le i \le m \bullet t_i$ is enabled at s_i. As mentioned earlier, an *infeasible* derivation results in an *infeasible state* (an infeasible state is still aware of its global program point). An infeasible state satisfies any safety property.

We define a *complete execution* trace, or simply trace, ρ as a sequence of transitions such that it is a derivation from s_0 and $s_0 \overset{\rho}{\Longrightarrow} s_f$ and s_f is a terminal state. A trace is infeasible if it is an infeasible derivation from s_0. If a trace is infeasible, then at some point, it takes a transition which is schedulable but is not enabled. From thereon, the subsequent states are infeasible states.

We say a given concurrent program is *safe* wrt. a safety property ψ if $\forall s \in SymStates \bullet$ if s *is reachable from the initial state* s_0 then s is safe, that is, $s \models \psi$. A trace ρ is *safe* wrt. ψ, denoted as $\rho \models \psi$, if all its states satisfy ψ.

Partial Order Reduction (POR) vs. State-Based Interpolation (SI)

We assume the readers are familiar with the traditional concept of POR. Regarding state-based interpolation, we follow the approach of [14,18]. Here our symbolic execution is depicted as a tree rooted at the initial state s_0 and for each state s_i therein, the descendants are just the states obtainable by extending s_i with a feasible transition.

Definition 1 (Safe Root). *Given a transition system and an initial state* s_0, *let s be a feasible state reachable from* s_0. *We say s is a* safe root *wrt. a safety property ψ, denoted* $\triangle_\psi(s)$, iff *all states s' reachable from s are safe wrt. ψ.*

Definition 2 (State Coverage). *Given a transition system and an initial state* s_0 *and s_i and s_j which are two symbolic states such that (1) s_i and s_j are reachable from s_0 and (2) s_i and s_j share the same program point ℓ, we say s_i covers s_j wrt. a safety property ψ, denoted by $s_i \succeq_\psi s_j$, iff $\triangle_\psi(s_i)$ implies $\triangle_\psi(s_j)$.*

The impact of state coverage relation is that if (1) s_i covers s_j, and (2) the subtree rooted at s_i has been traversed and proved to be safe, then the traversal of subtree rooted at s_j can be avoided. In other words, we gain performance by *pruning* the subtree at s_j. Obviously, if s_i naturally subsumes s_j, i.e., $[\![s_j]\!] \models [\![s_i]\!]$ or simply $s_j \models s_i$, then state coverage is trivially achieved. In practice, however, this scenario does not happen often enough.

Definition 3 (Sound State Interpolant). *Given a transition system and an initial state s_0, given a safety property ψ and program point ℓ, we say a formula $\overline{\Psi}$*

is a sound (state) interpolant *for ℓ, denoted by* $\mathsf{SI}(\ell, \psi)$, *if for all states $s \equiv \langle \ell, \cdot \rangle$ reachable from s_0, $s \models \overline{\Psi}$ implies that s is a safe root.*

What we want now is to generate a formula $\overline{\Psi}$ (called *interpolant*), which still preserves the safety of all states reachable from s_i, but is weaker (more general) than the original formula associated to the state s_i. In other words, we should have $s_i \models \mathsf{SI}(\ell, \psi)$. We assume that this condition is always ensured by any implementation of state-based interpolation. The main purpose of using $\overline{\Psi}$ rather than the original formula associated to the symbolic state s_i is to increase the likelihood of subsumption. That is, the likelihood of having $s_j \models \overline{\Psi}$ is expected to be much higher than the likelihood of having $s_j \models s_i$.

In fact, the perfect interpolant should be the weakest precondition [9] computed for program point ℓ wrt. the transition system and the safety property ψ. We denote this weakest precondition as $\mathsf{wp}(\ell, \psi)$. Any subsequent state $s_j \equiv \langle \ell, \cdot \rangle$ which has s_j stronger than this weakest precondition can be pruned. However, in general, the weakest precondition is too computationally demanding. An interpolant for the state s_i is indeed a formula which approximates the weakest precondition at program point ℓ wrt. the transition system, i.e., $\overline{\Psi} \equiv \mathsf{SI}(\ell, \psi) \equiv Intp(s_i, \mathsf{wp}(\ell, \psi))$. A *good* interpolant is one which closely approximates the weakest precondition and can be computed efficiently.

The symbolic execution of a program can be augmented by annotating each program point with its corresponding interpolants such that the interpolants represent the sufficient conditions to preserve the unreachability of any unsafe state. Then, the *basic* notion of pruning with state interpolant can be defined as follows.

Definition 4 (Pruning with Interpolant). *Given a symbolic state $s \equiv \langle \ell, \cdot \rangle$ such that ℓ is annotated with some interpolant $\overline{\Psi}$, we say that s is pruned by the interpolant $\overline{\Psi}$ if s implies $\overline{\Psi}$ (i.e., $s \models \overline{\Psi}$).*

Now let us discuss the the effectiveness of POR and SI in pruning the search space with an example. For simplicity, we purposely make the example *concrete*, i.e., states are indeed concrete states.

EXAMPLE 1 *(Closely coupled processes)*: See Fig. 1. Program points are shown in angle brackets. Fig. 1(a) shows the control flow graphs of two processes. Process 1 increments x twice whereas process 2 doubles x twice. The transitions associated with such actions and the safety property are depicted in the figure. POR requires a full search tree while Fig. 1(b) shows the search space explored by SI. Interpolants are in curly brackets. Bold circles denote pruned/subsumed states.

Let us first attempt this example using POR. It is clear that $t_1^{\{1\}}$ is *dependent* with both $t_1^{\{2\}}$ and $t_2^{\{2\}}$. Also $t_2^{\{1\}}$ is dependent with both $t_1^{\{2\}}$ and $t_2^{\{2\}}$. Indeed, each of all the 6 execution traces in the search tree ends at a different concrete state. As classic POR methods use the concept of *trace equivalence* for pruning, no interleaving is avoided: those methods will enumerate the full search tree of 19 states (for space reasons, we omit it here).

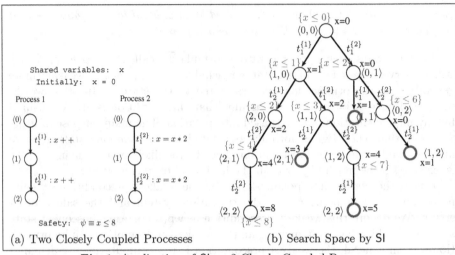

Fig. 1. Application of SI on 2 Closely Coupled Processes

Revisit the example using SI, where we use the *weakest preconditions* [9] as the state interpolants: the interpolant for a state is computed as the weakest precondition to ensure that the state itself as well as all of its descendants are safe (see Fig. 1(b)). We in fact achieve the best case scenario with it: whenever we come to a program point which has been examined before, subsumption happens. The number of non-subsumed states is still of order $O(k^2)$ (where $k = 3$ in this particular example), assuming that we generalize the number of local program points for each process to $O(k)$. Fig. 1(b) shows 9 non-subsumed states and 4 subsumed states.

In summary, the above example shows that SI might outperform POR when the component processes are closely coupled. However, one can easily devise an example where the component processes do not interfere with each other at all. Under such condition POR will require only one trace to prove safety, while SI is still (lower) bounded by the total number of global program points. In this paper, we contribute by proposing a framework to combine POR and SI *synergistically*.

4   Property Driven POR (PDPOR)

"Combining classic POR methods with symbolic algorithms has been proven to be difficult" [15]. One fundamental reason is that the concepts of (Mazurkiewicz) equivalence and transition independence, which drive most practical POR implementations, rely on the equivalence of two concrete states. However, in symbolic traversal, we rarely encounter two equivalent symbolic states.

We now make the following definition which is crucial for the concept of pruning and will be used throughout this paper.

Definition 5 (Trace Coverage). *Let ρ_1, ρ_2 be two traces of a concurrent program. We say ρ_1 covers ρ_2 wrt. a safety property ψ, denoted as $\rho_1 \sqsupseteq_\psi \rho_2$, iff $\rho_1 \models \psi \rightarrow \rho_2 \models \psi$.*

Instead of using the concept of trace equivalence, from now on, we only make use of the concept of trace coverage. The concept of trace coverage is definitely weaker than the concept of Mazurkiewicz equivalence. In fact, if ρ_1 and ρ_2 are (Mazurkiewicz) equivalent then $\forall \psi \bullet \rho_1 \sqsupseteq_\psi \rho_2 \land \rho_2 \sqsupseteq_\psi \rho_1$. Now we will define a new and *weaker* concept which therefore generalizes the concept of transition independence.

Definition 6 (Semi-commutative after a State). *For a given concurrent program, a safety property ψ, and a derivation $s_0 \stackrel{\theta}{\Longrightarrow} s$, for all $t_1, t_2 \in \mathcal{T}$ which cannot de-schedule each other, we say t_1 semi-commutes with t_2 after state s wrt. $\sqsupseteq_\psi$, denoted by $\langle s, t_1 \uparrow t_2, \psi \rangle$, iff for all $w_1, w_2 \in \mathcal{T}^*$ such that $\theta w_1 t_1 t_2 w_2$ and $\theta w_1 t_2 t_1 w_2$ are execution traces of the program, then we have $\theta w_1 t_1 t_2 w_2 \sqsupseteq_\psi \theta w_1 t_2 t_1 w_2$.*

From the definition, $Rng(\theta)$, $Rng(w_1)$, and $Rng(w_2)$ are pairwise disjoint. Importantly, if s is at program point ℓ, we have $Rng(w_1) \cup Rng(w_2) \subseteq \mathcal{T}_\ell \setminus \{t_1, t_2\}$. We observe that wrt. some ψ, if all important events, those have to do with the safety of the system, have already happened in the prefix θ, the "semi-commutative" relation is trivially satisfied. On the other hand, the remaining transitions might still interfere with each other (but not the safety), and do not satisfy the independent relation.

The concept of "semi-commutative" is obviously weaker than the concept of independence. If t_1 and t_2 are independent, it follows that $\forall \psi \, \forall s \bullet \langle s, t_1 \uparrow t_2, \psi \rangle \land \langle s, t_2 \uparrow t_1, \psi \rangle$. Also note that, in contrast to the relation of transition independence, the "semi-commutative" relation is *not symmetric*.

We now introduce a new definition for *persistent set*.

Definition 7 (Persistent Set of a State). *A set $T \subseteq \mathcal{T}$ of transitions schedulable in a state $s \in \mathrm{SymStates}$ is persistent in s wrt. a property ψ iff, for all derivations $s \stackrel{t_1}{\to} s_1 \stackrel{t_2}{\to} s_2 \ldots \stackrel{t_{m-1}}{\to} s_{m-1} \stackrel{t_m}{\to} s_m$ including only transitions $t_i \in \mathcal{T}$ and $t_i \notin T, 1 \le i \le m$, each transition in T semi-commutes with t_i after s wrt. $\sqsupseteq_\psi$.*

For each state, computing a persistent set from the "semi-commutative" relation is similar to computing the classical persistent set under the transition independence relation. The algorithms for this task can be easily adapted from the algorithms pre-

Safety property ψ and current state s
$\langle 1 \rangle$ $T := \emptyset$
$\langle 2 \rangle$ Add an enabled transition t into T
$\langle 3 \rangle$ **foreach** remaining schedulable transition t_i
$\langle 4 \rangle$ **if** $\neg (\forall tp_j \in T \bullet \langle s, tp_j \uparrow t_i, \psi \rangle)$
$\langle 5 \rangle$ Add t_i into T

Fig. 2. Computing a Persistent Set of a State

sented in [11]. For convenience, we show one of such possibilities in Fig. 2.

We note here that the computation of the persistent set assumes that the semi-commutative relation is given. As in traditional algorithms, the quality (i.e. the size) of the returned persistent set is highly dependent on the first transition t to be added and the order in which the remaining transitions t_i are considered. This is, however, not the topic of the current paper.

With the new definition of persistent set, we now can proceed with the normal *selective search* as described in classic POR techniques. In the algorithm presented in Fig. 3, we perform depth first search (DFS), and only accommodate safety verification (invariant property ψ).

Theorem 1. *The selective search algorithm in Fig. 3 is sound*[6].   □

In preparing for POR and SI to work together, we now further modify the concept of persistent set so that it applies for a set of states sharing the same program point. We remark that the previous definitions apply only for a specific state. The key intuition is to attach a pre-condition ϕ to the program point of interest, indicating when semi-commutativity happens.

```
Safety property ψ and initial state s₀
⟨1⟩ Initially : Explore(s₀)
function Explore(s)
⟨2⟩ if s ⊭ ψ Report Error and TERMINATE
⟨3⟩ T := Persistent_Set(s)
⟨4⟩ foreach enabled transition t in T do
⟨5⟩     s →ᵗ s'          /* Execute t */
⟨6⟩     Explore(s')
end function
```

Fig. 3. New Selective Search Algorithm

Definition 8 (Semi-commutative after a Program Point). *For a given concurrent program, a safety property ψ, and $t_1, t_2 \in \mathcal{T}$, we say t_1 semi-commutes with t_2 after program point ℓ wrt. $\sqsupseteq_\psi$ and ϕ, denoted as $\langle \ell, \phi, t_1 \uparrow t_2, \psi \rangle$, iff for all state $s \equiv \langle \ell, \cdot \rangle$ reachable from the initial state s_0, if $s \models \phi$ then t_1 semi-commutes with t_2 after state s wrt. $\sqsupseteq_\psi$.*

Definition 9 (Persistent Set of a Program Point). *A set $T \subseteq \mathcal{T}$ of transitions schedulable at program point ℓ is persistent at ℓ under a trace interpolant $\overline{\Psi}$ wrt. a property ψ iff, for all state $s \equiv \langle \ell, \cdot \rangle$ reachable from the initial state s_0, if $s \models \overline{\Psi}$ then for all derivations $s \xrightarrow{t_1} s_1 \xrightarrow{t_2} s_2 \ldots \xrightarrow{t_{m-1}} s_{m-1} \xrightarrow{t_m} s_m$ including only transitions $t_i \in \mathcal{T}$ and $t_i \notin T, 1 \leq i \leq m$, each transition in T semi-commutes with t_i after state s wrt. $\sqsupseteq_\psi$.*

Assume that $T = \{tp_1, tp_2, \cdots tp_k\}$. The trace interpolant $\overline{\Psi}$ can now be computed as $\overline{\Psi} = \bigwedge \phi_{ji}$ for $1 \leq j \leq k, 1 \leq i \leq m$ such that $\langle \ell, \phi_{ji}, tp_j \uparrow t_i, \psi \rangle$.

For each program point, it is possible to have different persistent sets associated with different interpolants. In general, a state which satisfies a stronger interpolant will have a smaller persistent set, therefore, it enjoys more pruning.

5   Synergy of PDPOR and SI

We now show our combined framework. We assume for each program point, a persistent set and its associated interpolant are computed statically, i.e., by separate analyses. In other words, when we are at a program point, we can right away make use of the information about its persistent set.

The algorithm is in Fig. 4. The function Explore has input s and assumes the safety property at hand is ψ. It naturally performs a depth first search of the state space.

---

[6] Proof outline is in [6].

Two Base Cases. The function Explore handles two base cases. One is when the current state is subsumed by some computed (and memoed) interpolant $\overline{\Psi}$. No further exploration is needed, and $\overline{\Psi}$ is returned as the interpolant (line 2). The second base case is when the current state is found to be *unsafe* (line 3).

Combining Interpolants. We make use of the (static) persistent set T computed for the current program point. We comment further on this in the next section.

The set of transitions to be considered is denoted by Ts. When the current state implies the trace interpolant $\overline{\Psi}_{trace}$ associated with T, we need to consider only those transitions in T. Otherwise, we

```
Assume safety property ψ and initial state s₀
⟨1⟩ Initially : Explore(s₀)
function Explore(s)
    Let s be ⟨ℓ, ·⟩
⟨2⟩ if (memoed(s, Ψ̄)) return Ψ̄
⟨3⟩ if (s ⊭ ψ) Report Error and TERMINATE
⟨4⟩ Ψ̄ := ψ
⟨5⟩ ⟨T, Ψ̄_trace⟩ := Persistent_Set(ℓ)
⟨6⟩ if (s ⊨ Ψ̄_trace)
⟨7⟩     Ts := T
⟨8⟩     Ψ̄ := Ψ̄ ∧ Ψ̄_trace
⟨9⟩ else Ts := Schedulable(s)
⟨10⟩ foreach t in (Ts \ Enabled(s)) do
⟨11⟩     Ψ̄ := Ψ̄ ∧ pre(t, false)
⟨12⟩ foreach t in (Ts ∩ Enabled(s)) do
⟨13⟩     s →ᵗ s'              /* Execute t */
⟨14⟩     Ψ̄' := Explore(s')
⟨15⟩     Ψ̄ := Ψ̄ ∧ pre(t, Ψ̄')
⟨16⟩ memo and return (Ψ̄)
end function
```

Fig. 4. A Framework for POR and SI (DFS)

need to consider all the schedulable transitions. Note that when the persistent set T is employed, the interpolant $\overline{\Psi}_{trace}$ must contribute to the combined interpolant of the current state (line 8). Disabled transitions at the current state will strengthen the interpolant as in line 11. Finally, we recursively follow those transitions which are enabled at the current state. The interpolant of each child state contributes to the interpolant of the current state as in line 15. In our framework, interpolants are propagated back using the precondition operation pre, where $\text{pre}(t, \phi)$ denotes a *safe approximation* of the weakest precondition wrt. the transition t and the postcondition ϕ [9].

Theorem 2. *The algorithm in Fig. 4 is sound*[7].   □

6   Implementation of PDPOR

We now elaborate on the remaining task: how to estimate the semi-commutative relation, thus deriving the (static) persistent set at a program point. Similar to the formalism of traditional POR, our formalism is of paramount importance for the semantic use as well as to construct the formal proof of correctness. In practice, however, we have to come up with sufficient conditions to efficiently implement the concepts. In this paper, we estimate the semi-commutative relation in two steps:

1. We first employ *any* traditional POR method and first estimate the "semi-commutative" relation as the traditional independence relation (then the

---

[7] Proof outline is in [6].

corresponding condition ϕ is just *true*). This is possible because the proposed concepts are *strictly weaker* than the corresponding concepts used in traditional POR methods.

2. We then identify and exploit a number of patterns under which we can statically derive and prove the semi-commutative relation between transitions. In fact, these simple patterns suffice to deal with a number of important real-life applications.

In the rest of this section, we outline three common classes of problems, from which the semi-commutative relation between transitions can be easily identified and proved, i.e., our step 2 becomes applicable.

Resource Usage of Concurrent Programs. Programs make use of limited resource (such as time, memory, bandwidth). Validation of resource usage in sequential setting is already a hard problem. It is obviously more challenging in the setting of concurrent programs due to process interleavings.

Here we model this class of problems by using a resource variable r. Initially, r is *zero*. Each process can increment or decrement variable r by some concrete value (e.g., memory allocation or deallocation respectively). A process can also double the value r (e.g., the whole memory is duplicated). However, the resource variable r cannot be used in the guard condition of any transition, i.e., we cannot model the behavior of a typical garbage collector. The property to be verified is that, "at all times, r is (upper-) bounded by some constant".

Proposition 1. *Let r be a resource variable of a concurrent program, and assume the safety property at hand is $\psi \equiv r \leq C$, where C is a constant. For all transitions (assignment operations only) $t_1 : r = r + c_1$, $t_2 : r = r * 2$, $t_3 : r = r - c_2$ where $c_1, c_2 > 0$, we have for all program points ℓ:*
$$\langle \ell, true, t_1 \uparrow t_2, \psi \rangle \wedge \langle \ell, true, t_1 \uparrow t_3, \psi \rangle \wedge \langle \ell, true, t_2 \uparrow t_3, \psi \rangle \qquad \square$$

Informally, other than common mathematical facts such as additions can commute and so do multiplications and subtractions, we also deduce that additions can semi-commute with both multiplications and subtractions while multiplications can semi-commute with subtractions. This Proposition can be proved by using basic laws of algebra.

EXAMPLE 2 : Let us refer back to the example of two closely coupled processes introduced in Sec. 3, but now under the assumption that x is the resource variable of interest. Using the semi-commutative relation derived from Proposition 1, we need to explore only *one complete trace* to prove this safety.

We recall that, in contrast, POR (and DPOR)-only methods will enumerate the full execution tree which contains 19 states and 6 complete execution traces. Any technique which employs only the notion of Mazurkiewicz trace equivalence for pruning will have to consider all 6 complete traces (due to 6 different terminal states). SI alone can reduce the search space in this example, and requires to explore only 9 states and 4 subsumed states (as in Sec. 3).

Detection of Race Conditions. [25] proposed a property driven pruning algorithm to detect race conditions in multithreaded programs. This work has achieved more reduction in comparison with DPOR. The key observation is that, at a certain location (program point) ℓ, if their conservative "lockset analysis" shows that a search subspace is race-free, the subspace can be pruned away. As we know, DPOR relies solely on the independence relation to prune redundant interleavings (if t_1, t_2 are independent, there is no need to flip their execution order). In [25], however, even when t_1, t_2 are dependent, we may skip the corresponding search space if flipping the order of t_1, t_2 does not affect the reachability of any race condition. In other words, [25] is indeed a (conservative) realization of our PDPOR, specifically targeted for detection of race conditions. Their mechanism to capture such scenarios is by introducing a trace-based lockset analysis.

Ensuring Optimistic Concurrency. In the implementations of many concurrent protocols, *optimistic concurrency* [21], i.e., at least one process commits, is usually desirable. This can be modeled by introducing a flag variable which will be set when some process commits. The flag variable once set can not be unset. It is then easy to see that for all program point ℓ and transitions t_1, t_2, we have $\langle \ell, \mathsf{flag} = 1, t_1 \uparrow t_2, \psi \rangle$. Though simple, this observation will bring us more reduction compared to traditional POR methods.

7   Experiments

This section conveys two key messages. First, when trace-based and state-based methods are not effective individually, our combined framework still offers significant reduction. Second, property driven POR can be very effective, and applicable not only to academic programs, but also to programs used as benchmarks in the state-of-the-art.

We use a 3.2 GHz Intel processor and 2GB memory running Linux. Timeout is set at 10 minutes. In the tables, cells with '-' indicate timeout. We compare the performance of Partial Order Reduction alone (POR), State Interpolation alone (SI), the synergy of Partial Order Reduction and State Interpolation (POR+SI), i.e., the semi-commutative relation is estimated using only step 1 presented in Sec. 6, and when applicable, the synergy of Property Driven Partial Order Reduction and State Interpolation (PDPOR+SI), i.e., the semi-commutative relation is estimated using both steps presented in Sec. 6. For the POR component, we use the implementation from [3].

Table 1 starts with parameterized versions of the *producer/consumer* example because its basic structure is extremely common. There are $2 * N$ producers and 1 consumer. Each producer will do its own non-interfered computation first, modeled by a transition which does not interfere with other processes. Then these producers will modify the shared variable x as follows: each of the first N producers increments x, while the other N producers double the value of x. On the other hand, the consumer consumes the value of x. The safety property is that the consumed value is no more than $N * 2^N$.

Table 1 clearly demonstrates the synergy benefits of POR and SI. POR+SI significantly outperforms both POR and SI. Note that this example can easily be translated to the resource usage problem, where our PDPOR requires only a *single* trace (and less than 0.01 second) in order to prove safety.

We next use the parameterized version of the *dining philosophers*. We chose this for two reasons. First, this is a classic example often used in concurrent algorithm design to illustrate synchronization issues and techniques for resolving them. Second, previous work [15] has used this to demonstrate benefits from combining POR and SMT.

The first safety property used in [15], "it is not that all philosophers can eat simultaneously", is somewhat trivial. Therefore, here we verify a *tight* property, which is (a): "no more than *half* the philosophers can

Table 1. Synergy of POR and SI

	POR		SI		POR+SI	
Problem	States	T(s)	States	T(s)	States	T(s)
p/c-2	449	0.03	514	0.17	85	0.03
p/c-3	18745	2.73	6562	2.43	455	0.19
p/c-4	986418	586.00	76546	37.53	2313	1.07
p/c-5	–	–	–	–	11275	5.76
p/c-6	–	–	–	–	53261	34.50
p/c-7	–	–	–	–	245775	315.42
din-2a	22	0.01	21	0.01	21	0.01
din-3a	646	0.05	153	0.03	125	0.02
din-4a	155037	19.48	1001	0.17	647	0.09
din-5a	–	–	6113	1.01	4313	0.54
din-6a	–	–	35713	22.54	24201	4.16
din-7a	–	–	202369	215.63	133161	59.69
bak-2	48	0.03	38	0.03	31	0.02
bak-3	1003	1.85	264	0.42	227	0.35
bak-4	27582	145.78	1924	5.88	1678	4.95
bak-5	–	–	14235	73.69	12722	63.60

eat simultaneously". To demonstrate the power of symbolic execution, we verify this property *without* knowing the initial configurations of all the forks. Table 1, again, demonstrates the significant improvements of POR+SI over POR alone and SI alone. We note that the performance of our POR+SI algorithm is about 3 times faster than [15][8].

We additionally considered a second safety property as in [15], namely (b): "it is possible to reach a state in which all philosophers have eaten at least once". Our symbolic execution framework requires only a *single trace* (and less than 0.01 second) to prove this property in all instances, whereas [15] requires even more time compared to proving property (a). This illustrates the scalability issue of [15], which is representative for other techniques employing general-purpose SMT solver for symbolic pruning.

We also perform experiments on the "Bakery" algorithm. Due to existence of infinite domain variables, model checking hardly can handle this case. Here we remark that in symbolic methods, loop handling is often considered as an orthogonal issue. Programs with statically bounded loops can be easily unrolled into equivalent loop-free programs. For unbounded loops, either loop invariants are provided or the employment of some invariant discovery routines, e.g., as in [5], is necessary. In order for our algorithm to work here, we make use of the standard loop invariant for this example.

To further demonstrate the power our synergy framework over [15] as well as the power of our property driven POR, we experiment next on the *Sum-of-ids* program. Here, each process (of N processes) has one unique *id* and will

---

[8] [15] is not publicly available. Therefore, it is not possible for us to make more comprehensive comparisons.

increment a shared variable *sum* by this *id*. We prove that in the end this variable will be incremented by the sum of all the ids.

See Table 2, where we experiment with Z3 [8] (version 4.1.2) using the encodings presented in [15]. #C denotes the number of conflicts while #D denotes the number of decisions made by Z3. We can see that our synergy framework scale much better than [15] with Z3. Also, this example can also be translated to resource usage problem, our use of property-driven POR again requires *one* single trace to prove safety.

Table 2. Comparison with [15]

	[15] w. Z3			POR+SI		PDPOR+SI	
	T(s)	#C	#D	T(s)	States	T(s)	States	T(s)
sum-6	1608	1795	0.08	193	0.05	7	0.01
sum-8	54512	59267	10.88	1025	0.27	9	0.01
sum-10	–	–	–	5121	1.52	11	0.01
sum-12	–	–	–	24577	8.80	13	0.01
sum-14	–	–	–	114689	67.7	15	0.01

Finally, to benchmark our framework with SMT-based methods, we select four *safe* programs from [7] where the experimented methods did not perform well. Those programs are micro_2, stack, circular_buffer, and stateful20. We note that safe programs allow fairer comparison between different approaches since to verify them we have to cover the whole search space. Table 3 shows the running time of SI alone and of the combined framework. For convenience, we also tabulate the *best* running time reported in [7] and C is the context switch bound used. We assume no context switch bound, hence the corresponding value in our framework is ∞.

Table 3. Experiments on [7]'s Programs

Problem	[7]		SI		PDPOR+SI	
	C	T(s)	States	T(s)	States	T(s)
micro_2	17	1095	20201	10.88	201	0.04
stack	12	225	529	0.26	529	0.26
circular_buffer	∞	477	29	0.03	29	0.03
stateful20	10	95	1681	1.13	41	0.01

We can see that even our SI alone significantly outperforms the techniques in [7]. We believe it is due to the inefficient encoding of process interleavings (mentioned in Sec. 2) as well as the following reasons. First, our method is *lazy*, which means that only a path is considered at a time: [7] itself demonstrates partially the usefulness of this. Second, but importantly, we are *eager* in discovering infeasible paths. The program circular_buffer, which has only one feasible complete execution trace, can be efficiently handled by our framework, but not SMT. This is one important advantage of our symbolic execution framework over SMT-based methods, as discussed in [18].

It is important to note that, PDPOR significantly improves the performance of SI wrt. programs micro_2 and stateful20. This further demonstrates the applicability of our proposed framework.

8   Conclusion

We present a verification framework which synergistically combines trace-based reduction techniques with the recently established notion of *state interpolant*. One key contribution is the new concept of property-driven POR which serves to reduce more interleavings than previously possible.

References

1. Abdulla, P., Aronis, S., Jonsson, B., Sagonas, K.: Optimal Dynamic Partial Order Reduction. In: POPL (2014)
2. Alur, R., Brayton, R.K., Henzinger, T.A., Qadeer, S., Rajamani, S.K.: Partial-Order Reduction in Symbolic State Space Exploration. In: Grumberg, O. (ed.) CAV 1997. LNCS, vol. 1254, pp. 340–351. Springer, Heidelberg (1997)
3. Bokor, P., Kinder, J., Serafini, M., Suri, N.: Supporting Domain-specific State Space Reductions through Local Partial-Order Reduction. In: ASE (2011)
4. Cadar, C., Godefroid, P., Khurshid, S., Păsăreanu, C.S., Sen, K., Tillmann, N., Visser, W.: Symbolic Execution for Software Testing in Practice: Preliminary Assessment. In: ICSE (2011)
5. Chu, D.-H., Jaffar, J.: A Complete Method for Symmetry Reduction in Safety Verification. In: Madhusudan, P., Seshia, S.A. (eds.) CAV 2012. LNCS, vol. 7358, pp. 616–633. Springer, Heidelberg (2012)
6. Chu, D.H., Jaffar, J.: A Framework to Synergize Partial Order Reduction with State Interpolation. Technical Report (2014)
7. Cordeiro, L., Fischer, B.: Verifying Multi-threaded Software Using SMT-based Context-Bounded Model Checking. In: ICSE (2011)
8. de Moura, L., Bjørner, N.S.: Z3: An Efficient SMT Solver. In: Ramakrishnan, C.R., Rehof, J. (eds.) TACAS 2008. LNCS, vol. 4963, pp. 337–340. Springer, Heidelberg (2008)
9. Dijkstra, E.W.: Guarded Commands, Nondeterminacy and Formal Derivation of Programs. Commun. ACM (1975)
10. Flanagan, C., Godefroid, P.: Dynamic Partial-Order Reduction for Model Checking Software. In: POPL (2005)
11. Godefroid, P.: Partial-Order Methods for the Verification of Concurrent Systems: An Approach to the State-Explosion Problem. Springer-Verlag New York, Inc. (1996)
12. Grumberg, O., Lerda, F., Strichman, O., Theobald, M.: Proof-guided Underapproximation-widening for Multi-process Systems. In: POPL (2005)
13. Gueta, G., Flanagan, C., Yahav, E., Sagiv, M.: Cartesian partial-order reduction. In: Bošnački, D., Edelkamp, S. (eds.) SPIN 2007. LNCS, vol. 4595, pp. 95–112. Springer, Heidelberg (2007)
14. Jaffar, J., Santosa, A.E., Voicu, R.: An interpolation method for CLP traversal. In: Gent, I.P. (ed.) CP 2009. LNCS, vol. 5732, pp. 454–469. Springer, Heidelberg (2009)
15. Kahlon, V., Wang, C., Gupta, A.: Monotonic Partial Order Reduction: An Optimal Symbolic Partial Order Reduction Technique. In: Bouajjani, A., Maler, O. (eds.) CAV 2009. LNCS, vol. 5643, pp. 398–413. Springer, Heidelberg (2009)
16. King, J.C.: Symbolic Execution and Program Testing. Com. ACM (1976)
17. Mazurkiewicz, A.W.: Trace Theory. In: Brauer, W., Reisig, W., Rozenberg, G. (eds.) Advances in Petri Nets. LNCS, vol. 255, pp. 278–324. Springer, Heidelberg (1986)
18. McMillan, K.L.: Lazy Annotation for Program Testing and Verification. In: Touili, T., Cook, B., Jackson, P. (eds.) CAV 2010. LNCS, vol. 6174, pp. 104–118. Springer, Heidelberg (2010)
19. Peled, D.: All from One, One for All: On Model Checking Using Representatives. In: Courcoubetis, C. (ed.) CAV 1993. LNCS, vol. 697, pp. 409–423. Springer, Heidelberg (1993)
20. Silva, J.P.M., Sakallah, K.A.: GRASP–A New Search Algorithm for Satisfiability. In: ICCAD (1996)
21. Sulzmann, M., Chu, D.H.: A Rule-based Specification of Software Transactional Memory. In: LOPSTR pre-proceedings (2008)

22. Valmari, A.: Stubborn Sets for Reduced State Space Generation. In: Rozenberg, G. (ed.) APN 1990. LNCS, vol. 483, pp. 491–515. Springer, Heidelberg (1991)
23. Wachter, B., Kroening, D., Ouaknine, J.: Verifying Multi-threaded Software with IMPACT. In: FMCAD (2013)
24. Wang, C., Chaudhuri, S., Gupta, A., Yang, Y.: Symbolic Pruning of Concurrent Program Executions. In: ESEC/FSE (2009)
25. Wang, C., Yang, Y., Gupta, A., Gopalakrishnan, G.C.: Dynamic Model Checking with Property Driven Pruning to Detect Race Condition. In: Cha, S(S.), Choi, J.-Y., Kim, M., Lee, I., Viswanathan, M. (eds.) ATVA 2008. LNCS, vol. 5311, pp. 126–140. Springer, Heidelberg (2008)
26. Wang, C., Yang, Z., Kahlon, V., Gupta, A.: Peephole partial order reduction. In: Ramakrishnan, C.R., Rehof, J. (eds.) TACAS 2008. LNCS, vol. 4963, pp. 382–396. Springer, Heidelberg (2008)
27. Yang, Y., Chen, X., Gopalakrishnan, G., Kirby, R.M.: Efficient Stateful Dynamic Partial Order Reduction. In: Havelund, K., Majumdar, R. (eds.) SPIN 2008. LNCS, vol. 5156, pp. 288–305. Springer, Heidelberg (2008)

Reduction of Resolution Refutations and Interpolants via Subsumption

Roderick Bloem[1,*], Sharad Malik[2,**], Matthias Schlaipfer[3,*],
and Georg Weissenbacher[3,***]

[1] Graz University of Technology, Austria
[2] Princeton University, NJ, USA
[3] Vienna University of Technology, Austria

Abstract. Propositional resolution proofs and interpolants derived from them are widely used in automated verification and circuit synthesis. There is a broad consensus that "small is beautiful" — small proofs and interpolants lead to concise abstractions in verification and compact designs in synthesis. Contemporary proof reduction techniques either minimise the proof during construction, or perform a *post-hoc* transformation of a given resolution proof. We focus on the latter class and present a subsumption-based proof reduction algorithm that extends existing single-pass analyses and relies on a *meet-over-all-paths* analysis to identify redundant resolution steps and clauses. We show that smaller refutations do not necessarily entail smaller interpolants, and use labelled interpolation systems to generalise our reduction approach to interpolants. Experimental results support the theoretical claims.

1 Introduction

Resolution proofs and interpolants are an integral part of many verification-related techniques such as abstraction [24] and model checking [17], vacuity detection [29], synthesis [18,20], and patch generation [32]. These techniques take advantage of the fact that refutations and interpolants direct the focus to the *core* of the problem instance (literally and metaphorically). In practice, small refutations provide concise abstractions in model checking [24], and small interpolants enable precise refinement and compact designs in synthesis [20].

Consequently, proof reduction as well as the minimisation of unsatisfiable cores has received ample attention. We roughly group the resulting reduction approaches into two categories: techniques that minimise the proof during construction, and techniques that rely on a *post-hoc* proof transformation. Algorithms for the extraction of minimal unsatisfiable subsets (such as [25,4]) typically fall into the former

---

* Supported by the Austrian Science Fund (FWF) through grants S11403-N23 (National Research Network RiSE) and W1255-N23 (LogiCS doctoral programme).
** Funded by C-FAR, one of six centers supported by the STARnet phase of the Focus Center Research Program (FCRP), a Semiconductor Research Corporation program sponsored by MARCO and DARPA.
*** Funded by grant VRG11-005 of the Vienna Science and Technology Fund (WWTF).

E. Yahav (Ed.): HVC 2014, LNCS 8855, pp. 188–203, 2014.

category and rely on iterative calls to a SAT solver. Representatives of the latter class reduce the proof size by identifying and eliminating redundancies (e.g. [3,16,28,7]). The focus of these reduction algorithms is not on minimality but scalability, which is why they avoid additional SAT calls. Naturally, there are also hybrid approaches: Gershman et al. [14], for instance, rely on a solver to detect redundancies in a given proof.

The focus of our work is on *post-hoc* proof transformations. The motivation for this decision is two-fold. Firstly, while small proofs and interpolants are desirable, minimality is often not necessary and comes at the cost of scalability [3]. Secondly, it is possible to harvest information from a complete proof that is not available during proof construction. This idea is very explicit in [16], where a *meet-over-all-paths* analysis identifies redundant literals and resolution steps (discussed in §3.1). Other authors [3,28] deploy a richer set of transformation rules (including pivot and unit recycling), but fail to exploit the information readily available in the proof. In §3, we cast pivot and unit recycling [3,16,13,28] more generally as *subsumption* and generalise them in a single concise transformation rule (Theorem 1). Subsumption has been successfully deployed during proof construction (in [33], for instance). We use subsumption as a post-processing step and carry forward the idea of [16] to use proof analysis to identify redundancies that were not eliminated during proof construction. proof construction (in [33], for instance, and implicitly in [15]). We use subsumption as a post-processing step and carry forward the idea of [16] to use proof analysis to identify redundancies not eliminated during proof construction.

Interpolation is often an after-thought to proof reduction. It is common practice to extract interpolants from a reduced proof [27] and to subsequently compact the result by removing structural redundancy [8]. We show in §4 that pivot and unit recycling can actually *increase* the number of variables in an interpolant. In §4, we lift the results from §3 to *labelled* clauses in the framework of labelled interpolation systems [12], thus avoiding transformations that introduce nonessential [10] (or peripheral [29]) variables.

Contributions. In §3, we present a single concise transformation rule (Theorem 1) which, based on subsumption, generalises existing proof reduction techniques [3,13,16]. We show in §4 that careless transformations may increase interpolant size, and lift the results from §3 to labelled clauses [12] to rule out detrimental reductions (Theorem 2). §5 covers our implementation and provides an experimental evaluation that demonstrates a small but consistent improvement over [13,16].

2   Notation and Preliminaries

This section introduces our notation and restates some prior results on proof restructuring [11] in §2.1, and labelled interpolation systems [12,10] in §2.2.

2.1   Formulae, Proofs, and Transformations

Propositional Formulae. We work in the standard setting of propositional logic. Formulas are defined over a set X of propositional variables, the logical constants

T and F (denoting true and false, respectively), and the standard logical connectives $\land$, $\lor$, $\Rightarrow$, and $\neg$ (denoting conjunction, disjunction, implication, and negation, respectively).

$\text{Lit}_X = \{x, \bar{x} \mid x \in X\}$ is the set of literals over X, where $\bar{x}$ is short for $\neg x$. We write $\text{var}(t)$ for the variable occurring in the literal $t \in \text{Lit}_X$, and $\text{Var}(F)$ to denote the variables occurring in a formula F. A clause C is a set of literals interpreted as a disjunction. A clause C *subsumes* a clause D if $C \subseteq D$. The empty clause $\square$ contains no literals and is interpreted as F. The disjunction of two clauses C and D is their union, denoted $C \lor D$, which is further simplified to $C \lor t$ if D is the singleton $\{t\}$. A propositional formula in Conjunctive Normal Form (CNF) is a conjunction of clauses, also represented as a set of clauses.

Resolution Proofs. The resolution rule is an inference rule deriving a new clause from two clauses containing complementary literals. The clauses $C \lor x$ and $D \lor \bar{x}$ are the *antecedents*, x is the *pivot*, and $C \lor D$ is the *resolvent*. $\text{Res}(C, D, x)$ denotes the resolvent of C and D with the pivot x.

Definition 1 (Resolution Proof, Refutation). *A resolution proof R is a directed acyclic graph $(V_R, E_R, piv_R, \ell_R, s_R)$, where V_R is a set of vertices, E_R is a set of edges, piv_R is a function mapping vertices to pivot variables, ℓ_R is a function mapping vertices to formulae, and $s_R \in V_R$ is a designated sink vertex. An initial vertex has in-degree 0. All other vertices are internal and have in-degree 2. The sink s_R has out-degree 0. For every internal vertex v with $(v_1, v), (v_2, v) \in E_R$, we have $\ell_R(v) = \text{Res}(\ell_R(v_1), \ell_R(v_2), piv_R(v))$. A resolution proof R is a* resolution refutation *if $\ell_R(s_R) = \square$.*

The subscripts above are dropped if clear from the context. A vertex $v_i \in R$ is a *parent* of v_j if $(v_i, v_j) \in E_R$. Let v^+ and v^- be the parents of v such that $piv(v) \in \ell(v^+)$ and $\neg piv(v) \in \ell(v^-)$. A vertex v_i is an *ancestor* of v_j if there is a path from v_i to v_j. A vertex v_i dominates v_j if all paths from v_j to s_R visit v_i. The substitution $R[v_1 \leftarrow v_2]$ replaces the sub-proof rooted at v_1 with the sub-proof rooted at v_2:

Definition 2. *Let $R = (V_R, E_R, piv_R, \ell_R, s_R)$, and let $v_1, v_2 \in V_R$ ($v_1 \neq v_2$) such that v_1 is not an ancestor of v_2. The* substitution *of v_1 with v_2 in R, denoted by $R[v_1 \leftarrow v_2]$, is the directed acyclic graph $G = (V_G, E_G, piv_G, \ell_G, s_G)$, where $V_G = V_R \setminus \{v_1\}$, $E_G = (E_R \setminus \{(u, v) \mid u = v_1 \lor v = v_1\}) \cup \{(v_2, v) \mid (v_1, v) \in E_R\}$, $\ell_G(v) = \ell_R(v)$ and $piv_G(v) = piv_R(v)$ for all $v \neq v_1$, and s_G is s_R if $v_1 \neq s_R$ and v_2 otherwise.*

The transformation $R[v_1 \leftarrow v_2]$ does not necessarily yield a valid resolution proof. The transformation $\text{RestoreRes}(G, v)$ as defined below restores the validity of the single resolution step at vertex v.

Definition 3. *Let G be the directed acyclic graph $(V_G, E_G, piv_G, \ell_G, s_G)$. The transformation $\text{RestoreRes}(G, v)$ yields G if v is an initial vertex of G. For an internal vertex $v \in V_G$,*

```
proc RECONSTRUCTPROOF (R, v)
    if v ∉ visited then
        visited ← visited ∪ {v}
        foreach (u, v) ∈ E_R
            RECONSTRUCTPROOF (R, u)
        R ← RestoreRes (R, v)
```

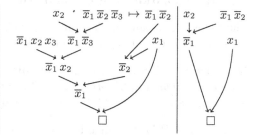

(a) RECONSTRUCTPROOF   (b) Reducing proof size

Fig. 1. Reconstructing proofs

— if $\exists (v^+, v), (v^-, v) \in E_G$ with $piv_G(v) \in \ell_G(v^+) \wedge \overline{piv(v)} \in \ell_G(v^-)$ then

$$\mathrm{RestoreRes}(G, v) = (V_G, E_G, piv_G, \ell, \mathsf{s}_G)$$

$$with\ \ell(u) \stackrel{\text{def}}{=} \begin{cases} \mathrm{Res}(\ell_G(v^+), \ell_G(v^-), piv(v)) & if\ u = v \\ \ell_G(u) & otherwise \end{cases}$$

— otherwise, let u and w be the parents of v, and $\mathrm{RestoreRes}(G, v) = G[v \leftarrow u]$, where u is chosen such that

$$(piv(v) \in \ell(u) \Rightarrow piv(v) \in \ell(w)) \wedge (\overline{piv(v)} \in \ell(u) \Rightarrow \overline{piv(v)} \in \ell(w)).$$

The second case in Definition 3 affords us a choice for u if neither parent contains the pivot or both parents contain the pivot literal in the same phase. The latter situation can arise in proofs that contain tautological clauses.

The algorithm RECONSTRUCTPROOF in Figure 1(a) (introduced in [3]) performs a linear time post-order (parents first) traversal of the graph, applying RestoreRes to re-establish $\forall (v_1, v), (v_2, v) \in E . \ell(v) = \mathrm{Res}(\ell(v_1), \ell(v_2), piv(v))$.

The following lemma is an adaptation of Lemma 2 from [11] to our setting.

Lemma 1. Let R be a resolution proof, and let $\pi = \{v_1 \mapsto u_1, \ldots, v_k \mapsto u_k\}$ be a mapping such that v_i is not an ancestor of u_j for $1 \le i, j \le k$. If $\ell_R(u_i) \subseteq \ell_R(v_i)$ for $1 \le i \le k$, then the proof P obtained by applying RECONSTRUCTPROOF to $R[v_1 \leftarrow u_1] \ldots [v_k \leftarrow u_k]$ has sink s_P with $\ell_P(\mathsf{s}_P) \subseteq \ell_R(\mathsf{s}_R)$.

Proof: By induction on the number of ancestors of s_R (cf. the more general proof of Theorem 1 on page 194). ∎

Example 1. Consider the left proof in Figure 1(b), in which the mapping π from Lemma 1 is indicated by $\mapsto$. The refutation on the right of Figure 1(b) shows the result of RECONSTRUCTPROOF after substituting $\overline{x}_1\overline{x}_2$ for $\overline{x}_1\overline{x}_2\overline{x}_3$.   ◁

2.2 Interpolation Systems and Labelling Functions

The following variant of Craig interpolants [9] has been introduced by McMillan [22] and is commonly used in the context of verification.

Definition 4 (Propositional Interpolant). *An* interpolant *for a pair of propositional formulae* (A, B), *where* $A \wedge B$ *is unsatisfiable, is a formula* I *such that* $A \Rightarrow I$, $B \Rightarrow \neg I$, *and* $\mathrm{Var}(I) \subseteq \mathrm{Var}(A) \cap \mathrm{Var}(B)$ *holds.*

Let A and B be formulae in CNF. A refutation R is an (A, B)-*refutation* of an unsatisfiable formula $A \wedge B$ if $\ell_R(v)$ is a clause in A or a clause in B for each initial vertex $v \in V_R$.

An interpolation system Itp is a function that given an (A, B)-refutation R yields a function, denoted $\mathrm{Itp}(R, A, B)$, from vertices in R to formulae over $\mathrm{Var}(A) \cap \mathrm{Var}(B)$. An interpolation system is *correct* if for every (A, B)-refutation R with sink $\mathbf{s}$, it holds that $\mathrm{Itp}(R, A, B)(\mathbf{s})$ is an interpolant for (A, B). We write $\mathrm{Itp}(R)$ for $\mathrm{Itp}(R, A, B)(\mathbf{s})$ when A and B are clear. Let v be a vertex in an (A, B)-refutation R. The pair $(\ell(v), \mathrm{Itp}(R, A, B)(v))$ is an *annotated clause* and is written $\ell(v) [\mathrm{Itp}(R, A, B)(v)]$ in accordance with [23].

In the following, we review the labelled interpolation systems introduced in [12], which generalise the propositional interpolation algorithms presented by Huang [19], Krajíček [21] and Pudlák [26], and McMillan [22]. A distinguishing feature of a labelled interpolation system is that it assigns an individual label $\mathsf{c} \in \{\bot, \mathsf{a}, \mathsf{b}, \mathsf{ab}\}$ to *each literal* in the resolution refutation.

Definition 5 (Labelling Function). *Let* $(\mathcal{S}, \sqsubseteq, \sqcap, \sqcup)$ *be the lattice below, where* $\mathcal{S} = \{\bot, \mathsf{a}, \mathsf{b}, \mathsf{ab}\}$ *is a set of symbols and* $\sqsubseteq$, $\sqcap$ *and* $\sqcup$ *are defined by the Hasse diagram to the right. A labelling function* $L_R : V_R \times \mathtt{Lit} \to \mathcal{S}$ *for a refutation* R *over a set of literals* $\mathtt{Lit}$ *satisfies that for all* $v \in V_R$ *and* $t \in \mathtt{Lit}$:

1. $L_R(v, t) = \bot$ *iff* $t \notin \ell_R(v)$
2. $L_R(v, t) = L_R(v^+, t) \sqcup L_R(v^-, t)$ *for an internal vertex* v, *its parents* v^+ *and* v^-, *and literal* $t \in \ell_R(v)$.

Definition 6 (Locality). *A* literal t is A-local *if* $\mathrm{var}(t) \in \mathrm{Var}(A) \setminus \mathrm{Var}(B)$. *Conversely,* t *is* B-local *if* $\mathrm{var}(t) \in \mathrm{Var}(B) \setminus \mathrm{Var}(A)$. *All other literals are* shared. *A labelling function* L *is* locality preserving *if for any initial vertex* $v \in V_R$ *and* $t \in \ell(v)$, $L(v, t) = \mathsf{a}$ *if* t *is* A-local *and* $L(v, t) = \mathsf{b}$ *if* t *is* B-local.

Shared literals may be labelled a, b, or ab. Given a labelling function L, the downward *projection* of a clause at a vertex v with respect to $\mathsf{c} \in \mathcal{S}$ is $\ell(v) \restriction_{\mathsf{c}, L} \overset{\mathrm{def}}{=} \{t \in \ell(v) \mid L(v, t) \sqsubseteq \mathsf{c}\}$. The subscript L is omitted if clear from the context.

Definition 7 (Labelled Interpolation System for Resolution). *Let* L *be a locality preserving labelling function for an* (A, B)-*refutation* R. *The labelled interpolation system* $\mathrm{Itp}(L)$ *maps vertices in* R *to partial interpolants as defined in Figure 2.*

For an initial vertex v with $\ell(v) = C$

$(A\text{-clause})$ $\dfrac{}{C \quad [C|_{\mathsf{b}}]}$ if $C \in A$ $\qquad$ $(B\text{-clause})$ $\dfrac{}{C \quad [\neg(C|_{\mathsf{a}})]}$ if $C \in B$

For an internal vertex v with $piv(v) = x$, $\ell(v^+) = C_1 \vee x$ and $\ell(v^-) = C_2 \vee \overline{x}$

$$\dfrac{C_1 \vee x \quad [I_1] \qquad C_2 \vee \overline{x} \quad [I_2]}{C_1 \vee C_2 \quad [I_3]}$$

$(A\text{-Res})$ $\quad$ if $L(v^+, x) \sqcup L(v^-, \overline{x}) = \mathsf{a}$, $I_3 \overset{\text{def}}{=} \quad I_1 \vee I_2$

$(AB\text{-Res})$ if $L(v^+, x) \sqcup L(v^-, \overline{x}) = \mathsf{ab}$, $I_3 \overset{\text{def}}{=} (x \vee I_1) \wedge (\overline{x} \vee I_2)$

$(B\text{-Res})$ $\quad$ if $L(v^+, x) \sqcup L(v^-, \overline{x}) = \mathsf{b}$, $I_3 \overset{\text{def}}{=} \quad I_1 \wedge I_2$

Fig. 2. Labelled interpolation systems

ltp yields interpolants of a highly redundant propositional structure. The structural redundancy is typically reduced in a subsequent step [8]. Therefore, we resort to the number of variables as a measure of interpolant size. Labelled interpolation systems support the elimination of *nonessential* (or *peripheral* [29]) variables from interpolants [10], as stated by the following lemma.

Lemma 2. *Let L and L' be locality preserving labelling functions for an (A, B)-refutation R, where $L(v, t) = \mathsf{a}$ if $\ell_R(v) \in A$ and $L(v, t) = \mathsf{b}$ if $\ell_R(v) \in B$ for all initial vertices of R. Then $\mathrm{Var}(\mathsf{ltp}(L)(v)) \subseteq \mathrm{Var}(\mathsf{ltp}(L')(v))$ for all $v \in V_R$.*

Example 2. Assume that the left refutation in Figure 1(b) is an (A, B)-refutation with $(\overline{x}_1 x_2 x_3), (\overline{x}_1 \overline{x}_2 \overline{x}_3), (x_1) \in A$ and $(x_2), (\overline{x}_1 \overline{x}_2) \in B$, and let L be the labelling function from Lemma 2. $\mathsf{ltp}(L, R)(v) = \mathsf{F}$ for all initial vertices v in A and $\mathsf{ltp}(L, R)(v) = \mathsf{T}$ for all remaining initial vertices. The internal vertices are annotated as follows:

$$\overline{x}_1 \overline{x}_3 \underbrace{[(x_2 \vee \mathsf{T}) \wedge (\overline{x}_2 \vee \mathsf{F})]}_{\overline{x}_2}, \quad \overline{x}_1 x_2 \, [\overline{x}_2 \vee \mathsf{F}], \quad \overline{x}_2 \underbrace{[(x_1 \vee \mathsf{F}) \wedge (\overline{x}_1 \vee \mathsf{T})]}_{x_1}$$

$$\overline{x}_1 \underbrace{[(x_2 \vee \overline{x}_2) \wedge (\overline{x}_2 \vee x_1)]}_{x_1 \vee \overline{x}_2}, \quad \square \, [(x_1 \vee \overline{x}_2) \vee \mathsf{F}]$$

Accordingly, $\mathsf{ltp}(L, R)(\mathsf{s}_R) = x_1 \vee \overline{x}_2$. For the same partition (A, B) and the right refutation P in Figure 1(b) we obtain $\mathsf{ltp}(L, P)(\mathsf{s}_P) = x_1$. $\qquad \triangleleft$

According to Lemma 2, the set $\mathrm{Var}(\mathsf{ltp}(L, R)(v))$ in Example 2 cannot be reduced any further by mutating L. The proof transformation in Figure 1(b), however, results in an interpolant with fewer variables.

We present a proof transformation technique aimed at reducing proof size in §3. In §4, we show that smaller proofs do not always yield interpolants with fewer variables, and specialise our reduction technique to eliminate variables (and Boolean connectives) from interpolants.

3 Proof Reduction via Subsumption

Example 1 in §2.1 demonstrates that the size of proofs can be reduced by means of clause subsumption. In general, let R be a resolution proof with vertices $u_i, v_i \in V_R$ such that $\ell_R(u_i) \subseteq \ell_R(v_i)$ for $1 \leq i \leq k$. Then the sub-proofs of R rooted at v_i can be pruned by means of substitution (see Def. 2) if no v_i is an ancestor of a u_j for $1 \leq i, j \leq k$ (cf. Lemma 1). The following example shows that the requirement $\ell_R(u_i) \subseteq \ell_R(v_i)$ is sufficient but not necessary.

Example 3. Let R be a refutation resembling the proof on the left of Figure 1(b) except that we replace the clause $\overline{x}_1\,\overline{x}_2\,\overline{x}_3$ with $\overline{x}_2\,\overline{x}_3$. In this setting, Lemma 1 does not justify the substitution proposed in Example 1 anymore, since $\overline{x}_1\,\overline{x}_2 \not\subseteq \overline{x}_2\,\overline{x}_3$. The substitution of $\overline{x}_2\,\overline{x}_3$ with $\overline{x}_1\,\overline{x}_2$ followed by RECONSTRUCTPROOF, however, still results in the proof on the right of Figure 1(b). The substitution is still valid because $\overline{x}_1$ is eliminated along all paths from $\overline{x}_1\,\overline{x}_2$ to $\square$ in the resulting graph. Intuitively, this situation arises since $\overline{x}_1$ is a *merge-literal* [2] of the resolution $\mathrm{Res}(\overline{x}_1\,x_2\,x_3, \overline{x}_1\,\overline{x}_3, x_3)$ in the original proof in Example 1.   ◁

The set of literals eliminated along all paths from $v \in V_R$ to s_R can be defined as the *meet-over-all-paths* in the terminology of data-flow analysis:

$$\mathrm{rlit}(v,w) = t \text{ s.t. } t \in \ell(v), \mathrm{var}(t) = piv(w), \exists u \neq w\,.\,(u,w) \in E \wedge \mathrm{rlit}(u,w) = \overline{t}$$

$$\sigma(v) = \begin{cases} \emptyset & \text{if } v = \mathsf{s}_R \\ \bigcap_{(v,w) \in E} (\sigma(w) \cup \{\mathrm{rlit}(v,w)\}) & \text{otherwise} \end{cases}$$

(1)

A solution to the data-flow equation 1 can be computed in linear time since the graph R is acyclic. Our definition of σ resembles the *safe literals* [13] and *expansion set* [16]. Unlike Gupta in [16] we do not rule out literals of opposing phase in $\sigma(v)$.

Given a resolution proof R and a solution of σ_R of Equation 1 for R, we call $\ell_R(v) \cup \sigma_R(v)$ the *augmented clause* of $v \in V_R$. The following theorem generalises Lemma 1 to use subsumption of augmented clauses.

Theorem 1. *Let R be a resolution proof, let σ_R be a solution of Equation 1 for R, and let $\pi = \{v_1 \mapsto u_1, \ldots, v_k \mapsto u_k\}$ be a mapping such that for all $1 \leq i \leq j \leq k$ it holds that a) no vertex v_i is an ancestor of u_j, and b) if v_j is an ancestor of u_i then $\sigma_R(u_i) \subseteq \sigma_R(v_i)$. If $\ell_R(u_i) \subseteq (\ell_R(v_i) \cup \sigma_R(v_i))$ for $1 \leq i \leq k$, then applying RECONSTRUCTPROOF to $R[v_1 \leftarrow u_1] \ldots [v_k \leftarrow u_k]$ yields a proof P with sink s_P such that $\ell_P(\mathsf{s}_P) \subseteq \ell_R(\mathsf{s}_R)$.*

The proof is led by nested structural induction on the number of substitutions and the number of ancestors of s_R. The core insight is that for every sub-proof of R rooted at s_R, RECONSTRUCTPROOF yields a proof P with sink s_P such that $\ell_P(\mathsf{s}_P) \subseteq (\ell_R(\mathsf{s}_R) \cup \sigma_R(\mathsf{s}_R))$.

The restrictions on the substitutions π in Theorem 1 are much weaker than in Lemma 1 (which corresponds to [11, Lemma 2]). Theorem 1 as well as Lemma 1 allow overlapping proofs in the range of π. In addition, Theorem 1 allows the substitution of vertices that are ancestors of preceding substitutions, and introduces

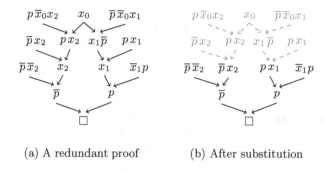

(a) A redundant proof   (b) After substitution

Fig. 3. Subsumption for elimination of redundant resolution steps

a more general notion of subsumption by considering augmented clauses. In the following section, we show that Theorem 1 justifies the redundancy elimination algorithms presented in [3,13,16].

3.1 Eliminating Redundant Resolution Steps

In the published version of his 1966 talk at a Leningrad seminar, Grigory Tseitin introduced the notion of regular proofs [30]. A resolution proof R is regular if, along any path from an initial vertex to the sink s_R, every pivot occurs at most once. If proofs are represented as trees rather than directed acyclic graphs, then refutations of minimal size are always regular [31, Lemma 5.1]. Consequently, pivots that repeatedly occur along a path in tree-shaped proofs are redundant. Bar-Ilan et al. [3] introduce an algorithm (RMPIVOTS) which eliminates such redundant resolution steps in the tree-shaped parts of a proof.

Fontaine et al. [13] generalise this algorithm to directed acyclic graphs considering all paths from a given vertex to the sink.[1] To this end, they introduce the notion of a *safe literals*, which resembles our definition of σ in Equation 1. The following example illustrates the algorithm from [13] on a redundant proof and shows that the resulting reduction is justified by Theorem 1.

Example 4. Consider the proof in Figure 3(a). Let v_1 and v_2 be the vertex for which $\ell(v_1) = x_1$ and $\ell(v_2) = x_2$, respectively. Then $\sigma(v_1) = \{p, x_1\}$ and $\sigma(v_2) = \{\overline{p}, x_2\}$, and the algorithm from [13] prunes the sub-proofs for $x_1 \overline{p}$ and $p x_2$.

Now let v_3 and v_4 be the vertices such that $\ell(v_3) = p x_1$ and $\ell(v_4) = \overline{p} x_2$. Since $\sigma(v_1) = \{p, x_1\}$ and $\sigma(v_2) = \{\overline{p}, x_2\}$, we may perform the transformation $R[v_1 \leftarrow v_3][v_2 \leftarrow v_4]$ by Theorem 1. This transformation corresponds to pruning the sub-proofs as described above. Figure 3(b) shows the corresponding proof returned by RECONSTRUCTPROOF.   ◁

---

[1] The resulting proofs are not necessarily regular. This is not a shortcoming of the algorithm, as minimal refutations are in general not regular [1].

```
proc RMPIVOTS (R, v)
    if v ∉ visited and
        {u | (v, u) ∈ E} ⊆ visited
    then
        visited ← visited ∪ {v}
        V± ← {v⁺, v⁻}
        R ← SubsumeRes (R, v)
        foreach u ∈ (V± ∩ VR)
            RMPIVOTS (R, u)
```

```
proc RMPIVOTSₜ (R, v)
    if v ∉ visited and {u | (v, u) ∈ E} ⊆ visited then
        visited ← visited ∪ {v}
        σ(v) = ⋂(v,w)∈E (σ(w) ∪ {rlit(v, w)})
        V± ← {v⁺, v⁻}
        R ← SubsumeRes (R, v)
        if v ∉ VR then σ(v) ← ⊤
        foreach u ∈ V±
            RMPIVOTSₜ (R, u)
```

(a) RMPIVOTS   (b) Optimised variant of RMPIVOTS

Fig. 4. Removing redundant resolutions

In the following, we provide a subsumption-based formalisation of the redundancy elimination algorithm RMPIVOTS which relies on σ to identify redundant resolution steps.

Proposition 1. *If $piv(v) \in \sigma(v)$ then $\ell(v^+) \subseteq (\ell(v) \cup \sigma(v))$. If $\overline{piv(v)} \in \sigma(v)$ then $\ell(v^-) \subseteq (\ell(v) \cup \sigma(v))$.*

Based on Proposition 1, the following proof transformation eliminates redundant resolution steps.

Definition 8. *Let R be the resolution proof $(V_R, E_R, piv_R, \ell_R, s_R)$, and let σ_R be a solution of Equation 1 for R. We define the following transformation:*

$$\text{SubsumeRes}(R, v) \stackrel{\text{def}}{=} \begin{cases} R[v \leftarrow v^+] \text{ if } piv(v) \in \sigma_R(v) \\ R[v \leftarrow v^-] \text{ if } \overline{piv(v)} \in \sigma_R(v) \end{cases}$$

The procedure RMPIVOTS in Figure 4(a) performs a pre-order traversal of the proof (starting at the root), which guarantees that the order of substitutions performed by SubsumeRes(R, s_R) satisfies condition *a)* in Theorem 1. The fact that $\sigma(v^+) = \sigma(v) \cup \{piv(v)\}$ and $\sigma(v^-) = \sigma(v) \cup \{\overline{piv(v)}\}$ in combination with the conditions of SubsumeRes in Definition 8 ($piv(v) \in \sigma(v)$ and $\overline{piv(v)} \in \sigma(v)$, respectively) establishes condition *b)*. Proposition 1 guarantees that $\ell(u_i) \subseteq (\ell(v_i) \cup \sigma(v_i))$. Therefore, applying RMPIVOTS followed by RECONSTRUCTPROOF yields a valid refutation.

Optimisations. The definition of σ is unnecessarily restrictive in the context of RMPIVOTS. Observe that $\sigma(v)$ is propagated even if RMPIVOTS prunes the node v. The constraints propagated along pruned paths may result in the unnecessary exclusion of literals from ancestors of v. We amend this by setting $\sigma(v)$ to the top element $\top$ of the power set lattice if a vertex v is pruned. Figure 4(b) shows the optimised version of RMPIVOTS, which intertwines the computation of σ and RMPIVOTS.

3.2   Limiting the Number of Candidates for Subsumption

RMPIVOTS (as introduced in §3.1) only considers a subset of all feasible subsumptions. For the proof in Example 1 in §2.1, for instance, RMPIVOTS substitutes x_2 for $\overline{x}_1\overline{x}_3$ (resulting in a different proof than the substitution suggested in Example 1). The algorithm RECYCLEUNITS [3], on the other hand, only considers unit clauses and would substitute $\overline{x}_2$ for $\overline{x}_1\overline{x}_2\overline{x}_3$. However, RMPIVOTS and RECYCLEUNITS may miss valid subsumptions.

Example 5. Consider the refutation to the right. Note that no pivots are eliminated more than once along any of the paths, and none of the unit clauses are valid candidates for substitutions, since their vertices violate the ancestor requirement of Definition 2. Let v be the vertex with $\ell(v) = x_1x_3$. Since $\sigma(v) = \{x_1, x_2, x_3, \overline{x}_4\}$, v is subsumed by x_1x_2 (as indicated by $\mapsto$ in the figure).   ◁

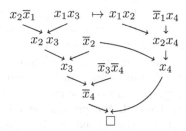

The computational cost for checking all pairs of clauses satisfying the ancestor requirement in Definition 2 for subsumption is substantial. In the following, we derive a lemma that allows us to reduce the number of subsumption checks.

Proposition 2. *If v_i dominates v_j then the following subset relations hold:*

$$a) \quad (\ell(v_j) \setminus \ell(v_i)) \subseteq \sigma(v_j) \qquad and \qquad b) \quad \sigma(v_i) \subseteq \sigma(v_j)$$

Corollary 1. *If R is a refutation, then $\ell(v) \subseteq \sigma(v)$ for all $v \in V_R$ that are ancestors of $\mathbf{s}_R$.*

Corollary 2. *Let R be a resolution refutation, and let $u_i, v_i \in V_R$ be such that $\ell(u_i) \subseteq (\ell(v_i) \cup \sigma(v_i))$. Then $\ell(u_i) \subseteq \sigma(v_j)$ for any $v_j \in V_R$ dominated by v_i.*

This is a simple consequence of Proposition 2b and Corollary 1. The following lemma allows us to exclude vertices that dominate a path segment of vertices with out-degree one from our search for subsumed vertices.

Lemma 3. *Let $v_j \to v_{j+1} \to \ldots \to v_k$ be a path in a refutation R such that all vertices v_i have out-degree 1 and $\mathrm{rlit}(v_i, v_{i+1}) \notin \sigma(v_k)$ (where $j \leq i < k$). Further, let u_k be such that $\ell(u_k) \subseteq (\ell(v_k) \cup \sigma(v_k))$ and v_j is not an ancestor of u_k. Then applying RECONSTRUCTPROOF to $R[v_k \leftarrow u_i]$ or $R[v_j \leftarrow u_i]$ yields the same refutation.*

Proof: We consider only the case that v_k is an ancestor of $\mathbf{s}_R$, since v_j and v_k are otherwise not visited by RECONSTRUCTPROOF. Since R is a refutation,

> **if** $\sigma(v) \neq \top \wedge (V_{\pm} = \emptyset \vee \exists u \in V_{\pm} . |\{w | (u, w) \in E\}| > 1)$ **then**
>   **pick** $u \in \{w \mid \ell(w) \subseteq \sigma(v) \wedge v \mapsto w$ satisfies Theorem 1$\}$
> $R \leftarrow R[v \leftarrow u]$

Fig. 5. Subsumption-based substitution of vertices

$\ell(u_k) \subseteq \sigma(v_k)$ (Corollary 1), and therefore $\ell(u_k) \subseteq \sigma(v_j)$ (Corollary 2). Since $\mathrm{rlit}(v_{i-1}, v_i) \not\subseteq \sigma(v_k)$ for $j < i \leq k$ and $\ell(u_k) \subseteq \sigma(v_k)$, we have $\mathrm{rlit}(v_{i-1}, v_i) \notin \ell(u_k)$ and $\overline{\mathrm{rlit}(w, v_i)} \in \ell(w)$ for $w \neq v_{i-1}$ and $(w, v_i) \in E$. Therefore, RestoreRes propagates vertex u_k until v_k is reached (cf. Definition 3). ∎

We claim that the restriction in Lemma 3 that v_j may not be an ancestor of u_k does not exclude viable candidates for subsumption: Every $\ell(v_i)$ $(j \leq i < k)$ contains a literal $\mathrm{rlit}(v_i, v_{i+1}) \notin \sigma(v_k)$ and therefore $\ell(v_i) \not\subseteq \sigma(v_k)$.

RMPIVOTS establishes the condition $\mathrm{rlit}(v_i, v_{i+1}) \notin \sigma(v_k)$ $(j \leq i < k)$ on paths as defined in Lemma 3. Consequently, we only need to search for clauses subsuming vertices with either no parent or a parent with out-degree greater than one (i.e., meets for σ in Equation 1). The corresponding pseudo-code is shown in Figure 5 and can be incorporated into RMPIVOTS$_\top$ (Figure 4(b)) before the recursive call. We present an efficient technique to detect clauses subsuming $\sigma(v_j)$ (i.e., the second line in Figure 5) in §5.

Lemma 3 reduces the computational burden, not least because contemporary SAT solvers such as PicoSAT [5] construct resolution chains whose intermediate vertices have out-degree one.

Finally, we point out that vertices v with $\{x, \overline{x}\} \subseteq (\ell(v) \cup \sigma(v))$ can be replaced with a fresh vertex $u \notin V_R$ with $\ell(u) = (x\,\overline{x})$. However, RMPIVOTS already guarantees that $\{x, \overline{x}\} \subseteq (\ell(v) \cup \sigma(v))$ only occurs on pruned traces.

4   Interpolant Reduction via Subsumption

It is tempting to apply the techniques of §3 with the intention to reduce interpolant size. The following example demonstrates that this approach may in fact have the opposite effect.

Example 6. Consider the (A, B)-refutation R with $(\overline{x}_0), (x_0\,\overline{x}_1), (x_1\,x_2) \in A$ and $(x_1\,\overline{x}_2), (\overline{x}_1) \in B$ on the left of Figure 6. We use a labelled interpolation system (Definition 7) with the labelling L (Definition 5) from Lemma 2. Each vertex is annotated with $\ell(v)\,[\mathsf{ltp}(L, R)(v)]$ as described in §2.2, and the label $L(t)$ of each literal $t \in \ell(v)$ is indicated using a superscript. The shared variable x_1 does not occur in $\mathsf{ltp}(L, R)(\mathbf{s})$, since the literals $\overset{a}{x_1}$ and $\overset{a}{\overline{x}_1}$ are *peripheral*.[2]

---

[2] Intuitively, since resolution corresponds to existential quantification and x_1 is eliminated *within* the A partition $((\exists x_1 . (x_0 \vee \overline{x}_1) \wedge (x_1 \vee x_2)) \Rightarrow (x_0 \vee x_2))$, the pivot can be "renamed" and treated as a local variable. As a side-effect, fewer logical connectives are introduced (prior to structural reduction), since the rule (AB-Res) introduces two more connectives than (A-Res) or (B-Res) (see Definition 7).

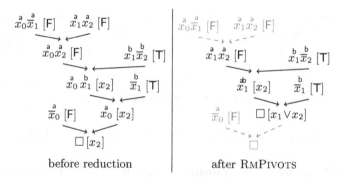

before reduction | after RmPivots

Fig. 6. Reduced proof size may increase number of variables in interpolant

We obtain the proof P on the right of Figure 6 by applying RmPivots and ReconstructProof to R. P is smaller than R, but the substitution has eliminated a peripheral resolution step and $\mathsf{ltp}(L, P)$ is forced to introduce x_1 when we resolve on $\overset{ab}{x_1}$ and $\overset{b}{\overline{x}_1}$.

Using a different interpolation technique (such as Pudlák's [26] or McMillan's [22]) or changing L does not resolve this problem. Labelled interpolation systems generalise Pudlák's and McMillan's interpolation systems [12], and according to Lemma 2, *any* labelling L would require $\mathsf{ltp}(L, P)$ to introduce x_1 at some point in P [10].   ◁

The elimination of the redundant vertex in Example 6 introduces a merge literal x_1 at the node v with $\ell(v) = x_1$ with $L(v, x_1) = ab$. In order to rule out substitutions that change the label of peripheral pivots from a or b to ab, we strengthen the subsumption requirement in Theorem 1 to include labels. Given a refutation R, we compute a mapping $\varsigma : V_R \times \mathtt{Lit} \to \mathcal{S}$ in lockstep with σ:

$$\mathrm{litlab}(u, v, t) = \begin{cases} L(v^+, \mathrm{var}(t)) \sqcup L(v^-, \overline{\mathrm{var}(t)}) & \text{if } t = \mathrm{rlit}(u, v) \\ \varsigma(v, t) & \text{otherwise} \end{cases}$$

$$\varsigma(v, t) = \begin{cases} \bot & \text{if } v = \mathbf{s}_R \\ \prod_{(v,w) \in E} \mathrm{litlab}(v, w, t) & \text{otherwise} \end{cases} \qquad (2)$$

In analogy to Corollary 1, we observe the following relationship between the labelling L and ς:

Lemma 4. *Let R be an (A, B)-refutation, L be a locality preserving labelling function for R, and $\varsigma_{R,L}$ be a solution of Equation 2. Then $L(v, t) \sqsubseteq \varsigma_{R,L}(v, t)$ for all $v \in V_R$ and $t \in \mathtt{Lit}$.*

Proof: By structural induction. The claim holds trivially for $\mathbf{s}_R$. Let $(v, w) \in E$ and $L(v, t) \neq \bot$. If $t \neq \mathrm{rlit}(v, w)$ then $t \in \ell(w)$ and $L(v, t) \sqsubseteq L(w, t)$ by

Definition 5, and $L(v, t) \sqsubseteq \varsigma(w, t)$ by the induction hypothesis. If $t = \text{rlit}(v, w)$ then $L(v, t) \sqsubseteq \text{litlab}(v, w, t)$. Therefore, $L(v, t) \sqsubseteq \prod_{(v,w) \in E} \text{litlab}(v, w, t)$.   ∎

Abusing our notation, we use $\sqsubseteq$ to denote the order on $\mathcal{S}$ (Definition 5) extended point-wise to the literals Lit. In the following, we lift Theorem 1 to labelled sets of literals using the product order $\preceq$ for the Cartesian product of the power set of Lit and (Lit $\to \mathcal{S}$), defined as follows:

$$\langle \ell(u), L(u) \rangle \preceq \langle \sigma(v), \varsigma(v) \rangle \quad \overset{\text{def}}{=} \quad (\ell(u) \subseteq \sigma(v)) \wedge (L(u) \sqsubseteq \varsigma(v))$$

Based on the definition of ς (Equation 2) and the order $\preceq$, Theorem 2 disallows substitutions that may introduce additional variables in an interpolant:

Theorem 2. *Let R be an (A, B)-refutation and let σ_R, ς_R be solutions of the Equations 1 and 2 for R. Let $\pi = \{v_1 \mapsto u_1, \ldots, v_k \mapsto u_k\}$ be a mapping such that for all $1 \leq i \leq j \leq k$ it holds that a) no vertex v_i is an ancestor of u_j, and b) if v_j is an ancestor of u_i then $\langle \sigma_R(u_i), \varsigma_R(u_i) \rangle \preceq \langle \sigma_R(v_i), \varsigma_R(v_i) \rangle$. If $\langle \ell_R(u_i), L(u_i) \rangle \preceq \langle \sigma_R(v_i), \varsigma_R(v_i) \rangle$ for $1 \leq i \leq k$, then applying* RECONSTRUCT-PROOF *to $R[v_1 \leftarrow u_1] \ldots [v_k \leftarrow u_k]$ yields a proof P such that $\text{Var}(\text{Itp}(L, P)) \subseteq \text{Var}(\text{Itp}(L, R))$.*

The proof is an extension of the proof of Theorem 1 to labelled clauses. For the labelling L that maps all shared literals to **ab**, $L(v) \sqsubseteq \varsigma(u)$ is always satisfied, allowing us to relax the labelling constraint.

In the setting of Example 6, let v be the vertex with $\ell(v) = x_0 \, \bar{x}_2$ and let u be the vertex with $\ell(u) = x_1 \, x_2$. We obtain $\varsigma(v, x_1) = $ **b**. Accordingly, the condition $L(u) \sqsubseteq \varsigma(v)$ in Theorem 2 rules out the substitution $R[v \leftarrow u]$. The following example, however, demonstrates that this restriction is not always beneficial.

Example 7. We continue working in the setting of Example 2. Let v_1, v_2 be the vertices such that $\ell(v_1) = (\bar{x}_0 \bar{x}_2 \bar{x}_3)$ and $\ell(v_2) = \bar{x}_1$, and u_1, u_2 be the vertices with $\ell(u_1) = \bar{x}_1 \bar{x}_2$ and $\ell(u_2) = \bar{x}_2$. Recall that the substitution $R[v_1 \leftarrow u_1]$ reduced the interpolant from $x_1 \vee \bar{x}_2$ to x_1. Theorem 2 disallows $v_1 \mapsto u_1$, since $\varsigma(v_1, \bar{x}_1) = $ **a** and $\varsigma(u_1, \bar{x}_1) = $ **b**. Detecting that it is safe to introduce x_1 at v_2 (where $\varsigma(v_2, x_1) = $ **a**) since $x_1 \in \text{Var}(\text{Itp}(R)(u_2))$ would require a computationally more expensive analysis. The substitution $R[v_1 \leftarrow u_2]$ is valid, however, since $\varsigma(v_1, \bar{x}_2) = $ **ab** and $\varsigma(u_2, \bar{x}_2) = $ **b**. The corresponding interpolant is x_1.   ◁

The conservative restrictions of Theorem 2, which enforce $\text{Var}(\text{Itp}(P)(v)) \subseteq \text{Var}(\text{Itp}(R)(v))$ for *all* $v \in V_P$, may prevent RECONSTRUCTPROOF from eliminating variables by pruning. One strategy to relax this restriction is to replace the meet in Equation 2 with the operation to the right. This modification

	a	b	ab
a	a	⊥	ab
b	⊥	b	ab
ab	ab	ab	ab

effectively enables the introduction of a variable at vertex v if it is already introduced along *one* path from v to s_R. In general, the detection of variables already introduced in other parts requires a more sophisticated analysis.

Table 1. We provide results for the benchmarks from synthesis and the HWMCC. We use a locality-preserving labelling function. For synthesis benchmarks, the partitions are acquired from the synthesis tool. For HWMCC benchmarks we use a random partition (A, B). We compare ALL-RMPIVOTS [16] to RMPIVOTS$_T$ without (T0) and with (T20) a search for subsumed clauses (limited to at most 20 minutes). We chose to implement ALL-RMPIVOTS rather than the algorithm from [13] because it is not clear how pruned edges are treated. In each comparison we use the intersection of solved benchmarks (no time- or mem-out in any configuration). Max size is the size of the largest solved proof measured in vertices. Size (%) is the average reduction in proof vertices. Vars (%) is the average reduction in variables in the final interpolant (analogous to interpolant size, cf. Footnote 2). Time (s) is the average run time (without proof creation). Mem (GB) is the average memory usage after proof creation.

synthesis	[16] vs. T0 vs. T20			[16] vs. T0		HWMCC	[16] vs. T0 vs. T20			[16] vs. T0	
solved	92/133			126/133		solved	38/131			111/131	
max size	367044			1150888		max size	311151			1710588	
size (%)	17.35	22.89	25.23	18.74	24.57	size (%)	11.49	14.12	16.61	20.60	25.66
vars (%)	0.62	0.68	0.68	0.65	0.69	vars (%)	1.61	1.99	1.99	1.87	2.47
time (s)	5	5	207	18	15	time (s)	3	3	218	30	23
mem (GB)	1.2	1.2	2.5	2.2	2.3	mem (GB)	0.8	0.8	2.5	3.4	3.4

5   Implementation and Experiments

We implemented (in Scala) the algorithms of §3.1 and §3.2 generalised to labelled clauses as described in §4. The performance of the algorithm in §3.1 and §3.2 hinges on an efficient check for the conditions of Theorems 1 and 2 (line 2 in Figure 5):

- *Subsumption check.* To identify clauses that subsume $\sigma(v)$, we maintain a single watch literal for each clause in R. By incrementally assigning the literals in $\sigma(v)$ to F, the watch literal enables us to identify clauses $\ell(u)$ that are inconsistent with $\neg\sigma(v)$. We may terminate before all subsuming clauses are found, in which case the algorithm favours shorter clauses. By prioritising literals in $\ell(v) \subseteq \sigma(v)$, we also avoid the unnecessary introduction of merge literals. The compatibility of $L(v)$ and $\varsigma(u)$ is checked separately.
- *Ancestor check.* Our algorithm performs a pre-order traversal starting from s_R. To detect cycles, we maintain ancestor information that is restricted to initial vertices and vertices with out-degree larger than one (see Lemma 3). If a substitution $v_i \mapsto u_i$ is performed, we remove the successors of v_i from the list of watched clauses up to the point where all literals in $\ell(u_i) \setminus \ell(v_i)$ have been merged or eliminated (to avoid invalid substitutions), and mark all ancestors of u_i as tainted. We currently disallow any v_j to be an ancestor of u_i $(j \geq i)$ in our subsumption check.

We present an experimental evaluation of our algorithms in Table 1. We use benchmarks from reactive synthesis [6] obtained via [20] and single safety property examples from the 2013 Hardware Model Checking Competition (HWMCC). We use PicoSAT [5] 957 (synthesis) and 959 (HWMCC) to obtain resolution proofs in TraceCheck format (-t option). We limited synthesis benchmarks to a TraceCheck file size between 100kB and 10MB (resulting in 133 benchmarks). We obtained the HWMCC proofs by unrolling until the file size grew beyond 10MB and pick the last file smaller than 10MB (resulting in 131 benchmarks). The experiments were run on an Intel Xeon E5645 2.40GHz with a 16GB JVM memory limit and a timeout of 30 minutes.

RMPIVOTS$_T$ provides small but consistent improvements over Gupta's algorithm [16], for proof as well as interpolant reduction. Subsumption beyond SubsumeRes yields additional proof reduction, but is significantly more expensive (in consistence with the results in [3]). Since we currently choose the first (and smallest) subsuming clause found, we believe that there is still room for improvement by adding heuristics for selecting better candidates.

6   Conclusion

We present a framework for the reduction of refutations and interpolants, generalising the proof analysis introduced in [16] to subsumption. We point out potential conflicts between the reduction of proofs and interpolants and introduce conservative criteria that prevent subsumptions that are detrimental to interpolant size. As future work, we intend to explore more sophisticated proof analyses enabling a more aggressive reduction of interpolant size.

References

1. Alekhnovich, M., Johannsen, J., Pitassi, T., Urquhart, A.: An exponential separation between regular and general resolution. In: STOC. ACM (2002)
2. Andrews, P.B.: Resolution with merging. J. ACM 15(3), 367–381 (1968)
3. Bar-Ilan, O., Fuhrmann, O., Hoory, S., Shacham, O., Strichman, O.: Reducing the size of resolution proofs in linear time. STTT 13(3), 263–272 (2011)
4. Belov, A., Lynce, I., Marques-Silva, J.: Towards efficient mus extraction. AI Communications 25(2), 97–116 (2012)
5. Biere, A.: PicoSAT essentials. JSAT 4(2-4), 75–97 (2008)
6. Bloem, R., Königshofer, R., Seidl, M.: Sat-based synthesis methods for safety specs. In: McMillan, K.L., Rival, X. (eds.) VMCAI 2014. LNCS, vol. 8318, pp. 1–20. Springer, Heidelberg (2014)
7. Boudou, J., Woltzenlogel Paleo, B.: Compression of propositional resolution proofs by lowering subproofs. In: Galmiche, D., Larchey-Wendling, D. (eds.) TABLEAUX 2013. LNCS, vol. 8123, pp. 59–73. Springer, Heidelberg (2013)
8. Cabodi, G., Loiacono, C., Vendraminetto, D.: Optimization techniques for craig interpolant compaction in unbounded model checking. In: Design, Automation and Test in Europe, pp. 1417–1422. ACM (2013)
9. Craig, W.: Linear reasoning. A new form of the Herbrand-Gentzen theorem. J. Symbolic Logic 22(3), 250–268 (1957)
10. D'Silva, V.: Propositional interpolation and abstract interpretation. In: Gordon, A.D. (ed.) ESOP 2010. LNCS, vol. 6012, pp. 185–204. Springer, Heidelberg (2010)
11. D'Silva, V., Kroening, D., Purandare, M., Weissenbacher, G.: Restructuring resolution refutations for interpolation. Technical report, Oxford (October 2008)
12. D'Silva, V., Kroening, D., Purandare, M., Weissenbacher, G.: Interpolant strength. In: Barthe, G., Hermenegildo, M. (eds.) VMCAI 2010. LNCS, vol. 5944, pp. 129–145. Springer, Heidelberg (2010)

13. Fontaine, P., Merz, S., Woltzenlogel Paleo, B.: Compression of propositional resolution proofs via partial regularization. In: Bjørner, N., Sofronie-Stokkermans, V. (eds.) CADE 2011. LNCS, vol. 6803, pp. 237–251. Springer, Heidelberg (2011)
14. Gershman, R., Koifman, M., Strichman, O.: Deriving small unsatisfiable cores with dominators. In: Ball, T., Jones, R.B. (eds.) CAV 2006. LNCS, vol. 4144, pp. 109–122. Springer, Heidelberg (2006)
15. Goldberg, E., Novikov, Y.: Verification of proofs of unsatisfiability for CNF formulas. In: Design, Automation and Test in Europe, pp. 886–891. IEEE (2003)
16. Gupta, A.: Improved single pass algorithms for resolution proof reduction. In: Chakraborty, S., Mukund, M. (eds.) ATVA 2012. LNCS, vol. 7561, pp. 107–121. Springer, Heidelberg (2012)
17. McMillan, K.L.: Applications of Craig Interpolants in Model Checking. In: Halbwachs, N., Zuck, L.D. (eds.) TACAS 2005. LNCS, vol. 3440, pp. 1–12. Springer, Heidelberg (2005)
18. Hofferek, G., Gupta, A., Könighofer, B., Jiang, J.-H.R., Bloem, R.: Synthesizing multiple boolean functions using interpolation on a single proof. In: Formal Methods in Computer-Aided Design, pp. 77–84. IEEE (2013)
19. Huang, G.: Constructing Craig interpolation formulas. In: Li, M., Du, D.-Z. (eds.) COCOON 1995. LNCS, vol. 959, pp. 181–190. Springer, Heidelberg (1995)
20. Jiang, J.-H.R., Lin, H.-P., Hung, W.-L.: Interpolating functions from large Boolean relations. In: ICCAD, pp. 779–784. ACM (2009)
21. Krajíček, J.: Interpolation theorems, lower bounds for proof systems, and independence results for bounded arithmetic. J. Symbolic Logic 62(2), 457–486 (1997)
22. McMillan, K.L.: Interpolation and SAT-based model checking. In: Hunt Jr., W.A., Somenzi, F. (eds.) CAV 2003. LNCS, vol. 2725, pp. 1–13. Springer, Heidelberg (2003)
23. McMillan, K.L.: An interpolating theorem prover. Theoretical Comput. Sci. 345(1), 101–121 (2005)
24. McMillan, K.L., Amla, N.: Automatic abstraction without counterexamples. In: Garavel, H., Hatcliff, J. (eds.) TACAS 2003. LNCS, vol. 2619, pp. 2–17. Springer, Heidelberg (2003)
25. Nadel, A., Ryvchin, V., Strichman, O.: Efficient MUS extraction with resolution. In: Formal Methods in Computer-Aided Design, pp. 197–200. IEEE (2013)
26. Pudlák, P.: Lower bounds for resolution and cutting plane proofs and monotone computations. J. Symbolic Logic 62(3), 981–998 (1997)
27. Rollini, S.F., Alt, L., Fedyukovich, G., Hyvärinen, A.E.J., Sharygina, N.: PeRIPLO: A framework for producing effective interpolants in SAT-based software verification. In: McMillan, K., Middeldorp, A., Voronkov, A. (eds.) LPAR-19 2013. LNCS, vol. 8312, pp. 683–693. Springer, Heidelberg (2013)
28. Rollini, S.F., Bruttomesso, R., Sharygina, N., Tsitovich, A.: Resolution proof transformation for compression and interpolation. The Computing Research Repository, abs/1307.2028 (2013)
29. Simmonds, J., Davies, J., Gurfinkel, A., Chechik, M.: Exploiting resolution proofs to speed up LTL vacuity detection for BMC. STTT 12(5), 319–335 (2010)
30. Tseitin, G.: On the complexity of derivation in propositional calculus. Studies in Mathematics and Mathematical Logic, Part II (1970)
31. Urquhart, A.: The complexity of propositional proofs. Bulletin of Symbolic Logic 1(4), 425–467 (1995)
32. Wu, B.-H., Yang, C.-J., Huang, C.-Y., Jiang, J.-H.: A robust functional ECO engine by SAT proof minimization and interpolation techniques. In: ICCAD (2010)
33. Zhang, L.: On subsumption removal and on-the-fly CNF simplification. In: Bacchus, F., Walsh, T. (eds.) SAT 2005. LNCS, vol. 3569, pp. 482–489. Springer, Heidelberg (2005)

Read, Write and Copy Dependencies for Symbolic Model Checking

Jeroen Meijer, Gijs Kant, Stefan Blom, and Jaco van de Pol

Formal Methods and Tools, University of Twente, The Netherlands
{j.j.g.meijer,g.kant,s.c.c.blom,j.c.vandepol}@utwente.nl

Abstract. This paper aims at improving symbolic model checking for explicit state modeling languages, e.g., PROMELA, DVE and MCRL2. The modular PINS architecture of LTSMIN supports a notion of event locality, by merely indicating for each event on which variables it depends. However, one could distinguish four separate dependencies: *read, may-write, must-write* and *copy*. In this paper, we introduce these notions in a language-independent manner. In particular, models with arrays need to distinguish overwriting and copying of values.

We also adapt the symbolic model checking algorithms to exploit the refined dependency information. We have implemented refined dependency matrices for PROMELA, DVE and MCRL2, in order to compare our new algorithms to the original version of LTSMIN. The results show that the amount of successor computations and memory footprint are greatly reduced. Finally, the optimal variable ordering is also affected by the refined dependencies: We determined experimentally that variables with a read dependency should occur at a higher BDD level than variables with a write dependency.

1 Introduction

Model checking [11] is a technique to verify the correctness of systems. Often these systems are made up of several processes running in parallel. Examining all possible execution paths of the system is hard, because of the well known state space explosion problem: because of the interleaving of the processes, the possible number of states is exponential in the number of processes. Symbolic model checking [6, 13] has proven to be very effective in dealing with that problem. Symbolic here means storing sets of vectors and relations between vectors as decision diagrams, such as Binary Decision Diagrams (BDDs) or Multi-Value Decision Diagrams (MDDs). A well known symbolic model checker is NUSMV [9], where systems are specified in the SMV language, directly describing transition relations.

We use the LTSMIN toolset [4], which also provides a symbolic model checker, but is different from NUSMV in several ways. LTSMIN provides a language independent interface, called PINS, to communicate states and transitions, and learns the partitioned transition relation on-the-fly, as in, e.g., [2,7]. New transitions are learned through an explicit NEXT-STATE function, which is the language specific

E. Yahav (Ed.): HVC 2014, LNCS 8855, pp. 204–219, 2014.
© Springer International Publishing Switzerland 2014

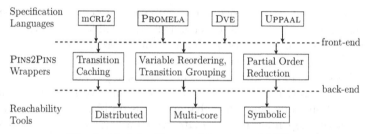

Fig. 1. Modular PINS architecture of LTSMIN

part of LTSMIN. Currently the languages that have been implemented on top of PINS include PROMELA [1], DiVinE, mCRL2, and UPPAAL. In [2] and [3], the PINS interface and underlying symbolic core algorithms of LTSMIN are described. An overview of the architecture is in Figure 1.

In PINS, states are represented as fixed-length *vectors* of values. Transitions are distinguished in separate disjunctive *transition groups*. A generalized definition of systems that is compatible with PINS is given in Section 2. Between slots of the state vector and the transition groups there can be dependencies, i.e., a transition group can be dependent on the value of a state variable for a condition to be true, or a transition may change the value of a state variable. The dependencies between transition groups and state slots are captured in a *dependency matrix*, which can be determined by static analysis of the model. Often it is the case that a transition group depends on a limited number of slots, which is known as *event locality*. This is the basis of many optimisations in symbolic model checking, as presented in, e.g., [5,8,10]. For symbolic state space generation it is best when the dependency matrix is sparse, i.e., when transition groups have a relatively local footprint, for the following reasons. First, a sparse matrix means that the transition relations for the transition groups depend on few variables and can be quite small. Also, because of the on-the-fly nature of LTSMIN, there will be fewer redundant calls to NEXT-STATE.

To further benefit from dependencies in the input models, in this paper we refine the notion of dependency and distinguish three types of dependencies: *read dependence* and two types of *write dependence*, *must-write* and *may-write*. To illustrate read and write dependence, we use a simple system with three variables $\langle x, y, z \rangle$ and two transitions:

$$
\begin{array}{ll}
1 : x = 1 \vee z = 0 \rightarrow y := 1, x := 0 \\
2 : y = 1 \qquad\quad \rightarrow z := 0, x := 1
\end{array}
\qquad
\begin{array}{c}
\begin{array}{c} x \ \ y \ \ z \end{array} \\
\begin{array}{c} 1 \\ 2 \end{array}
\begin{bmatrix} 1 & 1 & 1 \\ 1 & 1 & 1 \end{bmatrix}
\end{array}
\qquad
\begin{array}{c}
\begin{array}{c} x \ \ y \ \ z \end{array} \\
\begin{array}{c} 1 \\ 2 \end{array}
\begin{bmatrix} 1 & 0 & 1 \\ 0 & 1 & 0 \end{bmatrix}
\end{array}
\qquad
\begin{array}{c}
\begin{array}{c} x \ \ y \ \ z \end{array} \\
\begin{array}{c} 1 \\ 2 \end{array}
\begin{bmatrix} 1 & 1 & 0 \\ 1 & 0 & 1 \end{bmatrix}
\end{array}
$$

a. Transitions   b. Dep. matrix   c. Read matrix   d. Write matrix

In b), the dependency matrix indicates no event locality, but if read and write dependencies are considered separately, as in c) and d), then we see the transition groups depend on most variables only for reading or only for writing. Separating reads and writes helps in reducing the number of NEXT-STATE calls, the size of the transition relation, and the size of its symbolic representation. For instance, when a transition group is not read dependent on variable y, then the previous value of y can be discarded in computing the successors of a state.

However, it is not trivial to statically determine whether a transition group writes to a state slot. In the case of dynamic addressing of variables, e.g., writing a position in an array, it may be needed to mark an entire array as write dependent, even if only one position is changed. This problem is resolved by using two types of write dependence: *may-write*, which allows copying of values, and *must-write*, which does not.

In [8], a similar distinction is made between types of dependence. The main difference with this work is that we deal with dynamic variable addressing, both in the definitions of dependency and in the symbolic algorithms, where we use a special symbol in transition relations to mark that a variable should be copied.

The dependencies and the associated matrices are described in detail in Section 3. There also the *row subsumption* in dependency matrices and *variable reordering* are discussed. These two techniques improve the effect of the read-write distinction. In Section 4, we provide an adapted symbolic reachability algorithm that exploits the read and write dependencies.

We have benchmarked our work with the whole BEEM database and many PROMELA and mCRL2 models. There are many models that benefit from the distinction between read and write dependencies, but also several that do not. In Section 5, we highlight the results for six models. For mCRL2, performance is improved, because many calls to NEXT-STATE can be avoided. The NEXT-STATE function for mCRL2 is relatively slow, due to the term rewriter that was introduced to provide very expressive datatypes. For BEEM and PROMELA models, we find an improvement when a good variable ordering (a good reordering strategy) is chosen.

This work is based on Meijer's MSc thesis [14] and extends it with an extension to the transition relation to support copying values, and an analysis of the effect of variable ordering in the context of distinct read and write dependencies.

2   The Partioned Next-State Interface (Pins)

The starting point of our approach is a generalised model of systems, called *Partioned Next-State Interface* (PINS), which allows supporting several modeling languages within a single framework, without exposing language details to the underlying algorithms.

In PINS, states are vectors of N values. We write $\langle x_1, \ldots, x_N \rangle$, or simply $\boldsymbol{x}$, for vector variables. Each slot of the vector has a unique identifier, which is used in the language front ends to specify conditions and updates. Every language module, furthermore, has a NEXT-STATE function, which computes the successor of a state. This function is partitioned in K transition groups, such that $\text{NEXT-STATE}(\boldsymbol{x}) = \bigcup_{1 \leq i \leq K} \text{NEXT-STATE}_i(\boldsymbol{x})$. A model, available through PINS, gives rise to a partitioned transition system, defined as follows.

Definition 1. *A Partitioned Transition System (PTS) [3] is a structure $\mathcal{P} = \langle \langle S_1, \ldots, S_N \rangle, \langle \rightarrow_1, \ldots, \rightarrow_K \rangle, \langle s_1^0, \ldots, s_N^0 \rangle \rangle$. The tuple $\langle S_1, \ldots, S_N \rangle$ defines the* *set of states* $S_{\mathcal{P}} = S_1 \times \ldots \times S_N$, *i.e., we assume that the set of states is a* Cartesian product. *The* transition groups $\rightarrow_i \subseteq S_{\mathcal{P}} \times S_{\mathcal{P}}$ *(for* $1 \leq i \leq K$*) define the transition relation* $\rightarrow_{\mathcal{P}} = \bigcup_{i=1}^{K} \rightarrow_i$. *The initial state is* $s^0 = \langle s_1^0, \ldots, s_N^0 \rangle \in S_{\mathcal{P}}$. *We write* $s \rightarrow_i t$ *when* $(s, t) \in \rightarrow_i$ *for some* $1 \leq i \leq K$. *Also we write* $s \rightarrow_{\mathcal{P}} t$ *when* $(s, t) \in \rightarrow_{\mathcal{P}}$.

The partitioning of the state vector into *slots* and of the transition relations into *transition groups*, enables to specify the *dependencies* between the two, i.e., which transition groups touch which slots of the vector. The definition of these dependencies will be given in Section 3. Here we give an abstract description of how the variables in the state vector are read from and written to by the transition groups.

For every language module this is different, but there is a common pattern. In all of the supported languages, the specification of a transition is in the shape NEXT-STATE$_i(x) = cond_i \rightarrow$ action$_i$. $update_i(x)$.

The expression $cond_i$ is the condition that guards an action and may read variables from x. The symbol 'action$_i$' specifies the name of the action that is performed, i.e., the transition label. The expression $update_i(x)$ defines the state after the action. The update is a parallel assignment to the variables in the vector. However, these variables may be defined dynamically, e.g., they may be references to a location in an array.

Example 1. Given a state vector with variables $\langle c, a_0, a_1, i \rangle$, valid assignments would be, e.g., $c := c + 1$, $a_i := a_{1-i}$ and $i := c$.

We define the state updates more formally, abstracting away from the specific input languages of LTSMIN.

Definition 2 (State Update Specification). *The syntax of a state update of transition group i is as follows:* $\sigma_i ::= c_i \rightarrow a_i$. $\langle v_{i,1} := t_{i,1}, \ldots, v_{i,L_i} := t_{i,L_i} \rangle$, *where* $L_i \leq N$ *and* c_i, $v_{i,j}$, *and* $t_{i,j}$ *are expressions over* $x_1, \ldots, x_N$. *The conditions* c_i *are Boolean expressions and the left hand sides* $v_{i,j}$ *evaluate to variables in* $\{x_1, \ldots, x_N\}$. *The semantics of this state update is defined as the successor states after applying the update:*

$$s \rightarrow_i t \iff [\![c_i]\!]_s \wedge t = s[[\![v_{i,1}]\!]_s := [\![t_{i,1}]\!]_s, \ldots, [\![v_{i,L_i}]\!]_s := [\![t_{i,L_i}]\!]_s] .$$

A State Update Specification *(SUS) is a triple* $\mathcal{U} = \langle \langle x_1, \ldots, x_N \rangle, \{\sigma_1, \ldots, \sigma_K\}, s^0 \rangle$, *containing a vector of state variables* x_j *for* $1 \leq j \leq N$, *a set of state updates* σ_i *with* $1 \leq i \leq K$, *and an initial state* s^0.

Example 2 (1-safe Petri net). An example model is the Petri net in Figure 2, of which a specification is given in Listing 1.1. The behavior of this 1-safe Petri net is as follows. Initially, there is only one token in p_0. If transition t_0 fires then the token is moved from place p_0 to both p_1 and p_3. Transitions $t_{1..4}$ move the tokens between places $p_{1..4}$ independently. If the token is in both p_2 and p_4 then transition t_5 can fire to move the token to p_0. There are 5 reachable states for this Petri net. With booleans represented as $0, 1$, the states are: $\{\langle 1, 0, 0, 0, 0 \rangle, \langle 0, 1, 0, 1, 0 \rangle, \langle 0, 0, 1, 1, 0 \rangle, \langle 0, 1, 0, 0, 1 \rangle, \langle 0, 0, 1, 0, 1 \rangle\}$.

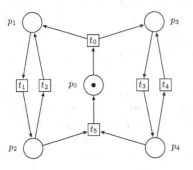

Fig. 2. Example 1-safe Petri net

Listing 1.1. State Update Specification (SUS) for a 1-safe Petri net

```
1    init ⟨true, false, false, false, false⟩
2    sus ⟨p₀, p₁, p₂, p₃, p₄ ∈ 𝔹⟩ = ⟨
3        p₀ →
4            t₀. ⟨p₀ := false, p₁ := true, p₃ := true⟩,
5        p₁ →
6            t₁. ⟨p₁ := false, p₂ := true⟩,
7        p₂ →
8            t₂. ⟨p₁ := true, p₂ := false⟩,
9        p₃ →
10           t₃. ⟨p₃ := false, p₄ := true⟩,
11       p₄ →
12           t₄. ⟨p₃ := true, p₄ := false⟩,
13       (p₂ ∧ p₄) →
14           t₅. ⟨p₀ := true, p₂ := false, p₄ := false⟩⟩
```

3   State Slot Dependencies

We exploit the notion of event locality by statically (a priori, before exploring any states) approximating dependencies between transition groups and state slots. We distinguish three types of dependencies: *read dependence* (whether the value of a state slot influences transitions), *must-write dependence* (whether a state slot is written to), and *may-write dependence* (whether a state slot may be written to, depending on the value of some other state slot). We provide formal definitions for the dependencies and dependency matrices for state update specifications.

Definition 3 (Read Independence). *Given a Partitioned Transition System* (PTS) $\mathcal{P} = \langle S_{\mathcal{P}}, \rightarrow_{\mathcal{P}}, s^0 \rangle$, *transition group i is read independent on state slot j if: for all $s, t \in S_{\mathcal{P}}$: whenever $\langle s_1, \ldots, s_j, \ldots, s_N \rangle \rightarrow_i \langle t_1, \ldots, t_j, \ldots, t_N \rangle$, it holds that*

- *either always$(s_j = t_j) \land \forall r_j \in S_j$: $\langle s_1, \ldots, r_j, \ldots, s_N \rangle \rightarrow_i \langle t_1, \ldots, r_j, \ldots, t_N \rangle$;*
- *or $\forall r_j \in S_j$: $\langle s_1, \ldots, r_j, \ldots, s_N \rangle \rightarrow_i \langle t_1, \ldots, t_j, \ldots, t_N \rangle$,*

i.e., the values t_k for $k \neq j$ do not depend on the value of slot j and either the value of state slot j is always copied, or always the value t_j is written, regardless of the value of s_j. In both cases the specific value of s_j is not relevant in transition group i.

Definition 4 (Read Dependency Matrix). *For a PTS $\mathcal{P}$, the Read Dependency Matrix (RDM) is a $K \times N$ matrix $RDM(\mathcal{P}) = RM_{K \times N}^{\mathcal{P}} \in \{0, 1\}^{K \times N}$ such that $(RM_{i,j} = 0) \Rightarrow$ transition group i is read independent on state slot j. For a State Update Specification (SUS) $\mathcal{U}$, the read dependency matrix $RDM(\mathcal{U})$ is defined as $RM_{K \times N}^{\mathcal{U}}$ with:*

$$
RM_{i,j}^{\mathcal{U}} = \begin{cases} 1 & \text{if } (x_j \text{ occurs in } c_i); \text{ or} \hfill \text{(a)} \\ & \text{if } \exists_{1 \leq k \leq L_i} : (x_j \text{ occurs in } t_{i,k}) \land (v_{i,k} \neq x_j \lor t_{i,j} \neq x_j); \text{ or} \hfill \text{(b)} \\ & \text{if } \exists_{1 \leq k \leq L_i} : (x_j \text{ occurs in } v_{i,k}) \land (v_{i,k} \neq x_j); \hfill \text{(c)} \\ 0 & \text{otherwise.} \hfill \text{(d)} \end{cases}
$$

In case (a), the condition c_i depends on x_j. In case (b), the right hand side of the update depends on x_j, but the assignment is not merely a copy. In case (c), variable x_j is used to dynamically determine a state slot for an assignment, but x_j is not directly used as left hand side, as in, e.g., the assignment $a_{x_j} := 1$. In that case, x_j is marked as read dependent, because it influences how the state vector is updated. In all other cases, x_j is read independent.

We say that a transition group is *must-write dependent* for variable x, if it modifies x definitely, i.e. by a static assignment. For instance, the assignment $x := 2y$ is must-write dependent for variable x, because the right-hand side does not depend on x. The assignment $x := 2x$ is must-write dependent on variable x because, independent of any other variables, it can modify the value of x. However, the assignment $x_i := 3$ is not must-write dependent on variable x_0, because for $i = 1$, the value of x_0 is never modified.

Definition 5 (Must-Write Dependency Matrix). *For a* PTS $\mathcal{P}$, *the* Must-write Dependency Matrix *(WDM) is a* $K \times N$ *matrix* $WDM(\mathcal{P}) = WM_{K \times N}^{\mathcal{P}} \in \{0,1\}^{K \times N}$ *such that* $(WM_{i,j} = 1) \Rightarrow$ *transition group i is* must-write dependent *on state slot j.*
For a SUS $\mathcal{U}$, *the must-write dependency matrix* $WDM(\mathcal{U})$ *is defined as* $WM_{K \times N}^{\mathcal{U}}$ *with:*

$$WM_{i,j}^{\mathcal{U}} = \begin{cases} 1 & \text{if } \exists_{1 \le k \le L_i} : (v_{i,k} = x_j) \wedge (v_{i,k} \neq t_{i,k}) \quad \text{(a)} \\ 0 & \text{otherwise.} \quad\quad\quad\quad\quad\quad\quad\quad\quad\quad\quad\quad\text{(b)} \end{cases}$$

In case (a), x_j is the left hand side of an assignment $v_{i,k} := t_{i,k}$. If the right hand side $t_{i,k}$ is the same, there is no must-write dependency, but instead the value is copied. If they are different, x_j is marked as must-write dependent. E.g., the assignment $x := x + 1$, x is marked both as must-write dependent and as read dependent.

Consider the case of an array assignment $a_i := c$. Then a_0 cannot be marked as must-write dependent. Still, we know that a_0 is either copied, or replaced by a constant. To exploit this knowledge for dynamic assignments, we introduce a third notion of independence.

3.1 The May-Write Dependency

In the case of assignment to a dynamically defined variable, using only read and must-write dependencies is not optimal, as is explained in the following example.

Example 3. Suppose we extend the specification of the 1-safe Petri net specification in Listing 1.1 by adding some data. We extend the state vector with variables $b_0, b_1 \in \mathbb{B}, i \in \{0, 1\}$. The initial state is extended with the values $\langle \text{false}, \text{false}, 0 \rangle$. We add two state updates: "$p_1 \to w . \langle i := 1 \rangle$" and "$\text{true} \to W . \langle b_i := \text{true} \rangle$". For the second assignment it cannot be statically determined if b_0 or b_1 is written to. This depends on the value of i. Therefore, b_0 and b_1 are marked as must-write independent. However, one of both may be changed, so our definition is not sufficient in this case. Changing it in a way that marks both b_0 and b_1 is safe, but requires that both are also marked as read dependent: one of the variables is copied and requires a read, but it cannot a priori be determined which one. Ideally, both variables are marked as write dependent, while allowing to indicate which variables are copied. Then they do not need to be read dependent.

To address the problem of dynamic resolution of variables, we introduce a weaker notion of write dependence: *may-write independence*.

Definition 6 (May-Write Independence). *Given a* PTS $\mathcal{P} = \langle S_{\mathcal{P}}, \rightarrow_{\mathcal{P}}, s^0 \rangle$, *transition group i is* may-write independent *on state slot j if:* $\forall s, t \in S_{\mathcal{P}}$, $\langle s_1, \ldots, s_j, \ldots, s_N \rangle \rightarrow_i \langle t_1, \ldots, t_j, \ldots, t_N \rangle \Rightarrow (s_j = t_j)$, *i.e., state slot j is never modified in transition group i.*

Thus, if transition group i is may-write-dependent on state slot j, then there are some states s, t and a transition $s \rightarrow_i t$, where the value in state slot j is changed: $s_j \neq t_j$.

Definition 7 (May-Write Dependency Matrix). *For a* PTS $\mathcal{P}$, *the May-write Dependency Matrix (MDM) is a $K \times N$ matrix $MDM(\mathcal{P}) = MM^{\mathcal{P}}_{K \times N} \in \{0, 1\}^{K \times N}$ such that $(MM_{i,j} = 0) \Rightarrow$ transition group i is may-write independent on state slot j.*
For a SUS $\mathcal{U}$, *the may-write dependency matrix $MDM(\mathcal{U})$ is defined as $MM^{\mathcal{U}}_{K \times N}$ with:*

$$MM^{\mathcal{U}}_{i,j} = \begin{cases} 0 \text{ if } \forall 1 \leq k \leq L_i \colon \forall s \colon (\llbracket v_{i,k} \rrbracket_s = x_j) \Rightarrow (v_{i,k} = t_{i,k}) & \text{(a)} \\ 1 \text{ otherwise.} & \text{(b)} \end{cases}$$

In case (a), if $v_{i,k}$ evaluates to x_j for some state s, i.e., an assignment to x_j is possible, then the assignment is a direct copy, i.e., the left hand side and right hand side are syntactically the same: $v_{i,k} = t_{i,k}$. This is determined statically by the language front-end before generation.

Example 4. In the extended Petri net example (Example 3), transition W is may-write dependent on both variables b_0 and b_1, because there exists both a state in which $i = 0$ and a state in which $i = 1$. Hence, both variables can be written to by the assignment $b_i := \text{true}$.

Definition 8 (Combined Dependency Matrix). *For a* PTS $\mathcal{P}$, *the dependency matrix (DM) is a $K \times N$ matrix $DM^{\mathcal{P}}_{K \times N} \in \{0, 1\}^{K \times N}$ with the elements $DM^{\mathcal{P}}_{i,j}$ as specified in Table 1. Note that $WM_{i,j} \Rightarrow MM_{i,j}$.*

Example 5. The combined dependency matrix for the extended 1-safe Petri net (Example 3) is shown in Table 2.

Note that here we say a transition group has a may-write dependency on a state slot if it is not must-write dependent. This differs from the definition of may-write independence. The definition of must-write dependence may seem superfluous, but it is necessary for language front-ends and symbolic back-ends which do not support copying values. So we have to take must-write dependence into account when applying transformations on the combined dependency matrix.

Table 1. Combined DM $DM^{\mathcal{P}}$

$DM^{\mathcal{P}}_{i,j}$		$RM^{\mathcal{P}}_{i,j}$	$WM^{\mathcal{P}}_{i,j}$	$MM^{\mathcal{P}}_{i,j}$
−	(copy)	0	0	0
r	(read)	1	0	0
W	(may-write)	0	0	1
w	(must-write)	0	1	1
+	(read/write)	1	{0, 1}	1

Table 2. DM for the Petri net

	p_0	p_1	p_2	p_3	p_4	i	b_0	b_1
t_0	+	w	−	w	−	−	−	−
t_1	−	+	w	−	−	−	−	−
t_2	−	w	+	−	−	−	−	−
t_3	−	−	−	+	w	−	−	−
t_4	−	−	−	w	+	−	−	−
w	−	r	−	−	−	w	−	−
W	−	−	−	−	−	r	W	W

3.2   Optimisation Operations on the Dependency Matrix

Combining transition groups and reordering variables are two techniques to enhance symbolic state space exploration. We adapted these techniques to benefit from read and write dependencies.

Definition 9 (Row Subsumption). *For matrix rows $\boldsymbol{m}, \boldsymbol{m}' \in M^N$ of length N, the* row subsumption *operator $\sqsubseteq: M^N \times M^N \to \mathbb{B}$ is defined as follows:*

$$\boldsymbol{m} \sqsubseteq \boldsymbol{m}' \iff \forall_{1 \leq j \leq N} : m_j \leq m'_j .$$

If a row $\boldsymbol{m}_i$ is *subsumed* by row $\boldsymbol{m}_k$, ($\boldsymbol{m}_i \sqsubseteq \boldsymbol{m}_k$), the corresponding transition groups i and k can be merged and the combined matrix row becomes the larger one, $\boldsymbol{m}_k$. In general, any two rows could be merged by taking their pointwise least upperbound. The result is that there are fewer transition groups and less applications of a transition relation, but the transition relations will be larger. For this to work, we

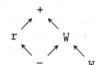

Fig. 3. Partial order on dependencies $\leq$

need a correct definition of $\leq$, i.e., a partial order on dependencies, which is given in Figure 3. Note that *may-write* dependency (W) may subsume a copy dependency (−), but *must-write* dependency (w) does not, because only W supports copying values.

Variable reordering is widely used to reduce the size of decision diagrams [16]. When using separate read and write dependencies, the order of read and write variables needs to be taken into account. In general it is a good idea to move variables that are read before variables that are written. Algorithm 1 uses the heuristic that every read which occurs after a write is increasingly expensive. Algorithm 2 shows a naive way to compute the cost of every column permutation of the Dependency Matrix (DM). The algorithm will choose the matrix with the lowest cost. Naturally, trying every permutation is exponentially expensive in terms of number of columns. LTSMIN implements more advanced column swap algorithms, for instance based on simulated annealing from [17]).

The dependency matrices have been implemented for the mCRL2, DVE and PROMELA input languages. For mCRL2, may-write dependencies are not needed,

Algorithm 1. COST	**Algorithm 2.** DM-OPTIMIZE
Input: DM	Input: DM
1 $cost \leftarrow 0$;	1 $best \leftarrow$ DM;
2 **for** $0 \leq i < K$ **do**	2 **for** $0 \leq i < N$ **do**
3 $writes \leftarrow 0$;	3 **for** $i < j < N$ **do**
4 **for** $0 \leq j < N$ **do**	4 $test \leftarrow$ SWAP-COLUMNS(DM, i, j);
5 **if** $\mathrm{DM}_{i,j} \in \{\mathtt{W},\mathtt{w}\}$ **then**	5 **if** COST($test$) < COST($best$) **then**
$writes \leftarrow writes + 1$;	$best \leftarrow test$;
6 **if** $\mathrm{DM}_{i,j} = \mathtt{r}$ **then**	6 **end**
$cost \leftarrow cost + writes$;	7 **end**
7 **end**	8 **return** $best$;
8 **end**	
9 **return** $cost$;	

because assignment to dynamic variables is not supported in the language. Still, may-write dependencies can arise by row subsumption.

4 Symbolic Reachability Analysis

To allow symbolic reachability analysis with read, write and copy dependencies we provide three definitions. The first contains projections on dependency matrices. Secondly, we provide a definition of the restricted NEXT-STATE function from read-projected states to their write-projected successors according to transition group $\rightarrow_i$, as it is used in PINS for on-the-fly reachability analysis. This technique is language independent, but depends essentially on the PINS-architecture, based on state vectors, disjunctive transition partitioning and read and write dependency matrices. Lastly, we provide a symbolic definition of NEXT that formalizes the transition relation and the application of the transition relation on a set of states.

Notation. For convenience, we introduce the function ind, the column indices of the cells that contain a '1' in row M_i: $ind(M_i) = \{j \mid 1 \leq j \leq |M_i| \wedge M_{i,j} = 1\}$. Given a vector s and a set of indices I, the notation $(s_j)_{j \in I}$ is used to represent the *subvector* $(s_{\bar{I}_1}, \ldots, s_{\bar{I}_\ell})$ of length $\ell = |I|$, where $\bar{I}$ is the sorted list of elements from I.

Definition 10 (Projections). *For any vector set $S = \prod_{1 \leq j \leq N} S_j$, transition group $1 \leq i \leq K$ and $K \times N$ matrix M, we define the projection $\pi_i^M : S \rightarrow \prod_{j \in ind(M_i)} S_j$ as $\pi_i^M(\boldsymbol{x}) = (x_j)_{j \in ind(M_i)}$, i.e., the subvector of $\boldsymbol{x}$ that contains the elements at indices in $ind(M_i)$, the indices that are marked in row i of matrix M. The projection function is extended to apply to sets in a straightforward way: $\pi_i^M(S) = \{\pi_i^M(\boldsymbol{x}) \mid \boldsymbol{x} \in S\}$. We also write π_i^{r} for π_i^{RM} and π_i^{w} for π_i^{MM}.*

Using these read and write projections, we can define how the read and write dependency matrices can be used to compute the successor states for a transition group, using only the dependent variables. We define the function NEXT-STATE$_i^{\mathrm{p}}$ that takes as input a read projected vector, and computes for transition group i

the set of may-write projected successor vectors. The input read projected vector may match a set of input states, and each of the output projected successor vectors may represent a set of successor states. In the case a variable is may-write dependent, but not changed, the symbol ▲ is used to mark that the variable should be copied from the input vector. This can occur, e.g., in the case an entire array $a_{1..10}$ is marked may-write dependent, because of an assignment $a_z := e$. If $z = 5$, the position a_5 is written to and all positions a_j with $j \neq 5$ are marked with ▲. We use $S_j^{\blacktriangle}$ for $S_j \cup \{\blacktriangle\}$ and $S_{\mathcal{P}}^{\blacktriangle}$ for the set $S_1^{\blacktriangle} \times \cdots \times S_N^{\blacktriangle}$.

Definition 11 (Partitioned Next-State Function). NEXT-STATE$_i^{\mathrm{P}}$: $\pi_i^{\mathrm{r}}(S_{\mathcal{P}})$ $\to \wp(\pi_i^{\mathrm{W}}(S_{\mathcal{P}}^{\blacktriangle}))$. *Given a read projected state* $(s_j)_{j \in ind(RM_i)}$,

$$\text{NEXT-STATE}_i^{\mathrm{P}}((s_j)_{j \in ind(RM_i)}) = \Big\{ \pi_i^{\mathrm{W}}(t) \mid$$

$$\exists s', t', t \in S_{\mathcal{P}}: \pi_i^{\mathrm{r}}(s') = (s_j)_{j \in ind(RM_i)} \wedge s' \to_i t' \wedge$$

$$\forall_{1 \leq j \leq N}: t_j = \begin{cases} \blacktriangle & \text{if } (j \notin ind(MM_i) \vee s_j = t_j), \\ t'_j & \text{otherwise} \end{cases} \Big\}.$$

The result vectors $(t_j)_{j \in ind(MM_i)}$, combined with the input vectors $(s_j)_{j \in ind(RM_i)}$ are stored in a symbolic transition relation $\hookrightarrow_i^{\mathrm{P}}$.

Definition 12 (Next). *We define the function* NEXT: $\wp(S_{\mathcal{P}}) \times (\pi^{\mathrm{r}}(S_{\mathcal{P}}) \times \pi^{\mathrm{W}}(S_{\mathcal{P}}^{\blacktriangle})$ $\to \mathbb{B}) \times M_N \times M_N \to \wp(S_{\mathcal{P}})$, *which applies a partial transition relation to a set of states, as follows. Given a set S, a partial transition relation* $\hookrightarrow^{\mathrm{P}}$, *a read matrix row r and a may-write matrix row w,*

$$\text{NEXT}(S, \hookrightarrow^{\mathrm{P}}, r, w) = \Big\{ y \in S_{\mathcal{P}} \mid \exists x \in S, z \in S_{\mathcal{P}}^{\blacktriangle}: \hookrightarrow^{\mathrm{P}}(\pi^r(x), \pi^w(z)) \wedge$$

$$\bigwedge_{j \in ind(w)} \Big(y_j = \begin{cases} x_j & \text{if } z_j = \blacktriangle, \\ z_j & \text{otherwise} \end{cases} \Big) \wedge \bigwedge_{j \notin ind(w)} (y_j = z_j) \Big\}.$$

The symbolic reachability algorithm that uses the functions NEXT-STATE and NEXT is in Algorithm 3. The algorithm is an extension of the symbolic reachability algorithm in [2, Table 6].

Variable $\mathcal{R}$ maintains the set of reachable states so far, while $\mathcal{L}$ stores the current level. After initialisation (lines 1–6), the next level $\mathcal{N}$ will be continuously computed and added, until the current level is empty (lines 7–15). In each iteration, first the new transitions must be learned (Algorithm 4). The next level is computed by calling NEXT for each transition group (line 11).

Our extension includes three subtle modifications compared to [2, Table 6], when growing the transition relations on-the-fly (Algorithm 4). *First,* the state is read-projected in line 2. The benefit being that fewer calls to NEXT-STATE are needed. *Secondly,* the tuples added to the partial transition relation in line 4 may contain the special value ▲. This allows dynamic assignments to be resolved

Algorithm 3. REACH-BFS-PREV	**Algorithm 4.** LEARN-TRANS

Algorithm 3. REACH-BFS-PREV

Input : $s^0 \in S_{\mathcal{P}}, K \in \mathbb{N}, RM, MM$
Output: The set of reachable states $\mathcal{R}$
1 $\mathcal{R} \leftarrow \{s^0\}$;
2 $\mathcal{L} \leftarrow \mathcal{R}$;
3 **for** $1 \le i \le K$ **do**
4 $\quad \mathcal{R}_i^{\mathrm{P}} \leftarrow \varnothing$;
5 $\quad \hookrightarrow_i^{\mathrm{P}} \leftarrow \varnothing$;
6 **end**
7 **while** $\mathcal{L} \ne \varnothing$ **do**
8 $\quad$ LEARN-TRANS();
9 $\quad \mathcal{N} \leftarrow \varnothing$;
10 $\quad$ **for** $1 \le i \le K$ **do**
11 $\quad \quad \mathcal{N} \leftarrow \mathcal{N} \cup \text{NEXT}(\mathcal{L}, \hookrightarrow_i^{\mathrm{P}}, RM_i, MM_i)$;
12 $\quad$ **end**
13 $\quad \mathcal{L} \leftarrow \mathcal{N} \setminus \mathcal{R}$;
14 $\quad \mathcal{R} \leftarrow \mathcal{R} \cup \mathcal{N}$
15 **end**
16 **return** $\mathcal{R}$

Algorithm 4. LEARN-TRANS

Output: Extends $\hookrightarrow_i^{\mathrm{P}}$ with new
$\qquad$ transitions on-the-fly
1 **for** $1 \le i \le K$ **do**
2 $\quad \mathcal{L}^{\mathrm{P}} \leftarrow \pi_i^{\mathrm{r}}(\mathcal{L})$;
3 $\quad$ **for** $s^{\mathrm{P}} \in \mathcal{L}^{\mathrm{P}} \setminus \mathcal{R}_i^{\mathrm{P}}$ **do**
4 $\quad \quad \hookrightarrow_i^{\mathrm{P}} \leftarrow \hookrightarrow_i^{\mathrm{P}} \cup \{\langle s^{\mathrm{P}}, d^{\mathrm{P}} \rangle \mid$
5 $\quad \quad \quad d^{\mathrm{P}} \in \text{NEXT-STATE}_i(s^{\mathrm{P}})\}$;
6 $\quad$ **end**
7 $\quad \mathcal{R}_i^{\mathrm{P}} \leftarrow \mathcal{R}_i^{\mathrm{P}} \cup \mathcal{L}^{\mathrm{P}}$;
8 **end**

efficiently at a lower (symbolic) level. *Thirdly,* the transition relation is applied using both the read and the may-write dependency matrices (line 11). That way, fewer levels of the underlying decision diagrams are affected.

Figure 4 clearly shows the difference between using the previously used projections (to the left) and using read-projections (to the right). Both can be used to compute successors for the states in Example 2, but when using read-projections, the function $\rightarrow_i$ is applied to only one of the four states with $p_0 = 0$, instead of to all.

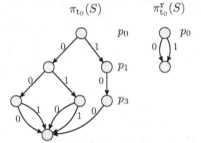

Fig. 4. Projection without and with read-separation for Ex. 2

4.1 Implementation

To investigate the effects of separating dependencies, we have implemented the transition relation and its application from Definition 12 in LTSMIN's native List Decision Diagram (LDD) library. An LDD is a form of Multi-way Decision Diagram MDD which was initially described in [2, Sect. 5]. The definition is as follows.

Definition 13 (List Decision Diagram). *A* List Decision Diagram *(LDD) is a* Directed A-cyclic Graph *(DAG) with three types of nodes:*

- $\{\epsilon\}$, *which encodes* true *and has no successors,*
- $\varnothing$, *which encodes* false *and has no successors,*
- $\langle v, down, right \rangle$, *a tuple with label v and two successors:* down *and* right.

The semantics $[\![s]\!]$ of an LDD node s is a set of vectors, as follows:

$$[\![\{\epsilon\}]\!] = \{\epsilon\}, \quad [\![\varnothing]\!] = \varnothing, \quad [\![\langle v, down, right \rangle]\!] = \{vw \mid w \in [\![down]\!]\} \cup [\![right]\!].$$

Algorithm 5. LDD-NEXT

Input: LDD nodes $s, \hookrightarrow^{\mathrm{P}}, r, w$ and level $l \in \mathbb{N}$
1 **if** $s = \varnothing \vee \hookrightarrow^{\mathrm{P}} = \varnothing$ **then** **return** $\varnothing$;
2 **if** $|r| = 0 \wedge |w| = 0$ **then** **return** s ;
3 **if** $s = \{\epsilon\} \vee \hookrightarrow^{\mathrm{P}} = \{\epsilon\}$ **then** ERROR ;
4 **if** $r_0 = l \wedge w_0 = l$ **then** // Read and write dependent
5 $\quad$ **if** $\hookrightarrow^{\mathrm{P}}_{\mathrm{v}} < s_{\mathrm{v}}$ **then** **return** LDD-NEXT$(s, \hookrightarrow^{\mathrm{P}}_{\mathrm{r}}, r, w, l)$;
6 $\quad$ **else if** $\hookrightarrow^{\mathrm{P}}_{\mathrm{v}} > s_{\mathrm{v}}$ **then** **return** LDD-NEXT$(s_{\mathrm{r}}, \hookrightarrow^{\mathrm{P}}, r, w, l)$;
7 $\quad$ **else** **return** LDD-WRITE$(s, \hookrightarrow^{\mathrm{P}}_{\mathrm{d}}, r_{\mathrm{d}}, w, l) \cup$ LDD-NEXT$(s_{\mathrm{r}}, \hookrightarrow^{\mathrm{P}}_{\mathrm{r}}, r, w, l)$;
8 **else if** $r_0 = l$ **then** // Only read dependent
9 $\quad$ **if** $\hookrightarrow^{\mathrm{P}}_{\mathrm{v}} < s_{\mathrm{v}}$ **then** **return** LDD-NEXT$(s, \hookrightarrow^{\mathrm{P}}_{\mathrm{r}}, r, w, l)$;
10 $\quad$ **else if** $\hookrightarrow^{\mathrm{P}}_{\mathrm{v}} > s_{\mathrm{v}}$ **then** **return** LDD-NEXT$(s_{\mathrm{r}}, \hookrightarrow^{\mathrm{P}}, r, w, l)$;
11 $\quad$ **else** **return** $\langle s_{\mathrm{v}}, $LDD-NEXT$(s_{\mathrm{d}}, \hookrightarrow^{\mathrm{P}}_{\mathrm{d}}, r_{\mathrm{d}}, w, l + 1), $LDD-NEXT$(s_{\mathrm{r}}, \hookrightarrow^{\mathrm{P}}_{\mathrm{r}}, r, w, l)\rangle$;
12 **else if** $w_0 = l$ **then** // Must-write or may-write dependent
13 $\quad$ **if** $\hookrightarrow^{\mathrm{P}}_{\mathrm{v}} = \blacktriangle$ **then** **return** LDD-COPY$(s, \hookrightarrow^{\mathrm{P}}_{\mathrm{d}}, r, w_{\mathrm{d}}, l) \cup$ LDD-WRITE$(s, \hookrightarrow^{\mathrm{P}}_{\mathrm{r}}, r, w, l)$;
14 $\quad$ **else** **return** LDD-WRITE$(s, \hookrightarrow^{\mathrm{P}}, r, w, l) \cup$ LDD-WRITE$(s_{\mathrm{r}}, \hookrightarrow^{\mathrm{P}}, r, w, l)$;
15 **else** **return** LDD-COPY$(s, \hookrightarrow^{\mathrm{P}}, r, w, l)$; // Copy

---

Algorithm 6. LDD-WRITE

Input: LDD nodes $s, \hookrightarrow^{\mathrm{P}}, r, w$ and $l \in \mathbb{N}$
1 **if** $\hookrightarrow^{\mathrm{P}} = \varnothing$ **then** **return** $\varnothing$;
2 **return** $\langle \hookrightarrow^{\mathrm{P}}_{\mathrm{v}},$
$\quad$ LDD-NEXT$(s_{\mathrm{d}}, \hookrightarrow^{\mathrm{P}}_{\mathrm{d}}, r, w_{\mathrm{d}}, l + 1), \varnothing \rangle$
$\quad \cup$ LDD-WRITE$(s, \hookrightarrow^{\mathrm{P}}_{\mathrm{r}}, r, w, l)$

Algorithm 7. LDD-COPY

Input: LDD nodes $s, \hookrightarrow^{\mathrm{P}}, r, w$ and $l \in \mathbb{N}$
1 **if** $s = \varnothing$ **then** **return** $\varnothing$;
2 **return** $\langle s_{\mathrm{v}},$
$\quad$ LDD-NEXT$(s_{\mathrm{d}}, \hookrightarrow^{\mathrm{P}}, r, w, l + 1),$
$\quad$ LDD-COPY$(s_{\mathrm{r}}, \hookrightarrow^{\mathrm{P}}, r, w, l)\rangle$

For some node $n = \langle v, down, right \rangle$, we use n_{v}, n_{d} and n_{r} to denote its elements v, down and right, respectively.

We assume (and enforce) in the implementation that the sequence of values in a level is ordered from small to large. E.g., $\langle 0, \ldots, \langle 1, \ldots, \varnothing \rangle\rangle$ is a valid node, but $\langle 1, \ldots, \langle 0, \ldots, \varnothing \rangle\rangle$ is not. We define $\blacktriangle$ to always be smallest.

A single vector $x = \langle x_1, \ldots, x_N \rangle$ (or singleton set $\{x\}$) can be represented as an LDD node as $\langle x_1, \langle x_2, \ldots, \varnothing \rangle, \varnothing \rangle$. Note that for vector x, encoded as LDD node x, the LDD node of the subvector $x_{1 < j \leq |x|}$, i.e., the vector x with the first element removed, equals x_{d}. An example LDD is given in Figure 5. This LDD encodes the set $\{\langle 0, 0 \rangle, \langle 0, 1 \rangle, \langle 1, 0 \rangle, \langle 1, 1 \rangle\}$ $(= \{0, 1\} \times \{0, 1\})$ with two variables x_0 and x_1.

In the implementation of the application of the transition relation NEXT in Def. 12, we use LDD's to encode the set $S_{\mathcal{P}}$, the relation $\hookrightarrow^{\mathrm{P}}$ and the matrix rows r and w.

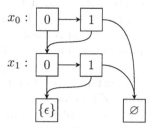

Fig. 5. $\{\langle 0, 0 \rangle, \langle 0, 1 \rangle, \langle 1, 0 \rangle, \langle 1, 1 \rangle\}$ as LDD

Here, $S_{\mathcal{P}}$ is encoded as an LDD of depth N and $\hookrightarrow^{\mathrm{P}}$ as an LDD of depth $|r| + |w|$. The rows r and w are actually encoded as LDD representations of the sorted vectors with the indices of dependent variables $ind(r)$ and $ind(w)$, respectively. The algorithm using LDD's, given in Algorithm 5, recursively traverses the LDD's level by level, maintaining a counter l to keep track of the current level, initially 0.

Lines 1–3 handle a few base cases. In the case the current level l (variable x_l) is both *read and may-write dependent* (lines 4–7), first a (read) value is matched (s_v and $\hookrightarrow^p_v$) and then each value from the next level of the relation is written using LDD-WRITE. The resulting node is united with all other values we may need to write. If the level is *read dependent* only (lines 8–11), then we first find a matching value and then create a new node with two recursive elements: downward matching the other levels, and, to the right, other nodes on the current level that may match the relation. If the level is *must-write or may-write dependent* only (lines 12–14), then for each value in the set we create a new node, where we either copy the value s_v or write the value from the relation. If the level has no read or write dependency (line 15), then a new node is created with the *down* and *right* nodes computed recursively with LDD-COPY. LDD-WRITE writes all values from the relation reachable on the current level. However, it needs to unite all the nodes with these values because they may occur in the wrong order. The unions are computed in the standard way for decision diagrams.

5   Results

To evaluate our work we have benchmarked with 266 DVE models from the BEEM database [15], 38 mCRL2 models, mostly from mCRL2's distribution, and 60 PROMELA models from different sources[1]. To compare our results to both the current version of LTSMIN and the effect of variable orderings we implemented the options w2W and W2+. These two options over-approximate must-write to may-write, and may-write to read and write, thus simulating the situation without read-write separation. Every experiment is run three times in both setups to determine the effect of our work. The machine we used has an Intel Xeon E5520 CPU, with 24 GB of memory. We have restricted the runtime of each experiment to 30 minutes.

Overall, we see that the mCRL2 models benefit from read-write separation, because of the reduced amount of NEXT-STATE calls. This is due to the fact that a NEXT-STATE call for mCRL2 is rather time consuming because of the term rewriting involved. The DVE and PROMELA front-ends run optimized C code. For these languages, the overhead of many unnecessary NEXT-STATE calls in the current version of LTSMIN is less noticeable. We see however that the runtime of DVE models is improved when we use a good variable ordering, which reduces the number of symbolic operations. We have highlighted six interesting experiments with relevant information in Table 4, of which a legend can be found in Table 3. Of all experiments which have a run time longer than one second, 101 out of 167 are faster. With optimized dependency matrices, 125 out of 160 experiments are faster.

With DVE models we see speedups mainly when the amount of symbolic (LDD) operations is reduced, such as in telephony.7. We were less successful in this for anderson.6. However, the runtime for blocks.3 is greatly reduced.

---

[1] Instructions to reproduce or obtain a copy of all models/results can be found at http://pm.jmeijer.nl/32ae74f74e

Table 3. Symbols used in Table 4

model	name of the model	**cs**	Column Sort, sorts columns such that writes are put on a diagonal
dm	dependency matrix operations		
$\overline{rt}$	average reachability time in seconds		
$\overline{mem}$	average peak memory usage in kilobytes	**rs**	Row Sort, sorts rows such that writes are put on a diagonal
#NS	number of NEXT-STATE calls		
#LDD	number of calls to LDD-NEXT (Alg. 5)	**cw**	Column sWap, minimizes distance between columns and puts reads before writes heuristically (Algs. 1 and 2)
$|\mathcal{R}|$	number of nodes of the set of reachable states		
$|\pi(\mathcal{R})|$	approx. number of nodes in the projections		
$|\hookrightarrow|$	approx. number of nodes of the whole transition relation		

The `anderson.6` model has 18,206,917 states, 36 groups and 19 state slots. In this model we see no speedup, because it is hard to find a good variable ordering. The bad ordering results in more recursive LDD-NEXT calls which slows down the reachability analysis. `blocks.3` is a model where we obtained very good results. The state space of this contains 695,418 states, there are 26 groups and 18 state slots. Because `blocks.3` contains many may-write dependencies we are able to greatly reduce the amount of NEXT-STATE calls. Furthermore the amount of nodes in the node table is reduced significantly. Telephony.7.dve is a model with 21,960,308 states, 24 state slots and 120 groups. Similar to `anderson.6` we see a slow down when we use separated dependencies. This slow down is the result of many more symbolic operations. However, opposed to `anderson.6` we are able to slightly speed up the reachability analysis by transforming the dependency matrix. We can reduce the amount of NEXT-STATE calls while only slightly increasing the amount of recursive LDD-NEXT calls.

In the first two mCRL2 models (`1394-fin` and `lift3-final`) we can see that the amount of reduced NEXT-STATE calls corresponds closely to the speedup attained. The model `1394-fin` has 188,596 states, 34 state slots and 1,069 transition groups. The second, `lift3-final`, has 4,312 states, 30 state slots and 60 transition groups. We obtained the most interesting result with the `vasy` model, a 1-safe Petri net submitted to the Petri net mailing list in 2003 [12] by Hubert Garavel. The model has 9.79×10^{21} states, 776 transition groups and 485 state slots. With our work we have managed to make reachability analysis for this model tractable for LTSMIN. Special about this model is the first transition, which removes the token from the initial place to several other places (like in Figure 2). Without read-write separations, this required exponentially many NEXT-STATE calls for this transition: $\leq 2^{61}$ calls, because there are 61 dependent state slots of boolean type. With our improvements it is identified that only one state slot is read, resulting in only 2^1 NEXT-STATE calls.

Table 4. Highlighted experiment results

model	dm	r̄t	m̄ēm	#NS	#LDD	|𝓡|	|π(𝓡)|	|↪|
anderson.6.dve		25.4	439,076	7,464	64,034,383	50,120	2,442	2,064
anderson.6.dve		34.6	439,076	4,080	127,725,604	50,120	1,470	1,386
anderson.6.dve	cs;rs;cw;rs	27.6	144,216	7,464	84,028,747	41,079	2,568	1,884
anderson.6.dve	cs;rs;cw;rs	29.9	144,216	4,080	109,711,771	41,079	1,533	1,386
blocks.3.dve		31.0	239,293	6,559,927	69,695,086	39,522	375,603	269,996
blocks.3.dve		10.9	144,064	262,543	62,467,909	39,522	12,314	1,604
blocks.3.dve	cs;rs;cw;rs	25.7	280,344	6,559,927	25,021,658	49,685	464,916	325,763
blocks.3.dve	cs;rs;cw;rs	4.6	144,196	262,543	12,281,723	49,685	12,076	1,478
telephony.7.dve		107.6	1,111,840	918,817	231,808,995	284,449	36,951	6,038
telephony.7.dve		123.7	696,188	730,841	393,099,843	284,449	31,473	5,337
telephony.7.dve	cs;rs;cw;rs	26.8	144,656	918,817	62,889,960	18,479	39,410	6,263
telephony.7.dve	cs;rs;cw;rs	25.4	144,656	730,841	63,110,689	18,479	33,144	5,478
1394-fin.mcrl2		22.6	208,084	3,372,554	1,995,202	7,384	870,142	12,505
1394-fin.mcrl2		3.4	188,944	443,813	1,800,912	7,384	229,251	8,399
lift3-final.mcrl2		5.3	184,624	190,347	313,868	5,452	162,956	7,023
lift3-final.mcrl2		2.5	181,372	79,941	378,179	5,452	54,249	5,496
vasy.mcrl2		-	-	-	-	-	-	-
vasy.mcrl2		152.6	1,149,592	2,694	241,432,226	9,387	4,340	5,444

6   Conclusion

Separating dependencies into read and write dependencies can speed-up symbolic model checking considerably. To do so, we had to solve two key problems. The first problem is that a *copy* dependency can in general not be over-approximated to a must-write dependency. Therefore we introduced the definition of may-write independence. This notion is used when it can not be statically determined whether a value needs to be written or copied. Separating dependencies introduced a second problem. Reachability algorithms that exploit our notions for read and write dependencies only work well with a good variable ordering. We have provided heuristics that try to put read dependencies before write dependencies.

Models for the PROMELA and DVE language front-ends for PINS are both highly optimized C programs. Thus a NEXT-STATE call is relatively fast compared to symbolic operations of the back-end. On the contrary, computing the state space of mCRL2 models involves the term rewriter of mCRL2. The increased expressiveness has a prize: term rewriting is a lot slower than the optimized C programs for PROMELA and DVE. So symbolic operations are relatively fast compared to a NEXT-STATE call to the mCRL2 language front-end.

Overall, we conclude that separating dependencies in the transition relation by default in LTSMIN is a good idea. We have observed only a few cases with a slow-down, and this slow-down was minimal. The observed speed-ups on the other hand were considerable, and in some cases necessary to make problems tractable for LTSMIN, e.g., for the vasy model.

Future work will split conditions into single guards, and consider their dependencies separately. Also, the distinction between read and write variables can be included in more advanced heuristics for static variable ordering strategies in the dependency matrix. We also recommend to implement our new definitions and algorithms for other modeling languages and connect them to LTSMIN through PINS.

References

1. van der Berg, F.I., Laarman, A.W.: SpinS: Extending LTSmin with Promela through SpinJa. ENTCS 296(2012), 95–105 (2013); pASM/PDMC 2012
2. Blom, S., van de Pol, J.: Symbolic Reachability for Process Algebras with Recursive Data Types. In: Fitzgerald, J.S., Haxthausen, A.E., Yenigun, H. (eds.) ICTAC 2008. LNCS, vol. 5160, pp. 81–95. Springer, Heidelberg (2008)
3. Blom, S., van de Pol, J., Weber, M.: Bridging the Gap between Enumerative and Symbolic Model Checkers. Technical Report CTIT, University of Twente, Enschede (2009), http://eprints.eemcs.utwente.nl/15703/
4. Blom, S., van de Pol, J., Weber, M.: LTSMIN: Distributed and Symbolic Reachability. In: Touili, T., Cook, B., Jackson, P. (eds.) CAV 2010. LNCS, vol. 6174, pp. 354–359. Springer, Heidelberg (2010)
5. Burch, J.R., Clarke, E.M., Long, D.E.: Symbolic model checking with partitioned transition relations. In: VLSI 1991 (1991)
6. Burch, J.R., Clarke, E.M., McMillan, K.L., Dill, D.L., Hwang, L.J.: Symbolic model checking: 10^{20} states and beyond. In: LICS 1990. IEEE (1990)
7. Ciardo, G., Marmorstein, R., Siminiceanu, R.I.: Saturation unbound. In: Garavel, H., Hatcliff, J. (eds.) TACAS 2003. LNCS, vol. 2619, pp. 379–393. Springer, Heidelberg (2003)
8. Ciardo, G., Yu, A.J.: Saturation-Based Symbolic Reachability Analysis Using Conjunctive and Disjunctive Partitioning. In: Borrione, D., Paul, W. (eds.) CHARME 2005. LNCS, vol. 3725, pp. 146–161. Springer, Heidelberg (2005)
9. Cimatti, A., Clarke, E., Giunchiglia, E., Giunchiglia, F., Pistore, M., Roveri, M., Sebastiani, R., Tacchella, A.: NuSMV 2: An OpenSource Tool for Symbolic Model Checking. In: Brinksma, E., Larsen, K.G. (eds.) CAV 2002. LNCS, vol. 2404, pp. 359–364. Springer, Heidelberg (2002)
10. Cimatti, A., Clarke, E., Giunchiglia, F., Roveri, M.: NuSMV: a new symbolic model checker. STTT 2(4) (2000)
11. Clarke, E.M.: The birth of model checking. In: Grumberg, O., Veith, H. (eds.) 25 Years of Model Checking. LNCS, vol. 5000, pp. 1–26. Springer, Heidelberg (2008)
12. Kordon, F., Linard, A., Beccuti, M., Buchs, D., Fronc, L., Hillah, L.M., Hulin-Hubard, F., Legond-Aubry, F., Lohmann, N., Marechal, A.: et al.: Model Checking Contest @ Petri Nets, Report on the 2013 edition (2013), ArXiv: http://arxiv.org/abs/1309.2485v1
13. McMillan, K.L.: Symbolic model checking. Kluwer (1993)
14. Meijer, J.J.G.: Improving Reachability Analysis in LTSmin. Master's thesis, University of Twente (2014)
15. Pelánek, R.: BEEM: Benchmarks for explicit model checkers. In: Bošnački, D., Edelkamp, S. (eds.) SPIN 2007. LNCS, vol. 4595, pp. 263–267. Springer, Heidelberg (2007)
16. Rudell, R.: Dynamic Variable Ordering for Ordered Binary Decision Diagrams. In: ICCAD 1993. IEEE (1993)
17. Skiena, S.S.: The Algorithm Design Manual. Springer (2008)

Efficient Combinatorial Test Generation Based on Multivalued Decision Diagrams

Angelo Gargantini and Paolo Vavassori

Dip. di Ingegneria, Università di Bergamo, Italy
{angelo.gargantini,paolo.vavassori}@unibg.it

Abstract. Combinatorial interaction testing (CIT) is an emerging testing technique that has proved to be effective in finding faults due to the interaction among inputs. Efficient test generation for CIT is still an open problem especially when applied to real models having meaningful size and containing many constraints among inputs. In this paper we present a novel technique for the automatic generation of compact test suites starting from models containing constraints given in general form. It is based on the use of Multivalued Decision Diagrams (MDDs) which prove to be suitable to efficiently support CIT. We devise and experiment several optimizations including a novel variation of the classical greedy policy normally used in similar algorithms. The results of a thorough comparison with other similar techniques are presented and show that our approach can provide several advantages in terms of applicability, test suite size, generation time, and cost.

1 Introduction

Combinatorial Interaction Testing (CIT) helps tester to find defects due to the interaction of components or inputs. It is based on the assumption that faults are generally caused by *interactions* among parameters. CIT tests the interaction in a systematic way. For instance, *pairwise* testing requires that every pair of parameter value be tested at least once. It can be generalized by the *t-way* testing. CIT has been proved to be very effective in finding faults [20].

A major problem in CIT is the generation of compact test suites, especially when the cost of executing each test case is high. Suitable tools can produce very compact test suites. For instance [20], a manufacturing automation system that has 20 controls, each with 10 possible settings –a total of 10^{20} combinations – can be tested by a test suite for the pairwise testing with only 180 tests in it. Applying CIT to highly configurable software systems is complicated by the fact that, in many such systems, the parameters are rarely independent from each other. There exist constraints that model dependencies among parameters that render certain combinations invalid or some combinations mandatory [12]. The presence of constraints increases the complexity of the test generation task: if constraints on the input domain are to be taken into account, even finding a single test or configuration that satisfies the constraints is NP-complete [5], since it can be reduced in the most general case to a satisfiability problem. Several

E. Yahav (Ed.): HVC 2014, LNCS 8855, pp. 220–235, 2014.

works, like this, target explicitly the test generation for CIT in the presence of constraints, CCIT in brief. In this paper we focus on reaching a good trade-off between the size of the generated test-suite and its time of generation.

Our algorithm is a classical greedy algorithm which produces a test at the time [7]. When building a single test, it chooses an *optimal* parameter and assigns an *optimal* value to it until a test is complete. However, we advance with respect to the state of the art by adopting the following original approaches:

– We employ a data structure, called Multivalued Decision Diagram (MDD), which is particularly suitable to combinatorial problems in order to represent inputs, their domains, and constraints over those inputs; MDDs offer several advantages w.r.t. the classical Binary Decision Diagrams.

– We soften the classical greedy algorithm by reducing the importance of the number of tuples covered by the test currently built, by weighting parameters and tuples depending on the constraints in order to reduce the test suite size;

The paper is organized as follows. In Sect. 2 we present some introductory material about constrained combinatorial interaction testing, about the framework called CITLAB, and about MDDs. Sect. 3 shows how MDDs are suitable to efficiently represent several aspects of CIT (models, tuples, tests, and constraints). In Sect. 4 we present our algorithm and several optimizations. Experiments are reported in Sect. 5. Section 6 presents relevant related work. Future works are discussed in Sect. 7, which concludes the paper.

2 Background

2.1 Combinatorial Interaction Testing

Combinatorial Interaction Testing (CIT) systematically explores t-way feature interactions inside a given system, by effectively combining all t-tuples of parameter assignments in the smallest possible number of test cases. This allows to budget-constraint the costs of testing while still having a testing process driven by an effective coverage metric [19]. The most commonly applied combinatorial testing technique is *pairwise* testing, which consists in applying a test suite covering all *pairs* of input values (each pair in at least one test case). Many CIT tools (see [24] for an up to date listing) and techniques have already been developed [16,19] and are currently applied in practice [4,18].

Combinatorial testing can be applied to a wide variety of problems: highly configurable software systems, software product lines which define a family of software, hardware systems, and so on. As an example, Listing 1 reports the input domain model of a simple smart-phone product line using the CITLAB [10]. The model contains three parameters: the display can have 16 or 8 million colors or be in black and white (BW), the frontCamera can have 1 or 2 megapixels (1MP and 2MP) or not be present (NOC). The phone can also have an emailViewer. We will use this simple example throughout the paper to explain our approach. While testing of all the possible configurations for the phone would require $3 \cdot 3 \cdot 2 = 18$ tests, pairwise coverage can be obtained by a test suite containing only 9 tests.

Listing 1. A mobile phone example

```
Model phone
Parameters:
    Enumerative display { 16MC 8MC BW };
    Enumerative frontCamera { 2MP 1MP NOC };
    Boolean emailViewer;
end
Constraints: # emailViever => display != BW # end
```

In most configurable systems, constraints or dependencies exist between parameters. Constraints were first described as being important to combinatorial testing in [11] and were introduced in the AETG system. In our approach, tests that do not satisfy the constraints are considered *invalid* and do not need to be produced. However, the generation of tests considering constraints is more challenging than the generation without them, and several test generation techniques still do not support constraints, at least not in a direct manner.

In CITLAB testers are allowed to specify constraints in a general form. For instance, the constraint that a phone with an email viewer cannot have a black and white display can be modeled as shown in Listing 1.

2.2   Multivalued Decision Diagram

A decision diagram is a graph that represents a function $f : \mathcal{D} \to B$ where $\mathcal{D} = \mathcal{D}_1 \times \ldots \times \ldots \mathcal{D}_n$ and B is the Boolean domain, i.e., $B = \{\mathbf{F}, \mathbf{T}\}$. A decision diagram is used to evaluate the truth value of f when applied to the variables $x_1, \ldots, x_n$. If all the domains $\mathcal{D}_i$ are binary, then we use Binary Decision Diagrams (BDDs) to represent Boolean functions. BDDs are widely used within the domain of system design verification. Multi-Valued Decision Diagrams (MDD) extend BDDs by allowing every variable to have a different domain with different size. A MDD is a directed acyclic graph used to encode a function f. The graph has only two terminal nodes each labeled $\mathbf{F}$ or $\mathbf{T}$. Every non-terminal node is labeled by an input variable x_i and has $|\mathcal{D}_i|$ outgoing labeled edges; one corresponding to each value. The diagram is ordered if the variables adhere to a single ordering on every path in the graph, and no variable appears more than once on any path from the root to a terminal node. An MDD can represent the values in $\mathcal{D}$ that are selected by f: if the values $x_1, \ldots, x_n$ for the variables in $\mathcal{D}$ are selected by f, then $f(x_1, \ldots, x_n) = \mathbf{T}$, otherwise $f(x_1, \ldots, x_n) = \mathbf{F}$.

Typical operations among MDDs include *unary* operations like complement and cardinality, and *binary* operations like union, intersection, and difference.

MDD operations can be mapped to logic operation between the Boolean functions represented by an MDD. Given an MDD m with function f, its complement $m^{\complement}$ represents the function $\neg f$. The union between two MDDs $m_1 \sqcup m_2$ represents the function $f_1 \vee f_2$. The intersection between two MDDs $m_1 \sqcap m_2$ represents the function $f_1 \wedge f_2$. Given the MDD m, its cardinality $|m|$ is the number of

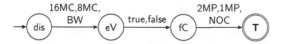

Fig. 1. MDD for the combinatorial problem of Listing 1

all the possible paths to the terminal node **T**. The cardinality can be used to check consistency among Boolean functions: if f_1 and f_2 are inconsistent, i.e. $f_1(x) \neq f_2(x)$ for any x, the intersection between their MDDs is empty.

MDDs can represent Boolean logic functions using less memory and shorter path then BDDs. From a theoretical point of view, Nagayama [22] demonstrated that the amount of memory used by mapping Boolean function with Boolean variables to heterogeneous MDD is lesser than using OBDD directly. This seems to suggest that MDDs are the preferred data structure when the domains are not simple Boolean values.

In order to achieve this performance improvement over BDDs, it is very important the use of techniques that can reduce the size of MDDs. To our knowledge, Meddly [3] is the only opensource C/C++ library that natively supports these DDs. According to our opinion, Meddly native support for MDDs and their variants, along with its performance makes it a good candidate for applications in areas where these DDs make sense.

3   Using MDD for CCIT

If one ignores the constraints, a combinatorial model with n parameters each with cardinality p_i can be very easily represented by an MDD that has n non-terminal nodes labeled by the name of every parameter and each node for parameter P_i has p_i outgoing labeled edges to the node for P_{i+1} for $i < n$ and to the **T** terminal node for P_n. We call this MDD M_{TS}. For instance, the MDD in Fig. 1 represents the M_{TS} for the phone given in Listing 1. In the following figures, edges sharing the same starting and final node are shown with a unique arch and the list of labels. Every path from root to the terminal **T** is a syntactically correct configuration. The M_{TS} represents all the tests, i.e., all the possible paths from the start to the terminal node. The cardinality of M_{TS} is equal to $\prod_{i=1}^{n} p_i$ which is equal to the total number of possible tests.

The equality formula that associates parameter P_i to one of its values v, i.e., the assignment $P_i = v$ can be easily represented by the following function.

$$f(p_1, \ldots, p_n) = \begin{cases} \mathbf{T} & \text{if } P_i = v \\ \mathbf{F} & \text{if } P_i \neq v \end{cases}$$

Such function can be represented by an MDD in which all the paths, traversing the edge outgoing the node P_i with label v, terminate to the terminal **T** while all the other ones terminate in **F**. For instance, the equality eV = true is shown in Fig. 2a. A similar MDD representation can be given for a tuple assigning

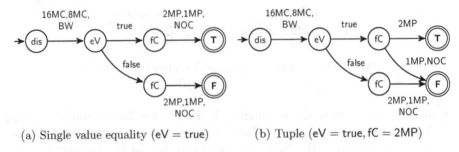

(a) Single value equality (eV = true)   (b) Tuple (eV = true, fC = 2MP)

Fig. 2. Representation by MDDs of assignments and tuples

values to a list of parameters. A path terminates to the node **T** if and only if it contains an assignment contained also in the tuple. For instance, the tuple (eV = true, fC = 2MP) is shown in Fig. 2b.

In most configurable systems, constraints or dependencies exist between parameters. Since we assume that the constraints corresponding to a CIT problem can be described by propositional logic with equality, we can describe every model constraint c_i using a Boolean general formula containing operators $\neg, \vee, \wedge$ over equalities among parameters and their values. Every constraint can be represented by an MDD modeling its truth function: it can be built using the representation of equality formulas proposed above and the operations between MDDs presented in Sect. 2.2.

In order to include the constraints in the MDD M_{TS} representing the unconstrained model, we can use the operations between MDDs. Let M_{TS} be the MDD representing the model and the whole test set from all the possible combinations. The conjunction of M_{TS} with all the constraints c_i restricts the set of satisfying interpretations of the function associated to M_{TS} such that it contains exactly those interpretations that correspond to valid test cases. Let m_{c_i} be the MDD for the constraint c_i, and the MDD M_{VS} be defined by the following formula: $M_{VS} = \prod_{i=1}^{n} m_{c_i} \sqcap M_{TS}$.

Integrating the constraints c_i into the MDD M_{TS} in order to obtain the MDD M_{VS}, changes the M_{TS} original topology by making one or more paths from valid to not-valid. In the original MDD there are n levels and n not-terminal nodes, where n is the number of parameter. In order to model not-valid paths it is necessary to duplicate some nodes. The MDD M_{VS} preserves the number n of levels but has some more not-terminal nodes. The M_{VS} represents all the *valid* tests, i.e. all the possible paths from the start to the terminal **T** node.

An example of the MDD M_{VS} representing the model and the constraints for the phone problem is shown in Fig. 3a. M_{VS} can be used to identify valid tests. For instance, the combination (dis = BW, eV = true) is not valid, regardless of the value of fC, as expected, since the requirements prohibit a BW display with the emailViewer. On the contrary, the test (dis = 16MP, eV = true, fC = 2MP) is a valid test, as shown by the corresponding path leading to the terminal **T** node in the MDD. An MDD with cardinality 1, i.e. with only one path to the **T**

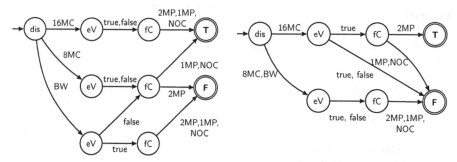

(a) M_{VS} for the phone with the constraints

(b) An MDD representing a single test case

Fig. 3. Representation by MDDs of models with constraints and test cases

terminal node, represents one valid test. The example shown in Fig. 3b identifies the test (dis = 16MP, eV = true, fC = 2MP).

4   An MDD-Based Algorithm for CCIT

We have devised an automatic algorithm for the generation of combinatorial test suites based on the use of MDDs. The algorithm takes as input the MDD M_{VS} representing the intersection between the model domain and the constraints, and produces as output the desired test suite R. It builds one test at the time until all the testing requirements are achieved. When building a single test, it proceeds in a greedy manner: it chooses one *optimal* parameter, which is not already set in the test, and its *optimal* value, according to our weighting criteria, and it adds this assignment to the test to be built. In the following we explain in details the algorithm that is reported in Alg. 1.

Firstly, we populate a list of tuples T_{TC} including all the combinations to cover based on a given coverage criterion C, usually *t-wise* coverage. We plan to use MDDs also to represent set of tuples like in [26]. Some tuples may be infeasible because of the constraints. In order to filter all the valid tuples, we use MDDs as well: the function *feasibleTuples* returns all the tuples required by the criterion C that have a non-empty intersection with the MDD M_{VS}.

We then start the iteration part where we generate, for each iteration, a test case M_{nc} represented by an MDD with final cardinality equal to 1. At the end of each iteration, we update T_{TC} removing the tuples covered by the generated M_{nc} until T_{TC} is empty.

In the single iteration we initialize M_{nc} to the valid set M_{VS}, we then sort all the parameters (*sortParamList*) by simply counting for every parameter p the number of tuples in T_{TC} that contain p. We then start assigning every P_i to the best value for it, by taking the *value* producing an assignment that is compatible with M_{nc} and that maximizes the coverage of tuples in T_{TC}.

This basic algorithm is a classical greedy algorithm that generates a test at the time and tries to cover as many uncovered tuples as possible. It can be improved in several directions, as explained in the following sections.

Algorithm 1. Generation of the test suite R

Input: M_{VS}: MDD for the model with the constraints
Output: R: set of MDDs representing the test set
   $T_{TC} \leftarrow feasibleTuples(M_{VS})$
   $R \leftarrow \emptyset$
   while $T_{TC} \neq \emptyset$ **do**   ▷ Build single test M_{nc}
      $M_{nc} \leftarrow M_{VS}$
      $P \leftarrow sortParamList(T_{TC})$
      for all $P_i \in P$ **do**   ▷ Fix every parameter in P
         $value \leftarrow chooseBest(P_i, M_{nc}, T_{TC})$
         $M_{nc} \leftarrow M_{nc} \sqcap P_i = value$
         if $|M_{nc}| = 1$ **then break end if**
      end for
      $T_{TC} \leftarrow removeCoveredTuples(M_{nc})$
      $R \leftarrow R \cup M_{nc}$
   end while

4.1   Optimization: Weighting Compatibility

Although most greedy algorithms consider only the number of remaining tuples that will be covered in order to determine the best choice [7], it is well known that such greedy policy can lead to bigger test suites, even for unconstrained models[1]. In the presence of constraints, this greedy policy can be even more inefficient since it tends to leave at the end all the tuples that are "difficult" to cover, because the constraints limit the number of valid test cases that can cover them. In this way, the last generated tests cover only a few tuples not covered yet, leading to bigger test suites.

We propose to *weight* every tuple depending on its compatibility with respect to the other tuples not covered yet considering also the constraints. Heavy tuples are more difficult to cover and they should be fixed sooner than light tuples. To weight tuples, we introduce a dynamic function *weigth* that measures the weight of every tuple and we modify the Alg. 1 by calling the function in Alg. 2 that assigns the weights before ordering the parameters. We modify the functions *sortParamList* and *chooseBest* accordingly in order to consider tuple weights.

The function ASSIGNWEIGHT increases the **weight** (initially set to 0) for all the tuple pairs (T_i, T_J) with T_i and T_j in T_{TC} that are mutually exclusive by considering also the constraints. Checking if two tuples are compatible can be performed by using the usual intersection operator among MDDs. For instance the tuples (dis = BW, fC = 2MP) and (fC = 2MP, eV = true) would have their *weight* increased because they are incompatible due to the constraints and this can be easily computed using the MDD of Fig. 3a.

Although we can rely on the efficiency of MDDs for the computation of weights, Alg. 2 has complexity $N^2/2$ where N is the number of remaining tuples

---

[1] Bryce and Colbourn report in [6] the example in which a simple greedy algorithm provides a solution of 1,222 tests. Relaxing the greedy behavior or other algorithms can provide much smaller test suites till 910 tests.

Algorithm 2. Computation of weights

---

function ASSIGNWEIGHT(T_{TC}, M_{VS})
    for all $T \in T_{TC}$ **do** $weight(T) \leftarrow 0$ **end for**
    for all $(T_i, T_j) \in T_{TC} \times T_{TC}$ **with** $i < j$ **do**
        if $M_{VS} \sqcap T_i \sqcap T_j = \emptyset$ **then**
            $weight(T_i) \leftarrow weight(T_i) + 1$
            $weight(T_j) \leftarrow weight(T_j) + 1$
        end if
    end for
end function

Algorithm 3. Approximate and faster computation of weights

---

function ASSIGNWEIGHTFROMPARAMS(T_{TC})
    for all $T \in T_{TC}$ **do** $weight(T) \leftarrow 0$ **end for**
    for all P_i **and** $T_i \in T_{TC}$ **with** $P_i \in T_i$ **do**
        $weight(P_i) \leftarrow weight(P_i) + 1$
    end for
    for all $T_i \in T_{TC}$ **and** $P_i \in T_i$ **do**
        $weight(T_i) \leftarrow weight(T_i) + weight(P_i)$
    end for
end function

---

to cover (T_{TC}) and this can increase the computation time. For this reason, we define a simplified algorithm (Alg. 3) that is less precise but it is much faster than Alg. 2. This algorithm 3 first assigns a weight to every parameter depending on the number of remaining tuples to cover (T_{TC}) that contain it. Then, every tuple gets a weight that is the sum of the weights of the parameters in it. It does not consider the model and its constraints (M_{VS}), it does not need to perform any operation among MDDs, and for this reason is much faster.

We devised the following policy. If the number of tuples to be covered ($|T_{TC}|$) is greater than a **threshold**, Alg. 3 performs the weighting otherwise, the more precise Alg. 2 is used.

4.2 Optimization: Repetitions

Our algorithm produces non deterministic results, since when ordering the parameters and when identifying the best value for the chosen parameter, it may occur that two or more choices are equally valid. In this case the algorithm randomly chooses one possibility. The choice may affect the behavior of the test generation only much later (typically only in the last steps). One possibility is to repeat with a different random seed the entire algorithm (except the evaluation of tuple feasibility) in order to see if by chance a better solution is found. We call this optimization *repetition*, as defined in [7]. We manage the repetition policy by setting the following three parameters $repeat_{\min}$, $repeat_{\max}$, and $repeat_{\text{better}}$. When repetition is activated, the algorithm generates at least $repeat_{\min}$ times a

Table 1. Characteristics of the CCIT benchmarks

	#Variable	#Constraints	Domain size	#Valid configurations	Ratio[3]
Minimum	3.00	0	8.00	1.00	2.44×10^{-29}
Maximum	259.00	388	$9.26 \times 10^{+77}$	$2.44 \times 10^{+62}$	1.00
Mean	44.85	27.46	$1.16 \times 10^{+76}$	$5.89 \times 10^{+60}$	0.25
Median	15.00	15	$8.35 \times 10^{+04}$	$2.60 \times 10^{+04}$	7.86×10^{-02}

new test suite. It keeps generating new test suites unless for $repeat_{better}$ the test suite is not smaller than the best found so far. In any case no more than $repeat_{max}$ generation runs will be executed. The smallest test suite found is returned.

5   Experiments

We have implemented the algorithm presented in the previous section in a prototype tool called MEDICI (MultivaluEd Decision diagrams for Combinatorial Interaction testing). We have integrated MEDICI in CITLAB, an extensible framework for combinatorial testing [10]. MEDICI is written in C++ and is based on Meddly [3] for the MDDs. It has been embedded in CITLAB and it is freely available[2]. CITLAB simply exports the necessary input file for MEDICI and executes it. Note that MEDICI accepts constraints in general form and thanks to the fact that it uses MDDs, it avoids the time-consuming conversion to CNF .

As benchmarks for CCIT problems we have gathered 117 models with constraints taken from the literature (Casa [13,15,12], FoCuS [26], ACTS [1], and IPO-S [9]) and from SPLOT SPLs repository, and used (in subsets) also by many other papers. The benchmarks can be found on the CITLAB web site and can be used for further comparisons. For the sake of brevity, we show, in Tab. 1, only some useful statistical summary about the models. We run the experiments on a PC with two Intel(R) Xeon(R) CPU E5-2630 @ 2.30GHz and 64 GByte of RAM. We exploit the multi-core architecture by running 20 threads in parallel and we run all the experiments with the pairwise coverage and 50 runs.

Let $\overline{size}_m$ be the average of the test suite size for model m over all the runs and $\overline{time}_m$ be the average of the time for model m, we introduce $size$ and $time$ defined as: $size = \Sigma \overline{size}_m$ which is the sum of the averages of the test suite sizes and $time = \Sigma \overline{time}_m$ which is the sum of the averages of the executions times (in seconds). We will use $size$ and $time$ as performance indexes.

Optimal Threshold Value. We perform an experiment in order to discover the impact of the threshold introduced in Sect. 4.1 over the test generation size

---

[2] CitLab and its MEDICI plugin can be found at
   http://code.google.com/a/eclipselabs.org/p/citlab/
[3] Ratio=(#Valid configurations / Domain Size).

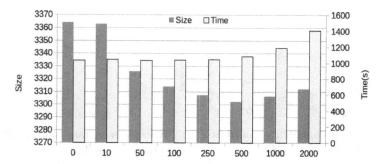

Fig. 4. Test suite *size* and *time* depending on the threshold

and time (with 1 repetition). Fig. 4 reports how the test suite size and time changes depending on the value of the threshold[4]. As the graph shows, the test suite size has a minimum for a threshold around 500, while it becomes sensibly greater with thresholds smaller than 250. The time becomes significantly greater for threshold greater than 250. From now on, we chose as optimal threshold the default value of 250.

Using Compatibility. We experiment the efficacy of the use of the compatibility and weights in order to choose the optimal parameter and value w.r.t. the classical greedy algorithm as explained in Sect. 4.1 by performing a comparison with a version of MEDICI that avoids this optimization and uses a greedy algorithm over the number of covered combinations. The results are shown in the chart of Fig. 5a.

We observe that using the compatibility leads to smaller test suites (*size* is around 4% smaller on average) with an increase of the time (*time*) of around 15%. Using the proposed technique slows the rate in which uncovered tuples are covered but reduces the final test suite size. For instance, Fig. 5b reports the size of still uncovered tuples (y-axis) while generating tests for one model (the number of tests already generated is on the x-axis). By maximizing the coverage of tuples (dotted line), the test generation covers more tuples at the beginning but at the end it needs new tests to cover the residual uncovered tuples. By using compatibility and by weighting the tuples (continuous line), the algorithm covers fewer tuples at the beginning but at the end all the residual tuples are easily covered with few tests. The figure shows that the problem of finding minimal test suites is not easily solvable by using pure greedy algorithms, since only near the end our proposed approach outperforms the classical greedy approach.

Number of Repetitions. Regarding the number of repetitions (options $repeat_{min}$, $repeat_{max}$, $repeat_{better}$ introduced Sect. 4.2), the situation is more clear, since the use of these options is purely incremental and increasing the

---

[4] Threshold values are in the set {0,10,50,100,250,500,1000,2000}.

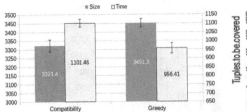 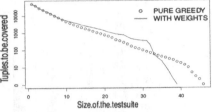

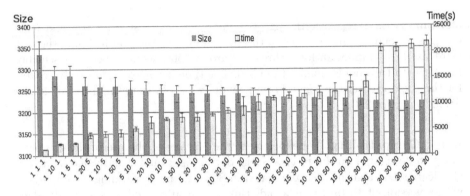

(a) Greedy vs Compatibility comparison with optimization of Sect. 4.1

(b) Tuple coverage rate for b_12 with optimization of Sect. 4.1

Fig. 5. Greedy vs Compatibility comparison

Fig. 6. Test suite *size* and *time* depending on the repetitions settings ($repeat_{\min}$ $repeat_{\max}$ $repeat_{better}$)

number of tries will always increase the time and decrease (or keep equal) the number of tests. The choice of the optimal values for these options, is however a typical multi-objective optimization, in which we try to optimize the two conflicting objectives of a small test suite size *and* a small generation time.

We test for the *repeat* options the values {1, 5, 10, 15, 20, 30, 50} which give rise to 27 valid configurations. The data for the execution of all the configurations is shown in Fig. 6 (and later in Tab. 2). The graph confirms that the two objectives of minimizing both *size* and *time* are conflicting: it is possible to obtain smaller test suite but at the expense of the test generation time. Our technique allows the tester to decide of spending more time in order to have smaller test suites. From all the configurations, we select one with ($repeat_{\min}$, $repeat_{\max}$, $repeat_{better}$) equal to (10,30,5) which represents a good compromise between time and speed and it can be considered as a good candidate for a default use of MEDICI. From now on, we will use this version for further comparison.

Comparison with Other Tools in CitLab. We perform a comparison of MEDICI with the other external tools supported by CITLAB, namely ACTS [1,21] and CASA [13,15]. ACTS is a tool developed by the NIST and implements several

Table 2. Comparison with
ACTS and CASA

	size	ΣσS	time	ΣσT
ACTS	3387.5	0.5	73.7	2.4
CASA	3185.4	4391.2	14781.2	14305.9
MEDICI	3214.4	6633.5	7871	965.4

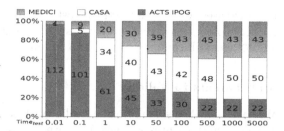

Fig. 7. Number of models that present the minimum cost for each generator for $time_{test}$ from 0.01 to 5000 secs

variants of the In Parameter Order (IPO) strategy. CASA is a tool developed at the University of Nebraska and it is based on simulated annealing, a well-studied meta-heuristic algorithm. Both support constraints, are freely available, have a large user base, and are very often used in comparison studies. Using CITLAB allows us to perform all the experiments in a very controlled environment on the same computer and using exactly the same examples.

Due to the high number of models and experiments, we can give only some cumulative results. Table 2 reports the results of the comparison: we have computed the mean, and the standard deviation (σ) of the size and time (in secs) among all the 115 runs for every model. Besides the sum of averages (*size* and *time*), the table displays the sum of the standard deviations.

Table 2 shows that ACTS is the fastest but it produces also the biggest test suites. ACTS has a deterministic algorithm and hence the standard deviation of its sizes is null. MEDICI is always slower than ACTS but it produces smaller test suites. MEDICI is around 200 times slower than ACTS, but it produces a test suite on the average 5.4% smaller than ACTS. On the other hand, CASA is the slowest of all, but it produces rather small test suites. CASA has a very high standard deviation both in time and in size (running CASA only once may not lead to the best solution of its). MEDICI is faster than CASA and it has a smaller standard deviation. CASA produces a test suite on the average 1% smaller than MEDICI, but its generation time is, on average, double that of MEDICI.

Overall, we can say that MEDICI performances are between CASA and ACTS. To better guide the user in the choice of the best test generator tool, we can roughly estimate the cost of testing (*cost*) as the total time for test generation ($time_{gen}$) plus test execution, which depends on the size of the test suite (*size*) and time necessary to execute every single test ($time_{test}$): $cost = time_{total} = time_{gen} + size \times time_{test}$. Using the data previously computed, we have also calculated the *cost* for each model and for each generator selecting a meaningful set of $time_{test}$. Fig. 7 shows the number of models that present the minimum average *cost* for each generator varying the $time_{test}$. ACTS outperforms both CASA and MEDICI if each test takes on average less than 10 seconds. This is in line with what was found by Garvin et al. [14]. If the time for executing a single test increases, CASA and MEDICI cost less than ACTS in most models. Even for very costly test execution (e.g. tests that require some human intervention), MEDICI can still compete with CASA in a meaningful number of models.

5.1 Threats to Validity

We have identified some threats to validity of the proposed study and we present some countermeasures we have employed. First, the benchmark data may be not representative. We have tried to collect models from many sources: to the best of our knowledge this is one of the biggest benchmark set of constrained combinatorial models used for test generation. The models represent a wide heterogeneous range of real life and academic models. Second, we are aware that our tool, MEDICI, may produce incomplete and incorrect test-suites that allow it to perform better than the other tools. To avoid this, besides performing unit testing we have used CITLAB "validator" [2] that checks that the resulting test suite actually cover all the required tuples (except those infeasible). We use this program for debugging MEDICI. In order to have confidence of the data obtained in the experiments, we have executed 50 runs for every configuration. Using multi-threads allows us to reduce the experimental time, but it may alter the running time, since an ordinary user will generally launch only one execution at the time. However, we believe that the comparison is still fair because we have treated all the generators in the same way.

6   Related Work

Combinatorial interaction testing has been an active area of research for many years. In a recent survey [23] Nie and Leung count more than 12 research groups that actively work on CIT area and many other groups and tools are missing in the count. In a previous survey, Grindal et al. [16] presented 16 different combination strategies, covering more than 40 papers. There are several web sites listing tools and approaches (like [24]), and publishing benchmarks and evaluations of tools and algorithms. The most studied area in CIT is the test suite generation, where several research groups continuously challenge existing algorithms and tools in order to provide better approaches in terms of execution times, supported features, and minimality of the produced test suites. Finding an algorithm that improves over the current state of the art has become a hard research task.

There are several families of CIT test generation tools, including bio-inspired, algebraic, logic-based [8], and greedy. In [7], Bryce et al. presented a general framework of *greedy* construction algorithms, in order to study the impact of each *type* of decision on the effectiveness of the resulting heuristic construction process. To this aim, they designed the framework as a nested structure of four decision layers, regarding respectively: (1) the number of instances of the process to be run, (2) the size of the pool of candidate rows from which select each new row, (3) the factor ordering selection criteria and (4) the level ordering selection criteria. The approach presented in this work fits exactly in the *greedy* category of algorithms modeled by that framework, and it is structured in order to be parametric with respect to the desired number of repetitions and the factor and level ordering strategies. Note that their study concluded that factor ordering is predominant on the resulting test suite size, and that *density*-based level ordering selection criteria was the best performing one out of those tested. In the present work, we explored original ways of redefining the *density* concept. In fact, while Bryce et al. compute it as the expected number of uncovered pairs, we weight tuple compatibility and we order parameters accordingly.

Comparison with BDD-based tools. Regarding the data structure we use, a comparison can be done with works using for CCIT binary decision diagrams (BDDs) which are similar to MDDs. Salecker et al. [25] developed a test set calculation algorithm which uses BDDs as efficient data structure to represent the combinatorial interaction testing problem with constraints. Both their and our approach are based on the modeling of the combinatorial interaction test problem with constraints as a single propositional logic formula. MDDs are a more efficient data structure for CCIT than BDDs: while modeling CCIT using BDDs requires a logic subformula corresponding to all possible alternatives for selecting values from each parameter P_i, MDDs permit to avoid the representation of these subformulas for single parameters; the benefit produced by this technique is the absence of the implicit constraints introduced to represent value selection. Unfortunately the tool presented in [25] is not available and a fair comparison is difficult. For sanity check, we found that on the same models presented in [25], MEDICI without repetitions was able to produce a smaller test suite (486.2 vs 547) and the time required in [25] was 2.3 times the time for MEDICI (687 vs 1606 secs), although our PC is only 1.8 times faster (considering the SPECint of around 42.6 vs 23.5).

Segall et al. [26] developed FoCuS, another BDD-based CCIT tool. In their approach each parameter is represented by one or more binary variables in the BDD. In order to build the BDD of valid tests, they first built for each constraint (called *restriction*) the BDD representing the set of tests allowed by it. A test is valid if and only if it is valid according to all restrictions, therefore the set of valid tests is exactly the intersection of the sets of tests allowed by the restrictions. This is computed by the conjunction of the BDDs representing these sets. Their approach is therefore very similar to ours in terms of problem representation, and we believe that also their approach would benefit from the use of MDDs instead of BDDs. Unfortunately FoCuS is not publicly available. However, again for sanity check, we found that on the same models presented in [26] MEDICI produced smaller test suites (923.5 vs 934) while published data for FoCuS do not include generation time.

7   Future Work and Conclusions

We plan to work in several directions in order to improve our approach and the tool. MEDICI (as most other test generation tools, with the notable exception of

ACTS) does not support constraints containing arithmetic expressions. CITLAB already adopts the language of propositional logic with equality and arithmetic to express constraints. To be more precise, it uses propositional calculus, enriched by the arithmetic over the integers and enumerative symbols. Although arithmetic expressions are quite rare in models published in the literature, we plan to extend MEDICI in order to deal with the arithmetic constraints expressed in CITLAB, since we believe that industrial studies often use them.

Moreover, we have experimented only pairwise coverage, even if MEDICI, ACTS, and CASA support n-wise coverage. Initial experiments shows that MEDICI performs well also with n-wise coverage, but further experiments are needed.

Overall, we believe that the technique presented in this paper and implemented in a prototype tool is a viable alternative to other commonly used tools for tests generation of combinatorial tests in the presence of constraints. Our techniques exploits an efficient data structure (MDDs) that proved to be suitable to represent and solve constrained combinatorial models and promise to scale better than BDDs [17]. We have also devised several optimizations, like *weighting*, that combined with a classic greedy approach allow us to obtain very good results, as demonstrated by our experiments. The use of the framework CITLAB has allowed us to define a wide body of benchmarks and to perform the comparison with other tools in a simple and fair way.

Acknowledgments. We thank Dario Corna for his valuable work on the implementation of MEDICI.

References

1. Advanced Combinatorial Testing System (ACTS),
   http://csrc.nist.gov/groups/SNS/acts/
2. Arcaini, P., Gargantini, A., Vavassori, P.: Validation of models and tests for constrained combinatorial interaction testing. In: The 3rd International Workshop on Combinatorial Testing (IWCT 2014) In conjunction with International Conference on Software Testing ICSTW, pp. 98–107. IEEE (2014)
3. Babar, J., Miner, A.: Meddly: Multi-terminal and edge-valued decision diagram library. In: 7th International Conference on the Quantitative Evaluation of Systems. IEEE (2010)
4. Brownlie, R., Prowse, J., Phadke, M.: Robust testing of AT&T PMX/starMAIL using OATS. AT&T Technical Journal 71(3), 41–47 (1992)
5. Bryce, R.C., Colbourn, C.J.: Prioritized interaction testing for pair-wise coverage with seeding and constraints. Information & Software Technology 48(10), 960–970 (2006)
6. Bryce, R.C., Colbourn, C.J.: One-test-at-a-time heuristic search for interaction test suites. In: Proceedings of the 9th Annual Conference on Genetic and Evolutionary Computation, GECCO 2007, pp. 1082–1089. ACM, New York (2007)
7. Bryce, R.C., Colbourn, C.J., Cohen, M.B.: A framework of greedy methods for constructing interaction test suites. In: ICSE 2005: Proc. of the 27th Int. Conf. on Software Engineering, pp. 146–155. ACM, New York (2005)

8. Calvagna, A., Gargantini, A.: A formal logic approach to constrained combinatorial testing. Journal of Automated Reasoning 45(4), 331–358 (2010)
9. Calvagna, A., Gargantini, A.: T-wise combinatorial interaction test suites construction based on coverage inheritance. Software Testing, Verification and Reliability 22(7), 507–526 (2012)
10. Calvagna, A., Gargantini, A., Vavassori, P.: Combinatorial interaction testing with CitLab. In: Sixth IEEE International Conference on Software Testing, Verification and Validation - Testing Tool Track (2013)
11. Cohen, D.M., Dalal, S.R., Fredman, M.L., Patton, G.C.: The AETG system: An approach to testing based on combinatorial design. IEEE Transactions On Software Engineering 23(7), 437–444 (1997)
12. Cohen, M., Dwyer, M., Shi, J.: Constructing interaction test suites for highly-configurable systems in the presence of constraints: A greedy approach. IEEE Trans. on Software Engineering 34(5), 633–650 (2008)
13. Covering Arrays by Simulated Annealing,
    http://cse.unl.edu/citportal/tools/casa/
14. Garvin, B.J., Cohen, M.B., Dwyer, M.B.: An improved meta-heuristic search for constrained interaction testing. In: Proceedings of the 2009 1st International Symposium on Search Based Software Engineering, SSBSE 2009, pp. 13–22. IEEE Computer Society, Washington, DC (2009)
15. Garvin, B.J., Cohen, M.B., Dwyer, M.B.: Evaluating improvements to a meta-heuristic search for constrained interaction testing. Empirical Software Engineering 16(1), 61–102 (2011)
16. Grindal, M., Offutt, J., Andler, S.F.: Combination testing strategies: a survey. Softw. Test, Verif. Reliab. 15(3), 167–199 (2005)
17. Hadzic, T., Hansen, E.R.: On automata, MDDs and BDDs in constraint satisfaction. In: Proceedings of the ECAI 2008 Workshop on Inference Methods based on Graphical Structures of Knowledge (2008)
18. Kuhn, D.R., Reilly, M.J.: An investigation of the applicability of design of experiments to software testing. In: Society, I. (ed.) 27th NASA/IEEE Software Engineering Workshop, pp. 91–95 (2002)
19. Kuhn, D.R., Wallace, D.R., Gallo, A.M.: Software fault interactions and implications for software testing. IEEE Trans. Software Eng. 30(6), 418–421 (2004)
20. Kuhn, R., Kacker, R., Lei, Y., Hunter, J.: Combinatorial software testing. Computer 42(8), 94–96 (2009)
21. Lei, Y., Kacker, R., Kuhn, D.R., Okun, V., Lawrence, J.: IPOG/IPOG-D: efficient test generation for multi-way combinatorial testing. Software Testing, Verification and Reliability 18(3), 125–148 (2008)
22. Nagayama, S., Sasao, T.: Compact representations of logic functions using heterogeneous MDDs. In: Proceedings of 33rd International Symposium on Multiple-Valued Logic, pp. 247–252 (2003)
23. Nie, C., Leung, H.: A survey of combinatorial testing. ACM Comput. Surv. 43(2), 11 (2011)
24. Pairwise web site, http://www.pairwise.org/
25. Salecker, E., Reicherdt, R., Glesner, S.: Calculating prioritized interaction test sets with constraints using binary decision diagrams. In: Proceedings of IEEE Fourth International Conference on Software Testing, Verification and Validation Workshops, pp. 278–285. IEEE Computer Society (2011)
26. Segall, I., Tzoref-Brill, R., Farchi, E.: Using binary decision diagrams for combinatorial test design. In: Proceedings of the 2011 International Symposium on Software Testing and Analysis, ISSTA 2011, pp. 254–264. ACM, New York (2011)

Formal Verification of Secure User Mode Device Execution with DMA

Oliver Schwarz[1,2] and Mads Dam[2]

[1] SICS Swedish ICT, Kista, Sweden
[2] KTH Royal Institute of Technology, Stockholm, Sweden
{oschwarz,mfd}@kth.se

Abstract. Separation between processes on top of an operating system or between guests in a virtualized environment is essential for establishing security on modern platforms. A key requirement of the underlying hardware is the ability to support multiple partitions executing on the shared hardware without undue interference. For modern processor architectures - with hardware support for memory management, several modes of operation and I/O interfaces - this is a delicate issue requiring deep analysis at both instruction set and processor implementation level. In a first attempt to rigorously answer this type of questions we introduced in previous work an information flow analysis of user program execution on an ARMv7 platform with hardware supported memory protection, but without I/O. The analysis was performed as a semi-automatic proof search procedure on top of an ARMv7 ISA model implemented in the Cambridge HOL4 theorem prover by Fox et al. The restricted platform functionality, however, makes the analysis of limited practical value. In this paper we add support for devices, including DMA, to the analysis. To this end, we propose an approach to device modeling based on the idea of executing devices nondeterministically in parallel with the (single-core) deterministic processor, covering a fine granularity of interactions between the model components. Based on this model and taking the ARMv7 ISA as an example, we provide HOL4 proofs of several noninterference-oriented isolation properties for a partition executing in the presence of devices which potentially use DMA or interrupts.

Keywords: Peripheral devices, DMA, separation, isolation, user mode execution, ARM, formal hardware/software co-verification, theorem proving, HOL4.

1 Introduction

Modern computing platforms usually execute multiple kinds of services together. Entertainment software runs next to online-banking applications. Personal communication services run next to business software. For security, there is a strong need to execute processes in isolation from each other, such that mutual influence is minimized and their integrity and confidentiality fully protected. Some

E. Yahav (Ed.): HVC 2014, LNCS 8855, pp. 236–251, 2014.

approaches attempt to achieve this level of isolation within the commodity operating system, while others base upon separation kernels, micro kernels or virtualization. In all cases, the hardware platform is required to allow for strong compartmentalization of process execution. Untrusted processes should neither be able to influence processes at higher trust levels nor to learn anything about their state of execution. Basic protection is enabled by several privilege rings of operation and memory protection/management units (MPU/MMU), controlled by control registers, coprocessors and configurations in memory. Information can potentially flow via multiple system components and operations, such as memory accesses by the CPU, directly accessible registers, side effects of control registers, coprocessors, timing channels, device ports, device accesses to memory, or interrupts, to just name a few. Therefore it is crucial to understand and document the information flows that are possible on a complex platform. These flows are not always obvious. For example, on some x86 processors it is possible for low-privilege code to overwrite higher privilege code by writing to an address that usually refers to the video card [5]. To enable this attack, it suffices to flip a configuration bit usually accessible from the low privilege level. On ARM, comparison instructions change flags in the current program status register (CPSR). When switching processes, those flags therefore need to be cleared or reloaded from the register bank of the invoked process. Peripheral devices further increase a system's complexity. Assigning them to only one process per device is sometimes insufficient to prevent information flow between processes. If a device has the capability of performing direct memory access (DMA), it can be programmed to circumvent the access policy of the MMU unless advanced hardware support for virtualization is provided and this support is soundly configured, which is by no means self-evident. Even if the configuration of DMA controllers is monitored to prevent copying between partitions, undesired information flows can still occur. For example, a device can fire an interrupt depending on the content of memory controlled by a user process, allowing for side channel communication based on the delays introduced by such interrupts. Given the complexity of modern hardware, it is not trivial to avoid misconfiguration. In previous work [10] we introduced a formal information flow analysis of ARMv7 user mode execution on instruction set architecture (ISA) level, however, not yet covering devices. With devices, the system's state increases and so does the set of possible information flows. CPU and multiple DMA devices with unknown behaviour can execute in parallel, possibly accessing the same memory, with an unknown interleaving.

This paper presents the following contributions. First, we extend the Cambridge HOL4 model of the ARM architecture [7] by a general device framework. To the best of our knowledge, this is the first theorem prover model for devices capable of reasoning on DMA. It is sufficiently detailed to capture possible information flows on modern systems. The adaptation to other processor architectures can be done with a minor effort. Second, we identify several secure device configurations. Since the focus is on platform information flow security rather than functionality, we do not restrict verification to concrete device specifications, but provide a suitable abstraction. For the verification of a system's separation properties, it is then sufficient to show that the configuration of the system devices complies with the identified abstract requirements. Finally, based on the proposed configurations and the device framework, we prove the following partitioning-related properties of the ARMv7 architecture with devices:

1. *Non-infiltration* states that the user mode execution of an ARMv7 processor is independent of devices that neither write to the memory accessed by the active process nor fire interrupts.
2. The integrity property of *extended non-exfiltration* states in turn that user mode processes are unable to influence devices that do not read from CPU-modifiable memory. Moreover, other protected resources[1], such as memory of neighboring processes, can not be modified by the process. That is true even if dedicated peripheral devices do access these resources in parallel. More specifically, the transformation of these resources depends only on such dedicated and inaccessible devices.
3. The third property, *filtered device non-infiltration*, states that devices which operate on disjunct resources can not influence each other without the interaction of the CPU.

One of the added challenges in the formulation and verification of the properties compared to [10] is that - with CPU and devices operating in parallel - different principles can cause different effects on the shared state. Covering separation during user mode execution, the results can be applied in the verification of hypervisors, separation kernels and operating systems. To the best of our knowledge, this is the first work on non-interference like platform properties for autonomous device execution.

2   Related Work

Hillebrand et al. [9] describe a pen and paper model, later formalized in Isabelle/HOL [1], for a memory-mapped hard disk integrated with a RISC architecture. The model includes side effects on device port reads/writes, interrupts and an external environment. The latter is also used to realize non-determinism, especially in timing matters. Direct memory access is not covered. Furthermore, unlike ARM, the processor model does not perform multiple memory operations per instruction (instruction fetches are assumed to not refer to device ports), which allows for executing processor and device steps in an interleaved way after one another, without considering device progress within a single processor step. In [1] they describe the exploitation of an oracle that enables the sequentialization of the concurrent execution of devices and CPU. While the concrete order of events in a system is hard to predict, this oracle allows for the quantification over all execution orders and external inputs. These results were applied in the functional correctness verification of a microkernel [2]. The system architecture includes concurrent devices; besides a hard disk used for page fault handling also

---

[1] See Section 6.3 for the complete list of protected resources.

devices accessible by user processes are considered. Using refinement techniques, the authors were able to establish a simulation relation between an abstract microkernel programming framework and the instruction level. On the abstract levels devices are represented as ghost data structures.

Duan and Regehr [4] describe a general device model framework integrated with the HOL4 model for ARM6 by Anthony Fox [6] in a lock-step manner. They provide a proof of concept for a UART device and its driver, presenting statements on functionality, (memory) safety and timing. Similar to [9] and [1], they model side effects of memory mapped accesses to device ports and exploit input streams. Again, DMA is not supported. The authors prove that the integration of new devices to the system does not cause new undefined behaviour and preserves already established system predicates. This allows to verify driver correctness for one device at a time, but clearly would not hold for DMA devices. In his PhD thesis [3], Duan integrates his model into the Cambridge model of ARMv7 and adds reasoning about interrupts. Since ARMv7 has instructions that perform multiple memory accesses, device port reads/writes have been integrated into the primitives for memory accesses. Also autonomous device transitions are integrated into the execution cycle, however, they occur only once per instruction. In a DMA setting this is not sufficient since physical memory can be changed by devices between two memory accesses from the CPU side. In order to reason about DMA with a finer granularity and to allow for non-deterministic device progress, we propose a different model in Section 5.

Monniaux modelled a USB controller in C and used an extended version of the Astrée static analyzer to verify that neither controller nor its driver will transfer data incorrectly [11]. He includes asynchronous DMA into his reasoning. By modelling the controller's behaviour with non-deterministic choices, an over-approximation is achieved. Isolation from untrusted software is not discussed.

XMHF [12] is a hypervisor framework for x86 exploiting virtualization support, in particular the DMA protection of Intel Vt-d and AMD's device exclusion vectors. The framework allows unmodified guests direct device access. System devices are included in the attacker model. Exploiting the model checker CBMC, mainly memory integrity is verified. As for direct memory access, CBMC verifies that the control register value written to the DMA protection hardware register has the bit set which enables DMA protection. The DMA table is manually audited. However, it seems that the actual effects of devices or the DMA protection unit are not part of the model. In the present paper we focus on systems without hardware support for virtualization.

The properties shown in this paper are inspired by Heitmeyer et al. [8], who formulated non-infiltration and non-exfiltration for a separation kernel. We adapt those properties to a platform with DMA devices and a CPU in user mode.

3   The HOL4 ARM Model

We base our work on Fox et al's monadic HOL4 ISA model [7] of ARMv7 platforms without hardware extensions such as TrustZone or virtualization support.

$$\texttt{arm\_state} = <|\ \begin{array}{ll} \texttt{psrs} & : \texttt{PSRName} \rightarrow \texttt{ARMpsr;} \\ \texttt{regs} & : \texttt{RName} \rightarrow \texttt{word32;} \\ \texttt{memory} & : \texttt{word32} \rightarrow \texttt{word8;} \\ \texttt{coproc} & : \texttt{coprocessors;} \\ \texttt{accesses} & : \texttt{memory\_accesslist;} \\ \texttt{misc} & : \texttt{Monitors}\ \#\ \texttt{ARMinfo}\ \#\ \texttt{bool}\ \#\ \texttt{bool}\ |>; \end{array}$$

Fig. 1. The ARM state in HOL4

Figure 1 shows a simplified definition of the processor state in this model. The function `psrs` returns the value of a processor state register (of type `ARMpsr`). The processor state registers include the current program status register, `CPSR`, in addition to the banked psrs `SPSR_m` for each privileged mode `m`, except for system mode. The ARMv7 core provides seven processor modes: one non-privileged user mode `usr`, and six privileged modes, activated when an exception (such as an interrupt) is invoked. The function `regs` takes a register name and returns its value. The ARM registers include sixteen general purpose registers ($\texttt{r0} - \texttt{r15}$) that are available from all modes in addition to the banked registers of each privileged mode that are available only in that mode. The function `memory` maps an address (`word32`) to a byte (`word8`). Caches are not represented in the model. The field `coproc` represents the set of coprocessor registers in `CP14` and `CP15` implicitly influencing execution, to a large extent even user-mode/exception execution. The field `misc` represents exclusive monitors for synchronization purposes, general information about the state, e.g. the architecture version, if the system is waiting for an interrupt etc, and `accesses` records the accesses to the memory.

A *computation* in the monadic HOL4 ARM model is a term of the type

$$\alpha\ \texttt{M} = \texttt{arm\_state} \mapsto (\alpha, \texttt{arm\_state})\ \texttt{error\_option}$$

where `error_option` is a datatype defined as:

$$(\alpha, \beta)\ \texttt{error\_option} = \texttt{ValueState of } \alpha \Rightarrow \beta\ |\ \texttt{Error of string}$$

Computations act on a state (`arm_state`) and return either `ValueState` a s, a new state s along with a return value a of type α, or an error e (if the computation is underspecified by the ARM specification). The monad unit `constT` injects a value into a computation, i.e. `constT` a $s = \texttt{ValueState}\ a\ s$, while binding is a sequential composition operation

$$f_1 \gg=_e f_2 = \lambda s.\texttt{case } f_1\ s \texttt{ of Error } c \rightarrow \texttt{Error } c$$
$$|\ \texttt{ValueState } a\ s' \rightarrow \texttt{if } e\ s' \texttt{ then } f_2\ a\ s' \texttt{ else } f_1\ s.$$

That is, if e holds in the final state of f_1, the return value of f_1 is passed to f_2 as the input parameter, otherwise f_2 is not executed. In addition to unit and binding, the ARM monadic specification uses standard constructs for lambda, full conditional, `let`, and `case`, as well as the monad operations parallel composition, positive conditional (`condT` e $f = \texttt{if } e \texttt{ then } f \texttt{ else constT } ()$), error (`errorT` $a = \texttt{Error } a$), and an iterator. Values of state components can be obtained and set by `readT` $f = \lambda y.(\texttt{ValueState } (f\ y)\ y)$ and `writeT` $f = \lambda y.(\texttt{ValueState } ()\ (f\ y))$.

4   Memory Management

The Memory Management Unit (MMU) enforces memory access policies and is therefore crucial for isolation. MMU configurations consist of page tables in memory and dedicated registers of CP15. Specific to ARM is the possibility of partitioning pages into collections of memory regions (*domains*), each representing one security role. The coprocessor registers involved are SCTLR, TTBR0 and DACR. The SCTLR register determines whether the MMU is enabled, TTBR0 contains the base address of the page table, and DACR manages the ARM domains.

In [10] we extended the ARM model with MMU functionality. The extended model defines two key functions, permitted, to account for access permissions, and mmu_setup, to reflect a "good configuration" property. The permission evaluation function permitted a b_w (v_s, v_t, v_d) b_p m takes as parameters an address a, a flag b_w indicating whether reading or writing access is to be evaluated, the values of SCTLR, TTBR0 and DACR, a flag b_p indicating whether permissions are to be checked against a privileged mode, and the memory m containing the page tables. The pair of booleans returned by permitted states whether the access permission on the specified location is defined in the given configuration, and the outcome of that decision (true if access is granted). Here, we apply a basic version of permitted, supporting one-level page tables with an identity address translation, but including the interpretation of ARM domains. It is shown that permitted is defined for all addresses in all reachable states.

The history of memory accesses is tracked in the accesses ghost field of the machine state, allowing to compute the set of memory locations accessed by an instruction. To stop computation after the first access violation, $\gg=_{nav}$ has been chosen as standard binding operator. The property nav s holds if there is no access violation recorded in state s. Formally, this is the case if there is no entry in the access list of machine state s that causes permitted to return a negative answer in the current configuration of s. The recording of an access always happens before the access itself.

We finally need to formulate a suitable well-formedness condition for the MMU configuration. Let accessible i a express that address a is readable and writable by user process i. Other, more refined, static user level access policies can be supported with minor effort. The predicate mmu_setup i s holds if (i) the MMU configuration $((d,p) = $ permitted a b_w (mmu_registers s) $\bot$ s.memory) for any address a and access type b_w is defined (i.e., d is true), (ii) the state s implements the desired access policy for process i (i.e., $p = $ accessible i a), and (iii) none of the active page tables in s (represented by the address set page_table_adds s) is accessible according to the policy.

mmu_setup i s :=
$\forall a, w, d, p.\ ((d,p) = $ permitted a b_w (mmu_registers s) $\bot$ s.memory)
$\quad \Rightarrow d \wedge (p = $ accessible i $a) \ \wedge \ (a \in ($ page_table_adds $s) \Rightarrow \neg$ accessible i $a)$

For the properties shown in Section 6 we furthermore prohibit user space processes to access device ports by assuming that the (state-independent) set of device addresses and accessible addresses are disjoint for every user process.

5   Device Model Framework

We present a general device model framework, capable of reasoning on DMA devices and with the ambition to cover all possible executions of a platform where the single-core processor and multiple devices run in parallel. In practice, changes to shared resources such as memory happen asynchronously and in a practically unpredictable order. We apply a non-deterministic approach that takes into account all possible interleavings and - to be conservative on timing behaviour - all possible durations of device and CPU actions, without restrictions on deadlines. Naturally, this does not allow to reason on whether an operation will be finished before a certain event or not. A timing accurate model would need to take CPU and system implementation specific details into account, including caches, MMU implementation specifics (such as the translation lookaside buffer), pipeline architecture and bus contention protocols. Models at this level of detail are surely interesting, but likely to be vastly more complex. The main challenge when integrating DMA into a device model is that memory can potentially change at any time, for example, between reading two words belonging to a multiple load instruction. Also inter-device communication can occur in any order and granularity. This precludes models that synchronize CPU and devices only between different CPU instructions. To address this challenge and allow for asynchronous device execution, we augment the CPU model with an abstract scheduler as suggested in [1], an oracle of the type

$$\texttt{oracle} : \texttt{num} \rightarrow (\texttt{dev\_name} \ \# \ \texttt{word32 option}) \ \texttt{option}$$

The oracle provides a non-deterministic sequence of activity entries where the n-th activity entry $\texttt{oracle} \ n$ is either $\texttt{NONE}$ (then the CPU is progressed rather than a device) or a tuple $\texttt{SOME} \ (d, e_{iopt})$, indicating the device with identifier ($\texttt{dev\_name}$) d to progress one step, possibly in the context of the optional external 32-bit input e_{iopt}. We assume processor liveness: $\forall n. \ \exists m. \ (m \geq n) \wedge (\texttt{oracle} \ m = \texttt{NONE})$. Liveness of devices can be optionally included, but is not required for the properties we show in this paper. To include devices into the machine state, $\texttt{arm\_state}$ is extended by the following components:

```
devices   : dev_rec;
ext_out   : dev_name → word32 list;
int_fired : bool;
counter   : num
```

The record $\texttt{devices}$ subsumes the states of all devices [2]. The external output is represented by a finite stream of 32-bit words for each device, accessible via the map $\texttt{ext\_out}$, mapping each device identifier to the list of outputs produced so far for that device. Whether an interrupt has been fired during the current execution cycle is stored in $\texttt{int\_fired}$. Fast interrupts or advanced interrupt controllers are not part of the model. Finally, $\texttt{counter}$ points to the current position in the oracle index and is incremented every time the oracle is invoked. Devices can progress in one of four ways:

---

[2] We notate $\texttt{devices}.d$ for the state of the device with identifier d in the record $\texttt{devices}$.

- *Autonomously*: A device may make processor-independent progress, either by entirely internal actions or by receiving external inputs, accessing memory, raising interrupts, or producing external outputs. The function

  ```
  progress : device ↦ (word32 option)
           ↦ (mem_req option # bool # word32 option # device) option
  ```

  takes as arguments a device state D and a possible external input e_{iopt}. It returns either an "error" (NONE) representing undefined behaviour or a tuple $(r_{opt}, b_{int}, e_{oopt}, D')$ with an optional read/write access request r_{opt} to the system's memory bus (including an address and the access type), a flag b_{int} indicating a possible interrupt, an optional external output e_{oopt} and the updated device state D'. This function is used to progress devices with a non-deterministic frequency after every executed CPU instruction and between memory accesses made by the CPU or other devices.
- *Upon reception of a pending reply to a memory bus read*: As a result of an autonomous step, a device can send a read request to the bus, in order to read from the system memory or from the port of another device. The result is communicated to the device by invoking the **receive** operation:

  ```
  receive : device ↦ mem_req ↦ mem_answer ↦ device option
  ```

  For a given device state D and request r being answered, **receive** D r v passes the read value v (as either byte or word) to D and returns either an error (NONE) or the updated device D'. Write operations requested by devices do not have an answer and thus change only the memory, but not the device. We assume that reads are atomic operations and the memory bus will always complete an issued read before handling new operations. In other words, we exclude scenarios where a device notices that one of its ports is being read and already starts side effect computations affecting memory or other system components without first returning the requested value. That is no limitation for the properties we show in this paper, since we do not consider port accesses in them. As for reads from physical memory, for any race condition outcome there is always one initiation of the oracle that represents this outcome within the model.
- *As side effect on port reads*: The CPU or another device may read from an address that is mapped to a device. This address can belong to a device register, but in general it is not required that such a register is physically existing, for example when the address is associated with a side effect. We therefore use the general term *port* rather than register. We assume atomic 32-bit accesses to device ports and that port accesses are not cached. The function

  ```
  d_read : device ↦ word32 ↦ (word32 # device) option
  ```

  takes as arguments a device state D and the port number indicating which port of the device is to be read. A special data structure of the model maps any virtual address to either physical memory or a device identifier together with a port number. The result of **d_read** is either NONE or the read 32-bit value together with a possibly updated device state D'.

advance_single f n := readT $(\lambda s.\ s.\text{devices})$ $\gg=_T$
$\qquad\qquad\quad$ $(\lambda \hat{D}.\ (\text{case oracle } n \text{ of NONE} \Rightarrow \text{constT } ()$
$\qquad\qquad\quad$ $|\text{SOME } (d, e_{iopt}) \Rightarrow$
$\qquad\qquad\quad$ condT $(f\ d)$
$\qquad\qquad\qquad$ $(\text{case progress } \hat{D}.d\ e_{iopt} \text{ of NONE} \Rightarrow \text{errorT } \epsilon$
$\qquad\qquad\qquad$ $|\text{SOME } (r_{opt}, b_{int}, e_{oopt}, D') \Rightarrow$
$\qquad\qquad\qquad\quad$ update_device d D' $\gg=_T$
$\qquad\qquad\qquad\quad$ $(\lambda u.$ update_output d e_{oopt} $\gg=_T$
$\qquad\qquad\qquad\quad$ $(\lambda u.$ condT b_{int}
$\qquad\qquad\qquad\qquad$ $(\text{writeT } (\lambda s.\ s \text{ with int\_fired} := \text{T}))$ $\gg=_T$
$\qquad\qquad\qquad\qquad$ $(\lambda u.\ \text{case } r_{opt} \text{ of NONE} \Rightarrow \text{constT } ()$
$\qquad\qquad\qquad\qquad$ $|\text{SOME } r \Rightarrow \text{mem\_acc\_by\_dev } r\ d))))))$ $\gg=_T$
$\qquad\qquad\quad$ $(\lambda u.$ increment_counter$))$

Fig. 2. The advance_single computation

– *As side effect on port writes*: the function

$$\text{d\_write : device} \mapsto \text{word32} \mapsto \text{word32} \mapsto \text{device option}$$

takes as arguments a device state D, the port number indicating which port of the device is to be written to and the 32-bit value to be written. It returns either an error (NONE) or the updated device state D'.

Different types of devices will have different behaviour. That is, the concrete functionalities of the device functions depend on the addressed device. While d_write and d_read are integrated into the existing memory access primitives of the ARM model (similar to [3]), progress and receive are used to realize autonomous progress of devices. Figure 2 defines advance_single f n that uses the oracle at position n to determine the next device to progress autonomously and that updates the state with the effect of this progress accordingly. Subsequently, resulting memory requests are realized (including possible side effects when directed to other devices) and finally counter is increased. A filtering predicate f can be used to apply those steps only to devices d for which f d holds. Here, update_device and update_output update the devices and ext_out components of the current state, respectively, and mem_acc_by_dev r d realizes the memory access request r on behalf of device d. Our model does not include any IOMMU. The repeated execution of advance_single is realized by advance, where for $n > 0$, advance f n traverses the oracle with filtering predicate f up to oracle position n and advance f 0 traverses the oracle until a NONE as activity entry indicates that execution will continue on the CPU side. The advance computation will synchronize devices and CPU before each memory bus access (for memory mapped ports and physical memory) of the CPU[3]

---

[3] Consequently, accesses to the shared state, in particular the memory bus, determine the granularity of the system.

```
next := (clear_alist ≫=
        (λu. readT (λs. s.int_fired ∧ ¬s.psrs(0, CPSR).I) ≫=
        (λb. if (¬b) then
                waiting_for_interrupt ≫=
                (λw. condT (¬w)
                    (fetch_instruction ≫=ᴛ
                    (λ(o, i). is_viol ≫=ᴛ (λa. clear_alist ≫=
                    (λu. if a then prefetch_abort
                         else (execute i ≫=ᴛ (λu. is_viol ≫=ᴛ
                                (λa. condT a
                                    (clear_alist ≫=
                                    (λu. data_abort)))))))))))) ≫=ᴛ
                (λu. advance all 0)
             else take_irq_exception ≫= (λu. clear_interrupts)))))
```

Fig. 3. The next computation

and additionally between two execution cycles. The model supports instruction fetching from device addresses, but we assume that page table walks are not performed on device ports. In the properties shown in this paper we assume an MMU setting that prohibits both, by choosing device addresses, page table addresses and user space accessible memory to be disjoint.

Incorporating the MMU and device extension, the instruction execution function next (Fig. 3) involves the following functionality: if an interrupt is pending and not masked, an interrupt exception is taken. Otherwise, the CPU may (if requested so by the previous instruction) wait for an interrupt or fetch and execute the next instruction pointed to by the program counter. If an access violation is recorded during instruction fetching or execution, a prefetch or data abort exception is initiated. The access list is cleared between the single steps and unconditional binding ≫=ᴛ is used occasionally, preventing the execution from halting and instead allowing the initiation of exceptions and the detection of possible further violations. In addition to the synchronization phases before any of the CPU's memory operations, possible autonomous device steps are considered after each instruction execution, in order to account for interrupt initiations.

As discussed earlier, our model is not clock accurate. While this is common with related work, usually a fixed duration is assumed for all instructions [3]. In our model, durations are non-deterministic, controlled by the oracle. However, given a specific oracle sequence, memory extensive instructions generally consume more oracle entries (i.e, time). For the properties of this paper and the targeted abstraction level, concrete instruction time is not relevant.

6   Security Properties

We next turn to formalizing several partitioning properties in terms of non-infiltration and non-exfiltration (cf. [8]), adapted to our setting, i.e., arbitrary and unknown user mode code executing on an ARMv7 CPU and in parallel with DMA devices. The isolation does not rely on an IOMMU. Together with a proper separation kernel (configuring devices, mediating user registers etc.) the discussed properties allow for establishing full process isolation within a system.

6.1   Suitable Device Configurations

Since isolation between CPU and DMA devices requires controlled device behaviour, we first describe possible device configurations that we consider secure. They allow the devices to change their internal state in an arbitrary way, but impose restrictions on DMA and interrupts. Kernels are responsible for realizing such a device configuration, in order to guarantee that process isolation is maintained when yielding to user mode. We expect those configurations to stay preserved throughout the whole user mode execution (while access to device ports is forbidden to both CPU and other devices). Formally, a configuration C is called *invariant* if it is preserved over autonomous steps, including the reception of replies to autonomously issued read requests:

$$\text{invariant } C := \forall D.\, C\, D \Rightarrow$$
$$(\forall e_{iopt},\, r_{opt},\, b_{int},\, e_{oopt},\, D'.$$
$$(\text{progress } D\, e_{iopt} = \text{SOME } (r_{opt}, b_{int}, e_{oopt}, D')) \Rightarrow C\, D')$$
$$\wedge\, (\forall r,\, v,\, D'.\, (\text{receive } D\, r\, v = \text{SOME } D') \Rightarrow C\, D')$$

A property P holds on a device D in a *stable* way if it is established by an invariant configuration C:

$$\text{stable } P\, D := \exists C.\, \text{invariant } C\, \wedge\, C\, D\, \wedge\, (\forall D'.\, C\, D' \Rightarrow P\, D')$$

The stable properties we are interested in guarantee that devices are configured in a way that prevents them from communicating with other devices, running into an undefined state, accessing memory out of well-defined boundaries or firing interrupts in dependency on DMA operations. We believe that many devices (e.g., timers or DMA controllers) can be configured to respect those restrictions. The `restricted_dma` predicate holds if a device is configured to restrict its DMA requests to a set A of memory addresses.

$$\text{restricted\_dma } A\, D := \forall e_{iopt},\, r,\, b_{int},\, e_{oopt},\, D'.$$
$$(\text{progress } D\, e_{iopt} = \text{SOME } (\text{SOME } r, b_{int}, e_{oopt}, D')) \Rightarrow (\text{access\_request\_map } r \subseteq A)$$

Here, `access_request_map` maps a memory request to the set of byte addresses it involves. A device is called `silent` if A does not include device ports. Devices not firing interrupts are called `interrupt_free`. We say that a device is `errorfree`, if `progress` and `receive` do not return NONE for any inputs. Based on those properties, we distinguish three specific device configurations: devices involving DMA operations on the memory of the active process, devices involving DMA operations on the memory of other processes, and devices that are allowed to fire an interrupt.

$$\text{own\_devices } i\, D := \text{stable (restricted\_dma (own\_add } i))\, D$$
$$\wedge\, \text{stable interrupt\_free } D$$
$$\text{foreign\_devices } i\, D := \text{stable (restricted\_dma (foreign\_add } i))\, D$$
$$\wedge\, \text{stable interrupt\_free } D$$
$$\text{interrupt\_devices } D := \text{stable (restricted\_dma empty\_set)}\, D$$

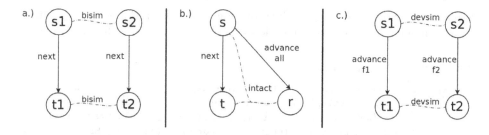

Fig. 4. a.) non-infiltration, b.) extended non-exfiltration, c.) filtered device non-infiltration

Here, `own_add` i is the set of addresses belonging to process or partition i, while `foreign_add` i spans exactly over the other user partitions. We do not allow a device to do both, accessing memory and firing interrupts. This is to prevent information flow from a user process' memory to another process' perception of execution time. [4] For a given user process i we assign each device d to one of three classes, `OWN` i d, `FOREIGN` i d or `INTERRUPT` d, that correspond to the configurations `own_devices` i D, `foreign_devices` i D and `interrupt_devices` D, respectively. While configurations refer to a concrete device state D, device classes are state-independent. We require that each device is in at least one of the three classes. The system properties discussed in the following subsections have a correct configuration of the devices as a prerequisite. The configuration of each device in the current state is supposed to follow the specification of the given class. Moreover, devices are not allowed to communicate with other devices or to run into an underspecified state.

> `device_setup` i $s := \forall d.$
>   (`OWN` i $d \Rightarrow$ `own_devices` i s.devices.d)
> $\wedge$ (`FOREIGN` i $d \Rightarrow$ `foreign_devices` i s.devices.d)
> $\wedge$ (`INTERRUPT` $d \Rightarrow$ `interrupt_devices` s.devices.d)
> $\wedge$ `stable errorfree` s.devices.d $\wedge$ `stable silent` s.devices.d

6.2   Non-infiltration

Confidentiality of the kernel and neighboring user processes (including their devices) and the integrity of the active user process is guaranteed by non-infiltration, a noninterference-like property at the user mode single instruction level. Consider two machine states in user mode that are *low equivalent* in the sense that the two states agree on the resources (devices, registers and memory) that are permitted to influence user mode execution, but do not necessarily

---

[4] Alternative configurations could allow DMA devices to fire interrupts, as long as those interrupts are masked while foreign processes are executing. However, this requires a very careful and more complex design at kernel level to avoid timing channels when interrupts occur close to context switches.

agree on other resources. Non-infiltration (Fig. 4.a) holds if the poststates, after execution of one instruction, remain low equivalent (or produce the same error).

Theorem 1. *Non-infiltration*

$$\forall s_1, s_2, i. (\text{mode } s_1 = \text{mode } s_2 = \text{usr}) \land \text{mmu\_setup } i \ s_1 \land \text{mmu\_setup } i \ s_2$$
$$\land \text{device\_setup } i \ s_1 \land \text{device\_setup } i \ s_2 \land \text{bisim } i \ s_1 \ s_2$$
$$\Rightarrow (\exists t_1, t_2. (\text{next } s_1 = \text{ValueState } () \ t_1) \land (\text{next } s_2 = \text{ValueState } () \ t_2)$$
$$\land \text{bisim } i \ t_1 \ t_2) \lor (\exists e. (\text{next } s_1 = \text{Error } e) \land (\text{next } s_2 = \text{Error } e))$$

The relation **bisim** is the low equivalence relation. User mode processes are allowed to be influenced by the user mode registers, the memory assigned to them, devices with access to that memory, interrupt devices, the CPSR, the coprocessors, pending access violations and the **misc** state component. Formally:

bisim $i \ s_1 \ s_2 :=$
  $(s_1.\text{counter} = s_2.\text{counter}) \land (s_1.\text{int\_fired} = s_2.\text{int\_fired})$
  $\land \text{equal\_user\_regs } s_1 \ s_2 \land (\forall a. \text{accessible } i \ a \Rightarrow (s_1.\text{memory } a = s_2.\text{memory } a))$
  $\land (\forall d. \text{ OWN } i \ d \lor \text{INTERRUPT } d$
    $\Rightarrow (s_1.\text{devices}.d = s_2.\text{devices}.d) \land (s_1.\text{ext\_out } d = s_2.\text{ext\_out } d))$
  $\land (s_1.\text{psrs}(\text{CPSR}) = s_2.\text{psrs}(\text{CPSR})) \land (s_1.\text{coproc.state} = s_2.\text{coproc.state})$
  $\land (\text{nav } s_1 = \text{nav } s_2) \land (s_1.\text{misc} = s_2.\text{misc})$

Non-infiltration guarantees that system components outside the **bisim** relation can not give rise to information flow. In particular, privileged registers, memory foreign to the current process and devices that operate on such memory can not influence the execution on the CPU. External output has no impact on other components either. However, it was included into the relation to obtain guarantees on that information from the kernel and neighboring processes can not be leaked through the system's output, as long as the configuration of the devices producing that output prevents them from accessing confidential memory.

6.3   Extended Non-exfiltration

Non-exfiltration guarantees the integrity of resources foreign to the active user process. Given a valid configuration for user process i active, the execution of a single instruction in user mode will not modify any other resources but those considered to be modifiable by i. In [10] this was expressed by the equality of protected components in pre- and poststate. However, when some of those protected components are modified by devices executing in parallel, this equality can not be proven. Therefore, we extend non-exfiltration to a triangle shaped property (compare Fig. 4.b), in which the poststate t of a system-wide progress is compared to both, the prestate s and a third state of comparison r that is the result of applying only the effects of the device operations to the prestate.

Theorem 2. *Extended Non-exfiltration*

$$\forall s, t, r, i. (\text{mode } s = \text{usr}) \land \text{mmu\_setup } i \ s \land \text{device\_setup } i \ s$$
$$\land (\text{next } s = \text{ValueState } () \ t) \land (\text{advance all } t.\text{counter } s = \text{ValueState } () \ r)$$
$$\Rightarrow \text{intact } i \ s \ t \ r$$

For synchronization, advance is applied up to the oracle counter state in post-state t. The intact relation between the prestate s with active process i, the poststate t and the comparison state r guarantees that coprocessors and memory not belonging to any user process remain unchanged. The memory of neighboring user processes, new interrupts, and devices that do not access memory of i, are determined by the device operations only. In particular, they can not be influenced by writing to the memory of i. The only modifiable registers are the CPSR, user mode registers, and the PSR and the link register of the mode in t.

intact i s t r :=
   $(t.\text{coproc} = s.\text{coproc}) \land (\forall a.(\forall j.\neg\text{accessible } j \ a) \Rightarrow (t.\text{memory } a = s.\text{memory } a))$
   $\land (\forall a, j. (i \neq j) \land \text{accessible } j \ a \Rightarrow (t.\text{memory } a = r.\text{memory } a))$
   $\land (t.\text{int\_fired} = r.\text{int\_fired})$
   $\land (\forall d. \text{FOREIGN } i \ d \lor \text{INTERRUPT } d$
      $\Rightarrow (t.\text{devices}.d = r.\text{devices}.d) \land (t.\text{ext\_out } d = r.\text{ext\_out } d))$
   $\land (\forall q. \ q \notin \text{accessible\_regs (mode } t) \Rightarrow (t.\text{regs}(q) = s.\text{regs}(q)))$
   $\land (\forall p. \ p \notin \{\text{CPSR}, \text{spsr\_(mode } t)\} \Rightarrow (t.\text{psrs}(p) = s.\text{psrs}(p)))$

6.4 Filtered Device Non-infiltration

In addition to the non-infiltration property of the overall system, we provide one for device activities only. It can be combined with extended non-exfiltration to guarantee that devices not accessing the active partition form their own group of resources which executes independently from the CPU. Formally, filtered device non-infiltration (Fig. 4.c) states that devices configured to not access more than the memory of active process i (devices d for which OWN i d holds) cannot influence devices not operating on that memory. Consequently, when comparing two systems and their executions, removing the activities of devices in the OWN class from one of the executions (through the filtering predicate of advance) will not change the effects that the other devices can observe.

Theorem 3. *Filtered Device Non-Infiltration*

$$f_2 = (\lambda d. \ f_1 \ d \land \neg\text{OWN } i \ d) \land \text{devsim } i \ s_1 \ s_2$$
$$\land \text{ device\_setup } i \ s_1 \land (\text{advance } f_1 \ n \ s = \text{ValueState } () \ t_1)$$
$$\land \text{ device\_setup } i \ s_2 \land (\text{advance } f_2 \ n \ s = \text{ValueState } () \ t_2)$$
$$\Rightarrow \text{devsim } i \ t_1 \ t_2$$

The devsim equivalence relation describes the resources visible to interrupt devices and to devices that operate on memory of non-active user processes.

devsim i s_1 s_2 :=
   $(s_1.\text{counter} = s_2.\text{counter}) \land (s_1.\text{int\_fired} = s_2.\text{int\_fired})$
   $\land (\forall a, j. (i \neq j) \land \text{accessible } j \ a \Rightarrow (s_1.\text{memory } a = s_2.\text{memory } a))$
   $\land (\forall d. \neg\text{OWN } i \ d \Rightarrow (s_1.\text{devices}.d = s_2.\text{devices}.d) \land (s_1.\text{ext\_out } d = s_2.\text{ext\_out } d))$

7   Implementation

We proved the theorems of Section 6 for the ARMv7 platform inside HOL4. This work extends the proof presented in [10], in which we showed non-infiltration, non-exfiltration and mode switching properties for ARMv7 user mode execution on ISA level without devices. Given the complexity of the ARM model and the instruction set, we exploited automation based on a sound, but incomplete inference system. For example, for two computations f and g that both preserve non-infiltration, the inference rule for sequential composition derives that also $f \gg_{\mathtt{nav}} g$ preserves non-infiltration. We have proven further rules for parallel composition, loops, alternatives, lambda abstraction and other constructors of the operational semantics. They enabled us to develop a proof tool for relational and invariant reasoning that - after being provided with the desired properties for primitive operations - was able to discharge large parts of the proof obligations (but not all) automatically. Details are discussed in [10].

In the present extended work, the separation properties had to be proven manually for advance, mainly because they would not hold for intermediate computations in isolation. Due to the complexity, this was one of the main challenges. We followed a bottom-up approach. Basic properties on mem_acc_by_dev, a rather extensive case analysis and automatic simplification allowed for the verification of properties on advance_single. This step often required to split the analysis into the effects on the device currently progressed by advance_single and the effects on all other devices. Finally, properties for advance were proven by induction. In order to allow for the continued application of the proof tool to the existing parts, we had to verify the transitivity of advance. Subsequently, the vast majority of the automatic proofs could be repeated without any interruptions, which gives confidence that our proof framework scales well for extensions of the platform model. The Cambridge model of ARM is 9 kLOC. In addition to the ARM model, we rely mainly on the relatively small inference kernel of the HOL4 theorem prover, our MMU extension (about 180 lines of definitions), the device framework (about 350 lines) and the formulation of the discussed properties (about 380 lines). The entire proof script has a length of about 20 kLOC and needs roughly two and a half hours to run on an Intel(R) Xeon(R) X3470 core at 2.9 GHz. We invested about five person months of effort into this work.

8   Conclusion and Future Work

We extended the Cambridge HOL4 ISA model for ARM by a general device framework for DMA devices. Based on the extended model we identified secure device configurations and proved several isolation properties for platforms where DMA devices execute in parallel with a CPU in user mode. The results can be used in separation proofs, be it in a hypervisor, separation kernel or operating system setting. Model, properties and verification approach can be adapted to other architectures. We gained confidence that our proof framework scales well for extensions of the model. The model allows for further interesting angles, which we plan to explore in future work: It is rather common that devices communicate with each other.

So far, we can only support such constellations by merging communicating devices into one block, so that the model understands the block as a single device. Removing this restriction comes with the challenge of ensuring that device configurations still remain secure when devices are allowed to write to ports of other devices. Probably easier to achieve is the augmentation of the set of device classes by devices that neither use DMA nor interrupts, but that can be accessed by user space processes. A UART interface managed by a single process is one such example. From a security perspective, such a device is similar to physical memory assigned to a process, in spite of the self-modifying nature and external influence that such components have. Even if devices (like a timer) are shared between different user processes, user mode access to their ports can still preserve isolation, for example, if that access is always reading. Further potential future work includes the investigation of connected external input/output channels or the enhancement of the model by an IOMMU.

Acknowledgments. Work supported by framework grant "IT 2010" from the Swedish Foundation for Strategic Research.

References

1. Alkassar, E., Hillebrand, M.A.: Formal functional verification of device drivers. In: Shankar, N., Woodcock, J. (eds.) VSTTE 2008. LNCS, vol. 5295, pp. 225–239. Springer, Heidelberg (2008)
2. Alkassar, E., Paul, W.J., Starostin, A., Tsyban, A.: Pervasive verification of an OS microkernel. In: Leavens, G.T., O'Hearn, P., Rajamani, S.K. (eds.) VSTTE 2010. LNCS, vol. 6217, pp. 71–85. Springer, Heidelberg (2010)
3. Duan, J.: Formal verification of device drivers in embedded systems. PhD thesis, the University of Utah (2013)
4. Duan, J., Regehr, J.: Correctness proofs for device drivers in embedded systems. In: Proceedings of the 5th International Conference on Systems Software Verification, SSV 2010. USENIX Association, Berkeley (2010)
5. Duflot, L., Etiemble, D., Grumelard, O.: Using CPU system management mode to circumvent operating system security functions. In: Proc. CanSecWest (2006)
6. Fox, A.: Formal specification and verification of ARM6. In: Basin, D., Wolff, B. (eds.) TPHOLs 2003. LNCS, vol. 2758, pp. 25–40. Springer, Heidelberg (2003)
7. Fox, A., Myreen, M.O.: A trustworthy monadic formalization of the ARMv7 instruction set architecture. In: Kaufmann, M., Paulson, L.C. (eds.) ITP 2010. LNCS, vol. 6172, pp. 243–258. Springer, Heidelberg (2010)
8. Heitmeyer, C., Archer, M., Leonard, E., McLean, J.: Applying formal methods to a certifiably secure software system. IEEE Trans. Softw. Eng. 34(1), 82–98 (2008)
9. Hillebrand, M.A., In der Rieden, T., Paul, W.J.: Dealing with I/O devices in the context of pervasive system verification. In: International Conference on Computer Design (ICCD): VLSI in Computers and Processors, pp. 309–316 (2005)
10. Khakpour, N., Schwarz, O., Dam, M.: Machine assisted proof of ARMv7 instruction level isolation properties. In: Gonthier, G., Norrish, M. (eds.) CPP 2013. LNCS, vol. 8307, pp. 276–291. Springer, Heidelberg (2013)
11. Monniaux, D.: Verification of device drivers and intelligent controllers: a case study. In: Embedded Software (2007)
12. Vasudevan, A., Chaki, S., Jia, L., McCune, J., Newsome, J., Datta, A.: Design, implementation and verification of an eXtensible and Modular Hypervisor Framework. In: Security and Privacy (2013)

Supervisory Control of Discrete-Event Systems via IC3

Mohammad Reza Shoaei[1,*], Laura Kovács[2,**], and Bengt Lennartson[1]

[1] Department of Signals and Systems
[2] Department of Computer Science and Engineering
Chalmers University of Technology, Gothenburg, Sweden
{shoaei,laura.kovacs,bengt.lennartson}@chalmers.se

Abstract. The IC3 algorithm has proven to be an effective SAT-based safety model checker. It has been generalized to other frameworks such as SMT and applied very successfully to hardware and software model checking. In this paper, we present a novel technique for the supervisory control of discrete-event systems with infinite state space via IC3. We introduce an algorithm for synthesizing maximally permissive controllers using a generalized IC3 to find (if any exists) a weakest inductive invariant predicate which holds in the initial state, is maintained as the system evolves, and implies safety and control properties. To this end, we use a variation of IC3, called Tree-IC3, as a bug finder to solve the supervisory predicate control problem by iteratively reporting all feasible counterexample traces using a tree-like search, while controlling the system to avoid them. The maximally permissiveness is achieved by finding the weakest of such controllers that is invariant under safety and control properties. Experimental results demonstrate the great potential of using IC3 technique for the purpose of the supervisory control problems.

Keywords: Discrete-event systems, Supervisory control theory, Incremental inductive verification, IC3.

1 Introduction

Supervisory Control Theory (SCT), established by Ramadge and Wonham [4,26,25], is a formal framework for modeling and control of discrete-event systems (DES). Problems that SCT can address include dynamic allocation of resources, the prevention of system blocking, etc. and, within these constraints, maximally permissive system behavior. Traditionally, there are a certain number of modeling formalisms that can be used for investigating feedback control of DES, such as state machines (SMs), automata, and extended finite-state

---

* This work was supported by the Wingquist Laboratory VINN Excellence Center within the Area of Advance – Production at Chalmers University of Technology, and the Swedish Governmental Agency for Innovation Systems (VINNOVA).

** This research was supported in part by the Swedish VR grant D0497701, the Austrian FWF RiSE grant S11410-N23, and the WWTF PROSEED grant ICT C-050.

E. Yahav (Ed.): HVC 2014, LNCS 8855, pp. 252–266, 2014.

machines (EFSMs), which are state machines with variables, see e.g. [28,5,30]. The control requirements on DES are expressed by specifications in terms of regular languages, in the case of DES modeled by SMs or automata, or in terms of constraints on the states (expressed by formula), in the case of DES modeled by EFSMs. The focus of this theory is on systematical synthesis of provably safe and nonblocking controllers for a given uncontrolled system, called *plant*.

Nevertheless, the industrial acceptance of SCT is still scarce due to the following two drawbacks: the computational complexity of synthesizing a controller and *state-space explosion*, owing to limited amount of memory when working with large state-space. Researchers in the DES community are therefore seeking effective synthesis techniques to avoid these pitfalls. For example, for systems with finite behavior, [21,10] propose an efficient synthesis technique using BDDs, in [23] an algorithm is presented that iteratively strengthens the formula on transitions so that forbidden or blocking states become unreachable, and in [7] a SAT-based approach is presented. Furthermore, for systems with infinite behavior, [16,24] propose approaches for synthesis of DES using predicates and predicate transformers. However, the approach in [16] works only with systems modeled by equations over an arithmetic domain and with very few uncontrollable events.

On the other hand, several researchers in the formal methods community have investigated safety of programs using verification techniques such as BMC [2], interpolation [18], k-induction [27], and recently IC3 [3]. The IC3 algorithm has proven to be an effective SAT-based safety model checker [29]. It has been generalized to other frameworks such as SMT and applied very successfully to hardware and software model checking [6,13]. Recently, Morgenstern et al. [22] proposed a property directed synthesis method for game solving, which is also inspired by IC3. However, [22] only checks whether a system is controllable, by computing an overapproximation for the winning states, but does not construct (synthesize) a winning strategy.

In this paper, we present a novel technique for supervisory control of DES with infinite state space via IC3. To this end, we use a generalized form of IC3 as reported in [6], called *Tree-IC3*, to find (if any exists) a weakest inductive invariant predicate which holds in the initial state, is maintained as the system evolves, and implies safety and control properties. In particular, for a DES modeled by EFSMs and a safety property expressed by a set of "legal" locations, we use Tree-IC3 to find violation of safety property by searching over abstract paths of the system. Whenever a violation is found, corresponding transitions of the system are strengthened by a controller to avoid violation of the safety properties. An evaluation of the proposed IC3-based technique on standard SCT benchmarks shows a radical improvement for systems with large domains compared to BDD-based and SAT-based approaches. It should be noted that, to the best of our knowledge, this work is the first attempt to use incremental, inductive techniques, such as IC3, for solving supervisory control problems, which opens new venues of research in supervisory control theory.

The remainder of the paper is organized as follows. Section 2 briefly describes the background. In Section 3, we introduce the incremental, inductive supervisory control (IISC) algorithm and in Section 4 we discuss our experimental results. Finally, we draw some conclusions and directions for future work in Section 5.

2 Background

In this paper, we use standard notion of first-order logic (FOL) and assume quantifier-free formulas. We denote formulas with ϕ, ψ, I, T, P, variables with x, y, and sets of variables with X, Y. A literal is an atom or its negation. A *clause* is a disjunction of literals, whereas a *cube* is a conjunction of literals. A formula is in conjunctive normal form (CNF) if it is a conjunction of clauses, and in disjunctive normal form (DNF) if it is a disjunction of cubes. With abuse of notation, we might sometimes denote formulas in CNF $\phi_1 \wedge \cdots \wedge \phi_n$ as sets of clauses $\{\phi_1, \ldots, \phi_n\}$, and vice versa. A subclause $p \subseteq c$ is a clause p whose literals are a subset of literals in c.

We write $\phi(X_1, \ldots, X_n)$ to indicate that all variables occurring in ϕ are elements of $\bigcup_i X_i$. For every variable x, we assume the existence of a unique variable x' representing the next value of x. Given a formula ϕ, we use $\phi^{\langle n \rangle}$ to denote the addition of n primes to every variable in ϕ, representing the value of variables in ϕ at n time units in the future. Similarly, for any set X of variables, we let $X' := \{x' \mid x \in X\}$ and $X^{\langle n \rangle} := \{x^{\langle n \rangle} \mid x \in X\}$.

Throughout the paper, we use the standard notion of theory, satisfiability, validity, and logical consequences. Given a theory $\mathcal{T}$, $\phi \models_{\mathcal{T}} \psi$ (or simply $\phi \models \psi$) denotes that the formula ψ is a logical consequence of ϕ in the theory $\mathcal{T}$. Furthermore, given a model $\mathcal{M} = (\mathcal{I}, \mathcal{D})$, where $\mathcal{D}$ is the domain of elements and $\mathcal{I}$ (over $\mathcal{D}$) is the interpretation function, we write $(d_1, \ldots, d_n) \models_{\mathcal{M}} \phi(X_1, \ldots, X_n)$ for some $d_i \in \mathcal{D}_{X_i}$ $(i > 0)$, or simply $d \models \phi$, to denote $(d_1, \ldots, d_n) \in (\phi)^{\mathcal{I}}$.

2.1 Modeling Discrete-Event Systems

State Machine. The behavior of a discrete-event system to be controlled, called the *plant*, is modeled as a state machine (SM) [15]. Let the tuple $G = \langle Q, \Sigma, \delta, Q^i \rangle$ denote an SM, representing a plant, where Q denotes the state set, Σ denotes the finite set of events (alphabet), $\delta \subseteq Q \times \Sigma \times Q$ denotes the transition relation, and $Q^i \subseteq Q$ denotes the subset of initial states. We say that a state $q \in Q$ is reachable in G if there is a sequence of transitions from an initial state q_0 to q, i.e., $(q_0, \sigma_0, q_1)(q_1, \sigma_1, q_2) \cdots (q_{n-1}, \sigma_{n-1}, q_n)$ in G where $q_0 \in Q^i$ and $q_n = q$. Let $C : Q \to 2^{\Sigma}$ be a function. For any $\sigma \in \Sigma$ and $q \in Q$, we say that σ is enabled by C in state q if $\sigma \in C(q)$. The *restriction* of G to C, denoted $G|_C$, is described by the state machine $G_C = \langle Q, \Sigma, \delta_C, Q^i \rangle$, where δ_C is defined according to: $(q, \sigma, r) \in \delta_C$ if and only if $(q, \sigma, r) \in \delta$ and $\sigma \in C(q)$.

Extended Finite State Machine. In practice, plants are often used for modeling programs or industrial systems with data dependency. In order to model such systems, in a compact and efficient way, we extend SMs with variables, in which FOL formulas are used to represent data flow in the system.

Let X denote the set of system variables. An *extended finite state machine* (EFSM) over X is a tuple $A = \langle L, \Sigma, \Delta, l^i, l^f, \Theta \rangle$, where L is the set of finite locations, Σ is the alphabet, Δ is the set of transitions, $l^i \in L$ is the initial location, $l^f \in L$ is a special location called *error* location (or forbidden location), and $\Theta(X)$ is a formula that describes the initial values of variables. A transition in Δ is a tuple (l, a, m), where $l, m \in L$ are respectively the entry and exit locations of the transition and $a = (\sigma, \varphi)$ is the *action of the transition*, where $\sigma \in \Sigma$ is the *event of the transition* and $\varphi(X \cup X')$ is the *formula of the transition*. When no confusion is possible, we often write $\sigma : \varphi$ instead of (σ, φ).

A path in A is a sequence of transitions of the form $(l_0, \sigma_0 : \varphi_0, l_1)(l_1, \sigma_1 : \varphi_1, l_2) \cdots (l_{n-1}, \sigma_{n-1} : \varphi_{n-1}, l_n)$. We say that the path (i) is an *error* path if $l_0 = l^i$ and $l_n = l^f$; (ii) is *feasible* iff the formula $\bigwedge_i \varphi_i^{(i)}$ is satisfiable; and (iii) is *spurious* if it not feasible. A plant is safe when all the paths leading to l^f are not feasible.

To simplify the presentation of the algorithms, it is assumed that every location has at least one outgoing transition. This can be done, say for location $l \in L$, by adding a self-loop $(l, \varepsilon : \top, l)$ to Δ, where $\varepsilon \notin \Sigma$ is an *empty event*.

State Machine Representation: Fix a model $\mathcal{M} = (\mathcal{I}, \mathcal{D})$. Then A can be described by SM $G_A = \langle Q_A, \Sigma, \delta_A, Q_A^i \rangle$, where $Q_A = L \times \mathcal{D}$ is the (possibly infinite) set of states, each of which is a pair of location and variables valuation, $Q_A^i = \{\langle l^i, d \rangle \in Q_A \mid d \models \Theta\}$ is the set of initial states, and δ_A is defined according to: $(\langle l, d \rangle, \sigma, \langle m, d' \rangle) \in \delta_A$ iff $(l, \sigma : \varphi, m) \in \Delta$ and $(d, d') \models \varphi$.

Symbolic Representation: The EFSM A can also be described symbolically by a *symbolic transition system* (STS) $S_A = \langle \hat{X}, T(\hat{X} \cup \hat{X}'), I(\hat{X}) \rangle$, where $\hat{X}$ is the extension of variables set X by adding two special elements x_L and x_Σ, with domain L and Σ respectively, $I(\hat{X}) = (x_L = l^i) \wedge \Theta$, and $T(\hat{X} \cup \hat{X}') = \bigvee_{(l, \sigma : \varphi, m) \in \Delta} (x_L = l) \wedge (x_\Sigma = \sigma) \wedge \varphi \wedge (x'_L = m)$. In what follows, we shall drop the hat on $\hat{X}$, as context will determine the intended meaning. Given S_A, the safety of EFSM A can be shown by proving that all the reachable states of S_A are a subset of the states symbolically described by the formula $P := \neg(x_L = l^f)$, namely, S_A satisfies the invariant property P.

Note that, for any EFSM A, S_A and G_A (which both represent low level behavior of A) are related in a way that S_A also symbolically represents the state machine G_A. Thus, any property that holds on S_A holds on G_A as well. In the sequel, to simplify the mathematical representation of the problem, we shall freely switch between these two low level descriptions of A and use the one that offers the simplest representation.

Abstract Reachability Tree.

Given an EFSM $A = \langle L, \Sigma, \Delta, l^i, l^f, \Theta \rangle$ over X, we further define an *abstract reachability tree* (ART) $\mathcal{A} = \langle V, E \rangle$ for A as follows: (i) V is a set of quadruples (l, ϕ, σ, k), where $l \in L$ is a location, $\phi(X)$ is a formula, $\sigma \in \Sigma$ is an event, and $k \in \mathbb{N}$ is a unique identifier; (ii) $v_\varepsilon := (l^i, \Theta, \varepsilon, 1)$ is the root of $\mathcal{A}$, where $\varepsilon \notin \Sigma$ is an empty event; (iii) for every non-leaf node $v := (l, \phi, \sigma, k) \in V$, for every transition $(l, \beta : \varphi(X \cup X'), m) \in \Delta$, v has a child node $w := (m, \psi, \beta, h)$ such that $\phi \wedge \varphi \models \psi'$ and $k < h$; and we call φ the *edge formula* of w. In the sequel, we shall use the following notations for any ART $\mathcal{A}$:

- For any node $v := (l, \phi, \sigma, k)$ in $\mathcal{A}$, ϕ and σ are called the *abstract state formula* and *event* of node v, respectively. If $l = l^f$, v is called an *error node*.
- A node $v := (l, \phi, \sigma, k)$ is said to be *covered* in $\mathcal{A}$ if either: (i) there exists an uncovered node $w := (l, \psi, \beta, h)$ in $\mathcal{A}$ such that $h < k$ and $\phi \models \psi$; or (ii) v has a proper ancestor for which (i) holds.
- $l_i \rightsquigarrow l_j$ denotes a path in $\mathcal{A}$ from a node (l_i, ψ, β, h) to a descendant node (l_j, ϕ, σ, k) with $h < k$.
- For any path $\pi := (l_0, \phi_0, \sigma_0, .) \rightsquigarrow \cdots \rightsquigarrow (l_n, \phi_n, \sigma_n, .)$ in $\mathcal{A}$, with (ab)use of notations, we let $\Sigma^{\mathcal{A}}(\pi)$ and $\Delta^{\mathcal{A}}(\pi)$ denote the sets of $[\sigma_0, \ldots, \sigma_n]$ events and $[\varphi_0, \ldots, \varphi_{n-1}]$ edge formulas of π, respectively. In the sequel, we sometimes view π as a subset of nodes $\pi \subseteq V$.

We say that $\mathcal{A}$ is *complete* if all its leaves are covered or their abstract state formula is equivalent to $\bot$; $\mathcal{A}$ is *safe* iff it is complete and for all error nodes (l^f, ϕ, σ, k) in $\mathcal{A}$, we have that $\phi \models \bot$. If an EFSM A has a safe ART, then A is said to be safe [12,19][1].

2.2 Supervisory Control

This section recalls the supervisory (predicate) control framework of [25,16]. Let $A = \langle L, \Sigma, \Delta, l^i, l^f, \Theta \rangle$ be an EFSM and let S be the STS over symbolic state space X (i.e. $\hat{X}$). The alphabet Σ is classically partitioned into the two disjoint subsets, the *controllable events* Σ_c, whose occurrence can be inhibited by the controller (also called supervisor) and the *uncontrollable events* Σ_u, which can never, or need not, be disabled. Let $P(X) := \neg(x_L = l^f)$ be the safety property that represents a set of good states. The control task is to design a static controller $C : X \to 2^\Sigma$ for S that guarantees safety property P by restricting the conduct of S, i.e., as the system (restricted to C) evolves (unrolls), it visits only the states where P holds. Note that, since a controller cannot restrict uncontrollable events, we also have that for each (symbolic) state $s \in X$, $\Sigma_u(s) \subseteq C(s)$, where $\Sigma_u(s)$ is the set of uncontrollable events defined at s.

In order to present formally the control task, we need the following notations. Given S, for any predicate $R(X)$ and for any $\sigma \in \Sigma$, let

$$\mathcal{F}_\sigma(R)(X) := \exists X_0 \, . \, R(X_0) \wedge T(X_0, X) \wedge (x_\Sigma = \sigma)$$

---

[1] In fact, e.g. in [19], this property is shown for systems modeled by program graphs. However, any EFSM can be transformed to the equivalent program graph by simply dropping their event set Σ and conjuncting Θ with formula of all outgoing transition of their initial location.

be the *strongest post-condition* predicate transformer for S w.r.t. σ, i.e., $\mathcal{F}_\sigma$ holds on the set of states of S that are reached by the transition with event σ from a state where R holds. We write $\mathcal{F}$, $\mathcal{F}_u$, and $\mathcal{F}^*$ for respectively $\bigvee_{\sigma \in \Sigma} \mathcal{F}_\sigma$, $\bigvee_{\sigma \in \Sigma_u} \mathcal{F}_\sigma$, and $\bigvee_{n \geq 0} \mathcal{F}^n$, where $\mathcal{F}^0$ is defined to be the identity predicate transformer. For given predicate R, $\mathcal{F}^*(R)$ holds in those states which are reachable from a state where R holds in zero or more number of transitions. Thus, $\mathcal{F}^*$ is useful in characterizing the *reachability set* of STS S. Furthermore, the restriction of $\mathcal{F}$ to R, denoted $\mathcal{F}|_R$, is a new predicate transformer defined by: $\mathcal{F}|_R(W) = \mathcal{F}(R \wedge W) \wedge R$ for any predicate $W(X)$.

Problem 1 (Supervisory Predicate Control Problem). The control task is to construct a static controller $C : X \to 2^\Sigma$ for S such that $\mathcal{F}^*_{S|_C}(I) \models P$.

That is, Problem 1 requires that the state trajectories in the controlled system $S|_C$, starting from the initial states I, remain confined to the set of states where the safety predicate P holds, and visit only the states where P holds. Thus, the controlled system guarantees safety.

Given any predicate $R(X)$, we say that R is a *controllable and safe invariant predicate (C-SIP)* for S if:

1) $R \models (\mathcal{F}|_R)^*(I)$,
2) $\mathcal{F}_u(R) \models R$, and
3) $R \models P$.

That is, 1) R is a *fixed-point* of the predicate transformer $\mathcal{F}|_R$ starting from the initial states I, 2) if S starts in a state where R holds, then under the execution of any transition with uncontrollable event it remains in a state where R holds, and 3) R implies the safety property.

The solution to the Problem 1 exists if and only if there exists a predicate R that is C-SIP for S^2. Indeed, $\bot$ is always a possible solution. Therefore, the notion of *permissiveness* has been introduced in SCT framework to compare the quality of different (predicate) controllers for given plant. For any two predicates R_1 and R_2, we say that R_1 is more permissive (less restrictive) than R_2 if $R_1 \equiv R_1 \vee R_2$. Now, for a family of C-SIPs for S, we let $R^\uparrow := \bigvee \{R \mid R \text{ is a C-SIP for } S\}$ denotes the *maximally permissive C-SIP* for S. The real challenge is to find $R^\uparrow$ for given S.

Discussion. In SCT framework, in addition to safety and control properties, it is desired for the controlled system to be *nonblocking*. This property guarantees that at least one *marked state* (which is also referred to as accepting state or final state) is reachable from any state in the controlled system. The nonblocking property is known to be a "global" behavior, as opposed to the "local" behavior of error (forbidden) states, so the condition that a state is nonblocking cannot be expressed as a property of the state alone, without considering possible progress from the state. However, *deadlocks*, unmarked states with no outgoing

---

[2] We refer the interested reader to [16] for proof of the above claim.

transitions, can be expressed (locally) as a property of each state. Thus, we consider deadlocks as a special form of error states. In this paper, however, we do not discuss the full supervisory control problem but instead we will focus on an important subclass of problems, i.e., safety and controllability problems.

2.3   Incremental, Inductive Verification

The term incremental, inductive verification has been used to describe algorithms that use induction to construct lemmas in response to property-driven hypotheses, e.g., the IICTL [11] and IC3 [3] algorithms. In this section, we briefly recall the original IC3 algorithm, as formulated in [9], and its extension to SMT, as described in [6].

IC3 Algorithm. Given a STS $S = \langle X, T(X \cup X'), I(X) \rangle$, let $P(X)$ describes a set of good states. The IC3 algorithm tries to prove that S satisfies P by maintaining formulas $F := F_0(X), \ldots, F_k(X)$, where F is called a *trace* and F_i $(i \geq 0)$ are called *frames*, such that:

- $F_0 = I$;
- for all $i > 0$, F_i is a set of clauses;
- $F_{i+1} \subseteq F_i$ (thus, $F_i \models F_{i+1}$);
- $F_i(X) \wedge T(X \cup X') \models F_{i+1}(X')$;
- for all $i < k$, $F_i \models P$.

For $i > 0$, F_i represents an over-approximation of the states of S reachable in i transition steps or less. Initially, F_0 is set to the initial states I. The algorithm proceeds incrementally, by alternating two phases:
(i) *Blocking phase*: The trace is analyzed to prove that F_k and $\neg P$ do not intersect, thus $F_k \models P$. More specifically, IC3 maintains a set of pairs (s, i), where s is a cube representing a set of states that can lead to a bad state and $i > 0$ is a position in the trace. New clauses are added to (some of) the frames in the trace by (recursively) proving that a set s of a pair (s, i) is unreachable starting from F_{i-1}. This is done by checking the satisfiability of the formula

$$F_{i-1} \wedge \neg s \wedge T \wedge s' \tag{1}$$

If it is unsatisfiable, i.e. F_{i-1} blocks $\neg s$, and s does not intersect with I, then IC3 strengthens F_i by adding $\neg s$ to it. If, instead, it is satisfiable, i.e. F_{i-1} is not strong enough to block s, then IC3 computes a (generalized) cube p representing a subset of the states in $F_{i-1} \wedge \neg s$ such that all the states in p lead to a state in s' in one transition step. Afterwards, IC3 tries to block the pair $(p, i - 1)$ (namely, it tries to show that p is not reachable in one step from F_{i-2}). This procedure continues recursively, possibly generating other pairs to block at earlier points in the trace, until either IC3 generates a pair $(q, 0)$, meaning that the system does not satisfy the property and a counterexample is constructed, or the trace is eventually strengthened so that the original pair (s, i) can be blocked.

(*ii*) *Propagation phase*: The trace is extended (if $F_i \models P$) with a new formula F_{i+1}, moving forward the clauses from F_i. If, during this process, two consecutive frames become identical, i.e. $F_i = F_{i+1}$, then a fixed-point is reached, and IC3 can terminate with F_i being an inductive invariant proving the property. For more elaboration on IC3 algorithm we refer to [3,9].

IC3 Extension to SMT. For proving safety property (and later for constructing $R^\uparrow$) of plants modeled by EFSMs, it is more convenient to work at a higher level of abstraction, using SAT modulo theories (SMT). To this end, as described in [6], we replace the underlying SAT engine with an SMT solver[3]. With the new solver, if the formula (1) is satisfiable, then a new pair $(p, i - 1)$ will be generated such that p is a cube in the *preimage of s w.r.t. T*. That is, to existentially quantify the variables X' in (1), eliminate the quantifiers, and then convert the result in DNF. This will generate a set of cubes $\{p_j\}_j$ which in turn generate a set of pairs $\{(p_j, i - 1)\}_j$ to be blocked at $i - 1$. In what follows, we shall assume that the SMT solver has a procedure PREIMAGE for computing the preimage.

3   Incremental, Inductive Supervisory Control via IC3

We now present the incremental, inductive supervisory (predicate) control (IISC) algorithm via IC3.

Outline. In high-level description, the algorithm constructs a controller (if any exists) for given plant by alternating between two phases:
(i) *Error-Finding,* which the algorithm searches for error location in the plant by *unwinding* it into an abstract reachability tree (ART). Whenever an error location is found, it tries to refute the abstract path to that location by applying a procedure that mimics the blocking phase of IC3. In case of failure to refute the error path, it returns a counterexample trace;
(ii) *Supervision,* which the algorithm tries to control the current counterexample trace from reaching the error location by strengthening the clauses attached to the *controllable nodes* (i.e. nodes with controllable event) in the path. Thus, the path is blocked from reaching the error location. In order to fulfill the maximally permissiveness criteria, the process strengthens only the nearest controllable node from the error location. This guarantees that the controller does not restrict the plant more than what is necessary to refute the error location. However, when there are no controllable nodes to be controlled (strengthen), the safety property is violated. Thus, the algorithm returns the counterexample trace. Otherwise, if the blocking process is successful, the counterexample is refuted and the algorithm continues the search.

---

[3] There are, however, some crucial steps which must be made before switching from SAT to SMT solver, for which we refer to [6].

```
procedure IISC(EFSM A = ⟨L, Σ, Δ, lⁱ, lᶠ, Θ⟩):
    global: The EFSM A and an ART 𝒜 = ⟨V, E⟩
    let vₑ := (lⁱ, Θ, ε, 1) be the root of 𝒜
    while there exists an uncovered leaf v ∈ V :
        if v := (lᶠ, φ, σ, k) and φ ⊭ ⊥ :
            (F, status) = IC3-BLOCK-PATH(π := vₑ ⤳ v)
            switch status :
                case CTX
                    /* in case π is a feasible error path */
                    if SUPERVISE(F, π) = false :
                        /* error path π cannot be controlled */
                        return the counterexample trace F
                case BLOCKED
                    /* in case π is refuted */
                    for i = 0 to size of π :
                        UPDATE-INV(F[i], π[i])
        else:
            STRENGTHENING(v) /* as in [6] */
            COVERING(v) /* as in [6] */
            UNWINDING(v) /* as in [6] */
    return /* the plant A is successfully supervised */
```

Fig. 1. Incremental Inductive Supervisory Control Algorithm

IISC Algorithm. Fig. 1 illustrates the IISC algorithm. The algorithm is built upon the Tree-IC3 technique in [6] as it arrives to finding and refuting abstract paths to the error location. The search proceeds in an "explicit-symbolic" fashion, i.e., the given plant is unwound into an ART, following a DFS strategy.

The algorithm starts by selecting an uncovered leaf, $v := (l, \phi, \sigma, k)$. If v is an error node (namely, $l = l^f$) then the algorithm tries to refute the abstract path to this node (i.e., $\pi^f := v_\varepsilon \rightsquigarrow v$) by calling the IC3-BLOCK-PATH procedure, see Fig. 2. Note that, in order to construct a correct ART, when IC3-BLOCK-PATH checks whether a cube c is blocked by a set of clauses F_{i-1}, the inductiveness check (1) is replaced with a weaker check

$$F_{i-1} \wedge T_{i-1} \models \neg c' \qquad (2)$$

However, because of this replacement, the requirement that $F_{i+1} \subseteq F_i$ is not enforced anymore. With this adaptation, the procedure tries to produce the clauses necessary to refute the abstract path and terminates successfully whenever an empty clause is generated. In case of failure to refute the path, the property is

---

procedure IC3-BLOCK-PATH($\pi := (l^i, \Theta, \varepsilon, 1) \rightsquigarrow \cdots (l_i, \phi_i, \sigma_i, .) \cdots \rightsquigarrow (l^f, \phi_n, \sigma_n, .)$):

   let $T := [\varphi_0, \ldots, \varphi_{n-1}] = \Delta^A(\pi)$ /* φ_i are the edge formulas */

   let $F := [\Theta, \ldots, \phi_i, \ldots, \phi_{n-1}]$ /* ϕ_i are the clauses of the nodes */

   while not exists $0 < j < n$ s.t. $F[j] \land T[j] \models \bot$:

      let stack $= \emptyset$

      foreach bad in PREIMAGE($\phi_{n-1} \land T[n-1]$) :

         /* bad is a cube in the preimage of $T[n-1]$ */

         stack.push((bad, $n-1$))

      while stack is not empty :

         $c, j = $ stack.top()

         if $j = 0$: /* π is a feasible error trace */

            let $B = [c_0, \ldots, c_{n-1}]$ be the counterexample trace

            return (B, CTX)

         if $F[j-1] \land T[j-1] \models \neg c'$:

            stack.pop() /* cube c is blocked */

            /* $\neg c$ can be generalized before adding to $F[j]$ */

            $F[j] = F[j] \land \neg c$

         else:

            foreach p in PREIMAGE($F[j-1] \land T[j-1] \land c'$) :

               stack.push(($p, j-1$))

   return $(F, \text{BLOCKED})$ /* path π is blocked */

Fig. 2. IC3 blocking path procedure

violated and a counterexample trace is returned[4]. If IC3-BLOCK-PATH returns a counterexample trace, then the algorithm tries to control the path π^f from reaching the error location by calling the SUPERVISE procedure, see Fig. 3. In the supervision phase, the nearest controllable ancestor of v, say $v_i := (l_i, \phi_i, \sigma_i, h)$ s.t. $\sigma_i \in \Sigma_c$, is controlled by strengthening (conjuncting) its incoming edge formula T_{i-1}, with negation of (bad) cube c, i.e. $T_{i-1} = T_{i-1} \land \neg c'$. Thus, the check (2) becomes satisfiable which implies that the cube c is blocked at v_i.

In case that the leaf node v is not an error node, the following procedures are applied to v: STRENGTHENING in which v is strengthened by forward propagating the clauses of its ancestor; COVERING in which v is covered thus can be closed, whenever the set of states of v is contained in the states of some previously generated node w having the same location; and UNWINDING, which expands the

---

[4] Note that, our formulation of the IC3-BLOCK-PATH procedure is slightly different from the original one in [6]. In particular, we set F_0 to denote initial formula Θ instead of $\top$. We also note that $\neg c$ can be generalized before being added to F_i. Although this is quite important in practice for effectiveness of IC3, here for brevity we shall not discuss this.

```
procedure SUPERVISE(B, π):                    procedure UPDATE-INV(vᵢ, ψ):
    if Σ^A(π) ⊆ Σ_u : return false              /* vᵢ := (lᵢ, φᵢ, σᵢ, .) */
    T := [φ₀, ..., φ_{n-1}] = Δ^A(π)             foreach cⱼ ∈ ψ s.t. φᵢ ⊭ cⱼ :
    let i be the size of π                           add cⱼ to φᵢ,
    while i > 0 :                                    uncover all nodes
        let vᵢ := (lᵢ, φᵢ, σᵢ, .) = π[i]            covered by vᵢ.
        UPDATE-INV(vᵢ, ¬B[i])
        if σᵢ ∉ Σ_u ∪ {ε} :
            /* strenghening edge formula */
            T[i − 1] = T[i − 1] ∧ ¬(B[i])'
            break
        i = i − 1
    return true
```

Fig. 3. Auxiliary procedures for the IISC algorithm

ART by generating the successors of v. Note that, for brevity, we have to omit several important details in each procedure, for which we refer to [6].

Finally, the IISC algorithm terminates when either the given plant couldn't be controlled or there are no uncovered leafs left, indicating that the plant A is controlled, by strengthening its transition formulas, thus guarantees the safety property. In the former case, a counterexample trace to the error location is returned. We also note that the termination of IISC algorithm is guaranteed whenever the given plant A is defined over a finite domain, see [6,3,9].

Theorem 1. *A maximally permissive C-SIP $R^\uparrow$ exists for a plant A if* IISC(A) *terminates without a counterexample trace.*

Proof. We sketch the proof as follows. Let $A^\uparrow := $ IISC(A) denote the EFSM obtained from A by applying IISC algorithm in Fig. 1, and let $R_{A^\uparrow}$ denote the transition formula of STS $S_{A^\uparrow}$. Let $\mathcal{F}$ be the strongest post-condition predicate transformer defined over S_A. Since the IISC terminates without a counterexample we immediately see that $R_{A^\uparrow} \models (\mathcal{F}|_{R_{A^\uparrow}})^*(I)$ and $R_{A^\uparrow} \models P$, where $P := \neg(x_L = l^f)$. Also, because IISC only controls the transitions with controllable events, clearly $\mathcal{F}_u(R_{A^\uparrow}) \models R_{A^\uparrow}$. Hence, $R_{A^\uparrow}$ is a C-SIP for S_A (see definition of C-SIP in Section 2.2). Furthermore, the maximally permissiveness of $R_{A^\uparrow}$ comes from the fact that A is controlled only when a feasible error path exists, and only the nearest controllable transition to the error location is controlled (strengthened). Thus, we conclude that $R_{A^\uparrow}$ is a maximally permissive C-SIP for $S_{A^\uparrow}$.

Corollary 1. *The solution to the Problem 1 exists if* IISC *algorithm terminates without a counterexample trace.*

Table 1. Performance statistics on benchmark examples

Model	IISC (s)	SC-BDD (s)	SC-SAT (s) [only verification]
CMT (1,5)	0.127	0.066	0.083
CMT (3,3)	0.430	1.639	2.128
CMT (5,5)	0.733	108	8.84
CMT (7,7)	0.975	T.O.	T.O.
EDP (5,10)	0.98	0.168	14.36
EDP (5,50)	0.124	0.374	T.O.
EDP (5,200)	0.124	1.382	T.O.
EDP (5,10E3)	0.124	16.746	T.O.
EDP (5,10E5)	0.124	T.O.	T.O.
PME	2.3	11.595	85.30

4   Experiments

The IISC algorithm has been integrated in the DES tool Supremica [1], in which we embedded Z3 [8] as our SMT solver. We use the theory of Linear Real Arithmetic for modeling formulas on transitions, which is well supported by Z3. To compute the exact preimage of a cube c and a transition formula $\varphi(X \cup X')$, we first convert the formula $\varphi \wedge c'$ to a DNF $\bigvee_i p_i$ and then use the quantifier elimination function in Z3 to project each cube p_i over current-state variables $X : \bigvee_i \exists X' . (p_i)$. The under-approximate preimage of c w.r.t. φ can then be constructed simply by picking only a subset of their exact preimage. In fact, similar to [6], we also under-approximate by simply stopping after the first cube.

Furthermore, as in work [6,19], we applied the following improvements to the implementation: A new instance of a program variable is used only when that variable is modified. This eliminates many constraints of the form $x^{\langle i+1 \rangle} = x^{\langle i \rangle}$ that occur when a variable is unmodified by a transition formula. Also, instead of always using an under-approximate preimage procedure as in [6], a threshold on the size of the clauses is introduced for deciding whether to use under-approximate or exact preimage procedure. In our industrial examples, however, this decision does not yield any substantial performance reduction. Moreover, in practice, before processing a node we first check if the node is covered. This often substantially reduces the overall run time of the algorithm.

For our evaluation, we compared the IISC algorithm with the Symbolic Supervisory Control using BDD (SC-BDD) algorithm in [21,10] and SAT-based Supervisory Control (SC-SAT) algorithm in [7], where we used the SC-SAT algorithm for the safety and controllability verification only and not for the synthesis. To this end, we used the following set of standard benchmarks in SCT: the parallel manufacturing example (PME) [17], cat and mouse tower (CMT), and extended Dinning Philosophers (EDP) [20].

Table 1 summarized the run time performance of the algorithms[5]. In this table, CMT(n, k) denote the CMT problem with a tower composed by n identical levels, k cats, and k mice; EDP(i, j) denote the EDP problem with i philosophers and j intermediate states of each philosopher, and T.O. indicates time out (5 min). As the table shows, for those examples with smaller domain, the SC-BDD is slightly better than the IISC algorithm. The performance difference might be because of the fact that once the BDD data structure is constructed, computing a controller can be done very efficiently. Although, SC-SAT only reports if the system is safe and/or it can be controlled, it performs poorly or time out in most of the examples. One possible reason is that the SC-SAT algorithm needs to enumerate all possible solutions (within the domain) using its underlying SAT solver.

As the systems become larger (namely, domain of variables become larger), the IISC approach obviously outperforms the SC-BDD and SC-SAT. With no surprise, this owes to the fact that the BDD-based approaches suffer from exponential space blow up of BDD nodes while representing a large state space, and SAT-based approaches have the disadvantage of search for a single, often complex, queries, which can in practice overwhelm the SAT solver. In contrast, the performance of our approach (and in general, IC3-based approaches) depends on the number of variables and transition formals rather than the actual number of explicit states and transitions.

5   Conclusions and Future Work

In this paper we have presented a novel technique to synthesizing controllers for discrete-event systems via IC3. More precisely, given a plant model and a safety property, we used a variation of Abstract Reachability Trees to keep track of both the invariants of reachable states and of permissible controller actions. The reachability tree is constructed iteratively using an adaptation of the Tree-IC3 algorithm. Whenever a feasible error trace is encountered, the algorithm attempts to strengthen the controller to rule out the error trace. If an error trace cannot be removed by strengthening the controller, the system is uncontrollable; if no more error traces can be found, the plant is successfully controlled. By the properties of the construction, the controller is maximally permissive. Our experiments demonstrate the potential of IC3-based techniques in supervisory control of discrete-event systems compared to BDD-based and SAT-based approaches.

There are some promising directions of future research. IISC can be extended to cover nonblocking control problem, in which IICTL technique [11] can be exploited. Moreover, abstraction and optimization techniques can be used to improve the overall performance of the controller synthesis. We also consider the possibility of parallel implementation and using a hybrid approach that combines IISC with interpolant-based approaches, such as [19,14], in order to get the benefits of both techniques.

---

[5] Benchmarks were performed on a workstation with a 2.67GHz Intel Core2 Quad processor and 2GB of available memory.

References

1. Åkesson, K., Fabian, M., Flordal, H., Malik, R.: Supremica - An integrated environment for verification, synthesis and simulation of discrete event systems. In: 8th Int. Work. Discret. Event Syst., pp. 384–385. Ann Arbor, MI (2006)
2. Biere, A., Cimatti, A., Clarke, E., Zhu, Y.: Symbolic model checking without bDDs. In: Cleaveland, W.R. (ed.) TACAS 1999. LNCS, vol. 1579, pp. 193–207. Springer, Heidelberg (1999)
3. Bradley, A.R.: SAT-Based Model Checking without Unrolling. In: Jhala, R., Schmidt, D. (eds.) VMCAI 2011. LNCS, vol. 6538, pp. 70–87. Springer, Heidelberg (2011)
4. Cassandras, C.G., Lafortune, S.: Introduction to Discrete Event Systems, 2nd edn. Springer US, Boston (2008)
5. Chen, Y.L., Lin, F.: Modeling of discrete event systems using finite state machines with parameters. In: IEEE Int. Conf. Control Appl. Conf. Proc., pp. 941–946 (2000)
6. Cimatti, A., Griggio, A.: Software model checking via IC3. In: Madhusudan, P., Seshia, S.A. (eds.) CAV 2012. LNCS, vol. 7358, pp. 277–293. Springer, Heidelberg (2012)
7. Claessen, K., Een, N., Sheeran, M., Sörensson, N., Voronov, A., Åkesson, K.: SAT-Solving in Practice, with a Tutorial Example from Supervisory Control. Discret. Event Dyn. Syst. 19(4), 495–524 (2009)
8. de Moura, L., Bjørner, N.: Z3: An Efficient SMT Solver. In: Ramakrishnan, C.R., Rehof, J. (eds.) TACAS 2008. LNCS, vol. 4963, pp. 337–340. Springer, Heidelberg (2008)
9. Een, N., Mishchenko, A., Brayton, R.: Efficient implementation of property directed reachability. In: Form. Methods Comput. Des., pp. 125–134 (2011)
10. Fei, Z., Miremadi, S., Åkesson, K., Lennartson, B.: A symbolic approach to large-scale discrete event systems modeled as finite automata with variables. In: 2012 IEEE Int. Conf. Autom. Sci. Eng., pp. 502–507. IEEE (2012)
11. Hassan, Z., Bradley, A.R., Somenzi, F.: Incremental, Inductive CTL Model Checking. In: Madhusudan, P., Seshia, S.A. (eds.) CAV 2012. LNCS, vol. 7358, pp. 532–547. Springer, Heidelberg (2012)
12. Henzinger, T.A., Jhala, R., Majumdar, R., Sutre, G.: Lazy abstraction. ACM SIG-PLAN Not., 58–70 (2002)
13. Hoder, K., Bjørner, N.: Generalized property directed reachability. In: Cimatti, A., Sebastiani, R. (eds.) SAT 2012. LNCS, vol. 7317, pp. 157–171. Springer, Heidelberg (2012)
14. Hoder, K., Kovács, L., Voronkov, A.: Interpolation and symbol elimination in vampire. In: Giesl, J., Hähnle, R. (eds.) IJCAR 2010. LNCS, vol. 6173, pp. 188–195. Springer, Heidelberg (2010)
15. Hopcroft, J., Motwani, R., Ullman, J.: Introduction to Automata Theory, Languages, and Computation, 3rd edn. Series in Computer Science,Education. Pearson Education India (2007)
16. Kumar, R., Garg, V., Marcus, S.: Predicates and predicate transformers for supervisory control of discrete event dynamical systems. IEEE Trans. Automat. Contr. 38(2), 232–247 (1993)
17. Leduc, R., Lawford, M., Wonham, W.M.: Hierarchical interface-based supervisory control-part II: parallel case. IEEE Trans. Automat. Contr. 50(9), 1336–1348 (2005)
18. McMillan, K.L.: Interpolation and SAT-Based Model Checking. In: Hunt Jr., W.A., Somenzi, F. (eds.) CAV 2003. LNCS, vol. 2725, pp. 1–13. Springer, Heidelberg (2003)

19. McMillan, K.L.: Lazy abstraction with interpolants. In: Ball, T., Jones, R.B. (eds.) CAV 2006. LNCS, vol. 4144, pp. 123–136. Springer, Heidelberg (2006)
20. Miremadi, S., Åkesson, K., Fabian, M., Vahidi, A.: Solving two supervisory control benchmark problems using Supremica. In: 9th Int. Work. Discret. Event Syst., pp. 131–136 (2008)
21. Miremadi, S., Lennartson, B., Åkesson, K.: A BDD-Based Approach for Modeling Plant and Supervisor by Extended Finite Automata. IEEE Trans. Control Syst. Technol. 20(6), 1421–1435 (2012)
22. Morgenstern, A., Gesell, M., Schneider, K.: Solving games using incremental induction. In: Johnsen, E.B., Petre, L. (eds.) IFM 2013. LNCS, vol. 7940, pp. 177–191. Springer, Heidelberg (2013)
23. Ouedraogo, L., Kumar, R., Malik, R., Åkesson, K.: Nonblocking and Safe Control of Discrete-Event Systems Modeled as Extended Finite Automata. IEEE Trans. Autom. Sci. Eng. 8(3), 560–569 (2011)
24. Ramadge, P.J., Wonham, W.M.: Modular Feedback Logic for Discrete Event Systems. SIAM J. Control Optim. 25(5), 1202–1218 (1987)
25. Ramadge, P.J., Wonham, W.M.: Supervisory control of a class of discrete event processes. SIAM J. Control Optim. 25(1), 635–650 (1987)
26. Ramadge, P.J., Wonham, W.M.: The control of discrete event systems. Proc. IEEE, Spec. Issue Discret. Event Dyn. Syst. 77(1), 81–98 (1989)
27. Sheeran, M., Singh, S., Stålmarck, G.: Checking Safety Properties Using Induction and a SAT-Solver. In: Johnson, S.D., Hunt Jr., W.A. (eds.) FMCAD 2000. LNCS, vol. 1954, pp. 108–125. Springer, Heidelberg (2000)
28. Skoldstam, M., Åkesson, K., Fabian, M.: Modeling of discrete event systems using finite automata with variables. In: 46th IEEE Conf. Decis. Control, pp. 3387–3392 (2007)
29. Somenzi, F., Bradley, A.R.: IC3: where monolithic and incremental meet. In: Form. Methods Comput. Des., pp. 3–8 (2011)
30. Yang, Y., Gohari, P.: Embedded supervisory control of discrete-event systems. In: Int. Conf. Autom. Sci. Eng., pp. 410–415 (2005)

Partial-Order Reduction
for Multi-core LTL Model Checking

Alfons Laarman[1,2] and Anton Wijs[3]

[1] Vienna University of Technology, Vienna, Austria*
[2] University of Twente, Enschede, The Netherlands
[3] RWTH Aachen University, Aachen, Germany
alfons@laarman.com, awijs@cs.rwth-aachen.de

Abstract. Partial-Order Reduction (POR) is a well-known, successful technique for on-the-fly state space reduction in model checking, as evidenced by the prestigious CAV 2014 award for its pioneers. The combination of POR with LTL model checking is long known to cause the so-called ignoring problem, i.e. relevant behavior is continuously ignored and never selected for exploration. This problem has been solved with increasing sophistication over the years, using various ignoring provisos, which include all necessary actions along cycles in the state space.

However, parallel model checking algorithms still suffer from a lack of an efficient solution; the best known ones causing severe decrease in reductions. We present a new parallel ignoring proviso for POR, which solves this issue by exploiting parallel DFS-based algorithms. Its similarity to the sequential solutions allows the combination with sophisticated earlier methods solving the ignoring problem. We prove correctness of the new proviso and empirically show that it maintains good reductions, runtime performance and parallel scalability.

1 Introduction

In explicit-state model checking, the correctness of a concurrent system description M is verified with respect to a property φ. This is done by exhaustively exploring $M's$ potential behavior in the form of a *state-space graph*. Explicit-state model checking is still an indispensable technique for formal verification of software systems. However, full verification is severely limited by the need to explore and store the entire state space, which is often exponential in the size of M.

For many years, Moore's law [25] guaranteed exponential advances in computation capabilities, which for model checking meant that larger state spaces – hence more complicated systems – could be analyzed. However, since a few years, due to physical limitations, CPUs no longer deliver sequential speedups with each new generation. Instead, now, the number of *cores* on CPUs grows

* Supported by the Austrian National Research Network S11403-N23 (RiSE) of the Austrian Science Fund (FWF) and by the Vienna Science and Technology Fund (WWTF) through grant VRG11-005.

E. Yahav (Ed.): HVC 2014, LNCS 8855, pp. 267–283, 2014.

exponentially. Only by exploiting this parallelism can one regain the previous growth trends, but parallelizing model checking algorithms is far from trivial.

Recently, it has been shown that original (sequential) verification algorithms based on depth-first search (DFS) can be parallelized efficiently for shared-memory multi-core machines [8,18,15]. These solutions *do not* attempt to parallelize DFS, but instead choose the optimistic approach to run several local DFS-based threads (workers) and lazily communicate sub-results. By randomized traversal, the workers are expected to explore different parts of the state space and communicate little. Results are typically shared in the DFS backtrack, which might not scale in theory, but in practice the algorithms have shown good speedups [8]. First, [19] demonstrated how to perform parallel LTL model checking based on the classic Nested Depth-First Search (NDFS) algorithm [7]. Since then, this technique has been improved in various forms of multi-core NDFS algorithms [8,18,20], and also employed for detecting Strongly Connected Components [24,23]. In the current paper, we focus on the currently best performing version of multi-core NDFS [8,18], which is referred to as a *Combination of MC-NDFSs* (CNDFS), because it is the state-of-the-art solution for multi-core LTL model checking (see Section 2).

Besides exploiting parallelism, another approach to handle larger state spaces is by *partial-order reduction* (POR), which prunes those concurrent interleavings of M' behavior that are irrelevant w.r.t. φ. For each reachable state of M, POR selects a subset of the locally executable transitions, based on a static analysis of the dependency relations in M' behavior. It can yield exponential reductions [31, Section 3]. Since the discovery and subsequent solving of the *ignoring problem* [29], POR can also preserve LTL properties [1]. The ignoring problem occurs when POR indefinitely postpones φ-relevant behavior by selecting similar subsets of transitions at the states along infinite execution traces of M (captured as cycles in its finite state-space graph). This problem can be solved by adding an *ignoring proviso*, i.e. a strengthening condition that limits the possible transition subsets allowed by POR. For LTL, practical ignoring provisos depend on cycles. Due to their heuristic nature and the difficulty of identifying cycles in a graph (see Section 2), efficient provisos have been studied for many years [9].

The combination of multi-core (LTL) model checking and POR benefits from both approaches. The ignoring problem however complicates matters, as its solution depends on detecting cycles in the state space, which are hard to detect in parallel algorithms. Not surprisingly, some existing parallel approaches either increase POR's time complexity and/or reduce reduction capability [3] (c.f. [15]).

In the current paper, we show how the ignoring problem can be handled efficiently using CNDFS and the novel *parallel cycle proviso*. We both mitigate the loss of reductions witnessed in previous parallel POR-enabled model checking algorithms, but also enable the use of several optimizations from [9].

The structure of the paper is as follows: in Section 2, preliminary notions are introduced, and CNDFS and POR are presented. In Section 3, we lift POR to the multi-threaded setting of CNDFS. Section 4 contains our experimental results, and Section 5 discusses related work. Finally, Section 6 draws conclusions.

2   Preliminaries

We choose an action-based representation of state spaces. The state-space graph $\mathcal{G}$ consists of a (finite) set of vertices or states $\mathcal{S}$, with an initial state $s_0 \in \mathcal{S}$, and a set of edges, the transitions $\mathcal{T} \subseteq \mathcal{S} \times \Sigma \times \mathcal{S}$, where Σ represents a set of actions in the system M, e.g. a statement for an imperative-language specification. We call s' a *successor* of s iff $\exists \alpha \colon (s, \alpha, s') \in \mathcal{T}$, denoted as $s \xrightarrow{\alpha} s'$, or $s \to s'$, in case α is not relevant. Furthermore, we write $s \to^+ s'$ for $(s, s') \in \mathcal{T}^+$ (transitive closure), and $s \to^* s'$ for $(s, s') \in \mathcal{T}^*$ (reflexive, transitive closure). A *path* through the state space between states s, s' is denoted by $s \xRightarrow{V} s'$, with $V \in \Sigma^*$ a sequence of actions $\alpha_0, \ldots, \alpha_n$ ($n \in \mathbb{N}$ and Σ^* the set of all finite sequences made up of actions in Σ) such that there exist states $s_0, \ldots, s_{n+1}$ with $s_0 = s$, $s_{n+1} = s'$, and $s_i \xrightarrow{\alpha_i} s_{i+1}$ for $0 \leq i \leq n$. We define the set of reachable states as: $\mathcal{R} \equiv \{ s \in \mathcal{S} \mid s_0 \to^* s \}$, i.e. a subset of $\mathcal{S}$, or all syntactically-allowed variable valuations in M.

To reflect the fact that the state space is generated *on-the-fly*, hence not known a-priori, we sometimes use a next-state function $en \colon \mathcal{S} \to 2^{\mathcal{S}}$ instead of $\mathcal{T}$ directly. On-the-fly checking procedures iteratively query all successors of all visited states, starting from the initial state.

To reason about correctness of *reactive systems*, φ may refer to infinite paths. We consider properties that are already incorporated in the state space of M. Well-known techniques exist to construct such so-called cross-products while still allowing on-the-fly verification [1, Ch.4]). Such state spaces are (finite) Büchi automata $\mathbb{B} = (\mathcal{G}, \mathcal{F})$, where $\mathcal{F} \subseteq \mathcal{S}$ is a set of accepting states. $\mathbb{B}$ accepts ω-regular words VW^ω with $V, W \in \Sigma^*$ and W^ω the infinite repetition of W. A word VW^ω is accepted by $\mathbb{B}$ iff there exists an infinite path labeled VW^ω that reaches an infinite number of accepting states. Since $\mathbb{B}$ is finite-state, this means that there must exist a path $s_0 \xRightarrow{V} s \xRightarrow{W} s$ and for some $XY = W$, $s \xRightarrow{X} s'$, we have $s' \in \mathcal{F}$. Since s' is an accepting state, we call $s \xRightarrow{X} s$ an *accepting cycle*. So, finite Büchi automata accept all traces that end in an accepting cycle, i.e. are lasso-formed. An accepted trace represents a counter-example in M to φ, hence the verification problem is reduced to finding accepting cycles that are reachable from the initial state, which can be done in time linear to the size of the state space using, for example, the well-known sequential algorithm NDFS [7].

Multi-core LTL checking. CNDFS [8] is a parallel LTL model checking algorithm, based on NDFS [7]. In NDFS, a DFS is run from s_0 to find reachable accepting states, and from each accepting state $s \in \mathcal{F}$, a *nested* DFS is launched to find a cycle containing s. Because of the order in which states are visited, NDFS runs in time linear to the state space size. For clarity, in the following, we refer to the outer DFS finding accepting states as the *blue* search, and to the nested DFS as the *red* search. These colors relate to how the searches affect the global state of the algorithm. Initially, all states are white. The blue search colors states cyan when it puts states on its stack, and blue when the state is fully explored and popped again from the stack (backtracked). The red search colors states pink when placed on its stack, and red when backtracking.

Algorithm 1.. CNDFS with parallel cycle proviso (in boxed lines)

Require: $\forall s \in \mathcal{S}: s.prov = ?$

1: **procedure** $cndfs(s_0, P)$
2:   $dfsBlue_1(s_0) \parallel \ldots \parallel dfsBlue_P(s_0)$
3:   **report no-cycle**

4: **procedure** $dfsRed_p(s)$
5:   $s.pink[p] := \mathbf{true}$
6:   $\mathcal{R}_p := \mathcal{R}_p \cup \{s\}$
7:   **stack** $sel_p(s) := por(s)$
8:   **for all** $s' \in mix_p(sel_p(s))$ **do**
9:     **if** $s'.cyan[p]$ **then**
10:       **report accepting cycle**
11:     **if** $s' \notin \mathcal{R}_p \wedge \neg s'.red$ **then**
12:       $dfsRed_p(s')$

13:   **if** $sel_p(s)=por(s)\wedge por(s) \subset en(s)$ **then**
14:     $new := \exists x \in por(s) : x.pink[p]$
15:     $cas(s.prov, ?, new)$
16:     **if** $s.prov = \mathbf{true}$ **then**
17:       $sel_p(s) := en(s)$
18:       **goto** l.8

19:   $s.pink[p] := \mathbf{false}$

20: **procedure** $dfsBlue_p(s)$
21:   $s.cyan[p] := \mathbf{true}$
22:   **stack** $sel_p(s) := por(s)$
23:   **for all** $s' \in mix_p(sel_p(s))$ **do**
24:     **if** $\neg s'.cyan[p] \wedge \neg s'.blue$ **then**
25:       $dfsBlue_p(s')$

26:   **if** $sel_p(s)=por(s)\wedge por(s) \subset en(s)$ **then**
27:     $new := \exists x \in por(s) : x.cyan[p]$
28:     $cas(s.prov, ?, new)$
29:     **if** $s.prov = \mathbf{true}$ **then**
30:       $sel_p(s) := en(s)$
31:       **goto** l.23

32:   $s.blue := \mathbf{true}$
33:   **if** $s \in \mathcal{F}$ **then**
34:     $\mathcal{R}_p := \emptyset$
35:     $dfsRed_p(s)$
36:     **await** $\forall s' \in \mathcal{R}_p \cap \mathcal{F} \setminus \{s\} : s'.red$
37:     **forall** $s' \in \mathcal{R}_p$ **do** $s'.red := \mathbf{true}$
38:   $s.cyan[p] := \mathbf{false}$

In CNDFS, several workers explore the state space mostly independently by each running a randomized NDFS; it is randomized w.r.t. the order in which the successors of each state are visited. Algorithm 1 without the boxed code (lines 13-18 and 26-31), and with $sel_p(s) = en(s)$ at l.7 and l.22, shows CNDFS. The algorithm is called for a given number of workers P. Each worker p starts by executing $dfsBlue_p(s_0)$, which starts the blue search. A local set of successor states $sel_p(s)$ is initialized to $en(s)$ at l.22. For clarity, we use a notation that distinguishes such sets for different p and s, but in practice, a stack-local variable is sufficient, i.e. the full definition of a function sel_p does not need to be maintained throughout the search. This is indicated with the **stack** keyword. Randomization of visiting successors of s is achieved through the function mix_p. If a state s is accepting, a red search is launched from it (l.35), to try to find a cycle containing s. In the red search, again local state sets are used to inspect successors (l.7). A cycle containing s is detected once a cyan state is reached (l.9). Since a cyan state is on the stack of the blue search, and accepting state s from which the red search has been launched is at the top of this stack, reaching any cyan state means that a complete cycle exists containing s.

CNDFS scales particularly well because some information is shared between workers. The blue color is shared between blue searches, hence when one worker has colored a state blue, other workers will not explore it anymore (l.24) (of course, local cyan states are also not added to the stack). In principle, one would also like to share the red color between red searches. It has been shown [8], however, that this cannot be done in a similar fashion. For correctness, one can only share this information once a red search has completely terminated. For this reason, we use a worker-local red set $\mathcal{R}_p$, consisting of the states that have been explored by the red search of worker p, which is constructed as a red search continues, and only made globally red (l.37) once the worker knows that all out-of-order red searches in the same search region have terminated (l.36).

CNDFS's complexity can be linear in the size of the graph, and its scalability is good (although for some graphs, its performance reduces to that of sequential NDFS). CNDFS has been shown to perform better than the fixpoint-based OWCTY algorithm [2] – for many years the best known algorithm for parallel LTL model checking – which has a worst-case quadratic complexity.

Partial-order reduction. POR prunes interleavings by constraining the next-state function *en*. This selection should preserve the property at hand (safety or liveness), and can be performed with the *state-local* information combined with some static analysis of M (mainly involving the commutativity of its operations).

A (state-local) POR function prunes $\mathcal{G}$ *on-the-fly* during exploration by selecting in each state s a subset of the enabled transitions, the *reduced set* $por(s) \subseteq en(s)$. POR definitions often allow multiple valid reduced sets, including trivially $por(s) = en(s)$. Smaller reduced sets often lead to smaller state spaces, but this is not necessarily the case [31]. Therefore, POR is heuristic in nature.

Over the years, several techniques have been developed to select sufficient subsets of enabled transitions, such as the stubborn set technique [30]. Since the selection of subsets of enabled transitions is orthogonal to our proposed CNDFS algorithm with POR, we consider the subset selection algorithm as a given, implemented with a function $por : \mathcal{S} \to 2^{\mathcal{S}}$. For a detailed explanation of the implementation of a POR subset selection algorithm, see [21].

The ignoring problem. Valmari identified the incompleteness of POR with respect to the preservation of liveness properties [29]. As liveness properties reason over infinite paths in $\mathbb{B}$, (state-local) POR may exhibit ignoring, i.e. continuously exclude actions leading to counter examples from the reduced set. The introduction of the *ignoring proviso* solved this, by forcing the involvement of all relevant transitions when constructing reduced sets. Because these ignoring provisos depend on *global* properties of $\mathbb{B}$, i.e. cycles in its $\mathcal{G}$, we first define a dynamic function *sel* which relaxes the *por* function such that $por(s) \subseteq sel(s) \subseteq en(s)$..

The exact dynamic definition of *sel* will be part of the on-the-fly exploration algorithms presented in the subsequent section. The definition of the proviso now depends on the reduced state-space graph induced by *sel* a posteriori (after the termination of the exploration algorithm). We denote this reduced graph $\overline{\mathcal{G}} = (s_0, \overline{\mathcal{T}}, \mathcal{S})$, with $\overline{\mathcal{T}} \subseteq \mathcal{T}$ such that each $(s, \alpha, s') \in \mathcal{T}$ is also in $\overline{\mathcal{T}}$ iff $s' \in sel(s)$. Transitions in this graph are denoted $s \Rightarrow s'$, and we define $\overline{\mathcal{R}} \equiv \{s \in \mathcal{S} \mid s_0 \Rightarrow^* s\}$. We define $\overline{\mathbb{B}}$ as $(\overline{\mathcal{G}}, \mathcal{F})$, so that any mention of $\overline{\mathcal{G}}$ and $\overline{\mathcal{R}}$ generalizes to $\overline{\mathbb{B}}$.

The ignoring proviso can now be defined on the reduced state space. (Ignoring provisos weaker than the follwoing exist, see e.g. [32], but their refinements are orthogonal to the cycle detection problem that we aim to solve here.)

Cycle. Along each cycle in $\overline{\mathcal{G}}$, at least one state s is *fully explored* ($sel(s) = en(s)$).

An implementation of the *Cycle* ignoring proviso thus needs to identify cycles on-the-fly and include all transitions of at least one state on each cycle. However, selecting the smallest set of states covering all (possibly overlapping) cycles is an NP-complete problem, known as the *vertex feedback set* in graph theory [13]. Therefore, in practice, this proviso is implemented using DFS, which guarantees full exploration of at *least one* state on each cycle, *and* can be performed efficiently [9]. In this (stronger) form, the proviso is as follows:

Stack. When running a depth-first search (DFS) over $\overline{\mathcal{G}}$, each state $s \in \mathcal{R}$ that has a successor $s' \in por(s)$ on the stack, should be fully explored.

The *Stack* proviso overestimates the amount of states to explore fully, but has been improved over the years to yield excellent reductions [9].

In the next section, we present how to detect cycles in parallel, enabling POR in that setting. The preciseness that is achieved by this method is expected to be better than in related parallel solutions (see Section 4 for experimental results).

3   Multi-core Partial-Order Reduction

In the current section, we present a parallel cycle proviso for both safety and liveness properties, for use in parallel DFS-based algorithms. The presented algorithms indirectly implement the *sel* function on which the reduced state space $\mathcal{R}$ was defined in the previous section. While we are mainly interested in a complete solution for LTL model checking, we commence with a solution for safety properties, in order to introduce the approach in a stepwise fashion.

3.1   Partial-Order Reduction for Safety Properties

Checking safety properties can be done through reachability analysis. To show how the ignoring problem can be solved for safety properties, we introduce a parallel algorithm that launches multiple DFS workers. We refer to this approach as *parallel DFS*. While it is not the most efficient approach to do reachability analysis – for a better approach see [16] – parallel DFS provides a nice first step towards combining POR with CNDFS.

Safety properties are preserved by a weaker version of the ignoring proviso. One such version concerns bottom Strongly Connected Components (SCCs), i.e. SCCs without outgoing transitions:

BottomSCC. For all states $s \in \mathcal{R}$ of $\overline{\mathcal{G}}$, there exists a fully explored state s' $(sel(s') = en(s'))$ such that $s \Rrightarrow^* s'$. (this boils down to having one fully explored state in each bottom SCC of $\overline{\mathcal{G}}$, c.f. [32]).

Our parallel DFS with POR should detect at least one state in all bottom SCCs in $\mathcal{G}$. Valmari's SCC method is optimal [29] for this purpose. However, we use the stronger *Stack'* condition, which serves our introductory purpose better as it resembles the ignoring proviso required to preserve LTL (see the *Stack* proviso in the previous section):

Algorithm 2.. Parallel DFS with POR

Require: $\forall s \in \mathcal{S}: s.blue = false$	4: **procedure** $dfs_p(s)$
Require: $\forall s \in \mathcal{S}, p: s.cyan[p] = false$	5: $s.cyan[p] :=$ **true**
1: **procedure** $pardfs(s_0, P)$	6: **stack** $sel_p(s) := por(s)$
2: $dfs_1(s_0) \| \ldots \| dfs_P(s_0)$	7: **for all** $s' \in mix_p(sel_p(s))$ **do**
3: **report** no-cycle	8: **if** $\neg s'.cyan[p] \wedge \neg s'.blue$ **then**
	9: $dfs_p(s')$

```
 10:    if sel_p(s)=por(s)∧por(s)⊂en(s) then
 11:       if ∀x ∈ por(s) : x.cyan[p] then
 12:          sel_p(s) := en(s)
 13:          goto l.7
```

```
 A: cas(s.prov, ?, ∀x ∈ por(s) : x.cyan[p])
 B: if s.prov = true then
 C:    sel_p(s) := en(s)
 D:    goto l.7
```

	14: $s.blue :=$ **true**
	15: $s.cyan[p] :=$ **false**

Stack'. When running a DFS exploration over $\overline{\mathcal{G}}$, each state $s \in \overline{\mathcal{R}}$ for which *all* successors in $por(s)$ are on the stack, should be fully explored.

Consider Algorithm 2 without the boxed lines (lines 10–13 and A–D) and with $sel_p(s) = en(s)$ at l.6. (We use a local sel_p to explain how workers communicate successor sets, the global sel is defined later.) It starts P parallel DFS workers at l.2, which initially each independently traverse the state space (see the local cyan color at l.5 and l.15, indicating that a state is currently on the DFS stack). When backtracking, the workers communicate by marking states globally as visited at l.14 (with the color blue). Clearly, this algorithm explores all reachable states, and hence terminates on finite state spaces, since a state s is only colored globally blue once all states reachable from s have either been explored (are colored blue) or are going to be explored in the future (are colored cyan).

To introduce POR for safety properties, the ignoring proviso *BottomSCC* needs to be satisfied. We show that this is done by adopting the *Stack'* proviso in parallel DFS as a parallel *Stack'* proviso at l.10-13. The resulting algorithm will find at least one state on each cycle, and this state will be fully explored by at least one worker. At l.6, $sel_p(s)$ is now actually set to $por(s)$, and l.10 checks whether this is still true. This ensures that the proviso check is performed at most once for each state s on the stack. When all successors of s are on the stack ($\forall x \in por(s) : x.cyan[p]$) (l.11), the premise of the *Stack'* proviso holds, and all successors are selected for visiting at l.12 (to satisfy the conclusion of the proviso), before restarting the for loop at l.13. (The redundant reselection of $por(s) \subset en(s)$ can be avoided, but is used here to simplify our proofs.) The second time that l.10 is reached, $sel_p(s)$ is no longer set to $por(s)$, so the check is not performed a second time. To handle the special case that $por(s) = en(s)$, we require at l.10 that $sel_p(s) \subset en(s)$. Otherwise, an infinite goto loop would occur.

In the following proofs, we assume that each line of the code is executed atomically. The global state of the algorithm is the coloring of $\overline{\mathcal{R}}$ and the program counter of each worker. We use the following notations: The sets C_p and B contain all the states colored cyan by worker p, and globally blue, respectively.

For example, $s.cyan[p] = \textbf{true}$ is expressed as $s \in C_p$. To reason on the a posteriori explored graph, we define $sel(s) = en(s)$ iff $\exists p \in \{1 \ldots P\}: sel_p(s) = en(s)$, and $sel(s) = por(s)$ otherwise (notice that $sel_p(s)$ only grows). Finally, we use the modal operator $s \in \square X$ to reason about the successors of s in $\overline{\mathcal{G}}$, i.e. $\forall s' \in sel(s): s' \in X$, and for local successors: $s \in \square_p X \Rightarrow \forall s' \in sel_p(s): s' \in X$. We write $F_p(s)@L$ to indicate that thread p is about to execute l.L of function F).

The first lemma shows colorings of local successors of backtracked states, while the second relates backtracked states to the coloring of global successors:

Lemma 1. *When worker p marks a state s blue, its local successors are blue or cyan local to worker p:* $dfs_p(s)@14 \Rightarrow s \in \square_p(B \cup C_p)$.

Proof. At l.14, each local successor s' has either been skipped at l.8 (so $s' \in B \cup C_p$), or $dfs_p(s')$ had been called at l.9 leading to $t \in B$. So $s' \in (B \cup C_p)$. $\square$

Lemma 2. *Global successors of blue states that are not cyan, are blue or cyan:* $\bigcup_p(B \setminus C_p) \subseteq \square \bigcup_p(B \cup C_p)$.

Proof. Initially, $\bigcup_p(B \setminus C_p)$ is empty and the lemma holds. A state s is added to this set when the last worker p reaches $dfs_p(s)@l.15$. Locally, we have $s \in \square_p(B \cup C_p)$ by Lemma 1, but since all workers backtracked $s \in \bigcup_p \square(B \cup C_p)$ holds as well. Finally, states are never removed from $B \cup C_p$. $\square$

To reason about states for which the proviso's conclusion holds, we consider all states s with $sel(s) = en(s)$, i.e. *inviolable* states, as belonging to a set I, and all others with $sel(s) \subset en(s)$ as belonging to a set N (violable states).

Lemma 3. *In Algorithm 2, each blue state s can reach an inviolable state s':* $\forall s \in B: (\exists s' \in I: s \Rightarrow^* s')$.

Proof. B is only modified at l.14. I and N are 'modified' right before l.14.

Initially, B is empty, so the lemma holds. By Lemma 1, when the first state s is marked blue, it will have blue and cyan successors. Since at that point, there are no blue states yet, all successors of s must be cyan. But then, s must be inviolable at l.14, so $s \in I$ (if $por(s) = \emptyset$, then $en(s) = \emptyset$, since POR does not introduce deadlocks). All subsequent states marked blue either are identified as inviolable, satisfying the lemma with $s \equiv s'$, or have at least one blue successor $s' \not\equiv s$, for which the theorem already holds. $\square$

Finally, by showing that from each state reached by parallel DFS, an inviolable state is reachable, we clearly show that *BottomSCC* is satisfied.

Theorem 1. *Algorithm 2 explores all $s \in \overline{\mathcal{R}}$, and satisfies BottomSCC:* $\forall s \in \overline{\mathcal{R}}: (\exists s' \in I: s \Rightarrow^* s')$.

Proof. Due to l.10 and l.12, the goto can only be executed once per state. And since the set $B \cup \bigcup_p C_p$ grows monotonically in Algorithm 2, eventually the algorithm terminates for finite input graphs (see Section 8). By the obvious post-condition of DFS-based algorithms, we have $s_0 \in B$ at that moment. By Lemma 2, and the fact that $\bigcup_p C_p = \emptyset$ (the stacks are empty), we have $B \subseteq \square B$. Hence, $\overline{\mathcal{R}} = B$, and it follows from Lemma 3 that *BottomSCC* is satisfied. $\square$

Algorithm 2 has the downside that it could identify more inviolable states than strictly necessary, as the following example shows.

Example 1. The cycle in the graph on the right has multiple entrypoints. When different workers (with different search orders) enter the cycle differently, they determine a different inviolable state: a worker A entering via a will choose d (as it finds a to be cyan after traversing the cycle), while a worker B entering via d chooses c.

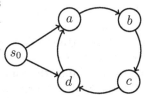

A coherent view of the state space. The problem that Algorithm 2 still exhibits, is that different workers obtain a different view of the state space, as they identify different inviolable states. As these are fully explored, the reduction can be limited. Therefore, we introduce synchronization between threads on their decision whether a state is inviolable or not. To realize this, we add a 3-valued variable per state called *prov*, initially set to *unknown* ('?'). This variable is global, hence workers can communicate with each other through the *prov* variables.

The boxed code at lines A–D should replace the parallel proviso check of lines 11–13. Upon backtracking, threads use the well-known atomic compare-and-swap (*cas*) operation to communicate their decision on a first-come-first-serve basis. The *cas* operation is defined as follows: $cas(x, v_1, v_2)$ atomically checks if variable x has value v_1, and if so, sets x to v_2. This solution does not completely prevent redundant inviolable states (w.r.t. to the *Stack'* proviso), but it can prevent some. For instance, in Example 1, c can be prevented from becoming inviolable, if worker A backtracks over c before worker B, marking c as violable.

Correctness of the modified algorithm follows from Lemma 4. It reasons on the states whose violability status has been determined ($s.prov \neq ?$) or is known upfront ($por(s) = en(s)$), captured by the final set: $F = \{s \in \mathcal{R} \mid s.prov \neq ? \vee por(s) = en(s)\}$. The lemma shows that when a state s is determined to be violable ($s \in F \cap N$), then s has a blue successor (for which Lemma 3 holds).

Lemma 4. *At least one global successor of a permanently violable state is blue:* $F \cap N \cap \Box B \neq \emptyset$.

Proof. A state s is added to $F \cap N$ after l.A sets $s.prov$ to **false**. By Lemma 1 and the fact that $\forall x \in por(s) \colon x.cyan[p]$ evaluated to **false**, we know there must be one blue successor (again if $por(s) = \emptyset$, then $en(s) = \emptyset$ and $s \notin N$). □

3.2 Partial-Order Reduction for Liveness Properties

For liveness properties, the *Cycle* proviso needs to hold (Section 2), which is met in finite state-space graphs if along all cycles at least one state is fully explored. In addition to this, CNDFS should search for accepting cycles, which constitute counter-examples (instead of $\mathcal{G}$, the algorithms now work on $\mathbb{B}$). In the current subsection, we show that CNDFS with POR and a novel *parallel cycle proviso*, similar to *Stack*, fulfills *Cycle*. First, we discuss how we solve a related problem.

Traditional (sequential) NDFS detects accepting cycles by launching a nested (red) DFS search from each accepting state found in the outer (blue) DFS search (see Section 2). Combining NDFS with POR and the *Stack* proviso yields a so-called *revisiting problem* [12]; in order for NDFS with POR to be complete, it is crucial that for every state s, the selection of $sel(s)$ is deterministic. This means that two constraints must be satisfied: (1) if a state is deemed inviolable, then all searches reaching it must be aware of this and select all successors, and (2) if a state is violable, the same subset must always be selected by the *por* function.

For the NDFS algorithm in [28], the revisiting problem can solved straightforwardly, by only selecting blue and cyan successors in the red search [28, Sec. 6]. This enforces that each state reached in a red search is explored in the same way as previously done in the blue search. However, in CNDFS, this approach does not apply because different searches run out of order executions; in particular, red searches may sometimes visit white states (see the proof of [8, Prop. 3]).

However, the revisiting problem of CNDFS with POR can be solved as follows. First of all, it is crucial that the subset selection mechanism is deterministic. This can be achieved efficiently, e.g. via guard-based POR [21]. Second of all, the decisions regarding proviso status of states is made global via synchronization methods similar to those used in the previous subsection, now also indicated by the boxed code in Algorithm 1. It implements the *Stack* proviso in both the blue and the red DFS. In the blue DFS, we check for the existence of at least one cyan successor (l.27), and in the red DFS for the existence of a pink successor (l.14). The mechanism to store the results using *cas* and *s.prov* is exactly as presented earlier for parallel DFS. This implements our parallel cycle proviso.

In the following correctness proofs, we refer with P_p to the pink states of worker p and with Red to the (globally) red states. We also construct a set of states backtracked in a red search: $R \equiv \bigcup_p(\mathcal{R}_p \setminus P_p) \cup Red$ (all states that are either in some local $\mathcal{R}_p$ but not on the pink stack, or globally marked red).

Now that we have $sel_p(s) = sel(s)$ at l.32, we can relate blue states to their (global) successor colorings (the proof is similar to that of Lemma 1):

Lemma 5. *Successors of blue states are blue or cyan:* $B \subseteq \Box\bigcup_p(B \cup C_p)$.

The next lemma expresses that for backtracked states, a decision has been made concerning their violability status.

Lemma 6. *Blue states and states backtracked in a red search have been considered for violability:* $B \cup R \subseteq F$.

Proof. A state s is colored blue at l.32. If $por(s) = en(s)$, then $s \in F$. If $por(s) \subset en(s)$, then l.28 has been executed, hence $s \in F$. A state s is colored red at l.37. There, we have $s \in \mathcal{R}_p \wedge s \notin P_p$, hence already $s \in R$. Also, at l.19, a state s is in R, since $s \notin P_p$. But then, either $por(s) = en(s)$, and $s \in F$, or $por(s) \subset en(s)$, and l.15 has been executed, so $s \in F$. $\Box$

The following lemmas help to prove Theorem 2, expressing that Algorithm 1 satisfies the *Stack* proviso, which implies that *Cycle* is satisfied.

Lemma 7. *Successors of states backtracked in the red search have also been backtracked in the red search or are pink:* $R \subseteq \Box \bigcup_p (R \cup P_p)$.

Proof. Since $R \equiv \bigcup_p (\mathcal{R}_p \setminus P_p) \cup Red$, we have $\bigcup_p (R \cup P_p) \equiv \bigcup_p ((\mathcal{R}_p \setminus P_p) \cup P_p) \cup Red$, so we need to prove that $R \subseteq \Box \bigcup_p (\mathcal{R}_p \cup Red)$. A state s is added to R when it is removed from P_p at l.19, since at that point $s \in \mathcal{R}_p$. At l.34, if $\mathcal{R}_p$ is non-empty, states are removed from $\mathcal{R}_p$, but those were added to Red at l.37 after the previous $dfsRed_p(s)$ terminated. Once added to Red (and R), states are never removed again. At l.19, all successors t have been considered at l.9–12. If $t \notin \mathcal{R}_p \cup Red$, then $dfsRed_p(t)$ is executed adding t to $\mathcal{R}_p$. So at l.19, we have $s \in \Box (\mathcal{R}_p \cup Red)$. □

Lemma 8. *Successors of permanently violable states are blue or backtracked in a red search:* $F \cap N \subseteq \Box (B \cup R)$.

Proof. A state s is permanently marked violable before l.19 and l.32. Because the conditions at l.14, resp. l.27, do not hold there, no successor s' of s can be pink, resp. cyan. By Lemma 7 (resp. Lemma 5), all s' are in R (resp. B). □

Theorem 2. *Algorithm 1 explores all states in $\overline{\mathcal{R}}$ of $\overline{\mathbb{B}}$, and fully explores one state on each cycle in $\overline{\mathbb{B}}$.*

Proof. The termination proof is analogous to that in Theorem 1.

We prove that the proviso holds by contradiction. Assume Algorithm 1 ran to completion, and as a result some cycle $C = s_1 \to \cdots \to s_n \to s_1$ contains no inviolable state: $\forall i \in \{1 \ldots n\}: s_i \in N$. Take the last time that a state s_x with $x \in \{1 \ldots n\}$ on C was permanently added to N ($s_x.prov$ is set to **false** at that moment). At this time, some worker p must be executing either l.15 or l.28. The immediate predecessor s_y of s_x on the cycle must have been in $F \cap N$ before s_x is marked, since s_x was the last state to be permanently marked violable. Therefore, by Lemma 8, $s_x \in B \cup R$. But then, by Lemma 6, $s_x \in F$. The latter contradicts our assumption that s_x is last marked permanently violable, which can only happen if its proviso flag is still set to '?', i.e. $s_x \notin F$ or $s_x \in I$. □

4 Experimental Evaluation

Experimental Setup. We implemented Algorithm 1 in the LTSMIN toolset. This toolset [17] is a language-independent model checker and supports POR since version 1.6. To this end, LTSMIN's PINS interface was extended with new funtions in order to export the necessary static information [21]. We experimented with DVE models from the BEEM database [27] and PROMELA models [11]; both are supported by LTSMIN via different language modules [4,17]. The selected models and properties are presented in Table 1, and include industrial case studies in PROMELA as well as representable instances from the large BEEM database. We focus on instances where the properties hold, because on-the-fly bug-hunting is not a bottleneck in our experience [8]. We performed experiments with version 2.1 of LTSMIN.[1] All experiments were repeated 10 times on a quadruple AMD Opteron 6376 CPU with 64 cores and 512GB RAM memory.

---

[1] http://fmt.cs.utwente.nl/tools/ltsmin/ (see [8] for command lines)

Table 1. DVE/PROMELA models and LTL properties used (all correct)

Model (DVE)	Property	Model (PROMELA)	Property
leader_filters.7	$\Diamond(\#elected \neq 0)$	garp	$\Box\Diamond progress$
elevator.3	$\Box(in \Rightarrow (\Diamond out))$	iprotocol-2	$\Box\Diamond progress$
leader_election.*	$\Diamond(\#leaders \neq 0)$	pacemaker_distibuted	$\Box(p \wedge (q \Rightarrow r))$
anderson.6	$\Box(req \Rightarrow \Diamond CS)$	pacemaker_concurrent	$\Box((p \Rightarrow q) \wedge (r \Rightarrow s))$

The results presented here focus primarily on the efficiency of the reduction of the parallel cycle proviso in LTL model checking. The main question that is answered is whether the parallel cycle proviso introduces too many inviolable states with respect to the sequential cycle proviso. We also did some analysis on the obtained scalability of CNDFS with POR, mainly to confirm that scalability is not lost; in the past, CNDFS has shown to scale well and often better than other parallel LTL model checking algorithms [4,8]. The complete set of experimental results are available at http://fmt.cs.utwente.nl/tools/ltsmin/hvc-2014.

We would have preferred to compare the parallel cycle proviso with the topological sort proviso [3] in DiVinE (see Section 5), the most sophisticated solution thus far, but the POR algorithm in DiVinE delivers less reductions than LTSmin's stubborn set implementation making a tool-by-tool comparison senseless. We did not reimplement the topological sort proviso because it seems impossible to combine it with CNDFS. Instead, we compare our conclusions with [3].

Reduction Performance. Sequentially, the CNDFS algorithm is equal to the NDFS algorithm modulo the fact that states are not instantly colored red, but only after the nested search [8]. Similarly, the parallel cycle proviso should be equal to the stack proviso when run with one thread. With increasing parallelism, the algorithm has the potential to select more states as inviolable as explained in Example 1. We are interested in determining these relative differences in reductions (between the stack proviso and the parallel cycle proviso). As

Table 2. POR reductions (percentages) without ignoring proviso, with stack proviso and with parallel cycle proviso (with multiple threads) averaged over 10 runs

Model	$|\mathcal{R}|$	None	Stack	Parallel cycle proviso (threads)					
				1	4	8	16	32	64
leader_filters.7	26,302,351	2.35	2.35	2.35	2.35	2.35	2.35	2.35	2.35
elevator.3	495,463	92.46	92.86	94.20	94.49	94.64	94.77	94.85	94.96
leader_election.4	746,051	3.02	3.02	3.02	3.02	3.02	3.02	3.02	3.02
leader_election.6	35,773,430	0.69	0.69	0.70	0.69	0.69	0.69	0.69	0.69
anderson.6	29,315,027	15.80	33.11	48.43	52.28	52.83	52.93	52.34	51.71
garp	67,108,837	6.25	18.68	18.69	20.23	20.85	20.69	20.64	20.79
peterson4	67,108,842	14.19	15.82	15.52	15.60	15.64	15.63	15.67	15.67
iprotocol-2	18,998,110	30.95	32.24	34.80	36.31	36.71	37.10	37.46	37.91
pacemaker_distributed	67,108,832	31.13	47.89	47.81	47.86	47.94	47.98	48.16	48.26
pacemaker_concurrent	18,092,815	42.06	46.05	45.90	45.88	45.92	45.92	45.96	46.00

Table 3. CNDFS runtimes (sec.) without POR (*Full*), without ignoring (*None*), with stack proviso (*Stack*), and with parallel cycle proviso averaged over 10 runs

Model	Full	None	Stack	Parallel cycle proviso (threads)					
				1	4	8	16	32	64
leader_filters.7	85.32	5.59	5.42	5.60	1.46	0.82	0.45	0.26	0.19
elevator.3		1.83	196.17	185.24	228.41	78.14	47.54	29.50	19.12	14.75
leader_election.4	5.68	6.33	6.16	6.51	2.28	1.93	1.23	1.23	1.93
leader_election.6	399.94	0.88	0.84	0.90	0.23	0.13	0.07	0.04	0.04
anderson.6	168.10	29.55	64.42	121.74	63.57	43.90	29.55	19.53	14.87
garp	426.06	15.66	52.09	62.52	28.54	18.75	12.03	7.69	5.94
peterson4	287.62	30.30	35.93	39.67	11.83	6.56	3.85	2.19	1.49
iprotocol-2	68.90	84.39	85.31	115.31	40.07	23.70	14.47	8.69	6.28
pacemaker_distributed	211.65	99.56	156.25	167.62	43.88	23.66	13.25	7.33	4.86
pacemaker_concurrent	55.16	256.92	332.50	342.65	88.68	46.01	24.72	12.88	7.97

a measurement, we choose the total number of states stored in the hash table. Although the relation between reduced state space size and number of inviolable states is only heuristic (exploring a different, but larger subset of states fully could yield a smaller reduced state space [10]), we are unaware of a better measurement.

Table 2 shows the size of the reduced state spaces relative to the original state space. For completeness, we also included the results without any ignoring proviso (which might miss counter-examples). All models show similar parallel reductions to the stack proviso, except anderson.6. We suspect that this is caused by a slightly more efficient implementation of the stack proviso, in particular concerning the revisiting problem, in the sequential nested search which does not work in a parallel setting (see [28] and discussion in Section 3.2).

A slight decrease in reductions when the number of threads is increased can be observed, the effect is however minimal and often sublinear with the most increase caused by 4 threads already. Hence we can conclude that CNDFS with POR does not cause too many redundant full explorations. This is a surprising result, as the parallel benchmarks in [3] seem to show a steep decrease in reduction performance.

We cannot explain precisely why the reductions sometimes improve with more parallelism, e.g. anderson.6 (recall that we present averages over 10 experiments). The behavior might be caused by different thread schedulings.

Runtime Performance. Table 3 shows that the runtimes of CNDFS with POR are similar to those of NDFS with stack proviso (discounting the state space difference for anderson.6). The overhead of the proviso bits is thus minimal.

Scalability. Figure 1 shows that CNDFS with POR exhibits good speedups for larger models (see Table 3). Comparing these speedups to those obtained earlier without POR [8], we see that they are largely unaffected. It is not surprising that the smaller (reduced) leader-election model with only a few thousand states exhibits sublinear speedup.

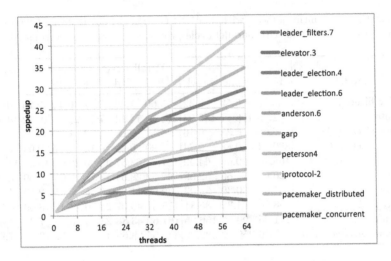

Fig. 1. Plot of parallel scalability (speedup) of CNDFS with POR

5   Related Work

Applying POR when model checking liveness properties involves an ignoring proviso which may cause orders of magnitude loss in reductions (c.f. [15,9]). In a sequential setting, the use of DFS-based algorithms could mitigate these losses almost completely in the past (c.f. [15,9,29]). However, those techniques cannot be used in parallel, i.e. multi-threaded, shared memory, model checking.

In related work, several other attempts have been made to implement the ignoring proviso for similar parallel settings.

1. The *topological sort proviso* [3] uses the distributed Kahn algorithm for topological sort. When the sort is incomplete due to cycles, these nodes are removed (fully explored) and the algorithm is restarted up to fixpoint.
2. The *two-phase proviso* [26] skips new states with singleton reduced sets, trivially avoiding cycles by fully exploring other states.
3. A distributed version of SPIN [22], implements the *Stack'* proviso for safety properties, while conservatively assuming that successors maintained by other workers are on their respective stacks.
4. A stronger alternative for the *Stack* proviso is one tailored for BFS, where all states reaching queued states are fully explored [5,6].
5. Static POR identifies cycles already in the system specification [14].

All of the above methods have either shown to offer significantly less reduction than the *Stack* proviso (4 and 5), only work for safety properties (3), or have shown a degrading performance when the amount of parallelism is increased, often already noticeable with 4–8 workers (1 and 2).

Finally, Evangelista and Pajault [9] further optimized the *Stack* proviso to avoid unnecessary full explorations on overlapping cycles and on cycles that already contain fully explored states. We are the first to adopt these optimizations in a parallel setting.

6 Conclusions

In this paper, we proposed how POR can be integrated in parallel DFS-based search algorithms, in particular in both a parallel DFS reachability algorithm, and CNDFS for on-the-fly LTL model checking. The used parallelization technique is very promising, since very good speedups occur in practice.

To integrate POR, the main challenge was to ensure that when confronted with cycles, the parallel threads explore beyond them, i.e. they do not continuously ignore actions that may lead to new reachable states. This is known as the ignoring problem. Furthermore, for completeness, the two DFS searches in NDFS need to agree on which transitions are explored from each state, and for CNDFS, earlier solutions for this revisiting problem are not correct. We proposed solutions for both these problems. Experimental results indicate that our solution for CNDFS does not harm the scalability of it, while reductions are achieved that are comparable when applying POR in a sequential NDFS.

For future work, the ideas from the color proviso [9] could be incorporated in the parallel cycle proviso, since both are based on a stack check. We expect similar improvements as witnessed in [9].

Acknowledgements. We thank Tom van Dijk for providing access to the 64-core machine at the FMT department of the University Twente.

References

1. Baier, C., Katoen, J.P.: Principles of Model Checking. The MIT Press (2008)
2. Barnat, J., Brim, L., Ročkai, P.: A Time-Optimal On-the-Fly Parallel Algorithm for Model Checking of Weak LTL Properties. In: Breitman, K., Cavalcanti, A. (eds.) ICFEM 2009. LNCS, vol. 5885, pp. 407–425. Springer, Heidelberg (2009)
3. Barnat, J., Brim, L., Ročkai, P.: Parallel Partial Order Reduction with Topological Sort Proviso. In: SEFM 2010, pp. 222–231. IEEE Computer Society (2010)
4. van der Berg, F., Laarman, A.: SpinS: Extending LTSmin with Promela through SpinJa. ENTCS 296, 95–105 (2013)
5. Bošnački, D., Holzmann, G.J.: Improving Spin's Partial-Order Reduction for Breadth-First Search. In: Godefroid, P. (ed.) SPIN 2005. LNCS, vol. 3639, pp. 91–105. Springer, Heidelberg (2005)
6. Bošnački, D., Leue, S., Lluch-Lafuente, A.: Partial-Order Reduction for General State Exploring Algorithms. STTT 11(1), 39–51 (2009)
7. Courcoubetis, C., Vardi, M., Wolper, P., Yannakakis, M.: Memory Efficient Algorithms for the Verification of Temporal Properties. In: Clarke, E., Kurshan, R.P. (eds.) CAV 1990. LNCS, vol. 531, pp. 233–242. Springer, Heidelberg (1991)

8. Evangelista, S., Laarman, A., Petrucci, L., van de Pol, J.: Improved Multi-Core Nested Depth-First Search. In: Chakraborty, S., Mukund, M. (eds.) ATVA 2012. LNCS, vol. 7561, pp. 269–283. Springer, Heidelberg (2012)
9. Evangelista, S., Pajault, C.: Solving the Ignoring Problem for Partial Order Reduction. STTT 12, 155–170 (2010)
10. Geldenhuys, J., Hansen, H., Valmari, A.: Exploring the Scope for Partial Order Reduction. In: Liu, Z., Ravn, A.P. (eds.) ATVA 2009. LNCS, vol. 5799, pp. 39–53. Springer, Heidelberg (2009)
11. Holzmann, G.: The model checker SPIN. IEEE TSE 23, 279–295 (1997)
12. Holzmann, G., Peled, D., Yannakakis, M.: On Nested Depth First Search. In: SPIN 1996, pp. 23–32. American Mathematical Society (1996)
13. Karp, R.M.: Reducibility among Combinatorial Problems. In: Complexity of Computer Computations. IBM Research Symposia Series, pp. 85–103. Springer (1972)
14. Kurshan, R., Levin, V., Minea, M., Peled, D., Yenigün, H.: Static Partial Order Reduction. In: Steffen, B. (ed.) TACAS 1998. LNCS, vol. 1384, pp. 345–357. Springer, Heidelberg (1998)
15. Laarman, A., Faragó, D.: Improved On-The-Fly Livelock Detection. In: Brat, G., Rungta, N., Venet, A. (eds.) NFM 2013. LNCS, vol. 7871, pp. 32–47. Springer, Heidelberg (2013)
16. Laarman, A., van de Pol, J., Weber, M.: Boosting Multi-Core Reachability Performance with Shared Hash Tables. In: FMCAD 2010, pp. 247–255. IEEE-CS (2010)
17. Laarman, A., van de Pol, J., Weber, M.: Multi-Core LTSMIN: Marrying Modularity and Scalability. In: Bobaru, M., Havelund, K., Holzmann, G.J., Joshi, R. (eds.) NFM 2011. LNCS, vol. 6617, pp. 506–511. Springer, Heidelberg (2011)
18. Laarman, A.: Scalable Multi-Core Model Checking. Ph.D. thesis, University of Twente (2014)
19. Laarman, A., Langerak, R., van de Pol, J., Weber, M., Wijs, A.: Multi-core Nested Depth-First Search. In: Bultan, T., Hsiung, P.-A. (eds.) ATVA 2011. LNCS, vol. 6996, pp. 321–335. Springer, Heidelberg (2011)
20. Laarman, A., Olesen, M.C., Dalsgaard, A.E., Larsen, K.G., van de Pol, J.: Multi-core emptiness checking of timed büchi automata using inclusion abstraction. In: Sharygina, N., Veith, H. (eds.) CAV 2013. LNCS, vol. 8044, pp. 968–983. Springer, Heidelberg (2013)
21. Laarman, A., Pater, E., van de Pol, J., Weber, M.: Guard-Based Partial-Order Reduction. In: Bartocci, E., Ramakrishnan, C.R. (eds.) SPIN 2013. LNCS, vol. 7976, pp. 227–245. Springer, Heidelberg (2013)
22. Lerda, F., Sisto, R.: Distributed-Memory Model Checking with SPIN. In: Dams, D.R., Gerth, R., Leue, S., Massink, M. (eds.) SPIN 1999. LNCS, vol. 1680, pp. 22–39. Springer, Heidelberg (1999)
23. Liu, Y., Sun, J., Dong, J.: Scalable multi-core model checking fairness enhanced systems. In: Breitman, K., Cavalcanti, A. (eds.) ICFEM 2009. LNCS, vol. 5885, pp. 426–445. Springer, Heidelberg (2009)
24. Lowe, G.: Concurrent Depth-First Search Algorithms. In: Ábrahám, E., Havelund, K. (eds.) TACAS 2014 (ETAPS). LNCS, vol. 8413, pp. 202–216. Springer, Heidelberg (2014)
25. Moore, G.E.: Cramming more Components onto Integrated Circuits. Electronics 38(10), 114–117 (1965)
26. Nalumasu, R., Gopalakrishnan, G.: An Efficient Partial Order Reduction Algorithm with an Alternative Proviso Implementation. FMSD 20(3), 231–247 (2002)

27. Pelánek, R.: BEEM: Benchmarks for explicit model checkers. In: Bošnački, D., Edelkamp, S. (eds.) SPIN 2007. LNCS, vol. 4595, pp. 263–267. Springer, Heidelberg (2007)
28. Schwoon, S., Esparza, J.: A Note on On-the-Fly Verification Algorithms. In: Halbwachs, N., Zuck, L.D. (eds.) TACAS 2005. LNCS, vol. 3440, pp. 174–190. Springer, Heidelberg (2005)
29. Valmari, A.: A Stubborn Attack On State Explosion. In: Larsen, K.G., Skou, A. (eds.) CAV 1991. LNCS, vol. 575, pp. 156–165. Springer, Heidelberg (1992)
30. Valmari, A.: Stubborn Sets for Reduced State Space Generation. In: Rozenberg, G. (ed.) APN 1990. LNCS, vol. 483, pp. 491–515. Springer, Heidelberg (1991)
31. Valmari, A.: The State Explosion Problem. In: Reisig, W., Rozenberg, G. (eds.) APN 1998. LNCS, vol. 1491, pp. 429–528. Springer, Heidelberg (1998)
32. Valmari, A.: Stubborn Set Methods for Process Algebras. In: POMIV 1996, pp. 213–231. AMS Press, Inc. (1997)

A Comparative Study of Incremental Constraint Solving Approaches in Symbolic Execution

Tianhai Liu[1], Mateus Araújo[2], Marcelo d'Amorim[2], and Mana Taghdiri[1]

[1] Karlsruhe Institute of Technology, Germany
[2] Federal University of Pernambuco, Brazil

Abstract. Constraint solving is a major source of cost in Symbolic Execution (SE). This paper presents a study to assess the importance of some sensible options for solving constraints in SE. The main observation is that stack-based approaches to incremental solving is often much faster compared to cache-based approaches, which are more popular. Considering all 96 C programs from the KLEE benchmark that we analyzed, the median speedup obtained with a (non-optimized) stack-based approach was of 5x. Results suggest that tools should take advantage of incremental solving support from modern SMT solvers and researchers should look for ways to combine stack- and cache-based approaches to reduce execution cost even further. Instructions to reproduce results are available online: `http://asa.iti.kit.edu/130_392.php`

1 Introduction

Symbolic Execution (SE) [14,18,19,22,27] is a technique for systematic test-input generation that has gained significant momentum in recent years. Unfortunately, SE is expensive. It needs to explore many program paths and the execution of each path is more expensive compared to a non-symbolic (i.e., concrete) execution. Improving both aspects – space and time – is therefore important and a significant amount of research has been done in this direction recently [17]. The focus of this paper is on time reduction.

SE tools heavily use constraint solvers to avoid the exploration of infeasible paths and to generate test inputs; it comes with no surprise that constraint solving is often reported as the execution time sink of the technique [13,16,33,35].

Incremental solving is an important feature to address this high cost; it leverages the similarity across similar constraints to reduce overall solving cost. Intuitively, when using such feature, solving a set of similar constraints can be faster compared to solving each constraint in the set separately. Considering the fact that constraints that SE generates are similar by construction, existing SE tools employ some form of incremental solving to speedup execution.

1.1 Incremental Constraint Solving Approaches

One simple alternative to incremental solving is to only solve the "changed parts" of the constraint. For example, consider that SE produces the constraint

E. Yahav (Ed.): HVC 2014, LNCS 8855, pp. 284–299, 2014.

pc_1 : $a>b$ $\wedge$ $x<y$ for which the solver outputs the following solution [a=2,b=1,x=3,y=4]. To compute the solution to the next constraint pc_2 : $a>b$ $\wedge$ $x\geq y$ this approach proceeds as follows: it invokes the solver to solve only the changed part of the constraint, namely $x\geq y$, which is a simpler problem, and combines the new solution [x=4,y=3] with the already-computed solution [a=2,b=1]. The combined solution clearly satisfies pc_2. This idea works under the assumption that SE explores similar paths in order (e.g., using depth-first search) and that not all variables in a constraint are dependent (e.g., x and y are mutually-dependent but do not depend on a and b).

The second alternative builds on the observation that the approach discussed above could be generalized to build on the solutions of all previously visited path constraints as opposed to only the last one visited. It caches solutions of every independent expression observed in every path constraint: two expressions are independent if they do not share any symbolic variables. Considering the previous example, a global cache stores solutions to the expressions $a>b$, $x<y$, and $x\geq y$ which appeared independently in the two individual path constraints pc_1 and pc_2. Despite the overhead in memory and time consumption related to caching (to store, lookup, and combine solutions), it has been observed that this optimization is beneficial. Popular symbolic execution tools, such as CREST [15], KLEE [16], PEX [32] and SPF [26], use similar features.

Another alternative to incremental solving makes use of built-in SMT solver support to solve similar constraints. It builds on the observation that as the paths that a SE explores gets longer chances of merging independent expressions increase since the number of input variables is limited. Unfortunately, the approaches to incremental solving presented above cannot help in this scenario. For example, the cached solution [x=3,y=2] to the constraint $x>y$ will not help to solve the constraint $x>y \wedge x>3$. In contrast, modern incremental SMT solvers, such as CVC4 [4], MathSAT5 [6], Yices [9], and Z3 [10] can help in this case: during constraint solving these tools learn lemmas, which can be later (re)used to solve similar *but not identical* constraints. To the best of our knowledge *no* existing SE tool uses such alternative for constraint solving.

1.2   Contribution

This paper reports the results of a study we conducted to assess how cache-based approaches compare with stack-based approaches to solve constraints incrementally. We considered various options of incremental solving and a large set of programs; both real (96 C programs from the KLEE [16] benchmark) and artificially-generated (300 randomly-generated programs of various sizes: 5, 10, and 20K). Overall, results indicate that stack-based approaches provide superior results. The median speedup obtained when using the support of a modern incremental SMT solver is of ∼5x (min.:∼1x, avg.:∼4.8x, max.: ∼9x).

In the light of these results, we investigated how to further improve stack-based approaches. We noticed that sharing of common expressions can facilitate the search for solution in SMT solvers [12]. We investigated the alternative of eliminating all common sub-expression from the constraint instead of of relying on the built-in heuristics from the solver. Results indicate that the speedup obtained with this alternative was of ~1.11x over the benefits obtained with the basic stack-based incremental approach.

2   Background

Symbolic Execution is comprised of two parts: constraint generation and constraint solving. We briefly explain each part below. More details can be found elsewhere [17, 25, 28].

2.1   Constraint Generation

When symbolic execution evaluates a branch instruction, it needs to decide which branch of the control flow to select. In a regular concrete execution, the evaluation of a boolean expression is either true or false. Thus only one branch of the conditional can be taken. In contrast, in symbolic execution, the evaluation of a boolean expression is a symbolic value, so both branches can be taken resulting in different paths to be explored in the program. Symbolic execution characterizes each path it explores with a *path-condition* over the input variables $\vec{x}$. This condition is defined with a conjunction of boolean expressions $pc(\vec{x}) = \bigwedge b_i$. Each boolean expression b_i denotes a branching decision made during the execution of a distinct path in the program under test. Symbolic execution terminates when it explores all such paths corresponding to the different combinations of decisions. Programs with loops and recursion may result in an infinite number of paths; in those cases, one needs to define a bound on the number of paths that symbolic execution can explore.

2.2   Constraint Solving

Symbolic execution uses constraint solving (i) to check path feasibility and (ii) to generate test inputs. In the first case, symbolic execution checks if the current path is feasible by checking if the current (partial) path-condition is satisfiable. Exploration of a path is interrupted as soon as the path-condition becomes unsatisfiable. In the second case, symbolic execution uses a constraint solver to solve constraints associated with complete paths. The solutions to these constraints correspond to test inputs. SMT-LIB[1] is a popular format for describing constraints in SMT solvers [2, 4, 8, 10]. The SMT-LIB syntax [29] uses a prefix notation for expressions. For example, the user writes (`assert F`) to declare that a logical formulas F must hold. One can combine multiple formulas with logical operators. Symbolic names can be introduced as uninterpreted functions without arguments. Incremental SMT solvers [4, 6, 10] provide an assertion stack to solving similar constraints. The assertion stack is equipped with **push** and **pop** operations to enable one to keep contextual information. Each stack frame

---

[1]See http://smtlib.cs.uiowa.edu

```int step(int a,int b){ if (a < 0) b = a + b; if (b < 1) b = 2; else b = 3; return a+b;}```	```int stepOpt(int a,int b){ if (a < 0) b1 = a+b; else b1 = b; if (b1 < 1) b2 = 2; else b2 = 3; return a+b2;}```
(a) Original	(b) Transformed (for illustration)

Fig. 1. Sample code

stores an *assertion set*, which includes locally-scoped declarations of functions, sorts, and logical formulas. The command (check-sat) holds if the conjunction of all assertion sets in the stack is satisfiable.

3   Techniques

We considered 5 techniques to evaluate effectiveness of cache-based and stack-based approaches to incremental solving. All techniques have been implemented in the same framework. We briefly describe them below.

- **Baseline** is the approach that does *not* use incremental solving. This approach conjoins all decisions reached along one path in a single constraint. That is, each constraint generated with SE results in a different potentially-long query to the solver.
- **Caching** refers to the technique that uses independent clauses optimization to simplify constraints before querying the solver (see Section 1.1). It incurs in overhead to partition constraints, lookup, and update the cache.
- **CachingOpt** optimizes *caching* by partitioning constraints incrementally. It keeps in memory the set of partitions and corresponding variables for the previously explored constraint. When reaching a control decision, it obtains new partitions by merging all partitions that have variables in common, considering the new variables involved in the decision. It incurs in additional overhead to merge partitions.
- **Stack** refers to the technique that creates a new frame on the assertion stack of an SMT solver when reaching a new control decision.
- **StackOpt** is as *stack* but builds constraints with new symbolic names so to facilitate identification of expression sharing.

3.1   Illustrative Example

This section illustrates the techniques. Figure 1 shows the code of function step; function stepOpt is obtained from code transformations on step. This function helps to illustrate the effect of common-subexpression elimination; new variables are introduced and each variable is defined only once. It is important to note that similar effect can be obtained without applying this transformation, e.g., by hash consing over assignment statements.

Figure 2 shows the SMT-LIB scripts produced by different techniques. In this example, each query terminates with the sequence of commands `check-sat` and `get-value` which indicate that the constraint was satisfiable and a solution could be retrieved. The solver context, that maintains the lemmas learned in previous computations, is destroyed with the command `exit`.

Figure 2(a) illustrates *Caching*. In this technique, each query starts with the construction of variables and terminates with the destruction of the solver context. For each query, only dependent constraints reach the solver; solutions are cached to avoid redundant queries. We show in comments the state of the cache and cache hit events. Figure 2(b) illustrates *Stack*. In this technique, the solver context evolves as new assertions are added to the stack; the context survives across the symbolic execution of different paths. To note that learned lemmas created on a stack frame are destroyed upon a `pop` of that frame.

3.2   Common Sub-expression Elimination: *StackOpt*

It is well known that sharing of structurally equal expressions can reduce space and time requirements in constraint solving, especially when dealing with large constraints. Modern SMT solvers identify those sharings automatically but there is cost associated with it and the mechanism to identify sharings is non-optimal.

Aware of that, we additionally evaluated the impact of translating the constraints to a representation that facilitates the identification of these sharings. In short, we eliminate common-subexpressions from input constraints. We want to evaluate how this feature works in conjunction with incremental SMT solving, which to the best of our knowledge is not used in these tools. We call the technique that uses this optimization *StackOpt*.

Consider, for example, the code fragment `if(.) a=x+y; if (a+z>10) {.}`. With traditional symbolic execution, the path corresponding to the traversal of the true branches is denoted by the constraint ... $x + y + z > 10$. *StackOpt*, however, translates this constraint to ... $a_1 = x_0 + y_0 \wedge a_1 + z_0 > 10$ as it identifies that the expression denoted by a_1 can be reused in other contexts. The use of such representation increases space requirements, i.e., it increases the number of variables and conjuncts in the constraint. On the other hand, it helps the constraint solver by letting it associate information with newly defined symbols (in this case, a_1).

Figure 2 shows side-by-side the scripts produced with this optimization disabled (*Stack*) and enabled (*StackOpt*). In contrast to *stack* and *caching*, that generate fresh constraints on decision points, *stackOpt* reuses expressions. For example, in Figure 2(c), *stackOpt* renames variable `b1` in query 1 to refer to `a+b`, and uses it in queries 2 and 3. We evaluate in this paper how such transformation can speedup stack-based constraint solving.

4   Evaluation

Our goal is to understand the extent to which constraint solving can be optimized for symbolic execution. We focused our attention to incremental solving, which

(a) Caching(Opt)	(b) Stack	(c) StackOpt

```
(a) Caching(Opt)
; query 1
(declare-fun a () Int)
(assert (< a 0))
(check-sat) ; sat
(get-value (a)) ; [a]:=[-1]
(exit)
; query 2
(declare-fun a () Int)
(declare-fun b () Int)
(assert (< a 0))
(assert (< (+ a b) 1))
(check-sat) ; sat
(get-value (a b))
; [a, b] := [-1, 0]
(exit)
; query 3
(declare-fun a () Int)
(declare-fun b () Int)
(assert (< a 0))
(assert (not(<(+ a b) 1)))
(check-sat) ; sat
(get-value (a b))
; [a, b] := [-1, 2]
(exit)
; query 4
(declare-fun a () Int)
(assert (not (< a 0)))
(check-sat) ; sat
(get-value (a)) ; [a]:=[0]
(exit)
; query 5
(declare-fun b () Int)
(assert (< b 1))
(check-sat) ; sat
(get-value (b)) ; [b]:=[0]
; cache hit : [!(a<0)]
; query 6
(declare-fun b () Int)
(assert (not (< b 1)))
(check-sat) ; sat
(get-value (b)) ; [b]:=[1]
; cache hit : [!(a<0)]
; cache: [a<0:[SAT,a:=-1],
; a+b<1:[SAT,a:=-1,b:=0],
; !(a+b<1):[SAT,a:=0,b:=2],
; !(a<0):[SAT,a:=0],
; b<1):[SAT,b:=0]]
```

```
(b) Stack
(declare-fun a () Int)
(declare-fun b () Int)
; query 1
(push)
(assert (< a 0))
(check-sat) ; sat
; query 2
(push)
(assert (< (+ a b) 1))
(check-sat) ; sat
(get-value (a b))
; [a, b] := [-1, 0]
(pop)
; query 3
(push)
(assert (not(<(+ a b) 1)))
(check-sat) ; sat
(get-value (a b))
; [a, b] := [-1, 2]
(pop)
(pop)
; query 4
(push)
(assert (not (< a 0)))
(check-sat) ; sat
;query 5
(push)
(assert (< b 1))
(check-sat) ; sat
(get-value (a b))
; [a, b] := [0, 0]
(pop)
;query 6
(push)
(assert (not (< b 1)))
(check-sat) ; sat
(get-value (a b))
; [a, b] := [0, 1]
(pop)
(pop)
(exit)
```

```
(c) StackOpt
(declare-fun a () Int)
(declare-fun b () Int)
; query 1
(push)
(assert (< a 0))
(check-sat) ; sat
(define-fun b1 () Int (+ a b))
; query 2
(push)
(assert (< b1 1))
(check-sat) ; sat
(get-value (a b))
; [a, b] := [-1, 0]
(pop)
; query 3
(push)
(assert (not (< b1 1)))
(check-sat) ; sat
(get-value (a b))
; [a, b] := [-1, 2]
(pop)
(pop)
; query 4
(push)
(assert (not (< a 0)))
(check-sat) ; sat
(define-fun b1 () Int b)
;query 5
(push)
(assert (< b1 1))
(check-sat) ; sat
(get-value (a b))
; [a, b] := [0, 0]
(pop)
;query 6
(push)
(assert (not (< b1 1)))
(check-sat) ; sat
(get-value (a b))
; [a, b] := [0, 1]
(pop)
(pop)
(exit)
```

Fig. 2. SMT-LIB scripts produced with various techniques. Comments indicate what happens during exploration.

is the basic principle to solve large sets of similar constraints. We describe in the following the experiment we conducted to evaluate the techniques from Section 3.

4.1 Research Questions

We pose the following research questions.

RQ1. How cache-based and stack-based approaches compare?
RQ2. What is the benefit of using common sub-expressions elimination?
RQ3. Where each technique spends most time?

4.2   Objects of Analysis

We used two sets of programs in our evaluation. The first set includes programs automatically generated with RUGRAT [7]. The second set includes programs collected from the benchmark of KLEE [5], an open-source symbolic execution tool for C programs.

RUGRAT is a grammar-based program generator that has been proposed to support empirical evaluation of testing and analysis techniques. It produces programs based on weights associated to grammar production rules. A practical challenge for these kinds of generators is to construct realistic programs. However, an empirical study indicates that it is statistically impossible for a program analysis technique to differentiate a program written by a human from one that the tool generates [20]. The study compared real and generated programs with 78 existing software metrics. We considered three options of program size: programs of 5, 10, and 20 KLOC. We generated a total of 300 programs, 100 programs for each program size and only considered programs whose symbolic execution produces integer linear constraints.

The KLEE Coreutils benchmark [16] contains 96 Unix core programs (4.5 KLOC together). As the tool handles C programs we could not use our infrastructure (see Section 4.7). Instead, we ran KLEE, collected constraints produced by the tool, and analyzed them in order, i.e., consecutive constraints in the list reflect exploration order and are similar. For this reason we could not evaluate the combination *stackOpt* on this program set.

4.3   Experimental Variables

The *independent* variables of our experiment are the exploration time, size of the program, and exploration bounds. The *control* variables (i.e., constants) of our experiment are the choice of constraint solver and the exploration order. We used Microsoft's Z3 [10] for solving constraints and bounded depth first search for exploring paths. Even though results are deterministic we ran our scripts multiple times to confirm environmental changes did not introduce noise in our measurements. We used an Intel Xeon E5-2670 CPU with 2.60GHz clock running on a 64-bit openSUSE, and set 8GB as the max heap size for a symbolic execution.

4.4   RQ1. How Cache-Based and Stack-Based Approaches Compare?

To answer this research question we compared the effectiveness of techniques on the RUGRAT and KLEE benchmarks. We only considered variants without applying common sub-expression elimination in this experiment.

The RUGRAT Benchmark. Figures 3 and 4 show results of various techniques for program generated with RUGRAT. We fixed the time budget for exploring paths in bounded depth-first order to 10 minutes.

	5K	10K	20K		5K	10K	20K
Solving Time (ms) per constraint				**Number of queries answered**			
baseline	8.100	16.750	25.565	*baseline*	29,154	9,115	5,856
caching	35.123	89.537	96.983	*caching*	34,870	4,875	3,416
cachingOpt	17.547	45.624	47.630	*cachingOpt*	58,988	10,097	5,047
stack	0.321	0.843	1.401	*stack*	441,353	185,236	101,408
stackOpt	0.309	0.752	1.258	*stackOpt*	1177,907	448,545	256,345

Fig. 3. Cost metrics

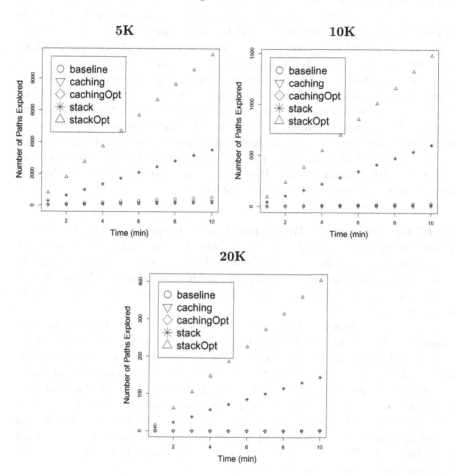

Fig. 4. Average number of complete paths explored (i.e., tests generated) using Z3. Time budget set to 10 minutes.

Figure 3 shows the average cost for solving a constraint for each technique and the total number of queries answered. The average cost of solving one constraint is the total constraint solving time divided by the number of queries issued to the solver within a 10m time slot.

Each datapoint in the plots from Figure 4 indicates the number of explored complete paths (/tests generated) for a pair of technique and point in time. These plots show progress of different solving approaches. All plots indicate that the use of incremental SMT solving is beneficial. Note from the y-axis that as the size of programs grows the number of explored complete paths decreases. However, note that the speedups remain relatively similar. We observed that as size of programs grow constraint solving also become much more expensive; this justifies the decrease in number of complete paths explored on longer programs. Note from Figure 3 that the number of queries answered by the constraint solver in fact increase for longer programs compared to other techniques.

All plots from Figure 4 show a linear x-y relationship, indicating that the cost of exploring one path remains nearly the same during state-space exploration. Note that results are averaged across several programs. This linear behavior was a surprise. In principle, it would be justified only when feasible complete paths are uniformly distributed across the exploration tree and the cost of exploring one path is constant. A close inspection on results revealed that this indeed occurs many times although not always. However, as many subjects are considered a linear behavior emerged in the averaged plots.

The KLEE Benchmark. We compared the techniques also using the benchmark of the SE tool KLEE [5, 16]. We analyzed the constraints it generates for 96 programs from KLEE's own benchmark. We set the time budget for SE to 30 seconds and used the default configuration for running KLEE. We confirmed as expected that KLEE spends most of its time budget (90%=~27s/30s) in constraint solving[2]

Figure 5 shows the speedup that the best technique, *stack*, obtains compared to the second best technique, *cachingOpt*. The table in the right-top corner shows the time cost of solving each constraint. We did *not* evaluate *stackOpt* in this experiment as that would require post-processing KLEE-generated constraints. Considering the 96 programs analyzed the median speedup of *stackOpt* over *cachingOpt* was ~5x. In absolute terms *stack* analyzed all constraint in 0.14s in the best case and 72.36s in the worst case, with a median cost of 6.3s and an average cost of 7.53s. For 91 of the 96 programs *stackOpt* was solved all constraints under 10s. 2 programs were solved under 30s and for only 2 programs it required more time: 54.9s and 72.36s.

It should be noted that the constraints from the KLEE benchmark build on the theory of bit-vectors whereas the constraints from the RUGRAT benchmark build on the theory of integers. We compared the techniques using different theories and obtained some evidence that the techniques we presented are effective for two relevant theories.

---

[2] http://klee.github.io/klee/klee-tools.html#klee-stats

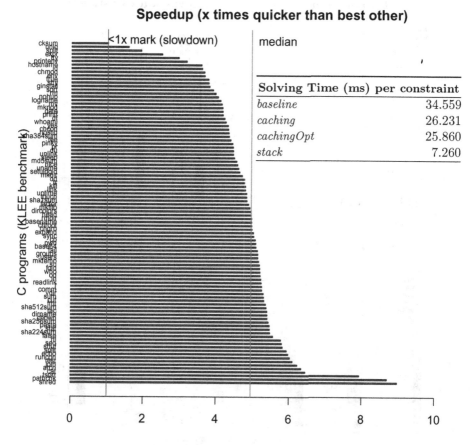

Fig. 5. Speedup of stack-based incremental SMT solving over best alternative solving approach using Z3 (KLEE benchmark). The table in the right-top shows the solving time per constraint in various approaches.

4.5 RQ2. What is the Benefit of Using Common Sub-expression Elimination?

Figure 4 shows that the *stackOpt* performs remarkably well. In contrast to *stack* this approach does not appear to degrade performance as the size of programs and constraints increase. The reason for the gain is justified: 1) On reaching each branch decision, *stackOpt* reuses the constraints constructed before path exploration while *stack* constructs new constraints when the variables involved in the branch condition were updated in the path leading to this branch. This is evidenced in Figure 4, in which *stack* has a notable overhead in path exploration. 2) To save search space and time, most modern SMT solvers (e.g., [1,2,4,6,9,10]) map structure-equal expressions to a singleton to construct a compact problem.

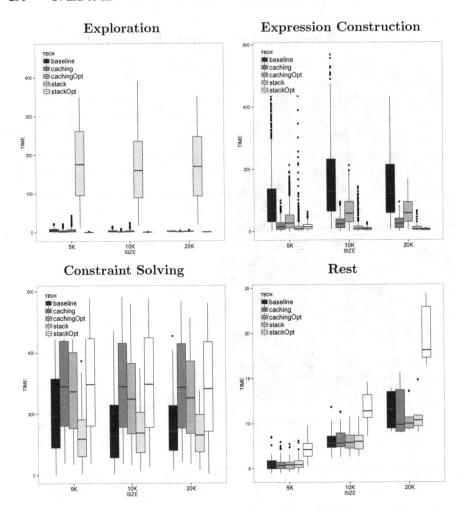

Fig. 6. Average time breakdown of different techniques using Z3 in 10 minutes

While modern solvers detect shared expressions at the syntactical level, *stackOpt* introduces intermediate variables as macros to shared expressions at the semantic level.

4.6   RQ3.   Where Techniques Spend Most Time?

Figure 6 shows the time breakdown of the techniques considering 4 sources of runtime cost: path exploration, expression construction, constraint solving, and rest. Path exploration time includes the cost of exploring paths (e.g., storing and restoring states), expression construction time includes the cost of creating Z3 expressions (we used Z3's programmatic interface for that), constraint solving time includes solving and and caching time, and rest includes the remaining parts, for example, the time of performing code transforms.

We make the following observations:

- *Baseline* spends more time in expression construction compared to other techniques. This happens because *baseline* needs reconstruct all Z3 expressions for a new query, while *caching* reduces the amount of constraints issued to the solver and consequently also reduces this cost.
- *Stack* spends more time in path exploration compared to other techniques. This happens because *stack* needs to update states on assignment statements and load states on decision points to generate fresh constraints, while *stackOpt* has constraints constructed before path exploration. That is even worse for those paths traversed multiple times; *stack* will reload the states and recompute the constraints for each traversing, while *stackOpt* has constraints constructed prior to the path exploration.
- All caching techniques and *stackOpt* spent most time on solving constraints and at least 70% of the time is spent in constraint solving.
- *stack* spent less time in constraint solving compared to other techniques, while it can solve more constraints than any other technique except *stackOpt*.
- *stackOpt* spent more time in rest than other techniques. This happens is because *stackOpt* has a code transformation to rename variables.

4.7   Infrastructure

We developed a SE tool prototype to support our experiments. The motivation was to evaluate the influence of SSA. The infrastructure has been implemented in Java in ~19.7KLOC, being~1.5KLOC from InspectJ [24]. We computed non-blank non-comment lines of source code with the CLOC tool [3]. We used the Soot optimization framework [30] to process Java bytecodes, the Jung graph framework [21] to construct and explore decision graphs, and InspectJ to unroll loops and inline methods. The infrastructure generates constraints in SMTLIB v2 so it can interface with any compliant solver. For example, Z3 [10] is called directly through its programmatic interface to create corresponding Z3 expressions.The infrastructure supports both integers and bit-vectors to assess the impact of various options of incremental solving to speedup symbolic execution. The infrastructure reuses the created objects to reduce the cost of time and memory allocation in constraint generation.

Static Transformations. We implemented a sequence of static code transformations before the construction of decision graph. For example, unroll loops according to the configurations, model the program in Static Single Assignment (SSA) representation and inline methods on each call site. Finally, we obtained a directed acyclic graph with unique variable names. We evaluated how costly code transformation can be relative to the other costs. We observed that the linearization (i.e., inlining methods and unrolling loops) procedure is significantly

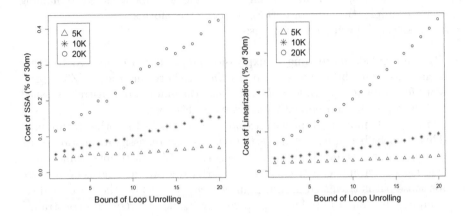

Fig. 7. Average percentage of static cost. For example, the average cost of linearization for a 20K program configured to unroll loops at most 3 times is approximately 34s(=(1.9/100)*30*60s).

more expensive compared to SSA, which is applied within each procedure prior to linearizing the code. But still linearization is relatively low cost. Figure 7 shows how each of these operations scale with program size and bound of loop unrollings. 60 subjects have been checked with a timeout 30m. The scale of the y-axis is the percentage of a 30m time budget. Results are averaged across all subjects considered for that size. In the worst case, linearization on 20K programs with 20 loop unrollings takes roughly 2m24s (=144s=8% of 30m).

4.8   Threats to Validity

As usual it is possible that results do not generalize much beyond our subject set. To mitigate this threat we used a set of 300 automatically-generated Java programs and a set of 96 real C programs from the GNU operating system.

Another threat to validity is the possibility of errors in our implementation. We carefully inspected our code and the consistency of our results. In summary, additional experiments are necessary to assess generality of our results.

5   Related Work

Symbolic Execution (SE) is expensive in time and space. We discuss below most-related recent work to reduce the high cost in constraint solving during SE.

5.1   Caching Schemes

Cadar *et al.* [16] proposed several optimizations to simplify constraints prior to calling the solver during SE. The SE tool KLEE implements *caching* as we described. In addition, KLEE implements constraint checking with a potential solution. It is based on the assumption that a solution of subset often satisfy extra constraints. We remain to investigate how this additional optimization compares with those we considered.

Visser *et al.* [34] proposed GREEN, an infrastructure to share results of symbolic executions across different environments. GREEN proposes canonical representations of path conditions to enable caching across different programs. The intuition is that after partitioning constraints w.r.t. dependent clauses the chance of finding structurally equal symbolic constraints increases. For example, solutions to constraints produced in the symbolic execution of one program could be used to solve constraints produced from SE for another program. Results of GREEN are encouraging. Although the goal of GREEN is the same (to speedup constraint solving), our contributions are complementary.

5.2 Incremental SMT Solving

Incremental SMT solving is an active field of research with the goal of optimizing problems that can be characterized by many similar sub-problems. For example, detecting the program execution trace which maximizes execution cost [23], solving scheduling problems [31]. As a basic decision procedure, incremental SMT solving searches for a satisfying assignment by performing various operations (e.g. unit propagation). When internal conflicts occur incremental SMT solvers extract and store conflict clause to prune exploration search space. More specifically, incremental solvers store learned and conflicting clauses in the assertion stack so that they can be reused upon backtracking. Recently, Wieringa *et al.* [11] proposed a technique to strengthen the clauses learned by the solver by extending an incremental SMT solver to execute in multiple threads. We observed that this development can directly improve symbolic execution.

6   Conclusions

This paper reports on a study to assess the impact of various options of incremental solving to speedup Symbolic Execution (SE). Results suggest that incremental solving is very important and that stack-based approaches provide superior results when compared to cache-based approaches for the benchmarks used in our experiments. Note that results are restricted to the use bounded depth-first search. More research is needed to find ways to combine caching- and stack-based approaches to improve results even further.

Acknowledgments. This work is partially funded by DFG grant TA764/1-1. Mateus is supported by the FACEPE fellowship # IBPG-0668-1.03/12. DFG is the German Research Foundation and FACEPE is the state of Pernambuco, Brazil, Research Foundation.

References

1. Alt-Ergo webpage, http://alt-ergo.lri.fr/
2. Boolector webpage, http://fmv.jku.at/boolector/
3. CLOC webpage, http://cloc.sourceforge.net/
4. CVC4 webpage, http://cvc4.cs.nyu.edu/web/
5. KLEE webpage, http://klee.github.io/klee/
6. MathSAT5 webpage, http://mathsat.fbk.eu/
7. RUGRAT webpage, http://www.rugrat.ws/
8. STP webpage, https://sites.google.com/site/stpfastprover/
9. Yices webpage, http://yices.csl.sri.com/
10. Z3 webpage, http://z3.codeplex.com/
11. Audemard, G., Lagniez, J.-M., Simon, L.: Improving Glucose for Incremental SAT Solving with Assumptions: Application to MUS Extraction. In: Järvisalo, M., Van Gelder, A. (eds.) SAT 2013. LNCS, vol. 7962, pp. 309–317. Springer, Heidelberg (2013)
12. Bankovic, M.: Argosmtexpression: an smt-lib 2.0 compliant expression library. In: Workshop of the SAT (June 2012)
13. Borges, M., Filieri, A., d'Amorim, M., Păsăreanu, C.S., Visser, W.: Compositional solution space quantification for probabilistic software analysis. In: PLDI, pp. 123–132 (2014)
14. Boyer, R.S., Elspas, B., Levitt, K.N.: SELECT - A Formal System for Testing and Debugging Programs by Symbolic Execution. In: International Conference on Reliable Software, pp. 234–245 (1975)
15. Burnim, J., Sen, K.: Heuristics for scalable dynamic test generation. In: ASE 2008, pp. 443–446 (2008)
16. Cadar, C., Dunbar, D., Engler, D.: Klee: unassisted and automatic generation of high-coverage tests for complex systems programs. In: OSDI, pp. 209–224 (2008)
17. Cadar, C., Godefroid, P., Khurshid, S., Pasareanu, C.S., Sen, K., Tillmann, N., Visser, W.: Symbolic execution for software testing in practice: preliminary assessment. In: ICSE, pp. 1066–1071 (2011)
18. Clarke, L.A.: A Program Testing System. In: ACM Annual Conference, pp. 488–491 (1976)
19. Howden, W.E.: Symbolic Testing and the DISSECT Symbolic Evaluation System. IEEE TSE 3(4), 266–278 (1977)
20. Hussain, I., Csallner, C., Grechanik, M., Fu, C., Xie, Q., Park, S., Taneja, K., Hossain, B.M.M.: Evaluating program analysis and testing tools with the RUGRAT random benchmark application generator. In: WODA, pp. 1–6 (2012)
21. Jung webpage, http://jung.sourceforge.net/
22. King, J.C.: Symbolic execution and program testing. Communications of ACM 19(7), 385–394 (1976)
23. Li, Y., Albarghouthi, A., Kincaid, Z., Gurfinkel, A., Chechik, M.: Symbolic optimization with smt solvers. SIGPLAN Not. 49(1), 607–618 (2014)
24. Liu, T., Nagel, M., Taghdiri, M.: Bounded program verification using an smt solver: A case study. In: ICST, pp. 101–110 (2012)
25. Pasareanu, C.S., Visser, W.: A survey of new trends in symbolic execution for software testing and analysis. STTT 11(4), 339–353 (2009)
26. Păsăreanu, C.S., Rungta, N.: Symbolic PathFinder: symbolic execution of Java bytecode. In: ASE, pp. 179–180 (2010)

27. Ramamoorthy, C., Ho, S., Chert, W.: On the automated generation of program test data. IEEE TSE 2(4), 293–300 (1976)
28. Schwartz, E.J., Avgerinos, T., Brumley, D.: All you ever wanted to know about dynamic taint analysis and forward symbolic execution (but might have been afraid to ask). In: SP, pp. 317–331 (2010)
29. SMT-LIB webpage, http://www.smtlib.org/
30. Soot webpage, http://www.sable.mcgill.ca/soot/
31. Steiner, W.: An evaluation of smt-based schedule synthesis for time-triggered multi-hop networks. In: RTSS, pp. 375–384 (2010)
32. Tillmann, N., de Halleux, J.: Pex–white box test generation for.NET. In: Beckert, B., Hähnle, R. (eds.) TAP 2008. LNCS, vol. 4966, pp. 134–153. Springer, Heidelberg (2008)
33. Visser, W., Geldenhuys, J., Dwyer, M.B.: Green: Reducing, reusing and recycling constraints in program analysis. In: FSE, pp. 1–11 (2012)
34. Visser, W., Geldenhuys, J., Dwyer, M.B.: Green: Reducing, reusing and recycling constraints in program analysis. In: Proceedings of the ACM SIGSOFT 20th International Symposium on the Foundations of Software Engineering, FSE 2012, pp. 58:1–58:11. ACM, New York (2012)
35. Yang, G., Khurshid, S., Pasareanu, C.S.: Memoise: A tool for memoized symbolic execution. In: ICSE, pp. 1343–1346 (May 2013)

Author Index